COMMAND OF THE WATERS

COMMAND
OF THE
WATERS

vvvvvvvvvvvvvvvvvvvvvvvvvvvvvvvvvvvvvvvvv

Iron Triangles, Federal Water
Development, and Indian Water

Daniel McCool

UNIVERSITY OF CALIFORNIA PRESS
Berkeley • Los Angeles • London

University of California Press
Berkeley and Los Angeles, California

University of California Press, Ltd.
London, England

Copyright © 1987 by The Regents of the University of California

Library of Congress Cataloging in Publication Data

McCool, Daniel, 1950–
Command of the waters.

Bibliography: p.
1. Water resources development—Government
policy—United States.   2. Water-rights—United States.
3. Indians of North America—Reservations—Water rights.
I. Title.
HD1694.A5M4   1987   333.91'00973   86–19232
ISBN 0–520–05846–1 (alk. paper)

Printed in the United States of America

1   2   3   4   5   6   7   8   9

For Patrice and Weston McCool

Contents

Acknowledgments

My interest in water policy developed when I was a graduate student at the University of Arizona, so it is only proper that I begin my acknowledgments there. Jeanne Nienaber Clarke and Helen Ingram introduced me to the subject and helped sustain my interest. Vine Deloria, Jr., graciously shared his understanding of Indian water rights with me. And Ken Godwin, Jeanne, and Vine guided me through the dissertation, which provided a starting point for this book.

A number of people read the draft manuscript; James Officer and Charles Wilkinson skillfully critiqued an early version. They did this simply as a favor and in the interest of scholarship. Imre Sutton and David Getches carefully read the manuscript for the University of California Press and helped me work out a number of problems.

During my research "outings" to Washington, D.C., many individuals gave me assistance. Most of them are listed in the Sources under the section entitled "Interviews." In addition, several people agreed to talk with me but prefer to remain anonymous. To all of these individuals I offer my heartfelt thanks. At the National Archives my work would have been impossible without the assistance of Renee Jaussaud, the librarian for the natural resources section. Her knowledge of the records is simply incredible.

Closer to home, a number of people helped. Sam Kirkpatrick and Bryan Jones provided the best kind of assistance there is: a job. William West served as a sounding board for my ideas on iron triangles. David White worked hard as my graduate assistant. Terry Schiefen typed the manuscript with consummate skill. And Texas A&M University, my employer, provided much support.

I also want to thank the people at the University of California

Press: Stanley Holwitz, Matthew Jaffe, Shirley Warren, Diana Feinberg, and others. I have never actually met any of these people but I know they are personable, efficient, professional, and a pleasure to talk with on the phone. In addition, Lois Smith did a masterful job of copy editing.

If there is anything of value in this book, it is in large part credited to the insights, comments, and contributions of those listed above. I alone claim responsibility for any errors or inadequacies.

And last, but most important, I want to thank my wife, Patrice, who, for the first three years of our marriage, saw only the back of my head. This book took more from her than it did from me.

CHAPTER ONE

Water, Indians, and Iron Triangles

What is of overriding significance gives way to what is immediate.
—Congressman Clem Miller, 1962:52

Introduction

In most areas of the western United States water is a scarce resource. To a great extent the course of western development followed the course of western waters. The possession of water and the ability to use it determine who thrives and who perishes.[1] Thus conflict over western water is not just a fight for economic advantage—it is a fight for survival. This is especially true for American Indians, whose culture and way of life are closely tied to their land. Most of that land is without substantial rainfall and therefore dependent upon streams, rivers, and groundwater for life-giving moisture.

Inadequate rainfall, however, recognizes no racial or cultural distinctions; non-Indians[2] also suffer from the lack of rain, and they too must depend on the same sources of water if they are to survive in the arid West. This places Indians and non-Indians in direct competition for a scarce resource—a resource that wanders in and out of Indian reservations, disappears one year and inundates the next, and respects neither political boundaries nor abstract legal doctrines. It is, however, a resource that can be stored, diverted, directed, or divided by physical structures. The conflict over water, then, involves more than just the water itself; it involves the structures necessary to put the water to use. This book is about the policy-making process that decides not only water rights but where and why water diversion structures are built.

Although many parties are in conflict over western water, one of the most troublesome facets of this conflict involves Indians and

1

non-Indians because it pits one legal doctrine against another: the Winters Doctrine, developed to protect the interests of Indians and other federal reservations, and the Prior Appropriation Doctrine, the basis of state-granted water rights. The Winters Doctrine (also known as the Reserved Rights Doctrine) was enunciated in the landmark case of *Winters v. U.S.* in 1908. Prior to *Winters* the federal government did not answer the question, when land was reserved for Indians, was water also reserved? In *Winters* the Supreme Court held that the government implicitly reserved water for Indians when their reservations were created; hence Indians hold a right to water created when their reservations were established. This right is exempt from state law and not limited by existing levels of beneficial use of water. In subsequent years a large body of case law evolved from the original *Winters* decision. The courts repeatedly reaffirmed the doctrine of reserved water rights, applied it to all federal reservations—not merely Indian lands, and attempted to clarify its precepts.

Winters Doctrine rights are federal rights established independent of state law. The states have adopted their own water laws, which are radically different from the Reserved Rights Doctrine. Beginning in the mid-1800s western states began formulating water codes tailored specifically to the arid conditions of the West. Called the Prior Appropriation Doctrine, this code of water law allocates water rights on the basis of priority of beneficial use; whoever puts the water to beneficial use first retains the rights to that water for as long as it is used. In times of shortage senior appropriators are allowed to consume their entire appropriation before junior appropriators receive any water. In addition, the right to water can be lost through nonuse.

Despite the existence of these two conflicting doctrines, water policymakers and water users have tended to view water policy in terms of one doctrine or the other without full consideration of the interactive relationship between the two. The architects of non-Indian water policy, principally Congress and state governments, have tended to ignore the existence of the Winters Doctrine and make significant water allocation and development decisions without regard to their impact on Winters Doctrine rights. Similarly, the architects of Indian water policy, principally the federal courts and some elements of the federal bureaucracy, have developed the water doctrine of reserved rights without clarifying, explaining, or attempting to compensate for its impact on non-Indian water rights and water development.

As a result of this tendency to develop two conflicting doctrines in nearly total isolation from each other, neither doctrine was designed to meet the needs or requirements of the other. They are on a collision course. It would be difficult to overstate the severity of the impact of this collision. Both Indians and non-Indians fear the consequences. Non-Indians fear that the Winters Doctrine will destroy the economy of the West and bring non-Indian development to a halt. Paul Bloom writes, "It cannot be stressed too much that the economic impact on the non-Indian economies of the western states would be severe and deleterious" if Winters Doctrine rights were developed to their greatest extent (1971:690). Indians fear that failure to develop Winters Doctrine rights will destroy not only tribal economies but their entire way of life. Rupert Costo argues, "There is no issue so critical to Indian affairs today, as the issue of water rights and resources. It cannot be too often emphasized, or too strongly insisted that this is THE most important problem confronting us . . . a problem concerning our very survival" (1972:4).

Although Indians and non-Indians often disagree as to how to resolve their conflicting water claims, all parties agree that the problem is severe. Phillip Fradkin calls it "the sword of Damocles that hangs over the West" (1981:155). According to a report by the Arizona Academy, "all other water conflicts and disputes pale into insignificance compared to the political effects Indian demands could have" (1977:12). Richard Foreman writes that "the controversy on the extent of such 'reserved' Winters Doctrine rights is now at the crux of Western water problems" (1981:58). Quite simply, "the magnitude of the problem cannot be overstated" (*Colville Confederated Tribes v. Walton* 1981:54).

Although the struggle over water has grown more intense in recent years, it is not of recent origin. In 1872 the Indian superintendent visited the Gila River Reservation and reported, "The water question is paramount to every condition affecting the progress and well-being of the tribes" (Superintendent's Annual Report for 1872:48). For many years almost nothing was done to stem the inevitable clash between the Winters Doctrine and the Prior Appropriation Doctrine. These two approaches to water rights developed independent of each other until the reality of increasing water scarcity in the face of increasing demands forced the doctrines into a showdown. This conflict (and therefore the conflict between Indians and non-Indians) is volatile politically because most western water has already been allocated. Hence the potential resolution of Indian claims is becoming more of a question of *re*allocation of water, not just another allocation of water. This increases the political costs of finding a solution to the conflict.

Unfortunately, the literature on water rights and water policy has also tended to isolate the Winters Doctrine from the reality of western water development under the Prior Appropriation Doctrine. There is an enormous body of literature that discusses the Winters Doctrine solely within a *legal* context. Many authors have debated the "true" meaning of the case law, and many have discussed what the Winters Doctrine should do, or will do, or could have done. But the actual impact of *Winters*—and its potential future impact—cannot be fully understood until the Winters Doctrine is examined within the larger *political* context of water development as a whole. In other words, to understand the impact of the Winters Doctrine on Indian water development, it is necessary to understand non-Indian water development.

This emphasis on the totality of water development is necessary because Indians and non-Indians are competitors not only for water but also for water *projects* and the federal funding used to finance them. In the American West water almost always must be stored and diverted before it is useful for economic development. If Indian tribes seek to apply their water rights for economic development—to turn "paper" water into "wet" water—it will be necessary to build water projects. Those projects, however, will compete with non-Indian projects that divert water away from Indian reservations.

The competition for water projects has assumed even greater relevance because, to a large extent, water *rights* decisions in the West have been made simply through the process of water *development*. Non-Indians have invested billions of dollars in water projects that in some cases divert water away from Indian reservations. They now argue that it would be too costly to abandon those projects and allow the water to be diverted to Indian projects. In a sense water rights decisions have been made through default. The relative allocation of water for Indians and non-Indians has been determined in many cases not by water rights decisions but by water development decisions. Whoever got the water projects got the water. The old adage "Possession is nine-tenths of the law" is particularly relevant to this situation. Therefore to understand the reality of water rights, it is necessary to understand the politics of water projects.

An understanding of the politics of water projects is impossible without examining *all* water projects, however, not just those in

the West. Funding for federal water projects is the result of a
policy-making process that involves all parts of the country and
many different aspects of water development. Politically all water
projects are related, as subsequent chapters will show.[3] Norris
Hundley argues convincingly that "to focus only on the West is to
obscure the national significance of the present crisis over Indian
water rights and to ignore the role of the federal government in
today's hotly contested battles" (1978:454). The present situation
in regard to Indian water development is not merely a product of
the case law related to *Winters*, nor is it simply a product of federal
Indian policy. These factors are important, but they are only two
variables in the broader question of national water resource development in the United States.

The following chapters place Indian water development within
the larger context of the politics of federal water resource development. To understand this political context, it is helpful to use the
concept of an "iron triangle."[4] Also known as a policy whirlpool
(Griffith 1961), a subgovernment (Cater 1964), or a subsystem
(Freeman 1965), an iron triangle is an informal political alliance that
forms to influence a specific public policy to its advantage. Consisting of congressional committees and subcommittees, administrative agencies, and interest groups, these tripartite coalitions
influence the allocation of government goods and services in such
a way that the congressional committee members get credit for
"bringing home the bacon" to their constituents, the administrative
agencies expand their budgets, personnel, and turf, and the interest groups get what they want from the government. Thus the
triangle works in a symbiotic fashion that creates advantages for
all three participants; by helping one another they help themselves.
Typically iron triangles operate in a quiet, methodical manner designed to maintain an uninterrupted flow of benefits to the participants and their constituencies (Dodd and Schott 1979:103–104;
Ripley and Franklin 1984:9–12, 103–107). Federal water resource
development is often cited as a classic example of policymaking
via iron triangles. The Bureau of Indian Affairs (BIA) is also involved in an iron triangle, as evidenced by J. Leiper Freeman's
seminal study, *The Political Process* (1965). The BIA's Indian water
development program is part of that iron triangle.

Not all iron triangles are equal, however. A variety of factors
affect the ability of a triangle to control relevant policy and reward
its participants. These factors must be identified in order to understand the differences between the federal water development iron
triangle and the BIA triangle. Although the central focus of the

book is on these two triangles, the Justice Department is also discussed because of the role it plays in this issue area and because it provides a third perspective: specifically, that of an agency not involved in an iron triangle.

Indian and non-Indian water development are particularly appropriate subjects for this type of study for two reasons. First, the Indian policy triangle has long suffered from a low level of political effectiveness, whereas the non-Indian water development triangle has been one of the best examples of a politically viable triangle. Thus we can compare and contrast two different kinds of triangles and examine how each responds to a changing political environment. Second, these triangles compete for the same resources under conditions of increasing scarcity. This focuses additional pressure on the factors that affect each triangle's political effectiveness. In short, this study compares a strong iron triangle, a weak iron triangle, and an agency (the Justice Department) that is not part of an iron triangle. All three are involved with the same issue.

Iron Triangles: Sources of Political Power

In order to understand why some iron triangles are more powerful than others, we must examine the three sets of participants, or "corners" of the triangle, as well as the general policy-making environment in which the triangle must operate. The important political factors affecting each of these will be discussed.

The general policy-making environment of an iron triangle is very specialized; specific types of policies, behavioral norms, and relationships predominate. The type of policy most commonly associated with iron triangles is distributive policy, meaning that the benefits of the policy are concentrated but the costs are dispersed. For example, when a congressman succeeds in bringing a federal project to his district, the benefits accrue only to his constituents but the costs of the project are borne by taxpayers nationwide. This makes the benefits very obvious to local constituents, but the costs are sufficiently spread out "as to be nearly invisible" (Ferejohn 1974:5). To accomplish this it helps if the program benefits are divisible—in other words, if they can be spread out to various localities. This kind of policy-making is sometimes pejoratively referred to as "pork barrel,"[5] meaning that allocations of government benefits are based on political gain rather than objective criteria (Murphy 1974:169). This combination of concentrated local benefits and dispersed costs contributes to an atmosphere of low conflict and stable, long-term relationships. Under normal circumstances the decision-making process takes place quietly behind closed doors. If someone objects, he or she can be converted into a supporter by being given additional distributive benefits.

The process of making distributive policy is nurtured by the congressional norms of reciprocity and logrolling,[6] which means that legislators trade votes for their "pet" projects and agree to "play the game according to the longstanding custom of live and let live" (Freeman 1965:54). The classic statement on how this system operates was provided by Senator Paul Douglas:

> The [Public Works] bill is built up out of a whole system of mutual accommodation, in which the favors are widely distributed, with the implicit promise that no one will kick over the applecart; that if senators do not object to the bill as a whole, they will "get theirs." It is a process, if I may use an inelegant expression, of mutual backscratching and mutual logrolling. (Quoted in Drew 1970:55)

This approach to distributive policy-making is self-perpetuating because legislators provide support for one another, always with the implicit understanding that the favor will be returned in the future. In an iron triangle the need for reciprocity goes beyond Congress to encompass the other participants in the triangle. There must be a process of mutual give-and-take so that each participant provides a necessary service to the others and in return receives expected benefits. Water development policy is particularly amenable to this process. Arnold writes that "when it comes to water, there is truly something for everyone. . . . Since all are included, the system survives and continues to create enormous local political capital" (1981:257).

The formulation of distributive policy via the logrolling process is simplified if the iron triangle operates as a fairly autonomous unit. This helps prevent outside interference and limits the number of participants and, hence, potential beneficiaries. To be insulated effectively from outside interference, both the congressional and the bureaucratic participants in a triangle must be autonomous. One threat to their independence is what is known as executive review, by which the president takes an interest in the triangle's policy area and attempts to inject himself into the policy-making process. Because the president's needs and objectives are often quite different from those of the triangle—he serves a national constituency, not a regional one—his involvement in the affairs of an iron triangle is usually fiercely resisted and politically costly. For example, when former president Jimmy Carter tried to reduce funding for water projects in 1977, he was told by several leading legislators that only Congress had the "right to select water resources projects" (H.R. accompanying P.L. 95–507, 1977).

A final element in the general policy-making environment concerns the implementability[7] of the iron triangle's programs. Some programs are easier than others to carry through to completion. In implementing distributive policy it is important that the iron triangle have a clear sense of *political* goals. In simplest terms this means that all participants understand and agree to the benefits that accrue from their participation. In some cases this may require ambiguity in *substantive* goals, so that the program may be expanded or altered to meet the needs of the participants.

Implementability is also affected by the perceived legitimacy of the program. Usually programs based on statutory authority (i.e., laws passed by legislators) are perceived as more legitimate than those based on case law (i.e., interpretations of statutory law by judges). In a political environment programs based on case law encounter a number of problems that do not typically occur with statute-based programs (Nakamura and Smallwood 1980:85–107; Johnson and Canon, 1984). This point is especially relevant to this book in light of the fact that Winters Doctrine rights are derived primarily from case law, but prior appropriation laws and the federal water development program are products of statutory law.

Another factor affecting implementability is the relative level of support for and opposition to an iron triangle's activities (Van Meter and Van Horn 1975:459). Opposition is not fatal so long as it is overshadowed by support. A high level of conflict between parties of relatively equal political strength can make program implementation difficult. Widespread support is easier to obtain if the program is congruent with prevailing social, economic, and political norms (Clarke and McCool 1985:7).

In sum, a favorable political environment for an iron triangle is characterized by distributive policies, the congressional norms of reciprocity and logrolling, an autonomous decision-making process, and a high degree of program implementability. When the iron triangle system is functioning effectively, it forms a feedback loop that connects all the participants in a reciprocal exchange of benefits. Thus it is self-perpetuating: it feeds on its own successes.

The triangle breaks down only when the loop is broken for an extended period of time.

The participants in an iron triangle—the congressional committees and subcommittees, administrative agencies, and interest groups—vary in terms of how well they fit into the triangle configuration and how effective they are in controlling policy to their own advantage.

In Congress the first step toward effective participation in an iron triangle is the creation of a specialized committee or subcommittee that deals exclusively, or at least primarily, with the issue at hand. For example, an "irrigation clique" was formed in Congress during the latter half of the nineteenth century but was not very effective until it was formalized as the Committee on Irrigation and Arid Lands. In recent years power in Congress shifted to the subcommittee level. Hence we would also expect the successful iron triangle to shift to a subcommittee devoted to its interests (Smith and Deering 1984:107, 116; Vogler and Waldman 1985:63).

Effective congressional participation in an iron triangle is further enhanced if the relevant committee or subcommittee is "packed" with legislators who support the goals and policies of the triangle. This can be accomplished through a selective recruitment process that results in ideological or regional overrepresentation. For example, agricultural committees are packed with legislators from farm states, and the irrigation committees are filled with westerners (see Horn 1970:30–32; Hinckley 1975:547–548; Davidson 1977:33, 1981:111; Smith and Deering 1984:106, 117).

An iron triangle's control over a committee or subcommittee can be further enhanced if the chair is fully devoted to the goals of the triangle. Until the early 1970s committee chairmen exercised almost dictatorial control over some committees, especially those dealing with distributive policy (Murphy 1974:176). Since that time congressional reforms have dispersed that power to a certain extent, but chairpersons are still important. A classic example is Representative Jamie Whitten, a longtime supporter of federal water development and chairman of the House Appropriations Committee. He recently explained that his position as chairman "doesn't mean you can run the [committee]. It just means you've got the first say" (*Wall Street Journal* 14 November 1985:58). Thus in the contemporary Congress an iron triangle is more likely to meet with success if the relevant committee and subcommittee chairpersons are in agreement with the goals of the triangle.

Administrative agencies must also meet certain conditions before they can effectively participate in an iron triangle. Of course, agencies that deal with distributive policies have a much greater potential for iron triangle participation because that is the principle area of activity for most triangles. If the agency's mission is flexible and open-ended, it can be expanded over time to meet the growing needs of the triangle.

Because iron triangles operate in a fairly stable manner, it is important that a participating agency also be stable over time. An agency that is repeatedly reorganized or placed under different authority lacks the stability necessary for effective participation. Under the best conditions the agency will remain relatively free of superior bureaucratic authority. This provides the autonomy alluded to earlier.

Another important element is the agency's ability to generate reliable, credible information, especially technical data (Meier 1979:62; Hamm 1980:410; Peters 1984:188; Rourke 1984:92–96). In politics information is a source of power and influence. An agency that cannot justify its programs or present data to convince others that its activities are beneficial will experience difficulty in establishing the kind of symbiotic ties that typify iron triangle relationships.

It takes more than scientific expertise and data to survive in a political environment, however. An agency must also be politically savvy, a characteristic that is often the result of inspired leadership (Meier 1979:66; Rourke 1984:108–111). Special political skills are needed to work closely and effectively with Congress and interest groups. These other participants in the triangle must be convinced—and remain convinced—that what is good for the agency is good for them. Hence a complex system of mutual adjustments and rewards must be developed and maintained.

These political tasks are easier if the agency has an image of being successful and powerful—one of the "movers and shakers" in Washington. A positive image is a product of both internal and external sources. Internally, agency personnel develop an image of themselves and their organization's effectiveness (Rourke 1984:103–108). A demoralized agency, or one that lacks self-confidence, will not inspire confidence from others (Clarke and McCool 1985:125–126). Conversely, agency personnel who are proud of their organization and devoted to its mission have more to offer their counterparts in the iron triangle. Agency image is also shaped by external sources: other actors and institutions. Bureaucracies, like individuals, have reputations.

Finally, an agency must have an adequate level of resources. Mazmanian and Sabatier write that "a threshold level of funding is necessary if there is to be any possibility of achieving statutory objectives . . . an inadequate level can doom a program before it begins" (1983:26). As we will see, that statement is acutely relevant to some of the programs discussed in the following chapters.

Interest groups compose the third corner of the triangle. According to Ripley and Franklin, iron triangles are "the most pervasive and effective channel for interest group effect on policy and program decisions" (1984:12). Like administrative agencies, interest groups vary in their ability to affect policy and steer government funds and programs in their direction. Groups that are generously funded and operated by a committed, highly professional staff have the greatest potential for success (Ornstein and Elder 1978:70; Schlozman and Tierney 1986:89). These resources become "a form of political currency which can be spent on various pressure group strategies and activities" (Ippolito and Walker 1980:313). In addition, to quote Freeman's seminal study of the Indian iron triangle, an interest group should be "vocal, organized, cohesive, clever, knowledgeable, and persistent" (1965:30).[8]

Iron Triangles, Water Policy, and Change

In 1979, Dodd and Schott wrote that "power within Washington depends largely on one's ability to influence subsystem (i.e., iron triangle) politics" (p. 173). There have been changes in recent years, however, which affected iron triangles (see, for example, Heclo, 1978; Gais, Peterson, and Walker, 1984), and these changes will be quite evident in the latter chapters of this book. At this point it is necessary only to identify four possible ways in which iron triangles respond to change.[9] First, political forces from outside the iron triangle often have a temporary impact on a triangle, which responds in an ad hoc fashion and then returns to policy-making as usual. Second, an iron triangle can coopt potential new enemies by allocating resources to them. Third, new demands sometimes result in new iron triangles with their own system of policy-making. Fourth, the rise of new interests, especially when accompanied by larger changes in the sociopolitical environment, may destroy an existing iron triangle. Each of these potential responses plays a role in the study of water policy, as subsequent chapters will demonstrate.

A final note on the concept of iron triangles is necessary to place it in theoretical perspective. The concept is a model, a simplification, and hence does not anticipate all of the nuances of political reality. We must look for trends that indicate the presence of these factors, not absolute conditions. As Hamm points out, the elements of iron triangles fall along a continuum (1983:415). To theorize we must generalize, however, and the iron triangle concept presented here is an attempt to identify the important factors that affect the political influence of an iron triangle. This permits us to compare iron triangles and identify their relative strengths and weaknesses.

Conclusion

This book is a comparative study of differential rates of water development. The primary focus is on the water development program of the Indian iron triangle and the non-Indian water development iron triangle. There is also considerable discussion of the Justice Department because of its important role in this issue area and because it provides another point of contrast, not being part of a triangle. Hence I will compare a traditionally weak iron triangle, a traditionally strong one, and an agency that is not part of a triangle.

There are several dimensions to this comparison. First, it is a longitudinal comparison. I will examine how water development programs have changed over time. Although the Army Corps of Engineers began its work in 1802, its programs and budget began to mushroom at the turn of the century, "a time of great federal water resources effort" (Holmes 1972:1). During the same period the Indian irrigation program began in earnest, the *Winters* decision was handed down, and the 1902 Reclamation Act initiated the federal government's irrigation program.

In addition, a comparative study of Indian and non-Indian federal water development provides an opportunity to compare and contrast the implementation of a judicially created water right with rights that were developed primarily in the legislative arena. Hence the special problems associated with the implementation of court-sponsored policy can be studied within a suitable comparative context. Studies of judicial implementation usually focus on controversial issues, such as school desegregation or abortion, that do not have a competing, legislatively created program to use as a reference point. In short, we can learn something about the relative policy-making powers of different branches of government.

Finally, this study provides an opportunity to compare programs across racial lines. The BIA water development program was designed to aid an oppressed and disadvantaged minority, whereas the Corps of Engineers and the Bureau of Reclamation primarily serve the dominant white majority. Thus we can compare how the racial status of these groups affected water development.

The book is organized as follows: chapter 2 explains the political context of the *Winters* decision by examining the politics of non-Indian water development during that period. Chapter 3 discusses the *Winters* decision and the response to it by the Justice Department, the courts, and Congress. Chapters 4 and 5 cover roughly the period from 1910 to 1975. The former traces the growth and development of the Corps of Engineers and the Bureau of Reclamation; the latter does the same for the BIA and its water development program for Indians. Chapter 6 examines the various conflicts among these water development programs. Chapters 7 and 8 concentrate on the "contemporary period": roughly the last ten years, when significant challenges have threatened to alter both federal water development policy and Indian policy. A final chapter offers some conclusions about the future of water policy, water rights, and iron triangles.

CHAPTER TWO

Federal Water Development at the Turn of the Century

Save the Forests; Store the Floods; Reclaim the Deserts; Make Homes On the Land.

—Slogan of the National Irrigation Congress

Introduction

This chapter concentrates on political phenomena of the early twentieth century that still have an impact on water policy; hence it is a selective rather than a comprehensive discussion of the period. The time frame ends about 1908 in order to provide a clear picture of political reality at the time of the *Winters* decision. The most significant event of that era was the passage of the 1902 Reclamation Act.

The Reclamation Act culminated a twenty-five-year struggle to enlist the aid of the federal government to irrigate the West. The act was unique in several ways. It created a special reclamation fund that funneled money from the sale of public lands into government-built irrigation projects. Participating farmers were required to repay the costs of the projects by making ten interest-free installments to this reclamation fund. This money would then be used to build other projects. In addition, the Reclamation Service was created in the U.S. Geological Survey to construct and maintain the projects in sixteen western states (Texas was added in 1906).

The unique features of the 1902 act were developed in response to a wide variety of conflicting inputs and reflected the prevailing political forces extant at the time. The development of an organized political effort to pass a reclamation law began soon after the publication in 1878 of John Wesley Powell's "Report on the Lands of the Arid Region," which argued that the West could be de-

14

veloped only through a coordinated, communal effort. By 1889 there was sufficient congressional interest in irrigation to establish a Select Committee on Irrigation and Arid Lands in each house, and in 1891 the first of a series of National Irrigation Congresses was held to promote western irrigation. Interest in a federal program was furthered in 1897 with the publication of the influential Chittenden Report, which concluded that the federal government should "build, own, and operate [water] works, holding the stored waters absolutely free for specific use under local regulations" (Reclamation Service Annual Report 1902:37). The Reclamation Act was not without its detractors, however. Many easterners objected to the use of federal funding for western projects.

These conflicting political inputs had an impact on the policy-making process that ultimately yielded the 1902 Reclamation Act. The law was a novel attempt to deal with the problems of western agriculture, and it brought life-giving water to millions of acres of arid land. Many of the conflicts generated by the passage of the bill persist to this day, however. Thus we can gain a greater understanding of contemporary water policy by examining the major political forces that were shaping national water policy at the turn of the century, when the modern era of water development began. In this chapter I will review not only the politics of western reclamation but also the rivers and harbors program of the Corps of Engineers. As the following pages will demonstrate, these two programs are inextricably linked in the policy-making process.

The Federal-State Relationship

There has long been a basic contradiction in the West's position in regard to water development; many westerners want federal funds for water development but do not want federal control. Politically this has required a difficult balancing act and exposed the West to potential federal hegemony. The national reclamation movement was acutely aware of this threat and had "mixed emotions" (Dunbar 1983:193) about a federal reclamation program.

The federal government's initial response to the West's plea for aid was the 1894 Carey Act, which was "designed to satisfy advocates of state action" (Glass 1964:14). This act ceded millions of acres of federal lands to western states, which were then supposed to use the proceeds from the sale of those lands for a state-level reclamation program. In other words, federal resources were distributed to western states without federal control. Although 9.75 million acres of federal land passed to the states by 1906 (National Irrigation Congress 1907:119), the states failed to establish viable reclamation programs. The land most susceptible to irrigation was already developed by private irrigators, and the remaining lands required a substantial investment per acre and a complex system of storage, diversion, and delivery before they could be successfully farmed. The "dismal and discouraging failure" (Worster, 1985:157) of the Carey Act convinced many westerners that only a program funded by the national government could succeed. As late as 1900, however, the reclamation movement was still badly divided:

> At that time there were two radically opposing views struggling for recognition. The first was for national development and the second was for turning over the public lands or their proceeds to the States. Messrs. Newlands [Congressman from Nevada] and Maxwell [founder of the National Irrigation Association] were particularly enthusiastic in their advocacy of the first course. (James 1917:14)

Thus when Congressman Newlands began the fight in Congress for an irrigation bill, the reclamation movement was far from united on the role of the federal government. The National Irrigation Congress, however, had gradually accepted the need for a federal program and used its considerable influence to push for a comprehensive bill. It is important to note that this shift toward federal aid was not intended to compromise state control over water. Rather, it was viewed as a federal investment in a water development program operating under the aegis of state prior appropriation laws.

This combination of federal money and state control was a compromise position between the opposing western factions and was embodied in nearly every pronouncement supporting a reclamation bill. For example, both Republican and Democratic party platforms for 1900 called for a federal irrigation program, the Republican platform "reserving control of the distribution of water for irrigation to the respective States and Territories" and the Democratic platform "preserving all rights to the states" (Reclamation Service Annual Report 1902:40–41). President Theodore Roosevelt declared that "irrigation works should be built by the National Government. . . . The distribution of the water, the diversion of the streams among irrigators, should be left to the settlers themselves, in conformity with State laws and without interference with those laws or with vested rights" (*Congressional Record* 1902:6677).[1]

When a reclamation bill was introduced in Congress in 1901 there arose considerable controversy over section 8, which dealt with the issue of federal versus state control. The original version introduced in the Senate read as follows:

> Sec. 8. That nothing in this Act shall be construed as affecting or intended to affect or to in any way interfere with the laws of any State or Territory relating to the control, appropriation, use, or distribution of water used in irrigation, but State and Territorial laws shall govern and control in the appropriation, use and distribution of the waters rendered available by the works constructed under the provisions of this Act: *Provided*, that the right to the use of water acquired under the provisions of this Act shall be appurtenant to the land irrigated, and beneficial use shall be the basis, the measure, and the limit of the right. (*Congressional Record* 1902:6762)

When the bill went to the House, however, the following language in section 8 was struck: "But State and Territorial laws shall govern and control in the appropriation, use, and distribution of the water rendered available by the works constructed under the provisions of this act." In its place a new phrase was inserted:

> . . . , or any vested right acquired thereunder, the Secretary of the Interior, in carrying out the provisions of this Act, shall proceed in conformity with such laws, and nothing herein shall in any way affect any right of any State or of the Federal Government or of any land owner, appropriator, or user of water in, to or from any interstate stream or the waters thereof. (*Congressional Record* 1902:6762)

This modification of section 8 was primarily the work of several legislators from nonwestern states and could be construed as a retreat from a position of total state control; the language prohibiting interference with state law was replaced by a guarantee of protection for state *or* federal rights. Ultimately the amended version was adopted. The changes made in section 8 would later create disagreement over Congress' intent.

Despite the proposed change in language, there were still numerous opponents of the bill who objected to the amount of state control. Congressman Ray of New York complained that under the bill "the United States surrenders all control. Congress surrenders all control. The laws of the several states are to control" (*Congressional Record* 1902:6766). Representative Robinson of Indiana complained that the bill was "a lame, bungling effort" to accomplish an "impossible blending" of the opposing ideas for national and state control, and as a result this "hotch-potch of a bill" was filled with "incongruities" (*Congressional Record* 1902:6670).

Although a number of congressmen remained critical of section 8 as drafted, the House refused to amend it to provide for full federal control (*Congressional Record* 1902:6766). Supporters of state control argued that section 8, as written, "follows the well-established precedent in national legislation of recognizing local and State laws relative to the appropriation and distribution of water" (*Congressional Record* 1902:6678). Congressman Mondell of Wyoming listed numerous statutes and regulations issued by the General Land Office that recognized the "doctrine of State control" (*Congressional Record* 1902:6679).

Section 8 as finally adopted was a confused amalgam of federal and state responsibilities, wrought by the necessity for political compromise. It "failed to clarify or define federal and state rights and responsibilities" (Pisani 1982:268). As a result, the argument over federal versus state control did not end with the passage of the 1902 Reclamation Act. Some federal policymakers were concerned that state water laws were too contradictory and inadequate to ensure a legally secure supply of water for federal reclamation projects. The Reclamation Service immediately began a campaign to convince western states to adopt uniform water codes. The first annual report of the service opined, "It appears probable that in some of the States radical changes in the laws must be made before important projects can be undertaken" (1902–1903:33).

In an effort to encourage state action, Morris Bien of the Reclamation Service drew up a model water code and, with the support of Chief Engineer Frederick Newell, began pressuring states to adopt it. The states resisted because the Bien plan "promised important new privileges to the federal government" (Pisani 1982:271). This dispute quickly developed into a full-scale conflict between the Reclamation Service and the reclamation movement. Despite this opposition Bien persisted and in an effort to justify his position formulated a new theory that the federal government had retained control over western waters. In a series of memoranda Bien argued that Congress never relinquished its control over water, and the modifications made to section 8 of the Reclamation Act indicated that the act did not consent to state control (Bien memorandum 1904, 1906, n.d.).

Predictably, many people in the reclamation movement reacted strongly. A speaker at the 1906 National Irrigation Congress warned that

> any plan or scheme that seeks to transfer the control and administration of irrigation affairs, from the several States to the general government at Washington, is regarded as an encroachment upon the rights of the State and an interference with individual prerogative acquired under local custom and law, and meets with more or less hostility on the part of those largely interested in irrigation affairs. (1906:65)

This states' rights position was supported in a crucial water rights case before the Supreme Court in 1907. In *Kansas v. Colorado* the high court declared that the federal government had very little control over nonnavigable water. Director Newell of the Reclamation Service feared that the case might "prove embarrassing in some of the litigation of the Reclamation Service" (Newell to Supervising and Project Engineers 28 May 1907).

The decision in *Kansas v. Colorado* was a definitive victory for the advocates of state control. Yet even western partisans could see the inadequacy of state water laws and urged the states to "put an end to the maddening uncertainty and endless litigation which has characterized the ownership and retention of water rights in many of the arid states" (National Irrigation Congress 1906:73). Even Theodore Roosevelt, the darling of the reclamation movement, remonstrated against the "lax and uncertain" water laws of western states (quoted in Reclamation Service Annual Report 1902:44). In short, the entire reclamation program rested upon laws that were entirely inadequate. Hays described some of the typical problems created by state water laws:

> No one knew how much water was available. Moreover, since the law provided that filings be recorded by counties instead of by watersheds, no one court could determine the total number of water rights claimed on a single stream. Consequently, judges often established rights far in excess of available supply. . . . Such confusion retarded both private and public irrigation development. (1959:16)

By the time the 1908 *Winters* decision was handed down, the situation in regard to federal-state conflict over water rights had become dismal. The Reclamation Service was at loggerheads with its principal constituency, the reclamation movement, a dangerous situation politically for any bureaucracy. The future of the federal program was in doubt, partly because of these legal problems.

Samuel Weil, in his famous 1911 water treatise, wrote that "the conflict between State and Federal jurisdiction . . . is becoming marked; and the law is in an uncertain and formative stage" (p. 478).

The U.S. Army Corps of Engineers and the Eastern Vote

By the time the Reclamation Service came into existence in 1902 the Corps of Engineers was already 100 years old. The corps is one of the oldest and most successful agencies in the federal executive branch. Its history is one of almost continuous expansion. Organized in 1802, the corps quickly developed a close relationship with project beneficiaries and members of Congress. In 1824 the first Rivers and Harbors Bill was passed, authorizing the corps to take charge of maintaining navigation on the Mississippi and Ohio rivers (Rivers and Harbors Act of May 24, 1824).

The 1824 act was only the first in a long litany of statutes that expanded the corps' responsibilities and hence its budget, power, and prestige. By 1900 the agency's activities had been expanded by a "waterway renaissance . . . a new enthusiasm for the improvement of [the nation's] navigable streams" (Hays 1959:91). The corps' enlarged mission included "responsibility for bridges, wharves, piers, channels and harbors, diversions of water, and deposits of refuse and other materials" (Holmes 1972:4).

With so many authorized activities the potential for pork barrel was great. The strength of the corps in Congress was illustrated by the way the Appropriations Committee organized its Subcommittee on Rivers and Harbors. Horn explains:

> In 1887, the Committee on Appropriations listed its River and Harbor Subcommittee as consisting of members of the Senate Committee on Commerce—a legislative committee. This was tacit recognition of the fact that neither Appropriations nor its predecessor, Finance, had ever been able to secure jurisdiction over the politically important pork barrel bills that appropriated federal funds for dams and channel improvements. (1970:40)

The corps' activities were not limited to eastern rivers and ports. The agency's engineers were "the principal agents of the Government in the exploration of the West" (Army Corps of Engineers 1973). When a federal reclamation program was being contemplated in the late 1800s the government turned to the Corps of Engineers for a detailed study. The resulting analysis, the Chittendon Report, was "instrumental in persuading a national audience to entertain the idea of federal dam construction" (Lee 1980:14).

Thus the Corps of Engineers was a force to be reckoned with when the federal government began to consider a reclamation program, and many of the opponents of the reclamation bill were easterners who strongly supported the Corps of Engineers. When the leaders of the reclamation movement initiated their drive for a reclamation bill, it was obvious they would have to overcome opposition from eastern congressmen. The slogan "Unite the West and convert the East" (National Irrigation Congress 1908:153) was adopted at the 1898 meeting of the National Irrigation Congress in preparation for the battle in Congress over a reclamation bill.

That battle materialized the following year when Senator Francis Warren of Wyoming introduced a bill to fund the construction of four western reservoirs. Congressman Newlands of Nevada introduced a similar bill for his state (Dunbar 1983:50). Both failed to pass because of opposition from eastern representatives. Several more bills were introduced in 1900 but again failed "because they were unable to command support outside the West" (Glass 1964:15). The following year Newlands tried again, this time receiving support from the new president, Theodore Roosevelt. An ardent supporter of reclamation, Roosevelt made the politically astute move of comparing the proposed reclamation program to the well-established Corps of Engineer's program for rivers and harbors:[2]

> It is as right for the National Government to make the streams and rivers of the arid regions useful by engineering works for water storage as to make useful the rivers and harbors of the humid regions by engineering works of another kind. (*Congressional Record* 1902:6677)

It took more than this, however, to overcome the East's opposition. Easterners' principal complaint was that the proposed reclamation bills were a drain on the national treasury, which was primarily stocked with taxes from the populous East. In other words, the reclamation program as originally envisioned was simply a transfer of money from the East to the West. The East was so hostile that, in Newlands' words, a "kind of guerrilla warfare" ensued in Congress (*Congressional Record* 1902:841–842). To mollify the East, Newlands modified his proposed program to include a revolving "arid lands reclamation fund" that would finance projects from the sale of public lands in the western states. Then eastern money would not be used to build western projects.

Still, many eastern congressmen objected, claiming that the plan imposed an unrealistic burden on project farmers, who would bear all construction costs. They argued that the debt would overwhelm the farmers and that the federal government would, by default, have to pay. Congressman Ray of New York called the proposed 1902 bill a "robbery or looting of the Treasury of the United States" (*Congressional Record* 1902:6766). Hepburn of Ohio called it "the most insolent and impudent larceny that I have ever seen embodied in a legislative filching from the common fund" (*Congressional Record* 1902:6742).

Despite such sentiments, the addition of the reclamation fund and the payback provision to the bill allayed the fears of many easterners. It also disappointed many westerners, who were clearly looking for a direct federal subsidy. Actually, they did receive a subsidy: the loans to project farmers were interest-free. Rucker and Fishback postulate why this particular form of subsidy was acceptable:

> The subsidy given to irrigators took the form of an exemption from interest charges on the loan for construction costs. Apparently this feature received little attention during the discussion of the bill. It was obvious that western interests wanted a subsidy, but why Congress opted for this particular form and not a direct payment is unclear. Since an interest subsidy is more subtle than a direct subsidy, it is possible that this form was chosen to make the subsidy more acceptable to nonwestern congressmen, whose constituents were subsidizing irrigation projects. (1983:51)

Thus the financing arrangement of interest-free loans from a revolving trust fund made the bill more palatable to easterners. But still the critics persisted, and proponents of the bill had to turn to a new strategy. Taking a cue from President Roosevelt, they made a "hostage" of the Corps of Engineers. Senator Carter of Montana filibustered to death the 1901 Rivers and Harbors Bill, or, in the words of one westerner, "he put the lid on the 'porkbarrel' so tight they could not get it off" (National Irrigation Congress 1910:112). Apparently this was the "only way to impress the eastern mind with the fact that the West was desperately in earnest" (National Irrigation Congress 1908:87). This hostage strategy worked, and the following year the Reclamation Act was passed.

The final vote on the bill in the House, where opposition was strongest, demonstrates the widespread support for the measure. As the voting results presented in table 1 indicate, both major parties and all regions of the country supported the measure. The final tally was 146 for and 55 against the bill (*Congressional Record* 1902:6778).[3] In this way the corps and the Reclamation Service became intertwined in the same net of congressional reciprocity, a condition that persists to this day.

Filibusters from western legislators were not the only threats the Corps of Engineers was facing at that time. The progressive notions then prevalent emphasized rational planning based on objective, scientific data (one of the many slogans of the National Irrigation Congress was "Science, not chance" [1908:86]). With the advent of federal programs for flood control, navigation, reclamation, and power, it soon became evident to progressive planners that comprehensive, multipurpose river basin planning was needed to coordinate all of these efforts. Theodore Roosevelt succinctly summarized this approach when he announced the appointment of an Inland Waterways Commission to study the possibilities of multipurpose water development: "Works designed to control our waterways have thus far usually been undertaken for a single purpose. . . . The time has come for merging local projects and users of the inland waters in a comprehensive plan designed for the benefit of the entire country" (quoted in Hays 1959:106).

Such a comprehensive approach constituted a direct threat to

TABLE 1

HOUSE VOTE ON THE 1902 RECLAMATION ACT,
BY PARTY AND REGION

	Yeas	Nays
Party		
Democrat	76	13
Republican	68	42
Populist	2	—
Region		
West	38	0
North	71	45
South	37	10

the autonomy of the Corps of Engineers, and the agency fought "tooth and nail" (Robinson 1979:26) against any plan that would "destroy their autonomy and subordinate them to men with an entirely different viewpoint" (Hays 1959:109). Autonomy is an important determinant of agency power because it permits the agency to make policy that meets its own needs. In this case the corps needed to maintain its political support by constructing locally oriented projects—the kind that create strong congressional and interest group support. This emphasis on local benefits was directly threatened by comprehensive planning, which, as the president pointed out, would concentrate on national, not local, priorities.

The corps was aided in its fight against comprehensive planning by demands for huge corps waterway projects. In a *quid pro quo* the corps agreed to support these projects, even some that it had previously disapproved, in return for widespread political support. The proposed projects included a waterway from Chicago to New Orleans and a coastal waterway that virtually ringed the entire eastern seaboard.

The reclamation movement also had an impact on the corps' fight against comprehensive planning. The West wanted its share of waterway projects, including a proposed Pacific Deep Waterway from "Lewiston [Idaho] to the sea" (National Irrigation Congress 1909:137). These waterways would provide cheap transportation for the products of irrigated agriculture. There was also fear and animosity between the two types of water development and their respective supporters, however. The corps had opposed the 1902 Reclamation Act, and the agency's supporters bitterly resented the 1901 filibuster. After the act became the law of the land, the Reclamation Service and the corps quickly developed into rival agencies. Paradoxically, however, the agencies were dependent upon each other; the reclamation program was essentially a modified western counterpart of the rivers and harbors program so popular in other regions of the country. In the atmosphere of congressional reciprocity, each program could be used to justify—or threaten—the other. This militated against any kind of coordinated planning.

In sum, by 1908 the Corps of Engineers was sufficiently strong politically to defeat proposals for comprehensive planning. To maintain that political strength, however, it had to acquiesce to the demands of congressmen, interest groups, and, to a certain extent, the demands of the reclamation movement. These forces produced an ever expanding federal water development program characterized by congressional logrolling across programs and an emphasis on local benefits.

Interest Group Support

Interest groups are critical to the success of an iron triangle. They form the organizational nucleus of an agency's constituency and a congressman's constituency. For policy issues in which benefits are locally oriented, as in the case of water projects, the power and influence of interest groups can be even more compelling. Thus it is necessary to examine the role that interest groups played in the early development of the federal water resources program.

In 1889 both houses of Congress formed irrigation committees. The Senate committee, chaired by Stewart of Nevada, immediately embarked on a tour of the West to promote government-aided irrigation. A coterie of legislators soon formed an "irrigation clique" (Stegner 1954:300) in Congress, but what was lacking was an active, organized response from potential beneficiaries of an irrigation program. Interest group activity on behalf of irrigation began in earnest with the formation of the National Irrigation Congress in 1891; following a severe drought five railroads provided funding and transportation for a series of annual meetings at which proponents of irrigation could generate publicity and understanding for their cause. Generously financed, these meetings were formal, grandiose affairs in which both political and technical problems were discussed. Irrigation was promoted with almost religious fervor, with proponents arguing in the florid tongue of the Gilded Age: "The Midas' touch, which turns the desert sands to gold, is the presence of water where empires shall be rebuilt for the child of the ages, heir of time" (National Irrigation Congress 1905:26).

The National Irrigation Congress was an effective engine of publicity when it was in session, but it met for only a few days each year. A permanent organization was needed, so in 1899 George Maxwell, a prominent California water lawyer, formed the National Irrigation Association to "strengthen and supplement" the activity of the Congress (Smythe 1911:272). This group consisted "largely of businessmen from both the East and the West" and had "considerable funds at its disposal" (Reclamation Service Annual Report 1902:40). By the time the battle in Congress over the reclamation bill began in 1901, a formidable and well-financed lobby had been organized to fight for federal reclamation.

These lobbying efforts were complemented by a number of publications committed to the task of influencing public opinion. The National Irrigation Congress produced a journal, *The Irrigation Age*, edited by William Smythe, which "launched the national reclamation crusade" (Pisani 1984:343). Smythe's 1899 book, *The Conquest of Arid America*, dramatized and glorified the effort to irrigate the West. Smythe's writings "were a mighty force on behalf of U.S. government-assisted reclamation in the West" (Lee 1980:12). Maxwell's National Irrigation Association also produced a monthly periodical called *Maxwell's Talisman*.

When the reclamation bill was introduced in 1901, an impressive and diverse array of interest groups endorsed it, including the National Association of Manufacturers, the National Board of Trade, the National Business League, the American Federation of Labor, the United Mine Workers, and many other business and labor associations (*Congressional Record* 1902:6729). These interest groups had a pervasive impact on Congress. Many of them were based in the East and represented powerful elements in society.

With the passage of the Reclamation Act a new source of interest group support developed. Section 6 instructed the secretary of interior to manage projects up to the point at which the "major portions" of the irrigated lands are paid for, and at that time ownership and management of the project would be transferred to the landowners. These owners formed water user associations based on model charters developed by the Interior Department. The Salt River Valley Water Users' Association was the first to be formed, in 1902. By 1908, the year of the *Winters* decision, the number of associations had grown to twenty-four (Reclamation Service Annual Report 1907–1908:11). Although the principal purpose of these associations was to fulfill the necessary contractual obligations of the projects, they became quite vociferous on all matters that influenced western irrigation. As conflict over water rights and repayment provisions intensified in the ensuing years, the associations became more politicized.

Although the irrigation program was heavily supported by many powerful interest groups, the Reclamation Service was not always able to capitalize on this strength because of conflicts over policy. The Reclamation Service's insistence on federal control over water rights and strict adherence to the payback requirement often angered the reclamation movement's organized interests.

While interest groups struggled over the passage and implementation of the Reclamation Act, the Corps of Engineers' program was also the focus of interest group activity. The "waterway renaissance" of the late nineteenth and early twentieth centuries was accompanied by the development of a highly organized constituency devoted to federal water development. The Interstate Mississippi River Levee Improvement Association was the first of many interest groups organized during that era. Established in 1890, the group lobbied hard for the corps' flood control program. In 1901 the Rivers and Harbors Congress began operation and developed into "the most powerful national force for expanded waterway improvement" (Hays 1969:94). The mission of this interest group was to promote "all phases of water development" (Maass 1951:45). Five years later another pro-Corps of Engineers interest group formed: the Lakes-to-the-Gulf Deep Waterway Association pushed for a ship channel from Chicago to New Orleans. Another massive project was promoted by the Atlantic Deeper Waterways Association. Organized in 1907, this group counted among its members many U.S. congressmen. In fact, the first president of the organization was Representative J. Hampton Moore from Philadelphia, a city that would profit from a coastal waterway stretching from New England to Florida (Maass 1951:41). By 1907 there were waterway lobbies in nearly every region of the country. In that year eight different conventions were held solely to promote waterway development (*Congressional Record* 1907:390).

Many of the interest groups pressing for increased funding for corps projects published newsletters and other types of promotional material. *The National Rivers and Harbors News* has long been one of the most influential publications. The corps' viewpoints also found an outlet in professional journals such as *Engineering News* and the *Proceedings of the American Society of Civil Engineers*.

While numerous groups were organizing to promote reclamation, flood control, or navigation, another group of individuals formed the National Drainage Congress in 1906 to press for federal funding to drain swamps and lowlands (Hays 1959:223). This group's demands were endorsed by the National Irrigation Congress (National Irrigation Congress 1907:266).

In sum, by the time the *Winters* decision was handed down in 1908, a formidable array of interest groups had been organized to pressure Congress for increased water development. For the most part these groups lobbied for projects with localized benefits that aided businessmen and farmers in specific locales. In some cases the Reclamation Service or the Corps of Engineers opposed project proposals on the grounds of objective engineering or economic analysis. The organized political pressure was usually too great for the agencies to resist, however, and they ultimately had to bow to the pressure. These agencies, and other Progressive Era bureaucracies, soon learned "a fundamental reality of American politics: power in the United States is primarily *local* power" (McConnell 1966:200).

Congress also proved to be quite responsive to the needs of locally oriented interest groups. Both houses had long-standing committees on rivers and harbors legislation. And beginning in 1889 both had a Committee on Irrigation and Arid Lands that were mandated to "consider the subject of irrigation and the best mode of reclaiming the arid lands" (*Congressional Record* 14 February 1889:1881). Typically these committees were filled with legislators from affected areas. For example, in 1901 the House Committee on Irrigation of Arid Land had a majority of western congressmen, who were a small minority in Congress at that time. Their counterpart in the Senate numbered eleven senators from the West, two from the North, and one from the South. Such membership increased the leverage of interest groups in Congress and created a greater potential for pork barrel.

Turn-of-the-Century Pork Barrel

By 1902 the Corps of Engineers had established an entrenched iron triangle that was routinely accused of building pork barrel water projects. In 1826 the first "omnibus" rivers and harbors bill was passed. That is, for the first time a large group of projects were lumped together in one bill. This prevents consideration of the merits of each project; if the good ones are to be built, then the questionable projects must be built also. According to one authority, the 1826 omnibus bill was the beginning of pork barrel water development in America (Maxey 1919:691–692).

The omnibus approach to rivers and harbors appropriations quickly became a congressional habit, and beginning with Andrew Jackson a litany of presidential vetoes attempted to stop them. Between 1832 and 1882 the omnibus rivers and harbors bill was vetoed five times. In each case the president's veto message contained references to three typical criticisms of alleged pork barrel legislation. First, the projects were strategically spread throughout many states and congressional districts in order to maximize the political payoff; second, many of the projects created only a localized benefit and therefore did not contribute to the national welfare; and third, the logrolling approach to omnibus legislation would lead to an ever expanding, self-perpetuating public works program.

For example, President Polk complained in his 1846 veto message that the Rivers and Harbors Act had a tendency to "embrace objects for the expenditure of the public money which are local in their character, benefiting but a few at the expense of the common Treasury of the whole" (*Congressional Record* 3 June 1896:6040). President Arthur's veto message explained how such bills would demand an ever increasing amount of funding: "As citizens of one state find that money, to raise which they, in common with the whole country, are taxed, is to be expended for local improvements in another state they demand similar benefits themselves. . . . Thus as the bill becomes more objectionable it secures more support" (*Congressional Record* 3 June 1896:6041). Arthur's veto created an important precedent that distinguished it from previous vetoes of rivers and harbors bills: Congress overrode it.

By the end of the nineteenth century "the annual authorization bill for waterway construction and maintenance became one of Capitol Hill's cherished political institutions" (Reid 1980:3). Congressional resolve to protect that institution was tested once again in 1896 when Grover Cleveland, who had a penchant for vetoes, vetoed the rivers and harbors appropriation for fiscal year 1897. The debate over the bill is instructive because it involved the same issues that are still being debated today.

Cleveland's veto message noted that "there are 417 items of appropriation contained in this bill, and every part of the country is represented in the distribution of its favors" (*Congressional Record* 3 June 1896:6027). Specifically, the projects were scattered throughout forty-one states and two territories. As one opponent of the bill put it, "the 'pork', as it is facetiously termed, is judiciously distributed" (*Congressional Record* 10 June 1896:6434).

The projects were not distributed randomly, however. Congressman Dockey of Missouri pointed out that the members of the House Committee on Rivers and Harbors were the principal recipients of the projects: "Appropriations and authorized contracts wholly within their States aggregate $31,094,135,91, or nearly one-half the entire bill. . . . An explanation is found for the enormous pressure exerted by members . . . for assignment to service on that committee" (*Congressional Record* 10 June 1896:6434). Opponents of the bill also pointed out that the Corps of Engineers refused to recommend a number of the projects but Congress authorized them anyway.

Congress' reaction to Cleveland's veto was swift. The Committee on Rivers and Harbors voted unanimously to recommend an override and warned that "if this bill should fail there are hundreds of useful projects . . . which would be suspended, whereby great waste would be incurred" (H.R. 2164, 1896:5). Under a suspension of the rules the House voted 219 to 61 to override. In the Senate a similarly lopsided margin of 56 to 5 also overrode the veto. Senator Stewart of Nevada, a leader in the reclamation movement, spoke in support of the bill because it funded a survey of reservoir sites in Wyoming and Colorado, which resulted in the Chittenden Report (*Congressional Record* 2 June 1896:6011, 3 June 1896: 6045, 10 June 1896:6433).

When the reclamation bill was under serious consideration in 1901, a number of federal policymakers wanted to avoid creating another pork barrel program similar to the rivers and harbors bill. President Roosevelt warned that "there should be no extravagance, and believers in the need of irrigation will most benefit their cause by seeing to it that it is free from the least taint of reckless expenditure of the public monies" (Reclamation Service Annual Report 1902:44). In addition, eastern congressmen were hesitant to set up an omnibus appropriation program for the exclusive benefit of the West. They knew from experience how expensive it could be.

The most common proposed solution to the pork barrel problem was to place control over project selection in the hands of administrative experts. This was not a new idea; during the debate over the 1896 rivers and harbors bill an opponent of the measure suggested that project selection be controlled by "some competent executive board or bureau" (*Congressional Record* 3 June 1896:6032). During the progressive years there was an unprecedented commitment to the ideal of objective, expert administration, so it is not surprising that such an approach would find its way into the reclamation bill. Congressman Newlands supported this idea of administrative rather than legislative control:

> Hoping to forestall disagreement among western congressmen over project locations, he suggested that the Secretary of the Interior have complete discretion in selecting projects and apportioning funds. Congressional control of annual appropriations frequently produced confusion, poor coordination, and inefficiency in rivers and harbors projects. The Nevada congressman proposed that expert planning based on thorough technical investigations, instead of logrolling, would direct the course of western irrigation. (Robinson 1979:16)

In response to this idea the 1902 act gave the secretary of interior complete control over project selection, a "radical delegation of power to the Executive" (Holmes 1972:9) that Congress "was later to regret" (Gates 1968:658).

The decision to delegate control of the new program to the secretary of interior was an attempt to meet the ideal of impartial administrative control (William Smythe boasted that it avoided the "hurly-burly of Congress" [1911:278]), but the secretary was a poor choice for such a responsibility. The secretary is a political appointee and, like congressmen, has a constituency; therefore he is subject to many of the same kinds of demands. The problem with congressional control over project selection is that the projects are distributed widely to maximize political support. The secretary of interior faced the same temptation. Political pressure to build a reclamation project in every western state surged even before the 1902 act was passed. In order to gain widespread support in the West, the leaders of the reclamation movement had to appeal to every state that wanted a project. During the debate on the bill Congressman Ray of New York predicted that the secretary of interior would yield to political pressure:

> The Administration . . . will have such a clamor from the West that it cannot resist. Therefore, to please Nevada, the Secretary will start a reservoir on the eastern slope of California; to please Wyoming there would be established a reservoir somewhere up in the Rocky Mountains; to please Arizona there would be a reservoir established in that section, and to please Colorado, a reservoir somewhere in that section. (*Congressional Record* 12 June 1902:6685)

Congressman Ray's prediction was uncannily accurate. By the time the act was passed there "arose from every part of the arid and semi-arid region insistent requests for examinations of all sorts of schemes" (Reclamation Service Annual Report 1911–1912:4). Soon after the Reclamation Service was organized, the secretary of interior authorized five projects, all in one day. By 1905 there were sixteen projects in thirteen states, and Texas was added to the list of eligible recipients. That same year Charles Walcott, director of the U.S. Geological Survey (the parent agency of the Reclamation Service until 1907) warned the National Irrigation Congress that the program was already in trouble:

> The Reclamation Service is constantly being importuned to make surveys in all parts of the country and expend the money broadly. The time has arrived, however, when it is necessary to limit general surveys, as there is not money in the [reclamation] fund to construct more than one or two projects in each state or territory, and general surveys will lead to expenditure without present adequate return. (National Irrigation Congress 1905:197)

The initiation of new projects continued, however, and by 1909 the secretary of interior had authorized thirty-three primary projects and thirty secondary projects; fifteen of the primary projects were less than half-finished, and only six were completed (Reclamation Service Annual Report 1908–1909:27–180). The secretary clearly let political considerations influence his selection of projects.

The secretary's overzealous authorization of projects placed a severe financial burden on the reclamation fund. This situation was exacerbated by the inability of project farmers to repay their loans, which were supposed to replenish the fund. Many of the farmers were inexperienced and unprepared for the rigors of irrigated agriculture. In addition, because most of the projects were not finished, the government could not collect fees for water deliveries (as no water was being delivered) and farmers had no source of income to pay off their loans. In short, the idea of avoiding pork barrel water projects through administrative control and repayment provisions was not being implemented as planned.

In sum, by the time of the 1908 *Winters* decision the Corps of Engineers had a long-established relationship with Congress and powerful interest groups (i.e., an iron triangle) and participated vigorously in the making of distributive policy. Much of its work was criticized as pork barrel because projects were often chosen to meet local rather than national needs. The corps was strong enough, however, to resist calls for reform, such as the drive for comprehensive planning. In contrast, the reclamation program was designed to avoid some of the pitfalls of rivers and harbors legislation, but these reforms were not implemented as anticipated, and the program immediately became mired in funding problems. Essentially the secretary of interior was using political criteria to allocate revenues from a fund that was responsive only to objective, nonpolitical variables. Sufficient funding for all of the projects initiated by 1909 would have to await congressional involvement in the funding—and project selection—process.

Conclusion

Relying upon the discussion of iron triangles presented in chapter 1, we can discern a number of critically important developments in the first decade of the twentieth century. That era was a momentous time for the federal government's water development programs. To an extraordinary extent these programs reflected the social, economic, and political context of that time. Several prevalent social and political trends heavily influenced the formulation and implementation of water policy, and each is worth

discussing because of its direct impact on the waterway renaissance, the 1902 Reclamation Act, and, after 1908, the implementation of the Winters Doctrine.

The imprint of the conservationist-utilitarian philosophy is
deeply embedded in the water development programs formulated
at the turn of the century. To the conservationist water that escaped to the sea without first serving mankind was wasted. The
National Irrigation Congress promulgated "reservoirs and engineering works necessary to safeguard against overflow, and save
for beneficial use the flood waters that now run to waste" (1908:
357). To the conservationist any policy that militated against beneficial use was anathema because it interfered with "the highest
utilization for all purposes of all our public lands" (National Irrigation Congress 1908:358).

The 1902 Reclamation Act also reflected the prevailing agrarian
populism of the era. The Jeffersonian ideal played an important
role in this movement and its campaign for an irrigation bill. The
promoters of irrigation argued that the family farm was the soul
of America; hence anything the government could do to put the
"landless man on the manless land" (National Irrigation Congress
1905:26) was worthwhile: "Irrigation restores the ideal of the American home, when it leads the unsuccessful from the slavery of the
city to the sovereignty of the country" (National Irrigation Congress 1905:26). Frederick Newell explained that "the object of the
Reclamation Act is not so much to irrigate the land as it is to make
homes" (National Irrigation Congress 1905:28). The move to put
people on western farms was aimed in part at eastern urbanites
because it was feared they would succumb to the sins of the city
(for example, anarchist thought). This was especially true for new
immigrants, who were thought to be even more vulnerable to such
temptations. (There were proposals to advertise the reclamation
program in Europe—*before* immigrants even got on the boat.) In
short, the 1902 act was a social program designed to bring the
"Democracy of the Desert" to the common man:

> No more noble, more sacrificing, more patriotic work can be done by
> the citizenship of this great republic than to engage in the sublime effort
> to enable its sturdy and home-loving people of small means to locate
> upon the land. This meets the need in social reform in all of its cryings!
> (National Irrigation Congress 1909:25)

The Corps of Engineers' waterway development program was
also aided by agrarian populism. It was thought that inexpensive

water transportation would solve small farmers' economic problems and free them from the tyranny of the railroads.

The progressive, "good government" impulse was also much in evidence in the water policy of early twentieth-century America.[4] The decision to delegate the selection of irrigation projects to the secretary of interior and the drive for river basin planning were both products of the progressive ideal of comprehensive, objective decision-making. The movement to take politics out of administration was at a high point, riding upon the theories of scientific management and "the new positive conception of government . . . the idea of a planned society" (Waldo 1948:32). Great faith in science and technology was developing, accompanied by the belief that people can—and should—alter nature for their benefit. While Congress was considering the Reclamation Act it also debated the placement of the "Isthmian Canal," to be built in Central America.

Finally, water development at the turn of the century was part of the larger phenomenon of nationalistic expansionism. Manifest Destiny had pushed aside Indians, Mexico, Spain, and the claims of Great Britain. Now it must push aside the desert and the shallow, meandering river.

A favorable social/political context does not guarantee successful implementation, however. For the iron triangle to function effectively certain conditions must be met; conditions the Corps of Engineers met with ebullience but that eluded the Reclamation Service. The latter agency suffered in three areas. First, an iron triangle requires a close working relationship between Congress and local constituent interest groups. An injection of executive control between these two points limits the effectiveness of the triangle. In the case of reclamation, the secretary of interior controlled the selection of projects. Therefore, congressmen could not take credit for selecting projects ("bringing home the bacon") and were reluctant to provide funding. A second and related issue concerned the payback provision of the reclamation law. Iron triangles are best at making distributive policy, whereby benefits are concentrated but costs are dispersed. The payback provision made that combination impossible, thereby reducing the political payoff from the projects. Additionally, the requirement that projects be funded from a revolving trust fund limited the potential expansion of the program and deprived Congress of the annual opportunity to appropriate funding for projects in home states or districts. The reclamation fund was a discrete source of revenue that would inevitably decline as time passed. The secretary of interior was authorizing projects as though he had a nearly unlimited source of funding, however. This left projects unfinished and angered important interest groups, which constitute a necessary element in an iron triangle. Finally, interest groups were further angered by the Reclamation Service's stand on water rights. As long as the service pushed for federal rather than state control over water allocation it would never develop the close relationship with western interest groups that is so critical to the success of an iron triangle.

In short, the Reclamation Service was in "serious trouble" (Gates 1968:663) by 1910. It lacked the stability and resources that are typical of agencies operating within an iron triangle. The reclamation program was experiencing so many problems that Director Newell felt compelled to begin his 1911 annual report with a section entitled "fallacies entertained" (1911–12:2), which listed the erroneous assumptions that had been made about the reclamation program.

In contrast, the Corps of Engineers was safely ensconced in a long-standing iron triangle. It had developed an unprecedented level of organizational autonomy and stability. This autonomy was disrupted occasionally by chief executives willing to risk meddling with a "sacred cow," but their long-term impact on water policy was minimal. Congress made sure of that. The agency was generously funded, and its engineer corps—an elite within the Army— enjoyed widespread respect and high morale. What its mission lacked in clarity it made up for in political responsiveness.

In sum, the Corps of Engineers was successfully implementing its policy objectives, which would best be defined as the distribution of government-financed benefits to specific localities or, in other words, distributive policy-making via an iron triangle. The Reclamation Service had yet to establish itself in a functioning iron triangle, but it held the potential for that *if* basic changes were made in the program. By 1908 those changes had yet to materialize.

Within this political context a conflict over water rights was brewing in a remote corner of Montana. It would pit Indians against Anglos, the Reclamation Service against the Bureau of Indian Affairs, local officials against national officials, and one doctrine of water law against another. It would have a lasting impact on the federal government's water development program, and vice versa. In other words, to understand the *Winters* case, which is the topic of the next chapter, it is necessary also to understand the extant political conditions analyzed in this chapter.

CHAPTER THREE

The *Winters* Decision and Its Progeny

The Indians had command of the lands and the waters . . . . Did they give up all this?

—*Winters v. U.S.*, 1908

Introduction

Concern for Indian water rights did not begin with the *Winters* decision. The first annual report of the Reclamation Service carried a stern admonition:

> The history of . . . Indians on arid lands has shown that unless pro-
> tected with great care the rights to the use of water on Indian lands
> have been gradually lost through neglect or oversight and the mere
> allotment of land without carefully guarding the future use of the neces-
> sary water has resulted disastrously to the Indians. (1902:289)

Despite this demonstration of concern for Indian rights, the reclamation program increased pressure on them to give up their water.
Many of the original reclamation projects immediately developed
conflicts with Indian tribes; the *Winters* case was one of these. Thus
the case typifies the water rights conflicts that were prevalent
during the initial stages of the reclamation program and continue
to this day.

The *Winters* decision also presents an opportunity to study the
interaction of several policy-making bodies; the Justice Department, the BIA, and the Reclamation Service represented various
points of view in the executive branch. Congress, which was actively involved in the move to irrigate the West, also had an opportunity to participate in the conflict. And the federal courts at the

district, appellate, and Supreme Court levels, participated in the decision-making process. To an extraordinary degree the *Winters* case set in motion a working relationship between these various decision-making bodies—and the relevant iron triangles—that persists to this day. Thus we can gain valuable insights into their contemporary relationships by examining the situation during and immediately after the *Winters* case.

Finally, the *Winters* decision presents an opportunity to examine the problem of program legitimacy. Reserved water rights were created by the courts and were never sanctioned by explicit statutory law. This creates difficulties in the implementation stage, especially when a program based on case law must compete with one mandated by statutory law. Lacking such authoritative congressional approval, the Indian water development program faced severe problems in implementing the spirit of the Winters Doctrine.

The Role of the Justice Department

When, in the spring of 1905, the BIA asked the Justice Department for assistance in protecting Indian water rights, the department was placed in an awkward position. As counsel for the federal government, the Justice Department was faced with the task of enforcing a contradictory and inconsistent set of water laws and policies. Stegner provides an incisive summary of western water rights at the turn of the century:

> [Western] water laws [were] a patchwork of improvisation, compromises, state law and federal law, interstate agreements and agreements between states and the federal government, riparian rights, appropriation rights, preferential uses, the "Wyoming Doctrine" . . . the "California Doctrine" . . . the "Colorado Doctrine." (1954:312)

By 1905, John Wesley Powell's warning that the West was "building up a heritage of conflict and litigation over water rights" (International Irrigation Congress 1893:112) was beginning to look like remarkably prescient thinking. Reclamation projects all over the West were encountering legal difficulties. In addition, the BIA had its own irrigation program, which was also experiencing extensive problems with water rights. It was inevitable that the two government programs would collide.

In the latter part of the nineteenth century an exceptionally hardy group of settlers moved to the Milk River Valley of northern Montana. The climate was harsh, dry, and unforgiving, but the new residents were willing to face such hardships in order to claim public lands recently made available by the breakup of the Great Blackfeet Indian Reservation. The remaining Indian lands were scattered along the Milk River in four separate parcels. One of these, the Fort Belknap Reservation, bordered the river in north-central Montana, and soon settlers established a number of small communities on the opposite side of the Milk. Both Indians and settlers began diverting water for irrigation, Indians aided by the BIA's irrigation program and non-Indians helped by the promise of a federal reclamation project—one of the first to be authorized.

The waters of the Milk River were the only dependable source to maintain these irrigation efforts. When settlers moved upstream from the reservation and began diverting water, the Indians were left with an insufficient supply. The BIA decided to attempt to retrieve some of the lost waters. In 1905 the secretary of interior (the parent department of the BIA) asked the Justice Department to file an injunction to protect the Fort Belknap Indian irrigation project from *subsequent appropriators* who were diverting the waters of the Milk River. The secretary's request was based on information from the BIA's Irrigation Office, which claimed a prior right to 11,000 miner's inches[1] of water that had been filed by the Indian agent in 1898 before the non-Indian settlers began diverting water. The Justice Department immediately cabled the U.S. attorney for the Montana district, Carl Rasch, to "take promptly such action as may be necessary to protect interests of Indians against interference by subsequent appropriators of waters of Milk River" (Justice Department memorandum n.d., about December 1905:1).

The U.S. attorney soon filed an injunction, but he evidently did not trust the filing evidence provided by the BIA. He was concerned that at least some of the defendants had in fact appropriated water before the Indians, so he framed his case "to enable the Government to invoke other grounds, or rights, in case there should be necessity for doing so" (Justice Department memorandum n.d., about December 1905:2).

The U.S. attorney's doubts about the BIA's filings were well founded. Two weeks after he filed the injunction, the defendants provided evidence proving that they, and not the Indian agent, were the first appropriators (by four days). This forced U.S. Attorney Rasch to "take the very grounds which [he] had sought to avoid" (Justice Department memorandum n.d., about December 1905:3). Specifically he based his argument on four propositions.

First, the Milk River was part of the Fort Belknap Reservation and therefore was never a source of public water subject to appropriation. Second, he argued that the reservation held riparian rights[2] in sufficient quantity to "carry out the objects and purposes for which said reservation was created" (Justice Department memorandum n.d., about December 1905:3). Third, he claimed that depriving the Indian reservation of water would violate the treaties and agreements made between the Indians and the government. Finally, he argued that state legislation cannot destroy the rights of the federal government as a riparian landowner. (This point was based on the Supreme Court's holding in *U.S. v. Rio Grande Dam and Irrigation Co.* 1898.) In short, Rasch knew his case was precarious at best, so he used a shotgun approach in hopes that at least one of his arguments would please the court.

When news of Rasch's amended complaint reached Washington, it caused a panic. Rasch's invocation of riparian rights not only contradicted his previous position, it contradicted official federal policy. At the same time that the *Winters* case was being litigated, the landmark case of *Kansas v. Colorado* (1907) was also in the courts. In that case the federal government was arguing that riparian rights did not apply to the arid states; the Reclamation Service, the Department of Agriculture, and even the Bureau of Indian Affairs had submitted briefs in support of exclusive prior appropriation water law. The Justice Department in the *Kansas* case argued that the Prior Appropriation Doctrine was "the doctrine the Government of the United States has sanctioned and approved, and the maintenance of which is essential to the interests of the United States and the general welfare of the citizens thereof" (Campbell memorandum n.d., about 1905:2). In that same case W. H. Code of the Indian Irrigation Service warned that if the riparian doctrine were applied to the western states, "a stop would be put to all development" on Indian reservations and it would "make the Indians dependent upon the Government for support to a large extent" (Campbell memorandum n.d., about 1905:4).

The Interior Department was mildly supportive of Rasch's strategy. The solicitor general argued that "the historical attitude of the Department in dealing with violations of the rights of Indians of whatever sort has been to use for the protection of such rights all means proper at the Government's disposal" (Solicitor General memorandum n.d., about December 1905). He justified creating an exception for the Indians because it would, in his opinion, be applied in a very narrow, specific manner and have little effect on the "great irrigation work in which the Government is now engaged." He admitted, however, that the doctrine of riparian rights was harmful to the irrigation program and that "further contention on the basis of riparian rights may well cease" (Solicitor General memorandum n.d., about December 1905:3).

Other federal policymakers were noticeably less supportive. When a claim concerning the Yakima Reservation was also based on riparian water rights, opposition intensified. The Reclamation Service issued a memorandum deploring the use of riparian rights to buttress Indian claims to water, claiming that such rights were "antagonistic to the possibilities of irrigation development" and "would overturn the foundations on which water rights for hundreds of thousands of acres of lands are based" (Reclamation Service memorandum 8 December 1905). The entire reclamation program rested upon the doctrine of prior appropriation, and the service was already experiencing severe water rights problems because of other inconsistencies in the law. The last thing the agency needed was another assault on its water rights. The Reclamation Service issued a second statement condemning Rasch's stand in the *Winters* case:

> it appears that to obtain for the Indians rights greater than could be claimed by any white man, the government has been placed in the position of using every available means to accomplish its immediate ends, ignoring broad general principles of policy necessary for the development of the entire arid region . . . [it] seems inconsistent and beneath the dignity of a great government. . . . If this brief can now be withdrawn, the irrigation policy established by the Reclamation Act . . . should be followed and the rights of the Indians based on prior appropriation. (Reclamation Service memorandum 12 December 1905)

The supervising engineer for the service's Milk River Project wrote to the Washington office that the local situation was "pretty bad" in the aftermath of the initial injunction and expressed fears that the case "would become a criteria [*sic*] for parallel cases" (Savage to Bien 10 March 1906). Another employee of the Reclamation Service informed local interests that he "deplored recent court decisions regarding Indian water rights" (Babb to Bien 10 April 1906).

In short, U.S. Attorney Rasch had limited support within his own department and faced intense opposition from other federal agencies. His contention that Indians had riparian rights contradicted not only his other claims on behalf of the Fort Belknap Reservation but the position of the federal government in other western water rights cases. Despite all of this opposition, Rasch chose to emphasize riparian rights more than the other three claims he made in his brief (Rasch to Bien 25 November 1905).

With practically the entire federal establishment vociferously opposed to the Indian's case in *Winters v. U.S.*[3] it must have been quite a shock when the federal district court issued the requested injunction against the non-Indian appropriators. The judge ignored Rasch's plea for riparian rights, however, and based the Indians' claim on treaty rights. At about the same time, another Indian water rights suit (*Conrad Investment Company v. U.S.* 1908) was filed by the Justice Department on behalf of the Blackfeet Indians, who also lived in Montana and claimed waters from the Milk River.

The non-Indian settlers on the Milk River did not take their defeat in the *Winters* case lightly. They appealed, lost in the ninth circuit, applied for a rehearing, lost the rehearing, then appealed to the U.S. Supreme Court. Again they lost, the high court reaffirming all lower court decisions. (The Court's decisions are examined in greater detail in the next section.) The settlers even attempted to gain a rehearing before the Supreme Court (it was denied), but their tenacity provided a trenchant precurser of their future behavior in regard to water rights.

The Justice Department's victory in the *Winters* case marked the beginning of a legal struggle that persists to this day. The department soon found itself immersed in Indian water rights cases. If it was unequivocally committed to the principles of the newly created doctrine, this would have been less problematic, but the agency's mission required it to pursue contradictory goals. As the official legal representative for the federal government the agency was supposed to litigate on behalf of all federal interests, but in the case of the Indians, their rights were in direct conflict with official policy. Practically all other elements of the federal government involved in water policy were committed to the prior Appropriation Doctrine, including the president, the Reclamation Service, and the Agriculture Department. Even the Justice Department and the BIA had come out strongly in favor of prior appropriation. This conflict of interest immediately began to cause problems. In 1910 a U.S. attorney wrote to the attorney general and complained about the situation:

> Owing to the apparent conflict of rights between the reclamation interests of the Government, and its duty to the Indians, I wish your office would carefully consider the matter, after a conference with the

reclamation officers and the Indian Department, and instruct me. At present, I am representing both conflicting interests. (McCourt to Attorney General 1 October 1910:4)

Given the power of the reclamation lobby and its institutional counterpart, the Reclamation Service, it should come as no surprise that the Justice Department would not pursue both sets of claims with equal vigor. Indeed, there is considerable evidence that Indian water rights were not a priority. In a letter to the commissioner of Indian affairs, the BIA's chief of irrigation described the role of the Justice Department in Indian water rights cases:

> The United States Attorney is usually willing to try the case in the courts, but does not get out and secure the evidence. He simply fights with the ammunition that is brought to him, and of course if this is not good and equal to that used on the other side, the case is usually lost. It is fair to assume that in cases where Indian water rights are affected, the other side will have good lawyers and will leave no stone unturned to have all the evidence possible to substantiate their contention. (Reed to Commissioner of Indian Affairs 26 March 1913)

It appears that the Justice Department's unwillingness to investigate its own Indian water rights cases was a matter of policy. A 1913 memorandum from the BIA's Irrigation Office noted that "the last report from the Attorney General was to the effect that the District Attorney had not had time to work up the mass of data necessary for a proper presentation of the complaint [filed by the BIA in the Ute Indians water rights case]" (memorandum entitled "Water Rights" n.d., about 1913). This same lack of effort also plagued the Pima Indian case (Reed to Commissioner of Indian Affairs 26 March 1913:1).

That same year (1913) the commissioner of Indian affairs requested that the Justice Department set up a special detail of U.S. attorneys in an attempt to solve the problems cited earlier. The Justice Department assigned to the Indian cases two attorneys who specialized in water rights. Despite this increase in attention, Indian rights still were not their highest priority; the annual report by the BIA's chief of engineers for 1914 noted that although the two attorneys' "work for the Indian bureau has been incidental to their other employment, it has been valuable" (1914:10). Of course, some of this "other employment" was work on behalf of the Reclamation Service. One BIA memorandum pointed out that the "District Attorney, having so many matters to attend to, not only for the Indian Service but for the Reclamation Service and other bureaus of the Department possibly, has undoubtedly had no time to work up the evidence affecting the Ute water rights" (from field irrigation memorandum 25 March 1913). The Justice Department's refusal to commit more resources to Indian water cases often irritated BIA personnel. The chief engineer for the BIA complained in his 1918 annual report that "in some instances there has not been satisfactory cooperation by U.S. Attorneys" (1918:6). Because of the Justice Department's refusal to do the legal legwork, the task fell to the BIA. Its ability to respond to this challenge was limited, which is explained in chapter 5.

Despite its halfhearted devotion to Indian water rights, the Justice Department still had an official duty to litigate these cases. Because the tribes involved in the suits did not have the resources to bring suit for themselves, they were totally dependent on the department to protect their rights in court. As private irrigation expanded and the reclamation program grew, more and more Indian projects faced difficult legal problems. The annual reports from the various Indian irrigation projects are filled with complaints about water theft. The following statement from the commissioner of Indian Affairs' annual report for 1919 is typical: "In past years considerable damage to the interests of the Indians has resulted from the whites taking and using the available water. Proceedings were instituted by the Department of Justice in behalf of the Indians" (1919:39).

In sum, the Justice Department was charged with conflicting and contradictory responsibilities. It was frequently in the position of acting as legal representative for both sides in water disputes. If a private firm engaged in such behavior, it would be a clear violation of conflict of interest laws, but the Justice Department had no choice. It was saddled with a mission that was so broad that it encompassed contradictory activities. Furthermore, none of this has changed; the department still represents both the BIA and the government's reclamation program, now administered by the Bureau of Reclamation (this is discussed further in chapter 6).

The Court's Response

The controversy over the waters of the Milk River produced four written court decisions that are remarkable in the degree of their consistency. The District Court concluded flatly that the "Indians . . . reserved the right to the use of the waters of Milk

River, at least to an extent reasonably necessary to irrigate their lands" (*U.S. v. Mose Anderson et al.* 1905). The court based this implied reservation of water on treaty rights and ignored U.S. Attorney Rasch's plea for riparian rights, which clearly contradicted much of the case and statutory law.

The invocation of implied treaty rights directly contradicted existing prior appropriation water law, however. The conflict between these two water rights doctrines is multidimensional; *Winters* rights exist *irrelevant of usage* whereas prior appropriation rights are *determined through usage*; the former is established by the federal government whereas the latter is granted by state governments; the amount of water reserved under the Winters Doctrine is indeterminate, but rights under the Prior Appropriation Doctrine are strictly quantified; and, perhaps most important, the Winters Doctrine is the principal source of water rights for Indians whereas the Prior Appropriation Doctrine is the principal source of water rights for non-Indians. Thus the two doctrines are inherently contradictory, competitive, and incompatible in a number of ways. The differences between the two doctrines are summarized in table 2.

The briefs submitted to the appeals court clarify the divergent approaches developed by each litigant. The settlers' arguments can be synthesized into one dominant theme: a reserved right for Indians violates a long tradition in public policy:

> It would be against public policy to hold that the agreement with the Indians contains a reservation of the use of the water of Milk River. If it is so held in this case the same rule will apply to every Indian reservation that has been opened to settlement, and the water of any stream bordering upon or running through any Reservation cannot be appropriated by White settlers. Surely it was not the intention of the officers of the Government or Congress, in dealing with the Indians in opening these Reservations to settlement to withhold the water on the lands ceded by the Indians from appropriation for useful and beneficial purposes under state law. . . . There is nothing in the policy of the Government or in the history of its dealings with the public lands to indicate any such intention on the part of Congress. (Brief for appellants filed 14 October 1907:46)

In short, the settlers could argue convincingly that the Reserved Rights Doctrine contradicted both the policy of Congress and its obvious deference to state prior appropriation laws and the case law established by the U.S. Supreme Court in *Kansas v. Colorado*, decided that same year. The appellants were quite capable of carrying their argument too far, however; they claimed that "irrigation

TABLE 2

COMPARISON OF WINTERS DOCTRINE AND PRIOR
APPROPRIATION DOCTRINE

Criteria	Winters Doctrine	Prior Appropriation Doctrine
Limit of right	Future need	Present use
Applicable uses	Meet purpose of reservation	Those defined by state law
Beneficial use required?	No	Yes
State permit required?	No	Yes
Source of right	Reservation of land	Diversion and use of water
Origin of doctrine	Federal courts	State courts, state legislatures
Officially sanctioned by	Federal courts	State and federal statutes, state and federal courts
Principal beneficiaries	Indians on federal reservations	Non-Indians

Note: The Criteria column lists eight aspects of water law that differentiate the Winters Doctrine from the Prior Appropriation Doctrine.

of Indian lands is not a government function" (p. 121). It is curious that they would make such a claim in a case that involved the government's Indian irrigation program. Perhaps it is a testament to the actual impact of the BIA's efforts (which is discussed in chapter 5).

The settlers' brief was a complex, 132-page summary of the case law and statutory law that militated against a reserved right. It was chock-full of substance. In contrast, the Justice Department's 34-page brief was by nature based on implication, allusion, and interpretation:

It may be conceded that the agreement [treaty] does not specifically reserve to the Indians any of the water of Milk River. We contend, however, that the import of the language . . . clearly evinces an intention by the parties thereto to make a reservation of so much of said water as should be found requisite to supply the reasonable needs of the Indians. (Brief for United States appellee filed 22 October 1907)

In essence the Justice Department was making an argument based on a moralistic view of the government's role rather than a literal view of policy. Official policy and political reality militated against reserved rights for Indians, but the Justice Department was essentially adopting an affirmative action approach, one in which the prejudice of de facto variables must be taken into account. Thus the Indians should be given the benefit of the doubt: "To presume and thus to construe the agreement as not reserving sufficient water to meet the reasonable needs of the Indians . . . would work a wrong and be prejudicial to them" (brief for United States appellee filed 22 October 1907:18).

When the case went to the Supreme Court, it was anybody's guess as to the outcome. The Court had handed down several relevant cases in the preceding decade that, when viewed as a whole, did not present a consistent approach. In *U.S. v. Rio Grande Dam and Irrigation Company* (1898) the Court ruled that state law cannot destroy the federal government's water rights "so far at least as may be necessary for the beneficial uses of the government property" (1898:690). In *Kansas v. Colorado* (1907), however, the Court recognized the power of states to control the waters within their own boundaries except for interstate navigable streams. This was a clear diminution in federal control over water and was viewed as a dangerous threat to the reclamation program because it brought into question the government's power to claim and store water for irrigation. In the area of Indian law the 1905 case of *U.S. v. Winans* was relevant because the Court ruled that a treaty concerning fishing rights should be construed not as "a grant of rights to the Indians, but a grant of rights from them—a reservation of those not granted" (1905:371). Given the unsettled state of both western water law and Indian law, in addition to these somewhat contradictory decisions, the Court could have gone in any number of directions.

The high court chose to affirm the lower court's decisions. The Court's response was succinct, and the enormous amount of attention the case has received belies its brevity. Justice McKenna's two-page opinion merely confirmed the reasoning of the lower courts; he asked rhetorically, "The Indians had command of the lands and the waters. . . . Did they give up all this?" and answered in the negative. Thus the high court set in motion an interpretation of the law that would become "a kind of legal Magna Carta for the Indian" (Hundley 1978:463) and the bane of states' rightists, non-Indian irrigators, and most of the federal establishment. It was, as Donald Worster recently noted, "potentially a bombshell that could blow the whole structure of western water rights . . . to ruins" (1985:298). The Court's decision appeared to be at odds with *Kansas v. Colorado*, and the author of that decision, Justice Brewer, provided the lone dissenting vote in the *Winters* case.

The brevity of the Court's decision was obtained at the expense of detail. The decision established certain principles of law, but it left many questions unanswered. These can be grouped into six categories. First, how does allotment affect the right? The Fort Belknap Reservation was unallotted, meaning it had not been divided into privately owned parcels pursuant to the General Allotment Act of 1887. By 1908 over five million acres of Indian land had been allotted. Did these privately owned parcels also enjoy a reserved water right? And what about the assignees and lessees of the allotted lands (see Getches 1981 and Collins 1985)?

Second, the *Winters* case involved non-Indians who had settled on lands that had previously been part of a recognized federal Indian reservation. The government's argument was, in essence, that when the Indians relinquished this land they did not relinquish the water associated with it. This leaves open the possibility that settlers on land that had never been part of a reservation would not be subject to the stipulations of the *Winters* decision. This would include, for example, diversions of water that take place upstream from a reservation, assuming the land irrigated by the diversion had never been part of that reservation.

Third, the *Winters* case involved a reservation created by treaty or, more accurately, an agreement recognized by Congress (Congress forbade making treaties with Indians in 1871). Many Indian reservations, however, were created by presidential proclamation, a unilateral congressional statute, or a declaration by the secretary of interior. Did these reservations also have some form of reserved rights?

Fourth, legal scholars have argued for years whether the Indians or the government reserved the rights to water. The distinction sounds academic, but it is not because it has an impact on who has the right to abrogate reserved rights. One school of thought argues that the Indians possess an "immemorial right," meaning that they were always in possession of the water, and therefore the Indians reserved *from* the government their water rights when the reservation was established. *U.S. v. Winans* (1905) is often cited in support of this view. The opposing argument contends that the government reserved the water *for* the Indians. Norris Hundley (1982) argues convincingly that *both* the Indians and the government reserved the water, but this still does not answer the question of who has the power to abrogate those rights. Can the federal government unilaterally alter the scope or extent of the reserved water right?

Fifth, an important unanswered question concerns the amount of water subject to the Reserved Rights Doctrine. In the *Winters* case the judge of the circuit court allocated 5,000 miner's inches to the Indians. This figure was chosen because it was the amount actually being used at the time of the decision. (The original complaint claimed that the Indians were diverting 11,000 inches, but it was later established that the actual amount was only 5,000—a case of bad data from the BIA.) The judge's decision made it fairly obvious that the amount could be expanded as the need grew for more irrigation water. Indeed, that appears to be the way a local newspaper interpreted the decision, exclaiming that "the worst feature of the decision [is] the possibility that an immense increase in that amount [5,000 inches] will be demanded after awhile in the name of the Indians" (*The Chinook Opinion*, quoted in Hundley 1982:37).

In theory, then, the reserved right of the Indians is completely open-ended, but there are some obvious practical limits to that claim. For example, do they apply to water sources running near but not contiguous to a reservation? Do they supersede other federal reservations of water? Do they apply to waters that are made available as a result of artificial retention? Could an Indian tribe claim water for any use—for example, the sale of water to non-Indians?

Finally, the courts ignored the problem of implementation, providing no clue whatsoever as to how the newly established doctrine of reserved rights should fit into the existing system of prior appropriation. This violated a cardinal rule of implementation: "Simple sequences of events depend on complex chains of reciprocal interactions. Hence, each part of the chain must be built with the others in view. The separation of policy design from implementation is fatal" (Pressman and Wildavsky 1979:xxiii).

In sum, the *Winters* decision left critically important questions unanswered. As a result the courts and other policymakers have been struggling with implementation almost continuously since the decision became law. The effort to clarify the new Reserved Rights Doctrine began almost immediately. The Ninth Circuit

Court of Appeals heard another Indian water rights case while the Supreme Court was still considering *Winters.* In *Conrad Investment Company v. U.S.* (1908) the court held that the Indians on the Blackfeet Reservation (also in Montana on the Milk River) had a paramount right to sufficient water to meet their *future* needs, thus reaffirming the view that reserved rights were open-ended.

Since 1908 the Reserved Rights Doctrine has been the subject of numerous court decisions: Secretary of Interior William Clark estimated in 1984 that there had been four thousand cases involving an interpretation of the doctrine (*Denver Post* 3 June 1984:6B). The Ninth Circuit Court of Appeals strongly reaffirmed its stand on reserved rights in 1956 (*U.S. v. Ahtanum Irrigation District*), and the Supreme Court in 1963 (*Arizona v. California*) also reaffirmed the doctrine and applied it to all federal reservations, not only those for Indians. Other cases have applied the doctrine to all Indian reservations, not only those created by treaty (*U.S. v. Walker River Irrigation District* 1939); permitted the transfer of reserved rights to lessees (*Skeem v. U.S.* 1921) and allottees (*U.S. v. Powers* 1939); and applied the doctrine to groundwater (*Cappaert v. U.S.* 1976). Most of these cases demonstrated the tendency of the courts to expand the doctrine, but in recent years the Court has reversed this trend (*Colorado River Water Conservation District v. U.S.* 1976; *U.S. v. New Mexico* 1978; *Arizona et al. v. San Carlos Apache Tribe of Arizona et al.* 1983; *Montana et al. v. Northern Cheyenne Tribe* 1983; *Nevada v. U.S.* 1983; *Arizona v. California* 1983).

This impressive legacy of litigation has yet to resolve many of the controversies surrounding the Winters Doctrine. This is a testament to the difficulty of implementing a vague, court-mandated policy, especially one that contradicts a long-standing policy with a statutory basis and strong political support.

The Congressional Response

Congress became involved in western water rights long before the *Winters* decision. Congressional enactments pertaining to this subject fall into two categories, one concerned specifically with projects on Indian reservations and the other consisting of general statements of policy regarding western water development.

In the latter category Congress has repeatedly indicated a deference to state water law, which, in the arid states, is based almost exclusively on the doctrine of prior appropriation. Beginning in

1862, Congress began passing laws that officially recognized and sanctioned state water appropriation laws. By the time the Reclamation Act was before Congress, seven separate congressional acts had been passed that specifically mandated compliance with state water law: The Homestead Act of 1862, the mining law of 1866, the Act of July 9, 1870, the Desert Land Act of 1877, the Act of March 3, 1891, and three statutes passed in 1897. However, there was—and still is—disagreement over the applicability of these acts to unappropriated waters, waters arising on federal reservations, and waters covered by other federal statutes (see Veeder 1965). Nevertheless, taken together these acts evince a fairly consistent congressional intent to abide by state law. And, of course, the Reclamation Act of 1902 (section 8) continued this long-standing policy.

In regard to statutes concerning Indian reservations, the intent of Congress is much less clear. Prior to 1908 the national legislature had authorized a number of specific Indian irrigation projects, appropriated funds for smaller Indian projects that required no authorization, and given the secretary of interior power to allocate water among Indians. There is little consistency in these laws in regard to water rights, however. For example, the Act of February 8, 1887 authorized the secretary of interior to "prescribe such rules and regulations as he may deem necessary to secure a just and equal distribution [of water] among the Indians residing upon any such reservations." This phraseology is reminiscent of the doctrine established in Kansas v. Colorado requiring an "equitable division of benefits" among states (1907:46), but the next section of the act refers to the rights of riparians. Another law instructs the secretary of interior to prescribe rules for Indian water use on the Fort Hall Reservation "as may be reasonable" (Act of March 3, 1891). Still another act provides that water from streams "shall be reserved for the Indians now using the same so long as said Indians remain where they now live" (Act of April 27, 1904). The latter act appears to be similar to the doctrine developed by the Court in Winters v. U.S.

Other laws, however, clearly indicate that Congress wanted at least some Indian irrigation projects to comply with state prior appropriation laws. For example, the act that authorized the Uintah Indian irrigation project stipulates that "such irrigation systems shall be constructed and completed and held and operated, and water therefore appropriated under the laws of the State of Utah" (Act of June 21, 1906). Similar language governed the Indian project on the Wind River Reservation (Act of March 3, 1905). Later, citing these acts, the BIA chief of irrigation admitted that "Congress has shown a tendency to legislate away from the law of implied reservation of water" (Chief Engineer Annual Report 1913:5).

In the aftermath of the *Winters* decision it was not clear what kind of response, if any, would emanate from Congress. Legislation on basic matters of water policy clearly acquiesced to the laws of the states, but Congress also showed at least some concern for the difficult situation of the Indians. And, as the Court in *Winters* pointed out, it was illogical to assume that Congress had agreed to establish Indian reservations in arid regions without providing any water to meet the purposes of the reservation. In the ensuing conflict over implementation of the Reserved Rights Doctrine, both sides turned to Congress for relief.

By the time of the first *Winters* decision the settlers in the Milk River Valley had organized into two interest groups: the Upper and Lower Milk River Valley Water Users Associations. When they lost in the district court they turned to their senator, Thomas Carter, for relief. Their strategy was simple: if the water belonged to the reservation, then they would obtain the reservation. Acquiescing, Senator Carter introduced a bill in 1906—one month before the case was to go to the appeals court. His bill provided for the opening of the northern part of the Fort Belknap Reservation—that is, the section that bordered the Milk River (*Congressional Record* 11 January 1906:943). It was thought that this would deprive the reservation of its reserved water right. A similar bill was proposed as an amendment to a bill opening the Blackfeet Reservation (where another reserved water rights case was developing). This bill, however, went even further; it proposed that all suits by the federal government that might enjoin settlers from diverting water be suspended and no future suits of like character be initiated (Babb to Newell 10 April 1906). The Reclamation Service was asked by prominent Montana citizens to help them introduce this bill, but the service directed them to Senator Carter's office for assistance.

To generate support for these bills, one resourceful Montanan who had been directly affected by the *Winters* decision wrote to J. J. Hill, the railroad magnate, and asked him to use his influence: "Your having so many representatives in Congress from the different states that you have property in [*sic*]. If it was brought to their notice the condition of affairs on the Milk River they might do something towards raising the injunction and throwing that Belknap reservation open and making the waters of the Milk River subject to the laws of Montana" (Matheson to Hill 14 April 1906).

Hill responded by writing directly to Charles Walcott, director of the Geological Survey (the parent agency of the Reclamation Service), and asking that the matter be investigated.

Despite the lobbying by Hill and the Milk River Valley interest groups, Carter's bills failed to pass. This was partly because of the opposition of the few but vociferous congressional proponents of Indian rights, such as John Stephens, who was on the House Indian Affairs Committee. These particular bills also faced another problem. Senator Carter of Montana was their principal legislative sponsor, but he was not on the Indian Affairs Committee, which considered bills of this sort. Montana's other senator, William Clark, was on the committee, but this hindered rather than helped Carter because the two were bitter enemies; Clark, a Democrat, had defeated Carter, a Republican, in 1901. Carter then regained a Senate seat in 1905 by defeating Montana's other Democratic senator. Clark was not about to let legislation out of the Indian Affairs Committee that would bring votes and publicity to his nemesis, Thomas Carter.

In 1907, Clark was defeated by Joseph Dixon, who was already well known for his opposition to a liberal Indian policy. Hence the Milk River Valley settlers had renewed hopes that they could obtain legislative relief. Adopting a different strategy, they asked Congress to appropriate $300,000 directly to them as compensation for losses they incurred as a result of the *Winters* decision. According to the local agent for the Reclamation Service, the Milk River settlers "were quite aggressive in desiring an appropriation from Congress to cover the loss to them consequent upon the recent court decision giving the Fort Belknap Indians prior water rights" (Savage to Newell 28 April 1908). But Montana's lone congressman, Charles Pray, opposed a bill of this nature, and again the settlers met with defeat.

Still undeterred, Senator Carter and his Milk River supporters persisted. In 1910, Carter got the Senate to agree to a resolution directing the secretary of interior to report on "the terms and conditions under which the United States may acquire and make available for settlement the northerly one-fourth of the Fort Belknap Indian Reservation" (*Congressional Record* 23 June 1910: 8794). Seven months later the secretary reported, "Apparently the Indians are not willing at this time to relinquish any part of their reservation. This is invariably the attitude of Indians when any proposition looking to the diminishing of their reservation is first presented to them" (U.S. Congress, Senate Document No. 805, 2 February 1911). The BIA Indian inspector and the project manager at Fort Belknap both recommended the bill, but Secretary of Interior Richard Ballinger argued against it. He pointed out that a unilateral reduction in the reservation without the approval of the Indians violated the 1888 agreement signed by Congress. He was also aware that his predecessor, Secretary Garfield, had visited the reservation just three years earlier and promised the Indians that their lands would not be reduced for at least another ten years. Again Congress refused to pass the bill.

When the settlers of the Milk River Valley became involved in the litigation that ultimately resulted in the *Winters* decision, they displayed remarkable tenacity. They sought four different court decisions and even asked the Supreme Court for a re-argument. When they turned to the national legislature for relief, they displayed the same kind of tenacity: in 1916 they asked Senator Myers, who had replaced Thomas Carter, to try once again to open the Fort Belknap reservation to settlement. He agreed, submitting a bill that not only opened the reservation but would have made all water rights on the diminished reservation subject to the laws of Montana. The superintendent for the Fort Belknap Indian irrigation project warned BIA headquarters that the bill "might prove disastrous to some of our Fort Belknap water rights" (Hanna to Reed 31 March 1916). The Justice Department joined the BIA in opposing the bill. Their strategy was to offer an amendment to the proposal that would reserve sufficient water for the Indians "to the extent that may be necessary or beneficial for the irrigation of Indian allotments . . . and all other purposes" (Truesdell to Reed 9 March 1916). This amendment would have defeated the purpose of the bill, but like its predecessors, the proposed law never made it out of committee.

A number of "schemes" generated by the persistent settlers of Milk River were reported by the project engineer on the Fort Belknap Reservation in 1920, among them a plan to apply state law to the Indians and a proposal to limit each Indian to forty acres of irrigable land and open the remaining "surplus land" to whites (Hanna to Reed 21 April 1920). Looking back on the settlers' continuing efforts to emasculate the *Winters* decision, a statement in 1906 by the Indian agent at Fort Belknap looks remarkably prescient: "[The Indians] don't know the white man with his bulldog tenacity and never give up spirit" (Logan to Leupp 29 April 1906).

Thus far this discussion of legislative action has focused on the settlers' efforts to negate the *Winters* decision, but there was also a concerted effort on behalf of the Indians to have the Reserved Rights Doctrine legitimated through statutory recognition. As the resistance to Indian reserved rights grew, policymakers in the Justice Department and the BIA began to realize that the Court's order would never be implemented unless additional steps were taken to emphasize the government's commitment to Indian rights. In late 1913 a bill was drawn up that reiterated the major tenets of the *Winters* decision. This attempt to protect Indian water generated little support, even among the supporters of such a measure. A simpler version of the bill was created that merely confirmed prior reserved rights for allotted Indian lands (memorandum entitled "Proposed Legislation" April 1913). Neither bill was ever introduced: Assistant Commissioner Merritt decided that the BIA would have a better chance of success if language protecting reserved water rights[4] was written instead into the appropriation bill that funded the Indian irrigation projects. And rather than use language that applied to all Indian reservations, Merritt rewrote the proposed amendment so it applied only to the four largest Indian projects and the Fort Belknap project. Why he decided on this strategy is unclear; perhaps he thought a piecemeal approach was less threatening and less visible. He seriously misjudged the potential risk of such a strategy, however. The insertion of policy-making language into an appropriation bill violated a point of order in both houses, and the only way it could be considered for passage was if no one objected. Given the widespread resistance to Indian reserved rights among western legislators, such a move stood little chance of being accepted. Indeed, the instant the amendment was proposed in the House, Congressman Mondell of Wyoming, a leader of the reclamation movement and an ardent opponent of reserved rights, objected. Congressman John Stephens of Texas, a persistent ally of the Indians, pleaded with Mondell to allow the amendment to be considered, but to no avail (*Congressional Record* 19 February 1914:3658–3664, 3672–3673). In the Senate the bill was stopped by a coterie of westerners led by Senator Myers of Montana (*Congressional Record* 20 June 1914:10769–10789).

The debate over the proposed reserved rights amendment to the Indian appropriations bill provides a valuable insight into Congress' attitude toward the problem. It is particularly relevant given the fact that precisely the same debate is currently taking place.

Senator Robinson of Missouri and Senator Page from Vermont were the principal proponents of the Indian reserved rights bill during the floor debate. After a point of order had been raised, Senator Myer of Montana agreed to accept the amendment if Indian reserved rights could be limited to three years; if by that time they had not been put to beneficial use the right would be lost.

Senator Page's response to that idea provides a succinct rationale for the Reserved Rights Doctrine:

> These appropriations [for Indian water projects that are reimbursable] may not be wrong if we will protect the Indian's rights, but, in my judgment, Mr. President, we are not doing this. We substantially say to the Indian "You must be a farmer. You must make beneficial use of this water." The Indian says, "I have no money; I have no horses, and I have no wagons: I have no plows. Help me to the wherewith and I will do it." Our reply to him is substantially this: "No, sir; we are going to tie your hands. We will not give you anything to work with; and yet if you do not make beneficial use of this water within three years—that is the amendment offered by the Senator from Montana—your rights under these irrigation projects may be taken away from you." (*Congressional Record* 20 June 1914:10770)

Senator Smith of Arizona was quick to rise in defense of state prior appropriation water laws. He viewed the issue in terms of its impact on states' rights:

> The Federal Government has no control or power or right over non-navigable streams in a State. The States own such streams by the very constitutions of the States. So the Federal Government's attempt to controvert the right of a State or the right of the people of a State as to the use of water is perfectly futile. Congress could not succeed in doing it if it tried to do so. . . . The law of the State would not permit such a thing; and the people who live there never would submit to it. (*Congressional Record* 20 June 1914:10071)

This debate also provides an insight into how the Reserved Rights Doctrine was viewed in a larger political context or, in other words, how it might or might not be implemented. In hearings on the bill Assistant Commissioner Merritt explained why such a law was necessary:

> We are asking that this proviso clause be incorporated in the bill in connection with a number of irrigation projects for the reason that we find it necessary if the water rights of the Indians are to be protected. Congress has appropriated in a number of cases a large amount of money for irrigation projects on various reservations and had required that those appropriations be made reimbursable out of the funds of Indians; otherwise the Indians stand a chance of losing their water rights or else taking their water-rights status to the courts for determination. (*Congressional Record* 20 June 1914:10787)

This is precisely what the Supreme Court tried to accomplish in *Winters v. U.S.*, but it is clear that the BIA did not think the decision would be implemented without congressional approval. Both proponents and opponents agreed that the concept of reserved rights was in conflict with prevailing congressional policy, the former arguing that that was why a protective bill was necessary and the latter arguing that that was why such a bill should never be approved.

At one point in the debate Senator Robinson, a strong proponent of reserved rights, had the *Winters* decision read into the record and cited from it extensively. He noted that the case "constituted an epoch in the history of Indian Affairs" (*Congressional Record* 20 June 1914:10773, 10777). The question of quantity also arose, and proponents of the bill made it clear that they considered the right to be open-ended but admitted that that caused problems for non-Indian irrigators.

Another interesting fact revealed by the debate was the low level of understanding and interest in the case. Senator Borah of Idaho offered an interpretation of the case that made it painfully evident he had confused the facts and misunderstood the Court's holding. Senators Smith of Arizona and Warren of Wyoming—two leading opponents of the bill—admitted they had never heard of the *Winters* case. And even Senator Robinson, when asked who the prior appropriators were in the case, could not answer. It appears that at that time, the Winters Doctrine was not a well-known case that had received a lot of attention. This has important implications for the implementation of the case; its potential impact on water rights was certainly not recognized at the time. When Robinson heralded the decision as an "epoch" he must have had little company. For the most part the decision appears to have been regarded as only marginally important.

With the demise of the amendments to the 1915 Indian appropriations act the BIA abandoned its legislative strategy. Congress was unwilling to settle the dispute over reserved water rights, apparently preferring to leave the matter to the courts. Although Congress was not amenable to broad statutory remedies that either eliminated reserved rights altogether or blessed them with the imprimatur of statutory law, it was willing to legislate less draconian measures. In four instances Congress passed laws that had a direct effect on Indian water rights. Two of them dealt with specific reservations (Yakima and Gila rivers) and the other two concerned funding for Indian irrigation projects that affected reserved rights.

Both of these will be discussed, for they provide additional insights into Congress' perception of Indian water rights.

The Yakima Reservation in Washington was created by treaty in 1859. Soon thereafter the Indians began diverting the Yakima River for irrigation purposes, using a crudely constructed system of canals and ditches. In 1896 the Indian Irrigation Division of the BIA began a project to help the Indians expand their facilities. The following year the system was capable of irrigating 50,000 acres, much of which was actually under irrigation. As in many other cases, however, there were inadequate records of the Indians' water use. In the meantime non-Indians developed an irrigation project (taken over by the Reclamation Service in 1906) that diverted water upriver from the Indian project. By 1906 the non-Indian diversions were sufficiently extensive to deprive the Indians of their customary usage of water. A long and bitter struggle ensued for control over the waters of the Yakima River. The white settlers in the area sent "various petitions" to Washington in hopes of persuading Congress to give them clear title to the water (Holt to Reed 17 February 1913).

The dispute dragged on for years. In the meantime the BIA stopped working on the Indian project until the water rights question was settled. Being upstream, the non-Indian irrigators exercised the right of possession and left the Indians with little or no water in the dry months. Finally, in 1913 the secretary of interior arbitrarily divided the water between the Indian project and the reclamation project. The amount he awarded the Indians was insufficient to irrigate most of the lands they had historically irrigated. The decision was so unfair to the Yakimas that a public outcry arose for an amended settlement. The lawyer for the Indians wrote a pamphlet entitled "The Crime Against the Yakimas," which was distributed to members of Congress. The Reclamation Service also pressed Congress for action because the water rights controversy was impeding its plans to build a dam and irrigation project in the area.

In an effort to resolve the conflict, Congress created a joint congressional committee to investigate the problem and recommend a solution. The committee was packed with friends of the Indians, including Senator Robinson of Missouri,[5] Congressman John Stephens of Texas, and Congressman Charles Burke (author of the Burke Act, which helped protect Indians during the allotment process, and later a commissioner of Indian Affairs). Their final report concluded that the secretary of interior's 1913 allocation order was "inadequate, inequitable, and unfair" because it did not "meet the actual demands for water on the reservation at the time and totally failed to make provision for future needs" (*Congressional Record* 20 December 1913:1282–1283). The report recommended that the Indian allocation be increased from 147 second-feet to approximately one-half the flow of the river (about five times as much).

A bill was introduced to appropriate sufficient funds to buy the needed water from the Reclamation Service's project on the Yakima River. Again Congressman Mondell led the opposition to the Indian bill, arguing that no water right should be based on anything other than beneficial use, and that "some day these lands will be occupied by American citizens of more or less Indian blood, but they will not differ greatly from the people of the surrounding territory, nor will their lands or region differ" (*Congressional Record* 29 July 1914:12948).

Congress decided that the circumstances were sufficiently severe that direct congressional intervention was needed. The publicity attending the case had been substantial, and it involved a situation in which the Indians had historically used the water; in other words, it did not contradict the principle of beneficial use. The BIA assured Congress that its irrigation system could utilize the entire amount recommended by the joint commission. Congress responded by amending the 1915 Indian appropriation bill to provide funds to purchase the needed water from the Reclamation Service's project on the Yakima River.

The new law enraged the settlers in the area and did not put an end to the Indians' water rights difficulties. In 1915 the chief engineer for the BIA wrote that the situation at Yakima "was delicate and might blow up like a powder magazine at most any time" (Reed to Conner 14 July 1915). Disputes and litigation continued for years, the BIA chief of irrigation concluding in his 1917 annual report that in the Yakima Valley "the ownership of irrigation water apparently will always be subject to more or less successful assaults" (1917:5). Today the Yakima Tribe and non-Indian irrigators are still locked in bitter conflict (see Conservation Foundation 1984:44–45).

At the same time that Congress was considering the problems of the Yakimas, a similar situation developed on the Gila River Reservation, home of the Pima Indians. This tribe had a long history of irrigated farming and was quite prosperous until settlers moved in and diverted the Gila River, the Indians' only source of irrigation water. The government did nothing to stop these diversions, and by the turn of the century this once prosperous tribe was starving and destitute (see Welsh 1985:128–130). The tribe's fortunes plummeted so rapidly that the first decade of the twentieth century is known among the Pimas as the "black decade" (Bowden 1977:85). As in the case of the Yakimas, the injustice to the Indians was obvious; they were the first to appropriate water and farm. Considerable publicity was generated in their defense. For example, Arthur Davis, later to become director of the Reclamation Service, wrote an article in 1903 entitled "What Irrigation Is Doing for Arizona: With a Plain Statement of How the Government Has Sanctioned a Grave Wrong Against Peaceful and Industrious Indian tribes; How by the Building of a Storage Reservoir this Wrong May Be Righted, Great Good Result, and Public Money be Saved" (Velasquez 1982:16). Davis's desire for a dam on the Gila did not arise entirely from his concern for Indians; it was thought that by including Indians in the project proposal—especially Indians who were so obviously mistreated—the non-Indians in the area would get a larger reclamation project.

Congress ultimately responded to the needs of the Pima Indians (and the nearby settlers) but in a very untimely manner. In 1912 a survey of the problem was authorized (Reclamation Service *Annual Report* 1913–1914:336). The final report recommending a project came out in 1915, but Congress did not authorize a dam until 1924. The authorization allocated half of the stored waters to the Indians and half to the white settlers. The dam was completed in 1929. The commissioner of Indian affairs noted that funding for the dam would be "the first important steps to rectify the injustice which had been done these Pima Indians for the 30 or 40 years that their water supply had been encroached upon by the whites" (Commissioner of Indian Affairs *Annual Report* 1916:43).

Two other laws were passed during this period that provide some insight into Congress' attitude toward Indian water rights. In 1908, Congress passed a law instructing the secretary of interior to develop allotted lands in accordance with the 1902 Reclamation Act and in the best interest of the Indians (35 Stat. 85). This could be interpreted as evidence of a congressional intent to apply the Reclamation Act's section 8, requiring that state prior appropriation law be observed, to Indian reservations.

In 1914, Congress passed another law that had a bearing on Indian water rights. The BIA had requested that a special position be created for a superintendent who specialized in water law. The chief engineer explained that "the necessity for a person skilled in the knowledge of water law has been apparent for some time. Many of the Indian irrigation projects have started off well but have soon found themselves in deep water [we must assume he intended no pun] on account of legal holes in their rights" (Reed to Sells 9 August 1914). Congress provided for the position beginning in fiscal year 1915.

Considered in total, the activity of Congress during the period following the *Winters* decision does not offer a clear-cut impression of congressional intent in regard to Indian water rights. A few general observations can be made, however. First, Congress clearly preferred to leave the broader question concerning Indian water rights to the courts. There were plenty of opportunities to legislate the Winters Doctrine out of existence or officially recognize it. Congress did neither. It appears that both sides in the conflict had sufficient political clout to exercise a veto effect on such legislation but insufficient strength to overwhelm the opposition. As a consequence congressional action in regard to Indian water rights was piecemeal and ad hoc, which is typical of water policy legislation. With Congress exercising a passive and intermittent role, the courts were obligated to fill the policy-making vacuum. This raises important questions regarding policy implementation, which are discussed in the conclusion of this chapter.

Second, the controversy over water rights illuminates a consistent pattern of congressional behavior as it affects Indians. The foes of reserved rights were always led by western legislators who had a large Anglo constituency and a tiny, nonvoting Indian constituency. Politically it would have been suicidal for them to support such measures. In contrast, the "friends" of the Indian were almost exclusively from nonwestern states. In addition, they were usually from safe districts and could afford to invest their political capital in an issue that was not directly relevant to their constituents. They were not subject to a political backlash, which was a definite possibility in the West. Instead there was an opportunity to gain political credit for spearheading a moral issue. This latter point was especially true in the Yakima and Pima cases.

Finally, Congress' preference for development and beneficial use is evident in nearly all of its activity. In the Yakima and Pima cases Congress was supportive because the Indians were prior appropriators. And even though Congress refused to pass a bill that would have abolished the Reserved Rights Doctrine, nothing Congress did during this period could be construed as a deliberate endorsement of the Winters Doctrine. In short, resolution of the problem would be worked out in the courts and in the battles between federal water development agencies.

Conclusion

The *Winters* case, the doctrine that developed from it, and the political response to that doctrine provide an interesting study of program legitimacy and how it affects the implementability of iron triangle policy. The case created a situation in which two existing programs, both represented in the federal bureaucracy and supported by some members of Congress and interest groups, were placed in direct conflict over a precious resource. In other words, two iron triangles were forced to compete with each other. This creates an opportunity to see how iron triangles respond to outside threats and competition and to identify the factors that enable them to compete effectively. The early development of the non-Indian water iron triangle was discussed in the previous chapter, and chapter 5 will describe the development of the BIA and its water development program. First, however, it was necessary to explain the origin of the case law that forms the foundation of Indian water rights. The fact that these rights are based on case law rather than statutory law has a profound impact on congressional, bureaucratic, and judicial implementation. To help place these three policy-making processes in perspective, each will be discussed at some length, focusing on problems of program legitimacy and how it affects implementability.

In 1979 the state water engineer for New Mexico stated, "Historically, Congress forgot to address the issue [of Indian water rights]. Today the potato's gotten so hot Congress wouldn't touch it with a ten-foot pole" (Simms 1980*a*:72). That is an accurate and succinct description of Congress' attitude throughout the seventy-year tenure of the Reserved Rights Doctrine. Traditionally Congress acquiesced to the states; or, as the Supreme Court explained it, western water policy has been characterized by "a consistent thread of purposeful and continued deference to state water law" (*California et al. v. U.S.* 1978). Yet that deference has not been so complete that Congress quickly dumped the Reserved Rights Doctrine. Rather, for the most part it adopted a hands-off approach, with occasional but discreet recognition of the special problems of Indians. The few times Congress became involved in Indian water rights it demonstrated a preference for development and beneficial use. Not surprisingly, this led Congress to make distributive policy; in both the Yakima and the Pima case the problem was ultimately resolved by congressional consent to build large reclamation projects that would provide more water for everyone. Politically that was much easier than reallocating water, even in situations in which it was fairly obvious that existing rights had been infringed upon. For the most part, however, Congress avoided the really tough decisions, leaving them to other policy-making entities.

In terms of bureaucratic implementation this void in policy-making left the BIA and the Reclamation Service in a difficult position. Both programs were relatively new at the time of the *Winters* decision, and both agencies faced numerous problems in implementing their respective programs. Conflict and competition were the last things either needed. This conflict (which is developed more fully in chapter 6) was inevitable for a number of reasons. First, the ambiguity of the *Winters* decision left much of the problem of interpreting and then allocating water up to the agencies involved. With the line between them unclear, it was necessary for each agency to fight for all it could get in this "no-man's land" of undefined water rights. Second, the best farmland in the West was already irrigated by private agriculture. It was the marginal lands that the Reclamation Service tried to irrigate, and this was precisely where most Indian reservations were established. Third, there were political reasons for the conflict. Indian land was easier and cheaper to obtain for reclamation reservoirs than private land. In addition, the allotment program, which stipulated that all "surplus land" be given or sold to settlers, provided a source of land for reclamation projects. In short, the conflict between the two agencies was bound to increase and thus complicate efforts to implement the programs.

Caught in the middle of this conflict was the Justice Department, saddled with the nearly impossible and ethically questionable mission of representing both sides. The Justice Department did not pursue both functions with equal vigor. Like all bureaucracies, it has a constituency, which is primarily the rest of the federal government. It is not surprising that the department would respond to the strongest elements within this constituency, and that included the non-Indian water iron triangle. Indian water rights were not the agency's top priority, especially when these rights threatened other federal interests. Still, the Justice Department made an effort to protect Indians when it was not popular to do so. In sum, bureaucratic implementation of Indian water rights was a confused and contradictory process with unclear goals, unclear lines of authority, and inequality in relative bureaucratic resources.

The foregoing discussion emphasizes the importance of both congressional and bureaucratic implementation, but first and foremost, the Winters Doctrine is a case of judicial implementation. The courts created the doctrine, and, as the subsequent four thousand or so cases attest, the courts have continued to attempt to implement the doctrine. It is important, then, to understand the special circumstances of judicial implementation.

The courts, because of their passive, highly constrained policy-making environment, face special difficulties in implementing court decisions. All branches of government encounter serious problems at the implementation stage—the recent literature on the subject makes this clear—but the judicial branch has few remedial alternatives when policymakers refuse to implement court directives. In the absence of congressional and/or executive branch support, the judiciary faces formidable barriers to implementation. Mazmanian and Sabatier write that "the courts, while capable of making new policy, are unable to enforce it effectively in the face of hostility from Congress and the president" (1983:169). When executive and legislative branches resist court decisions, they usually prevail. Robert Dahl examined a sample of Supreme Court cases and concluded, "It is an interesting and highly significant fact that Congress and the President do generally succeed in overcoming a hostile court on major policy issues" (1968:362). Johnson and Canon recently reiterated this point (1984:229–269).

The problems of judicial implementation are exacerbated when funding is required, as in the case of Indian water projects. Lawrence Baum writes, "Through legislation Congress can influence the implementation of Supreme Court decisions. Its most important tool is budgetary. Congress can provide or fail to provide funds to carry out a decision" (1981:205).

In addition to the power of the purse, the Congress also uses its oversight function to enforce its decisions. In contrast to the courts, Congress can rely upon oversight to ensure implementation:

> [A] judge has no means for systematically following up his or her orders. . . . The contrast with the legislature is clear: statutes . . . almost always mandate some enforcement activity by the executive branch. It is the responsibility of the legislative committees, either through oversight or appropriation hearings, to be sure that enforcement is taking place and producing the desired result. Courts simply do not have the same oversight capability or authority. (Birkby 1983:6)

The executive bureaucracy can also inhibit the implementation of court decisions. Stephen Wasby writes that "the degree to which government officials enforce or attempt to enforce court rulings

. . . is critical because those rulings are not self-enforcing. Executive branch officials do not often directly attack Supreme Court decisions but they may severely damage the possibilities for compliance by refusing to take firm action to implement them" (1978: 235). The activities of the Justice Department and the Reclamation Service are examples of this. And as chapter 5 will demonstrate, the BIA itself was a part of this problem.

Because of the Court's limited capacity to enforce its decisions, the judicial branch is ill-prepared to give substance to court-created rights that are bestowed upon specific groups or subpopulations. Scheingold calls this the "myth of rights":

> The myth of rights leads us to believe that litigation is an obvious and effective answer to any footdragging by opponents of the new order. . . . Direct deployment of legal rights in the implementation of public policy will not work very well, given any significant opposition. Litigation may be helpful to individuals who have the resources and determination to pursue remedies through the court system. But courts cannot be relied upon to secure rights more generally in the society for reasons rooted in legal policy and political power. (1974:117)

Reliance on "the myth of rights" may obscure substantive issues, increase conflict, and have a limited impact on target groups. "The consequence," Scheingold concludes, "is to sharply restrict the effective range of courts in the implementation of public policy" (1974:130).

To make this point clearer and more relevant to the case at hand, it is worthwhile to return to the Fort Belknap Reservation and see what happened in the aftermath of the landmark decision of *Winters v. U.S.* In 1915, seven years after the case, the local superintendent cabled the commissioner of Indian affairs: "About entire flow Milk River being diverted by white appropriators above our diversion point. No water passing our dam and little available for our ditch" (Sweeney to Gregory 8 May 1915). In 1920 the farm foreman on the Fort Belknap Reservation wrote a terse letter to his superiors at BIA regional headquarters: "The Indians absolutely do not receive the attention that's due them and its a shame and disgrace for our government to be a party to any such work" (Coates to Hanna 20 January 1920). In 1928 the BIA once again asked the attorney general to do something about the continued "interference by white people with Indian water rights of the Fort Belknap Reservation" (Edwards to Attorney General 1928). An investigation of the reservation's irrigation project in 1928 concluded flatly that the water rights gained in the *Winters* case would never be secure until put to beneficial use (Preston and Engle 1928:2307).

These quotes are all from white men speaking on behalf of the Indians on the reservation. But the Indians spoke for themselves when the Indian inspector came to the reservation in 1910 to see if he could convince the Indians to give up one-fourth of their land. Hawk Feather, an Assiniboine, explained why the Indians would not give up their land:

> When the big men came from Washington and talked with these people they told us that we would be the last Indians living on earth, but we are dying off nearly every day, and the cause of it is that we are starving to death. And you say, you have traveled all over this Milk River Valley and you ought to know and see that you can't find anything that we make our living on. There was a man here once and he told us that this water right belonged to us. He said we would use the water first and raise a crop and make a living on that, but we do not get enough water yet.

Another Assiniboine, named Eyes-in-the-Water, also spoke:

> The water rights belong to the Indians, but we don't get enough water. This year all these ditches are dry, and we will not raise anything, and I think we will starve off this winter. I wish you would help us and take all these words in for us. (U.S. Congress, Senate Document No. 805 2 February 1910:8)

Why was the irrigation project at Fort Belknap such a failure? What role did the BIA and its water development program play in this struggle over water, a struggle over the means to survive? These questions will be explored in chapter 5, but first I will examine the Indians' competitors for water and water projects: the federal water development programs of the Bureau of Reclamation and the U.S. Army Corps of Engineers.

CHAPTER FOUR

Non-Indian Water Development: The Bureau of Reclamation and the U.S. Army Corps of Engineers

There is nobody, not a member of the House, that's not interested in water. . . . Nobody escapes.

—House subcommittee chairman
(quoted in Murphy 1974:182)

Introduction

Federal water development is often cited as a classic case of distributive policy made by a coalition of congressmen, interest groups, and administrative agencies. One of the reasons Indian tribes have experienced difficulty obtaining water is because they must compete directly with these powerful non-Indian programs. To a great extent the larger political context of the BIA water development program can be defined in terms of the Bureau of Reclamation and the U.S. Army Corps of Engineers. In chapter 2 I examined the development of these programs to about 1910. This chapter will trace the growth and development of the federal water development program to the early 1970s, when shifting political forces disrupted the traditional approach to water policy.

An analysis of non-Indian water development programs provides an opportunity to identify the sources of strength of a classic iron triangle. We can then compare this to the analysis presented in chapter 5 of a comparatively weak iron triangle—the BIA. Even the strongest iron triangle is not immune to change and shifting political attitudes, however, as evidenced by attacks on the "sacred cow" of water development in recent years. Hence this and subsequent chapters afford an opportunity to examine how iron triangles respond to a changing political environment.

66

The Bureau of Reclamation

THREE PROBLEMS

By 1910 the Reclamation Service was in serious trouble, caused by three basic problems. First, Congress delegated the power to authorize and fund projects to the secretary of interior, which deprived congressmen of the opportunity to take credit for projects. In addition, this delegation of power failed to free the selection process from politics, and the secretary, for political reasons, authorized too many projects and overburdened the reclamation fund. The second problem concerned water rights. Some people in the Reclamation Service wanted to extend federal control over water rights, but most westerners—especially those in state office—adamantly refused to accept federal control. This created a wedge between the agency and its principal clientele, a serious impediment to iron triangle policy-making. Third, the original reclamation act required full repayment, without interest, within ten years. This placed an unreasonable financial strain on project farmers and threatened to bankrupt the reclamation fund, which was to be replenished by the sale of public lands and payments from project farmers. Together these problems prevented the Reclamation Service from functioning effectively in an iron triangle. As support for reclamation grew, however, efforts were made to remedy all three problems.

The easiest to rectify was the problem concerning the secretary of interior. Because the secretary authorized too many projects, there was insufficient funding to complete most of them. This infuriated the settlers, who felt they had been misled. They turned their wrath on the Reclamation Service and complained to their elected representatives in Congress. When a new secretary of interior took office in 1913, he told an associate, "Senators and Congressmen have been overwhelming me with curses upon the Reclamation Service" (quoted in Robinson 1979:42). Congress responded by revoking the secretary's authority to authorize and fund projects, beginning with fiscal year 1915.

The amendment to the act that revoked the secretary's authority was not intended to depoliticize the decision-making process. Rather, it was an attempt by Congress to gain greater control over—and thereby greater credit for—project selection and funding. The change in the law was also prompted by eastern congressmen, who demanded the right to participate in the process. They worried that future secretaries of interior, who are usually from the West, would continue to be overly generous to western irrigators. By moving the decision nexus to Congress they hoped to check the flow of money to western states. Western congressmen also had reason to support the revocation of the secretary's power of authorization. Without control over project selection and funding they could not claim credit for the project. The glory went to the secretary of interior (and the blame to the Reclamation Service, even though it was the secretary's fault that too many projects were authorized). Western legislators had another reason to support the amendment, however; they needed eastern votes in order to pass a relief act to help solve the second problem: farmers' inability to repay their loans to the reclamation fund.

Agitation for a more relaxed repayment schedule arose almost immediately after farmers began settling on the projects. The 1902 act required that all funds be repaid within a ten-year period, but the loan was interest-free. According to one estimate, that amounted to a subsidy of about 39 percent of project costs (Rucker and Fishback 1983:52). Still, farmers could not repay their loans. As early as 1909 the National Irrigation Congress recommended that the Reclamation Fund be augmented by the sale of gold bonds (National Irrigation Congress 1909:28). Two years later the Irrigation Congress formally requested that the repayment period be extended (1911:13). Congress was quick to respond. Table 3 is a list of the numerous provisions passed by Congress to alleviate the farmers' debt problems. The table makes it obvious that Congress was willing to go to extraordinary lengths to accommodate project beneficiaries. Beginning in 1910 with a $20 million loan, Congress provided successively more generous subsidies for reclamation projects. The 1914 Reclamation Extension Act was intended to "create an irrigated empire in the West" (*Congressional Record* 7 August 1914:13453), and to achieve that end the repayment period was extended to twenty years with a five-year grace period. Throughout the 1920s numerous deferrals and extensions were passed, and in 1926 the repayment period was extended again, this time to forty years. An article in *World's Work* from that year was entitled "Reclamation Becomes a Pork Barrel" (February 1926: 354). More relief acts were passed throughout the 1930s, culminating in the 1939 Reclamation Project Act, which endeavored to avoid placing "an undue burden on water users" by basing repayment on the ability to pay (not project costs, as originally planned) and again extending the repayment period (Reclamation Project

TABLE 3
Statutes Providing Relief for Irrigation Projects

Year	Statute
1910	$20 million loaned to reclamation fund.
1911	Curtis Act, February 13 (36 Stat. 902). Gave secretary of interior power to renegotiate repayment contracts.
1914	Provided a congressional appropriation of $13.53 million. Extension Act of August 13 (38 Stat. 686). Extended period to twenty years with ten-year grace period.
1920	Act of February 25. Funds from the sale of oil and coal leases to be transferred to the reclamation fund.
1921	Joint Resolution of May 17 (41 Stat. 4). Gave secretary of interior power to deliver water to farmers even if they were a year or more behind on repayment.
1922	Act of March 31 (42 Stat. 489). Provided deferments to individual farmers.
1923	Act of February 28 (42 Stat. 1324). Provided deferments to individual farmers.
1924	Act of May 9 (43 Stat. 116). Provided deferments to individual farmers.
1926	Act of May 25 (44 Stat. 636). Repayment extended to forty years. $17.3 million written off on twenty-one projects.
1928	Boulder Canyon Project Act (45 Stat. 1057). Funded from the general treasury.
1931	Act of February 6 (46 Stat. 1064). Payments from the reclamation fund to the general treasury suspended for two years.
1932	Act of April 1 (47 Stat. 75). Provided one-year moratorium on construction charges.
1933	Act of March 3 (47 Stat. 1427). Extension of the 1932 act.
1934	Act of March 27 (48 Stat. 500). Extension of the 1932 act.
1935	Act of June 13 (49 Stat. 337). Extension of the 1932 act.
1936	Act of April 14 (49 Stat. 1206). Extension of the 1932 act.
1939	Act of May 31 (53 Stat. 792). Allowed repayment exemptions for settlers for up to four years.
1939	Reclamation Project Act of August 4 (53 Stat. 1187). Repayment period extended to at least forty years with ten-year grace period. Repayment to be based on ability to pay (as determined by the Bureau of Reclamation), not on actual project costs.

Act of August 4, 1939). The final report of the 1968 Public Land Law Review Commission summarized the result of these numerous congressional provisions:

> Under these . . . extension acts the average contract life for the repayment of construction charges became 50 years, with payments on 12 projects to extend over 50 to 64 years, on six projects over 65 to 79 years, on four projects from 80 to 99 years and on three projects from 100 to 150 years. (Gates 1968:688)

Congress' generous attitude was not initially shared by the Reclamation Service. It feared that the program would lose legitimacy if it abandoned the original principle of full payback (excepting interest costs). This concern was shared by the secretary of interior in 1913, when he presciently argued that "the descent through successive general postponements to complete repudiation of a just debt may now be clearly discerned and easily made" (quoted in Chandler 1913:130). In 1925 the commissioner of Reclamation (Elwood Mead) devoted three pages of his annual report to a diatribe against the repayment moratoriums, arguing that they would violate "the integrity of reclamation" and "discredit the whole reclamation policy" (Commissioner of Reclamation Annual Report 1925:8–11). The commissioner also opposed the liberalized repayment provision passed in 1931 (Commissioner of Reclamation Annual Report 1932:5).

The Reclamation Service's resistance to repayment liberalization was based on sound economics but bad politics. For many years the agency and its clientele had a hostile relationship because of the repayment issue. As pointed out in chapter 1, a successful iron triangle allocates benefits that are concentrated, but the costs must be dispersed. The payback provision violated the latter part of that formula. It also prevented reclamation interest groups and the agency from developing a close political relationship. Although the Reclamation Service resisted modifications to repayment, it was quite willing to subsidize irrigation through the sale of oil and coal leases and water power. The service was candid about its intentions to rely upon hydropower, the "paying partner," to pay for irrigation development. The agency's official newsletter, the *Reclamation Record*, editorialized in 1926 that "with the increased cost of irrigation works in the future, the revenues from power must be depended upon to lessen the burden on the irrigator" (1926:1).

Not until after the passage of the 1939 Reclamation Project Act did the most serious disputes over repayment subside. At that time the agency began to develop much closer relations with its clientele or, as William Warne delicately phrased it, "The period of major adjustment of relationships between the Bureau and the water-users occurred during the two decades between the great wars" (1973:64). In other words, both the agency and the interest groups realized it would be better to work as allies in an iron triangle than as antagonists fighting over repayment schedules.

Also, by that time the original idea of funding projects from a revolving reclamation fund had been modified in so many ways that it had lost a great deal of relevance; the 1928 Boulder Canyon Project Act was funded from the general treasury, not the reclamation fund (it would ultimately cost more than all previous projects combined). President Franklin Roosevelt used funds from the Public Works Administration to build projects (see Lowitt 1984:81–99). Later other "nonreimbursable" costs such as recreation and flood control were added to help minimize the burden of repayment on irrigators. In time these other benefits paid an increasing portion of project costs, although irrigated agriculture remained the principal beneficiary (Burness et al. 1980:817–826).

Ultimately the various revisions to the 1902 act created a substantial subsidy to project farmers. Leveen (1978) found that irrigators would repay only 3.3 percent of the $3.62 billion the bureau spent on irrigation construction. A study in 1980 by the Interior Department's Office of Policy Analysis found that per acre subsidies ranged from 57 to 97 percent (1980:38–41). Frederick and Hanson reviewed the available data and concluded that the irrigation subsidy "averages at least $500 per acre over all Bureau of Reclamation projects" (1982:70). The General Accounting Office reviewed six reclamation projects and found that irrigation repayments cover less than 10 percent of actual project costs (*GAO Report to the Congress* 13 March 1981; also see GAO Reports dated 10 October 1985, 31 January 1986, and 7 March 1986). And a study by Rucker and Fishback estimated that the interest subsidy, figured at a 10 percent discount rate over fifty years, amounts to 91 percent (1983:53). In short, the Bureau of Reclamation solved its second problem for the most part: it managed to disperse a large part of the costs and concentrate benefits in classic distributive fashion, thereby endearing the agency to its clientele and strengthening its position in the iron triangle.

The third factor inhibiting the Bureau of Reclamation's political growth concerns the conflict between federal and state governments over the control of water rights. Early leaders in the bureau wanted to establish a uniform system of federal water rights that would have clarified the bureau's rights and created consistency across states. This was vehemently resisted by state-level policymakers, who traditionally controlled water rights. Like the repayment issue, the conflict over water rights threatened to drive a wedge between the bureau and its principal constituency. On this matter, however, the agency was willing to recognize the realities of politics, even when Morris Bien and Frederick Newell were still leading the agency: "Fearful of losing political support in the West, Reclamation Service officials rarely discussed federal water rights in public and they filed for water under state laws just as individual appropriators did" (Pisani 1982:274).

The bureau has continued this policy of deference to state law. King, writing in 1959, stated that "the federal government has always carefully followed state law in the administration of the Reclamation Act" (1959:11). William Warne, a former assistant secretary of the interior, also made this point (1973:176).

In sum, the Bureau of Reclamation solved all three of its problems, with minor exceptions. Project beneficiaries still had to repay some project costs, and in that sense the bureau was at a disadvantage compared with the Corps of Engineers, which had few repayment provisions. The proportion of reimbursable costs grew progressively smaller, however. And the bureau still felt some residual heat from the controversy over federal versus state control, but the agency was clearly aligned with the states' rights forces after about 1930. Overall the conditions were ripe for the development of a strong iron triangle.

CONGRESS AND RECLAMATION

The reclamation iron triangle began to develop soon after both houses created a Committee on Irrigation and Arid Lands in 1889. Four years later Arid Lands was transferred to another committee, and a new committee devoted solely to irrigation and reclamation was formed. This committee was packed with a group of pro-irrigation westerners who soon earned the sobriquet "the irrigation clique" for their single-minded devotion to the reclamation cause.

In the ensuing years the Committee on Irrigation and Reclamation became well known for its regional and ideological bias. In the 1946 reorganization of Congress the responsibility for reclamation authorization was transferred to a new subcommittee on irrigation and reclamation in each house. The western bias of the original committee survived this reorganization. Table 4 indicates the regional bias of the House and Senate subcommittees that were responsible for authorizing reclamation projects from 1956 to 1984. The table indicates the region of membership as well as the chairmen of the subcommittee, whose names appear in parentheses under the region they represented. The extent of western over-representation is truly phenomenal. For many years the Senate subcommittee had no members whatsoever from other regions, and in only one case (the Senate in 1980) was there not a majority of westerners on both subcommittees. And there were only two Congresses in which the West did not control the chairmanship (1978–1980). Thus in terms of authorization, the reclamation iron triangle clearly managed to pack the relevant committee (see also Andrews and Sansone 1983:259–265).

In terms of appropriation, a somewhat different story emerges. For many years there was significant divergence between the full committee and the subcommittee in regard to western overrepresentation. Historically the West was overrepresented at the full committee level. Horn compiled data on the Senate Appropriations Committee from 1867 to 1966 and concluded,

> As the American people moved westward, need for internal improvements and federal assistance in taming the frontier increased. Few committee assignments were more helpful than Appropriations. From the plea to establish military posts to protect settlers against hostile Indians in bygone days, to the current quest for vast reclamation and hydroelectric power projects, the demands by westerners have been successfully pressed on Appropriations. (1970:32)

One of the reasons reclamation did so well on the Appropriations Committee was because of the chairmanship of Senator Carl Hayden of Arizona. If one individual were to be plucked from the panorama of American politics and credited with the success of the reclamation program, it would be Hayden. Elected to the House in 1912, then to the Senate in 1926, he began his service on the Appropriations Committee in 1928. He became chair in 1953 and "ruled" (Reisner 1986:149) until his retirement in 1969. His service in Congress gave a whole new dimension to the term "seniority." Throughout his career he pushed reclamation with a single-minded devotion that won many projects for the West, including his lifelong dream of a Central Arizona Project, "his swan

TABLE 4

	West		South		North
1956					
House	20	(Aspinall)	2		7
Senate	5	(Anderson)	—		—
1958					
House	20	(Aspinall)	2		6
Senate	5	(Anderson)	—		—
1960					
House	18	(Rogers)	2		3
Senate	6	(Anderson)	—		—
1962					
House	16	(Rogers)	1		4
Senate	8	(Anderson)	—		—
1964					
House		(Rogers)			
Senate	9	(Moss)	—		—
1966					
House	17	(Rogers)	1		2
Senate	9	(Anderson)	—		—
1968					
House	18	(Johnson)	1		3
Senate	9	(Anderson)	—		—
1970					
House	18	(Johnson)	1		2
Senate	10	(Anderson)	—		—
1972					
House	16	(Johnson)	2		—
Senate	10	(Anderson)	—		—
1974					
House	17	(Johnson)	1		—
Senate	7	(Church)	—		—
1976					
House	16	(Johnson)	—		1
Senate	7	(Church)	3		1
1978					
House	11	(Meeds)	—		2
Senate	8		1	(Bumpers)	1
1980					
House	10	(Kazen)	—		2
Senate	5		2	(Bumpers)	3

TABLE 4 (Continued)

MEMBERSHIP AND CHAIRMANSHIP OF AUTHORIZATION SUBCOMMITTEES
FOR BUREAU OF RECLAMATION, BY REGION, 1956–1984

	West	South	North
1982			
House	12 (Kazen)	—	—
Senate	5 (Murkowski)	—	4
1984			
House	12 (Kazen)	—	—
Senate	5 (Nickles)	1	3

Note: Subcommittee chairmen are listed in parentheses.

song in the Congress" (Johnson 1977:226). One of the reasons Hayden's chairmanship of the full committee was so important was the absence of western domination at the subcommittee level.

From 1947 to 1955 appropriations for reclamation in both houses was handled by the Subcommittee on the Interior Department. During that time the subcommittee in the House was never chaired by a westerner because of a conscious policy on the part of House Appropriations Committee chairmen of avoiding the "interest-sympathy-leniency syndrome" (Fenno 1966:141). This meant that if a congressman wanted to be on a subcommittee that concerned appropriations directly relevant to his district, the chair would put him elsewhere to avoid inflating the budget. In regard to reclamation, this helped to counterbalance the West's domination in the Senate. It also infuriated people like Carl Hayden, who often saw their handiwork pared down by a subcommittee that was less sensitive to the needs of the arid West.

One of the committee chairmen who espoused this strategy was Clarence Cannon, who was always looking for ways to increase his control over the appropriations process. He reorganized the subcommittees in the House in 1955 and moved the responsibility for reclamation appropriations from the Subcommittee on the Interior Department to the existing Subcommittee on Public Works, which also handled funding for the Corps of Engineers. The political significance of this new "super" public works subcommittee can be assessed by the fact that Cannon appointed himself chair.

Cannon's reorganization had three important impacts. First, it made it nearly impossible for westerners to gain control of subcommittee appropriations. With all public works being funded by the same subcommittee, legislators from every part of the country were clamoring to get on it. Second, it made logrolling for funding much more direct and convenient. Even more than in the past the Bureau of Reclamation and the Corps of Engineers were locked together in a web of vote-trading and mutual support. Third, Cannon's reorganization was mimicked by the Senate.

However, complications arose in the Senate. Hayden was upset that the new arrangement might disrupt the politics-as-usual in regard to his control over reclamation funding. To ensure continuity with past policy he subdivided the new subcommittee into three "units": one concerned with funding for the corps (all members of the subcommittee were members of this unit), a unit for the Tennessee Valley Authority and Atomic Energy Commission, and a third unit dealing exclusively with irrigation. Hayden made himself chairman of the latter unit, thereby ensuring continued control over his favored programs. These units were not dissolved until Hayden's retirement in 1969.

The difference between House and Senate public works subcommittees is readily apparent in the data presented in table 5. In the House the dominant area, at least as long as Cannon was chair, was the North, an area traditionally known for its hostility toward federal reclamation (recall the debate over the 1902 act). Even after Cannon retired, however, the westerners on the subcommittee were still a minority. This contrasts with the situation in the Senate, where the West was better represented, but still had a numerical majority for only one Congress (1980). In neither house did the West control the subcommittee chairmanship. Of course, in the Senate this was largely offset by Hayden's chairmanship of both the unit on reclamation and the full committee.

Because of the difference between the two branches, Hayden and his Senate allies were often in the position of adding projects to the appropriations bill that had been cut by House members. Richard Fenno tells of one such situation during the budget-cutting years of the Korean War. House members cut several projects from the bill, including funds for the Bureau of Reclamation. Then Hayden went into action: "On the Senate floor, three decreases were proposed. Senator Hayden opposed all, and all were defeated. Three increases were also proposed; Senator Hayden agreed to each of them and they passed" (Fenno 1966:606).

Despite the differences between the House and Senate in regard to western representation, the reclamation program achieved a relatively high level of support in Congress, as evidenced by the level of funding and generous statutory provisions. The first truly impressive increase in funding was the 1928 Boulder Canyon Project Act, which authorized Hoover Dam and ultimately absorbed more money than all other projects authorized at that time. Congress' willingness to forgive repayment debts, as evidenced by table 3, is an indication of the strength of reclamation sentiment in the national legislature.

Another indication of congressional support is the level of funding over time. Table 6 provides the annual appropriations for the bureau from 1936 to 1975 in five-year increments. These data include the monies from the reclamation fund, which remained solvent through the years because Congress transferred the proceeds from oil leases to the fund. This obviously injected a great deal of money from nonagricultural sources into the fund to subsidize irrigation. The data indicate a significant bulge in appropriations after World War II, a time when "Congress took the brakes off reclamation development in the West" (Gates 1968:691–692). There was so much demand for projects during that era that the Interior Committee's proposed budget was constantly being subjected to proposed amendments as various legislators tried to pass pet projects. Fenno writes that from 1947 to 1954 "the Bureau of Reclamation appropriation was considered in the Interior Department bill. . . . The presence of this constituency- and regionally-oriented bureau helped swell the number of proposed amendments" (1966:458).

Funding for reclamation fell during the 1950s as a result of pressure from the Eisenhower administration but bounced back during the Kennedy years: "The early 1960's were a period of growth in all the Bureau's water programs" (Holmes 1979:14). The agency again experienced a funding decline in the late 1960s, primarily because of President Lyndon Johnson's policy of cutting some domestic programs in order to allocate more funds to the Vietnam War (Holmes 1979:100). The bureau received a giant boost in 1968 with the passage of the Colorado River Basin Project Act, the largest and most expensive reclamation program authorized. This act is an excellent example of the logrolling that typically accompanies distributive policy-making. The Colorado River is divided into the Upper Basin and the Lower Basin. The Upper Basin, led by Congressman Aspinall from Colorado (known as "Mr. Reclamation"; Fradkin 1981:106), feared that increased development of the Lower Basin would utilize all the remaining water in the river and not leave enough for Upper Basin development. As chairman of the House Interior Committee, Aspinall was in a position to do something about it. In a classic case of vote-trading he agreed to

TABLE 5

MEMBERSHIP AND CHAIRMANSHIP OF APPROPRIATIONS SUBCOMMITTEES
(PUBLIC WORKS) FOR BUREAU OF RECLAMATION AND ARMY CORPS OF
ENGINEERS, BY REGION, 1956–1984

	West		South		North	
1956						
House	1		2		12	(Cannon)
Senate	7		6	(Ellender)	5	
1958						
House	2		2		9	(Cannon)
Senate	7		7	(Ellender)	4	
1960						
House	1		2		10	(Cannon)
Senate	9		8	(Ellender)	2	
1962						
House	1		2		9	(Cannon)
Senate	9		8	(Ellender)	2	
1964						
House	1		2		7	(Cannon)
Senate	10		7	(Ellender)	4	
1966						
House	1		2		5	(Kirwan)
Senate	10		7	(Ellender)	4	
1968						
House	2		2		4	(Kirwan)
Senate	10		6	(Ellender)	4	
1970						
House	1		3		4	(Kirwan)
Senate	7		5	(Ellender)	5	
1972						
House	1		3	(Evins)	4	
Senate	7		3	(Stennis)	8	
1974						
House	1		3	(Evins)	4	
Senate	9		3	(Stennis)	6	
1976						
House	1		4	(Evins)	3	
Senate	7		3	(Stennis)	5	
1978						
House	3		4	(Bevill)	4	
Senate	4		4	(Johnston)	5	

TABLE 5 (Continued)
MEMBERSHIP AND CHAIRMANSHIP OF APPROPRIATIONS SUBCOMMITTEES
(PUBLIC WORKS) FOR BUREAU OF RECLAMATION AND ARMY CORPS OF
ENGINEERS, BY REGION, 1956–1984

	West		South		North
1980					
House	3		4	(Bevill)	2
Senate	9		4	(Johnston)	3
1982					
House	5		3	(Bevill)	3
Senate	6	(Hatfield)	6		3
1984					
House	4		4	(Bevill)	1
Senate	6	(Hatfield)	6		3

Note: Subcommittee chairmen are listed in parentheses.

TABLE 6

ANNUAL APPROPRIATIONS FOR THE BUREAU OF RECLAMATION,
IN FIVE-YEAR INCREMENTS, 1936–1975
(in thousands of dollars)

Year	Appropriations
1936*	17,338
1940	78,665
1945	27,287
1950	372,917
1955	165,919
1960	260,265
1965	327,408
1970	391,801
1975	490,170

Source: Annual Budget for the U.S., 1937–1977.

*1936 was the first year in which all funds were aggregated as general fund appro-
priations for the Bureau of Reclamation.

support the Central Arizona Project in the Lower Basin in return for five projects in Colorado. Additional projects in New Mexico and Utah were included to gain additional support for the bill (*Congressional Quarterly Almanac* 1968:807–813; Ingram 1969).

In sum, the Bureau of Reclamation enjoyed a relatively high level of support in Congress most of the time. Its funding history reveals that the reclamation program has sometimes been vulnerable to exogenous forces such as presidential interference and the larger political environment (for example, the war in Vietnam), but for the most part the agency was quite successful in obtaining funding for reclamation projects. It was also successful in persuading Congress to amend the original reclamation statute to aid farmers and the agency itself. By one count the act had been amended 175 times by 1950 (President's Water Resources Policy Commission 1950:286). The close relationship between an agency and congressional subcommittee that is so critical to the political effectiveness of an iron triangle was clearly evident.

THE BUREAU AS
ADMINISTRATIVE AGENCY

For a period of nearly fifty years congressional support for reclamation closely approximated the ideal set forth in chapter 1. The Bureau of Reclamation also met many, but not all, of the requirements for effective agency participation in an iron triangle. The mission of the agency clearly involved the distribution of divisible goods and services (as late as 1961 the bureau was still giving away project lands; see Holmes 1979:13). There was a limit on mission expandability, however. The bureau was originally authorized to operate in only sixteen western states. This was later expanded to include Texas, Hawaii, and Alaska, but that still left thirty-one states beyond the purview of the bureau's programs. This hampered the agency's ability to participate in a policy-making arena that involved water development in every state and locality in the nation.

The bureau was able to expand its mission into new substantive functions, however. Its original task of irrigation grew to encompass nearly every phase of water development, including

> planning, constructing, maintaining and operating works of improvement for irrigation, hydropower development, municipal and industrial water supply, navigation, flood control, fish and wildlife preservation and propagation . . . recreation . . . comprehensive basin investiga-

tions, preauthorization project planning. . . . In addition to its planning and construction responsibilities, the Bureau marketed electricity . . . created and administered new towns at construction sites . . . established model farms . . . and engaged in agricultural research and farmer service activities. (Holmes 1979:13)

Hence the bureau was able to expand its mission within the geographical limits of the western states.

In terms of organization the Bureau of Reclamation has been remarkably stable. In 1907 the agency was removed from the U.S. Geological Survey and made a separate agency in the Department of Interior and has remained there ever since. In 1923 the name was changed from the Reclamation Service to the Bureau of Reclamation after a major internal reorganization. The name was changed again briefly in the late 1970s by Jimmy Carter, but Ronald Reagan immediately restored the traditional title. The autonomy of the agency is compromised somewhat by its subordination in the Department of Interior, but it has long been one of the more powerful agencies within that department.

Another important agency asset is the ability to exercise expertise, generate reliable information, and build a favorable image from both internal and external sources. In this area the bureau did very well, at least until recently. The agency quickly established a reputation for expertise in engineering. As Rourke points out, an agency that can claim some form of scientific expertise is at a distinct advantage because of the public's high regard for all things scientific (1984:92–95). Robinson writes that the bureau "pioneered designs and construction methods and assembled an outstanding public works organization" (1979:21). Respect for the bureau's engineering prowess is evident in the final report of the 1924 investigation by the Committee of Special Advisors on Reclamation: "The skill displayed in the building of the engineering structures of the Reclamation Service is of the highest order. Monuments to this skill will stand throughout the years to come in the form of great dams and water distribution systems. Some of these structures are already famous throughout the world" (U.S. Congress, Senate Document No. 92, 1924:30). An effusive article in a 1941 issue of *National Geographic* celebrated the opening of the bureau's Grand Coulee Dam and expressed similar sentiments: "[The] Bureau of Reclamation is stirring in its foresight and in its scientific approach to the age-old problem of helping the earth serve mankind" (Williams 1941:772). In 1964 the American Society of Civil Engineers voted Glen Canyon Dam to be the "outstanding engineering achievement of the year."

The giant dams built by the agency, such as Hoover, Glen Canyon, and Grand Coulee, became symbols, massive concrete metaphors of the bureau and its mission. Indeed, some argued these projects were metaphors for the entire American experience:

> Boulder Dam is the Great Pyramid of the American Desert, the Ninth Symphony of our day, and the key to the future of the whole Colorado River Basin.
>
> No other single piece of man's handiwork in this vast wilderness hinterland has epitomized so well during its construction all the strange and complex ramifications of our American Way—all its democratic faults and virtues, the political interlocking of local, state and federal governments, the meshed and rival economies of public and private enterprise, the conflicting needs of urban, agrarian and industrial groups. (Waters 1946:337)

Equally effusive references to the bureau's big dams are found throughout the water literature of the last fifty years (see Holbrook 1956:319; Taylor 1969:165; Fradkin 1981:238; Lear 1985:82; *New York Times* 17 March 1985:L22). The agency literally "remade the map of the West" (Stegner 1954:353). Indeed, Lowitt calls the bureau "the primary instrument in the modernization of the West" (1984:225).

In later years, when the most obvious sites for massive dams had already been developed or ruled off-limits by environmentalists, the bureau turned to ever more ambitious projects—some would call them "fantastic and bizarre" (Fradkin 1981:255)—that would transfer massive amounts of water from one river basin or region to another.[1] Yet even these projects were "reported in the popular media with a certain amount of respect for their long planning horizons and promethean audacity as engineering feats" (Holmes 1979:144).

The bureau also benefited from several inspiring leaders and a high level of organizational morale. Frederick Newell, the agency's first director, was well respected and "set a high standard" (Warne 1973:14). Newell was replaced by Authur Davis, "an outstanding engineer-administrator and an international authority on irrigation works" (Robinson 1979:42). Elwood Mead, an "illustrious reclamationist" (Reisner 1986:153), (director from 1924 to 1936) proved to be an able leader as well as politically astute:

Mead kept closely in touch with the people on the projects and had their support as well as that of the business interests and the engineering fraternity. Through masterful use of publicity he molded them into a power group effectively supporting the reclamation program. (Gates 1968:675)

With such leaders to guide them, and the public mesmerized for many years by their engineering feats, it is no wonder that the agency developed a strong sense of purpose and morale. Warne's book, a gushing tribute to the bureau, emphasized this point: "From its inception, the Bureau has been a 'high-morale outfit'" (1973:v).

The bureau's professional image has become tarnished somewhat in recent years because of the increasing emphasis on environmental factors and the failure of Teton Dam in 1976, the first bureau dam to collapse (see Reisner 1986:393–424). For most of this century, however, the agency displayed nearly all of the attributes necessary for effective participation in an iron triangle.

RECLAMATION INTEREST GROUPS

The Bureau of Reclamation has a long history of intimacy with several powerful interest groups. Typically the agency maintains close contact with grass-roots local interests that benefit from bureau projects. By the 1920s the bureau had such a close relationship with local beneficiaries that the 1924 report by the Committee of Special Advisors on Reclamation felt compelled to comment on the mutually dependent aspects of that relationship: "A dependence on Federal paternalism has settled down upon nearly all the projects, and a corresponding bureaucratic tendency has grown up within the Reclamation Service. The water users have come to look upon themselves as wards of the Government, a specially favored class with special claims upon governmental bounty" (U.S. Congress Senate Document No. 92, 1924:xiii).

Organized support for reclamation began in the late nineteenth century with the first National Irrigation Congress. After the bureau (the Reclamation Service) was created in 1902 these groups proliferated. Their first lobbying victories were the numerous extension acts passed by Congress, which responded repeatedly to these "special interests" (Hays 1959:248). Foremost among these groups was the National Water Users Association, formed in 1911 specifically to fight for more liberal repayment terms (Hays 1959: 247; Robinson 1979:42).

By the late 1930s most of the original interest groups established to support reclamation had fallen by the wayside. Elwood Mead, then head of the bureau, knew the necessity of organized constituency support, so he and several western governors formed the National Reclamation Association in 1932. This "powerful pressure group" (Lowitt 1984:98) was made up of state-level associations and often had the backing of powerful economic interests, such as western chambers of commerce and business interests that profited from the bureau's construction activities (Warne 1973:190). This organization developed very close ties with the bureau. The commissioner of reclamation often spoke at their annual meetings, and in turn the officials from the group had "easy access" to the commissioner (Warne 1973:191). Originally the National Reclamation Association's purpose was to deal only with matters concerning irrigation, but it later broadened its mission to include other forms of water development and changed its name to the National Water Resources Association.

Throughout its history this organization has strongly supported state prior appropriation laws, or, in Dunbar's words, it became "the watchdog of state-created water rights" (1983:198). Organized support for state prior appropriation laws, from the National Water Resources Association and many other groups, ultimately became a potent lobbying force. Indeed, Harrison calls it "the most powerful water policy lobby in the nation" (1981:S-11). Although that is probably an overstatement, it is significant that the vast political power of the western water development lobby was devoted to the fight against Indian reserved rights and other federal water rights.

The National Water Resources Association has not been alone in its efforts to promote western water development. The Bureau of Reclamation made it a point to establish powerful water user groups and strong irrigation district organizations that provided constituency support (Holmes 1979:19–20; Robinson 1979:32). As the bureau expanded its mission into new activities it created an enlarged potential for clientele support. For example, the American Public Power Association lobbied hard for the bureau's hydropower production activities. In the late 1960s this organization's policy was to support "the maximum development of the nation's hydroelectric sites" (U.S. Congress, House 1968, Part 2:840).

The western states themselves also formed a potent lobbying force for the Bureau of Reclamation. Once the bureau dropped its support for federal control of water rights, the agency and the states became close partners. Warne explains: "The legal requirement that the Bureau file water rights applications with the state engineers . . . has made it necessary to maintain close liaison with water officials in the state capitols of the West" (1973:174–175). The involvement of western state governments with reclamation lobbying has taken several forms. State legislatures have allocated funds to the National Water Resources Association (Warne 1973:192–193). State officials have also formed their own organizations. For example, in 1927 the Association of Western State Engineers was formed to fight against federal reserved rights (Dunbar 1983:197). State officials also played an important role in the establishment of the Western States Water Council in 1966. This group became an ardent supporter of increased water development and a vociferous opponent of Indian water rights. Perhaps the most effective lobbying activity is done by western congressmen and senators. They often testify on behalf of water projects at public hearings, and they personally lobby their colleagues.

It should be noted that interest group support for the Bureau of Reclamation is conditional. These groups have opposed the agency when there is a disagreement in policy direction, the best example being the issue of state versus federal control of water rights. Furthermore, any attempt by the bureau to cut back on the distribution of divisible goods and services always meets with cries of protest from organized constituents. Thus to maintain a high level of interest group support the agency needs to minimize any claim or support for federal reserved water rights and maximize subsidized federal water development and associated services.

In sum the Bureau of Reclamation enjoyed the advantages of a classic iron triangle. The agency operated in a favorable political and social environment and was supported by strong interest groups and a coterie of devoted legislators. As a result, "Reclamation in this century has grown beyond the wildest hopes of its sponsors" (Coggins and Wilkinson 1981:106). The cohesiveness of this iron triangle depended in part on its ability to minimize claims for federal reserved water rights and divert as much water as possible, even water that might be subject to future application to Indian reservations. Hence the lobbying activity of this iron triangle often included a persistent effort to minimize both Indian water rights and water development. This inevitably led these two programs into conflict. It also led the bureau into conflict with environmentalists and fiscal conservatives, which is discussed later. The rising conflict created a political environment less conducive to the classic operation of the reclamation iron triangle, but for at least half a century the reclamation program expanded relatively unrestrained. By 1974 the bureau had invested $6 billion in completed project facilities (U.S. Congress, House 1975, Part 4:85) and accomplished the following:

—11 million acres of land currently provided with irrigation service, and an additional 9 million acres to be irrigated upon completion of ongoing construction;

—50 power plants with 6 million kilowatts of hydropower generation capacity in operation, and an additional 4.5 million kilowatts of capacity under construction;

—14,590 miles of canals, 990 miles of pipelines, 230 miles of tunnels, 35,160 miles of laterals, 15,750 miles of project drains, 16,236 miles of transmission system;

—3.5 million acre-feet of municipal and industrial water deliveries, and an additional 1.6 million acre-feet upon completion of future construction; and

—345 diversion dams. (U.S. Congress, House 1975, Part 4:3; Water and Power Resources Service November 1979)

Despite the Bureau of Reclamation's recent problems, there is no doubt that the agency has functioned effectively as an agent of non-Indian water development. Billions of dollars have been allocated to the bureau and vast amounts of water have been diverted by its projects.

The U.S. Army Corps of Engineers

The relationship among the Corps of Engineers, organized constituencies, and Congress is something of a legend. Superlatives are often used to describe this relationship and the policies that result. Secretary of Interior Harold Ickes called the corps "the most powerful and most pervasive lobby in Washington" (from the foreword; Maass 1951:IX). Congressman Tom Bevill, a principal congressional supporter, called the corps the "most outstanding agency in our government" (U.S. Congress House, 1981b: 668). And William O. Douglas, a vocal critic, referred to the corps as "public enemy number one" (quoted in Florman 1977:26). In short, the corps, its congressional supporters, and organized constituencies constitute a classic iron triangle. In this section I will examine each of the corners of this triangle, concentrating on the factors identified in chapter 1 as affecting the triangle's political effectiveness.

CONGRESS AND THE CORPS

Immediately after World War II the Corps of Engineers returned to its civilian duties and, at the instigation of Congress, embarked on an ambitious water development program. Like the Bureau of Reclamation, the Corps enjoyed an extraordinary level of support from the authorization committees (the House committee was so cozy it was called the "public works club"; Anagnoson 1980:83) but sometimes met with resistance from budget-minded members of Appropriations. Congressmen Cannon and Tabor, who both served as House Appropriations chair during the postwar period, tried to minimize the potential for self-serving expenditures (the "interest-sympathy-leniency syndrome" mentioned earlier). Both Cannon and Tabor felt so strongly about the corps' activities that they made themselves subcommittee chair and ranking minority member to maintain close control over public works expenditures. Cannon's interest in the corps' budget was not stimulated totally from budgetary parsimony; one of Cannon's "great legislative passions" (Fenno 1966:145) was the development of public power, so he used his position as committee chair to further that goal.

By 1956 the authorization subcommittees for Corps of Engineers activities in both houses had achieved truly national representation. This reflects the corps' nationwide activity, which militates against the development of regional overrepresentation. Table 7 contains the data for both membership and chairmanship for the corps' authorization subcommittees. This table includes two House subcommittees from 1956 to 1974 because flood control and rivers and harbors were handled by separate subcommittees. The data reflect the combined membership of both of these House subcommittees.

As shown in table 7, for many years a northerner chaired the House Subcommittee on Rivers and Harbors and a southerner chaired the House Subcommittee on Flood Control. For most of the years in the sample a westerner (Bob Kerr of Oklahoma) chaired the Senate subcommittee. In terms of membership no single region has dominated either the House or Senate subcommittee, although

TABLE 7

MEMBERSHIP AND CHAIRMANSHIP OF AUTHORIZATION SUBCOMMITTEES
FOR THE ARMY CORPS OF ENGINEERS, BY REGION, 1956–1984

	West		South		North	
1956						
House	9		10	(Davis)[3]	17	(Blatnik)[2]
Senate	5	(Kerr)[1]	1		4	
1958						
House	7		9	(Davis)[3]	19	(Blatnik)[2]
Senate	6	(Kerr)[1]	2		3	
1960						
House	10		7	(Davis)[3]	17	(Blatnik)[2]
Senate	4	(Kerr)[1]	—		9	
1962						
House	8		8	(Davis)[3]	18	(Blatnik)[2]
Senate	6	(Kerr)[1]			9	
1964						
House	10		8	(Davis)[3]	15	(Blatnik)[2]
Senate	5		2		10	(McNamara)[1]
1966						
House	12		9	(Jones)[3]	16	(Blatnik)[2]
Senate	9		1		7	(McNamara)[1]
1968						
House	12		12	(Jones)[3]	18	(Blatnik)[2]
Senate	5		1		5	(Young)[1]
1970						
House	13		10	(Jones)[3]	19	(Blatnik)[2]
Senate	3		2		6	(Young)[1]
1972						
House	17	(Roberts)[2]	12	(Jones)[3]	23	
Senate	3		1	(Jordan)[1]	5	
1974						
House	7	(Roberts)[1]	7		12	
Senate	4	(Gravel)[1]	1		4	
1976						
House	7	(Roberts)[1]	4		12	
Senate	6	(Gravel)[1]	1		3	
1978						
House	7	(Roberts)[1]	7		11	
Senate	6	(Gravel)[1]	—		1	
1980						
House	7	(Roberts)[1]	4		13	
Senate	6	(Gravel)[1]	—		1	

TABLE 7 (Continued)

MEMBERSHIP AND CHAIRMANSHIP OF AUTHORIZATION SUBCOMMITTEES
FOR THE ARMY CORPS OF ENGINEERS, BY REGION, 1956–1984

	West	South	North
1982			
House	4	7	15 (Roe)[1]
Senate	5 (Abdnor)[1]	1	1
1984			
House	5	3	15 (Roe)[1]
Senate	4 (Abdnor)[1]	—	3

Note: Subcommittee chairmen are listed in parentheses.

[1] Chairmen of Senate (and House after 1972) Flood Control/Rivers and Harbors Subcommittee.

[2] Chairman of House Rivers and Harbors Subcommittee.

[3] Chairman of House Flood Control Subcommittee.

the West was overrepresented on the basis of population. After 1978, when the Bureau of Reclamation joined the Corps of Engineers in the Senate Subcommittee for Water Resources (under the Committee on Environment and Public Works), the West began to dominate the subcommittee even more (also see Andrews and Sansone 1983:225–269).

Table 5, shown earlier, depicts the regional makeup of the appropriations subcommittees that dealt with both the corps and the Bureau of Reclamation beginning in 1956. The national distribution of membership on this committee helped the corps as much as it hurt the Bureau of Reclamation. Membership was fairly evenly distributed, with some underrepresentation of western states. In terms of the chairmanship, a regional imbalance favoring the South is readily apparent. For many years southern legislators from safe one-party districts or states dominated many chairs throughout the congressional committee system, including the prestigious Public Works Subcommittee for Appropriations. This was especially true in the Senate but diminished after the 1974 reforms and the Republican takeover in 1981. Still, the domination of southern chairs on public works subcommittees resulted in many large corps projects in southern states such as Louisiana (home of Senators Johnston and Ellender), Mississippi (home of Senator Stennis), and Alabama (home of Congressman Bevill, whom Jack Anderson called, in typically indelicate language, "the pasha of pork"; *Washington Post* 26 July 1985:E-10).

In short, the favorable orientation of Congress toward the Corps of Engineers was a result of some regional bias among subcommittee chairmen, but for the membership their devotion to the agency must be explained in terms of the political payoff of corps projects rather than regionalism. Although the corps is sometimes perceived as predominantly associated with the South, the membership of the relevant subcommittees indicates that legislators from all regions are interested in water development. As a result the corps has responded by building projects in all regions.

Given the bias in chairmen and the perceived advantages of distributive politics, it should come as no surprise that the corps has received "favored treatment" (Ferejohn 1974:233). This treatment is reflected in both the decision-making process that selects corps projects and the funding for those projects. Maass called the process of project selection "a truly unique procedure" (1950:579). It is specifically designed to meet the demands of local interests, maximize the opportunities for claiming credit, and increase the probability that projects will be approved if there is sufficient political payoff. For example, the use of omnibus authorization bills permits congressmen to attach questionable projects to strong projects, forcing the president either to kill the good projects with a veto and risk alienating a large number of voters or to accept the bad projects with the good ones.

Congress protects this favorable decision-making process by attempting to minimize input from other sources. As a result it is one of the best examples of an autonomous process. Arthur Maass's well-known study, *Muddy Waters,* found that the corps "reported directly to the Congress, made little effort to clear its plans and programs with other executive agencies, and in a sense, took its orders directly from the Congress. . . . The chief executive was denied the right of veto; he could not intervene between the committees of Congress and one of his executive bureaus" (1951:62). A later study by Grant McConnell reached a similar conclusion, determining that the corps' autonomy was a principal source of power for the agency (1966:215–216). To ensure that the corps' program meets their needs, congressmen participate to an unprecedented extent in the implementation stage. This increases their control over the allocation of benefits and maximizes their association with such benefits (Horn 1970:187; Ripley and Franklin 1986:95).

The project selection process is so biased toward approval that the corps itself has at times attempted to reform it. In the early part of the twentieth century the corps suggested several reforms that were very unpopular in Congress. Exercising its well-known political aptitude, the agency quietly abandoned talk of reform: "When its suggestions for changes elicited no favorable response, the Engineers quickly ceased to give advice. . . . If they insisted on a more constructive approach to waterway problems, Congress might limit seriously their administrative independence" (Hays 1959:214). In the 1960s a similar situation arose. The corps attempted to introduce more restrictive project criteria, but again Congress resisted, preferring more liberal criteria that increased the potential for pet projects (Holmes 1979:11). On occasion Congress even approved projects that were not recommended by the corps on the basis of such liberal criteria (Maass 1951:31; we will see more examples of this in chapter 7).

Given the political value of corps projects, Congress has been quite willing to fund them liberally. Horn's study of the Senate Appropriations Committee in the 1960s discovered a rather novel approach to corps budgeting:

> Senators interested in public works development are especially concerned with the amount that the Corps of Engineers can use during the next fiscal year in planning or constructing a given project. Throughout the hearings of the Public Works Subcommittee, the Army Engineers, whose working relations with Congress generally transcend any direction secretaries of the army and even presidents have been able to exert, are repeatedly asked by the chairman and members: "What is your capability?" which means: "How much do you need?" (1970:118)

As a result of this attitude, corps funding has experienced meteoric growth for most of this century. Like that of the Bureau of Reclamation, the corps' budget skyrocketed after World War II and then was temporarily diminished by President Eisenhower's quest for frugality. Table 8, which presents a sample of the corps' annual appropriations from 1950 to 1975, demonstrates this budgetary growth. In the early 1960s, under President Kennedy, another period of rapid budgetary growth occurred, and after a brief relapse in the latter part of that decade the corps' fortunes once again rose dramatically. It also experienced extensive growth in the number of personnel assigned to the agency. Additionally, very little of the corps' expenditures is reimbursable (Holmes 1972:35).

After 170 years of congressional generosity the Corps of Engineers can boast of an impressive record of accomplishment. By

TABLE 8

ANNUAL APPROPRIATIONS FOR THE CORPS OF ENGINEERS,
IN FIVE-YEAR INCREMENTS, 1950–1975
(in thousands of dollars)

Year	Appropriations
1950	640,575
1955	447,823
1960	872,637
1965	1,253,879
1970	1,237,259
1975	1,756,877

Source: Annual Budget for the U.S., 1952–1977.

1976 the agency had constructed over 4,000 projects with a real property investment of $88 billion (Corps of Engineers 1976:25–26). These projects included

—19,000 miles of waterways,
—500 harbors,
—350 reservoirs,
—9,000 miles of flood control structures,
—7,500 miles of "improved" channels,
—50 hydropower projects with a generating capacity of 12 million kilowatts, and
—100 emergency responses. (Army Corps of Engineers 1973)

Clearly Congress and the corps have historically enjoyed an unusually close relationship. James Murphy's study of the House Public Works Committee illuminated one of the principal reasons why both the agency and Congress have fought to preserve this relationship: "The wide-spread constituency interest in the Corps' projects provides substantial incentive for cooperation. Virtually every committee member, sooner or later, will have a project somewhere in the Corps' labyrinthine evaluation process" (1974:173). In a particularly relevant comparison Freeman contrasts the BIA/Congress relationship with that of the corps:

The obverse of the [BIA] case can be found in those situations in which leaders of bureaus or similar units are, more or less, permanently divorced from strong identification with the Administration and perm nently wedded to Congress. Among the clearest examples of this typ are leaders of the Corps of Engineers of the Army. (1965:45)

THE CORPS AS
ADMINISTRATIVE AGENCY

The Army Corps of Engineers is one of the more remarkable agencies in the federal government. The corps has proven to be amazingly adept at meeting the needs of congressmen and local constituent groups and in so doing has become "a rich, powerful, and influential federal agency" (Mazmanian and Nienaber 1979:1). Its mission is close to the ideal for an iron triangle participant. Its projects and programs can be concentrated while costs can be dispersed, and the list of distributive activities can be easily expanded. And expand they have; throughout the corps' 183-year history Congress has incrementally added new functions and responsibilities, nearly always accompanied by increased funding. Additions to the corps' mission include the following:

1802   Corps established with responsibility to build structures such as roads, lighthouses, and bridges
1834:   Navigation, including rivers and harbors
1850:   Lead agency in the Mississippi River Commission's flood control projects
1899:   Regulatory authority over waterways, including refuse control
1909:   Hydroelectric power development
1917:   Comprehensive planning and development
1925:   Comprehensive river basin surveys
1928:   Comprehensive flood control for Mississippi River
1930:   Coastal protection and beach erosion prevention
1936:   National flood control policy
1941:   Irrigation and small boat navigation
1944:   Park and recreation facilities, fish and wildlife conservation
1950:   Municipal and industrial water supply, pollution abatement
1955:   Hurricane protection
1960:   Comprehensive flood plain studies for all rivers
1962:   Disaster relief operations

1971:   Expansion of pollution control activities
1972:   Responsibility for issuing permits for all dredge and fill
        activities, including wetlands
1972:   Wastewater treatment program
1976:   Water supply and water transfer studies

In recent years the corps expanded its activities into the areas of environmental mitigation and protection, and water quality (Allee and Dodge 1970; Nienaber 1975).

The corps' organizational stability is equally impressive. The agency was established as an autonomous unit of the Department of Defense (then called the Department of War) and has remained there ever since. Numerous attempts to reorganize the agency and place it under the control of some other bureaucratic body have failed completely.

The agency's professionalism is also widely recognized. The corps has effectively capitalized on the mystique of science to generate respect for its programs and projects. This image is enhanced by the aura of military efficiency and discipline that pervades the organization. Leadership positions in the agency are reserved for members of the military (although civilian employees greatly outnumber them), and it is considered an elite assignment to be an officer serving with the corps. Not surprisingly, the agency's partners in the water iron triangle nurture the corps' reputation for scientific rationalism. For example, the annual meeting of the Atlantic Deep Waterways Association traditionally adopted a resolution recognizing the corps' capabilities. Language such as this was typical: "The improvement of our rivers and harbors has, for more than a century, been delegated to the Corps of Engineers. . . . Many notable engineering achievements have been accomplished. Their work has been marked by engineering skill and fidelity in execution" (quoted in Maass 1951:42). Congressmen are equally effusive. Senator Robert Kerr of Oklahoma, whose state profited greatly from corps projects, offered the following opinion in 1962: "If there is an agency in the government that is staffed by men and women who are technically qualified to perform the duties assigned to them, it is the Corps of Engineers" (*Congressional Record* 4 October 1962:22168).

The corps' expertise in political matters is also widely recognized (see Reisner 1986:251). Maass's (1951) well-respected study of the corps in the 1930s and 1940s detailed the agency's skill in maintaining the water iron triangle. John Ferejohn's study (1974) of corps budgeting from 1947 to 1968 reached a similar conclusion. And

Mazmanian and Nienaber's analysis of the ability of the corps to respond to new political stimuli concluded that "the Army Corps of Engineers has once again proved to be a most politically astute organization" (1979:194).

The corps' morale is also impressive. Arthur Morgan's *Dams and Other Disasters* is bitterly critical of the agency, but he notes the corps has "a strong spirit of solidarity" (1971:67). The agency's morale is enhanced by the elite nature of the assignment for military officers. There are no enlisted personnel in the Corps of Engineers.

CORPS INTEREST GROUPS

The corps has been very adept at cultivating a clientele. Maass found that its planning process provided for thirty-two stages at which interest groups could inject their input (1951:37). The list of organized interests is impressive. By all accounts the National Rivers and Harbors Congress has been the most powerful. Its influence in Congress was enhanced by overlapping membership; all congressmen and senators are ex-officio members of the organization and have at times occupied leadership positions in it while they were serving in Congress. At one time, in the late 1940s, the president of the National Rivers and Harbors Congress and all three of its national vice-presidents were members of Congress and served on the committees and subcommittees that dealt with the corps' projects and budget (Stong 1949:13). In the 1950s, when President Eisenhower was attempting to cut back on project expenditures, a caucus of affected congressmen (i.e., those from districts where projects were cut) rebelled. They were led by Congressman Overton Brooks, who at the time was also president of the National Rivers and Harbors Congress (Fenno 1966:493). According to the group's official policy statement, they had achieved "semi-official status" because of their "close liaison with governmental agencies, both legislative and executive" (quoted in Stong 1949:14).

The corps has also received support from a menagerie of local and regional interest groups. A list of groups that are specific to just one area or river basin would include the Atlantic Deep Waterways Association, the Ohio Valley Improvement Association, the Mississippi Valley Association, the Columbia Basin Development League, and the Missouri-Arkansas Basin's Flood Control and Conservation Association (Holmes 1979:12). Powerful business interests have also lobbied the corps and participated in its project selection process. For example, the Ohio Valley Conservation and Flood Control Congress was established in 1933 by a coalition of chambers of commerce in the area (Maass 1951:43). In the late 1960s Ferejohn discovered that a "powerful coalition of local interest groups" was allied with the corps in an effort to resist any outside input into the water iron triangle (1974:80). And Mazmanian and Nienaber found that the corps, always conscious of the need for interest group support, solicited new clientele groups in the early 1970s when the political climate was shifting (1979:193).

In sum, the Corps of Engineers has enjoyed an unusually close alliance with Congress and relevant interest groups. It has long been the classic iron triangle. As Ferejohn pointed out, "there is always considerable demand in Congress to expand the program of the Engineers" (1974:76).

The General Policy Environment

Thus far in this chapter I have examined the non-Indian water development iron triangle and found that the participants rank high on most of the determinants of effective participation in an iron triangle. To a great extent the success of the triangle in obtaining funds for projects can be attributed to these factors, but we must also consider the general policy environment. Chapter 1 cited four areas of this environment: the nature of distributive policy, the norm of reciprocity/logrolling, autonomy, and implementability. To understand fully the politics of water development, we must examine these factors and how they affect the policy environment.

DISTRIBUTIVE POLICY

The essential characteristic of distributive policy is the combination of concentrated benefits and dispersed costs. Congress has gone to great lengths to preserve that combination. To maximize benefits Congress and its executive branch allies have adopted a number of policies to that end. First, Congress has always supported a very liberal definition of benefits. In 1936 a law was passed requiring a positive benefit/cost ratio (benefits must be equal to or greater than costs) for flood control projects. Subsequently the requirement was applied to all federal water projects. In order to maximize the flow of expenditures to home districts and states, however, Congress took a broad view of what constituted a benefit and, conversely, a very restrictive view of costs. Responding to this need, federal agencies developed benefit/cost analyses that were biased toward project acceptance. Scholarly reviews of these benefit/cost formulas generally have been critical. A selection of studies from various periods confirm this. Statements such as the following are representative: benefit/cost analysis consists of "a considerable accumulation of absurdities" (Clarenbach 1955:1298); "the techniques of benefit/cost analysis have been abused" (Hirshleifer, De Haven, and Milliman 1969: 227); "The result, of course, is to misinform high-level decision makers in both the executive and legislative branches" (Marshall 1964:407); "It is safe to say that existing evidence indicates that the Corps routinely overestimates project benefits" (Ferejohn 1974:46); "both Congress and the Corps have sanctioned methods that allow creative accounting of benefits, conservative estimates of costs" (Arnold 1981:257).

The use of biased benefit/cost analysis results in the concentration of benefits in specific localities. Distributive policy also requires that costs be dispersed, however, which Congress has accomplished by absorbing most costs at the federal level rather than charging beneficiaries. Every president since Franklin Roosevelt has attempted to revise this practice by instituting what is known as cost-sharing, meaning that states or local beneficiaries would be required to pay part of the costs. As we have seen, Congress fought this bitterly, first by making most corps expenditures nonreimbursable and then by repeatedly revising the repayment formula used by the Bureau of Reclamation.

Another proposed reform that would require beneficiaries to bear a greater share of costs is to charge a fee for the use of federal facilities. Proposals for user fees have been introduced in nearly every session of Congress, usually with presidential approval, since the 1930s. As of the mid-1970s, however, none had survived the congressional process (Reid 1980:2–6).

In short, Congress effectively stifled attempts to alter significantly the distributive nature of water development projects. As a result congressmen continued to place great emphasis on such projects. In the 1960s Horn found that the Public Works Appropriation Subcommittee, which handled funding for both the Bureau of Reclamation and the Corps of Engineers, was considered to be the most attractive and prestigious committee assignment and, because of the competition, the most difficult assignment for a newcomer to obtain (1970:44–49). A study of Congress in the 1970s concluded that "virtually no congressmen oppose public works" (Arnold 1979:46).

THE NORM OF RECIPROCITY

The norm of reciprocity, the second factor in the policy environment, also remained a standard feature of water development policy. A clear example was the passage of the 1968 Colorado River Basin Project Act, whereby support for projects in one state was traded for support for projects in another. As described by Dean Mann, "the lobbying effort [in Congress] was vigorous and explicit 'you vote for my project and I'll vote for yours'" (1975:105).

One of the most direct and continuous consequences of logrolling was the inability of the government to plan projects adequately on a comprehensive basis. The norm of reciprocity requires that projects be chosen according to a political quid pro quo, not whether they fit into a plan worked out through a rational, apolitical formula. The 1950 president's Water Resources Policy Commission complained that "there is today no single, uniform Federal policy governing comprehensive development of water and land resources" (1950:5). The same accusation is still being made, so often that it is almost a cliché (see, for example, Doerksen 1977; Chan 1981; Harrison 1981; Sander 1983).

The dysfunctions of the norm of reciprocity are exacerbated by cross-agency vote-trading. Planning might be at least partially feasible if logrolling occurred only among projects of the same agency or genre—for example, trading one flood control project for another. Congressmen also trade across agencies and programs, however. The first example of this was the filibuster of the Rivers and Harbors Act of 1902 by proponents of a reclamation bill, which was then followed by congressional approval of both the reclamation bill and the rivers and harbors bill. It worked, and it is still being used. This means that a reclamation project in the West might be traded for a harbor improvement on the east coast. Support for this type of policy-making comes from the notion that such activity maintains regional equity and fairness. For example, westerners believe that federal projects in their region simply help them to get their fair share of the federal pie (see Mann 1973). As a result Congress has continued to think of water policy as a "disparate assemblage of specific projects" (Fesler 1964:394) that can be thrown together in omnibus bills and basinwide authorizations.

AUTONOMY

The autonomy of the water development program is something of a legend, not because it has never been questioned or challenged, but because it has successfully withstood an almost constant barrage of challenges. The history of water resources policy is peppered with studies, presidential directives, and august commissions that have attempted to tame the independence of the water development iron triangle.

The first such endeavor was initiated by President Theodore Roosevelt in 1907, and others have recurred frequently ever since. A partial list of studies that examined water resources administration and made recommendations to diminish the autonomy of the water iron triangle include the following:

1907: Inland Waterways Commission
1908: National Waterways Commission
1924: Joint Congressional Commission on Water Resources
1937: President's Committee on Administrative Management (Brownlow Report)
1949: First Hoover Commission
1950: President's Water Resources Policy Commission
1952: Temple University Survey of Federal Reorganization
1953: Missouri Basin Survey Commission
1955: Presidential Advisory Committee on Water Resources Policy
1955: Second Hoover Commission
1971: President's Advisory Council on Reorganization (The Ash Council)
1973: National Water Commission

This list includes only the more important efforts; in 1959 the Senate Select Committee on Water Resources noted that it had been preceded by at least twenty committees and commissions that had examined the problems of disjointed water development and administration. The reforms espoused by these studies generally fall into two categories: proposals to consolidate all water development functions into one agency or department, and the establishment of an "independent" agency (i.e., an agency the principal constituency of which is the president) that has the power to establish project criteria and review proposed projects.

The 1907 Inland Waterways Commission was the first study to recommend that the Corps of Engineers and all other federal water development programs be consolidated into one agency "that can be held accountable" (U.S. Congress S. 325, 1908). This proposal was made by every major study of the problem until the 1952 Temple University Survey. Fesler wrote in 1964 that this "was the last official study to recommend a transfer of the civil functions of the Army Corps of Engineers. From then on, the Corps was to be treated as an immovable object against which no irresistible force could be effectively mobilized" (1964:383). This moratorium on the impossible lasted until President Nixon's effort to create a new Department of Natural Resources, which, like all of its predecessors, never got beyond the proposal stage. As a result, the corps continued to enjoy a "remarkable degree of autonomy" (McConnell 1966:215), the Bureau of Reclamation continued to operate without being forced to coordinate with other agencies, comprehensive planning remained impossible, and logrolling remained the principal method of project selection.

The second approach to limiting the autonomy of the water development iron triangle was to establish an independent agency to review proposed projects and to pass judgment on their acceptability. The Bureau of the Budget was created in 1921 to perform just such a review function for all federal programs and expenditures, but in the area of water development the autonomy of the decision-making process prevented the bureau from having much of an effect. The first attempt to establish a review agency specifically for water development and associated issues was President Franklin Roosevelt's creation in 1939 of a National Resources Planning Board with a Water Resources Committee. This organization was authorized to impose a number of criteria on water development agencies to improve coordination and planning (Executive Order 8455, June 1940). Congress responded by abolishing the National Resources Planning Board in 1943 and forbidding the president to transfer the agency's review function to another agency (Marshall 1964:412).

The next attempt to establish some sort of review was to increase the power of the Bureau of the Budget. Another executive order was issued by Roosevelt (Executive Order 9384, 4 October 1943) that authorized the bureau to develop a long-range program of water development. Every agency was required to submit a report on every project proposal for review *before* the proposal was sent to Congress. In order to handle the increased workload created by this new task, the Bureau of the Budget tried to establish a new division, but Congress refused to fund the division and as a result "the extent of the Budget Bureau's review of construction agency programs was very limited" (Holmes 1972:37). Congress also developed administrative procedures that permitted it to bypass the Budget Bureau and review for itself all project proposals that had been investigated, even those that had been judged unfavorably by the corps (Maass 1950:57). Roosevelt's successor, Harry Truman, also made an effort to rationalize water development but "accomplished little" (Coate 1983:61).

Despite the obvious failure of these early efforts, the idea of an independent review agency remained popular with reformers (but not with Congress). The president's 1950 Water Resources Policy Commission proposed the establishment of a federal board of review, appointed by the president, to review all water development programs (1950:11). A similar idea was put forth in the 1955 President's Advisory Committee on Water Resources Policy (Fesler 1964:368). The Second Hoover Commission sought to strengthen the Bureau of the Budget *and* to create a new review agency in the Executive Office of the President (U.S. Commission on the Organization of the Executive Branch of the Government 1955:I-35–36), but until the 1960s "little positive action" (Maass 1950:258) was taken to review water projects.

The next significant effort to establish a review grew out of an effort by President Kennedy and the Senate Select Committee on National Water Resources (1959–1961) to improve and expand the federal water development program. This effort culminated in the passage of the 1965 Water Resources Planning Act, which established an independent executive agency called the U.S. Water Resources Council. This agency was not truly independent in the sense that the president was the agency's primary constituency, however; the council was originally composed of the secretaries of Agriculture, Interior, Army, and HEW (Health, Education and Welfare). In other words, the members of the council represented the interests that were supposed to be reviewed, given that the Bureau of Reclamation is in Interior, the corps is in the Department of the Army, and other aspects of federal water development (such as the Soil Conservation Service, which is in Agriculture) were represented on the council.[2] Thus the members had a vested interest in the existing federal water development program (see Liebman 1967; Holmes 1979:249–272). The director of the Budget Bureau was given "observer status" on the council. (Later the council was expanded to include the secretaries of the Departments of Commerce, Transportation, and Housing and Urban Development, the administrator of the Environmental Protection Agency, and the chairman of the Federal Power Commission.)

Despite the failure to diminish the autonomy of the water development iron triangle, it would be a serious mistake to conclude that the chief executive has not tried diligently to do so. Almost every president in this century has criticized the independence of the water triangle and noted the conspicuous lack of planning and coordination. Theodore Roosevelt, initially an ardent supporter of federal water development, became more skeptical in later years. The failure of his 1907 Inland Waterways Commission to accomplish anything and the continued expansion of the Corps of Engineers led him to lament in 1913 that federal water development had become "a disconnected series of pork-barrel problems whose only real interest was in their effect on the reelection or defeat of a Congressman" (Roosevelt 1913:211).

Although nearly every president has criticized the water iron triangle, only some of them have been willing to commit their political capital to a concentrated effort to reform water policy, an effort many considered inevitably futile. Eisenhower was one of those who thought a reduction in public works expenditures merited a battle. It is worthwhile to examine Eisenhower's efforts in some detail because of their similarity to earlier—and later—challenges to the water development iron triangle. These efforts can be grouped into two categories: attempts to cut funding directly by vetoing authorization and appropriation bills, and attempts to alter the decision-making process by which projects are selected.

Eisenhower used the veto quite often in an effort to curb what he thought was excessive government spending, and he considered water projects to be one of the more gratuitous examples of government waste. His distaste for such projects was sufficiently intense that he made the politically risky move of appearing before the influential National Rivers and Harbors Congress and telling them he was "very cold and unsympathetic" to "piecemeal" water development (*Public Papers*, Eisenhower 1954:505). He apparently meant what he said, for in 1956 he vetoed the omnibus water project authorization act, citing the fact that ninety-nine projects had either not been properly reviewed or had not been recommended by the corps' initial investigation (*Public Papers*, Eisenhower 1956:680–683). There were numerous protestations in Congress, but the veto was sustained.

Eisenhower vetoed the next omnibus bill also, passed in 1958, citing many of the same reasons (*Public Papers*, Eisenhower 1958:307–310). Again the veto was sustained. Because these bills were biennial this meant that no new omnibus corps projects were authorized for a period of six years. However, a $5 billion backlog of authorized but unfunded or incomplete projects minimized the immediate impact of these vetoes. The president was somewhat more predisposed to authorize reclamation projects. In 1956 he approved three important reclamation authorizations: the Colorado River Storage Project Act, the Small Reclamation Project Act, and the Washita River Project. Yet even these approvals contained language critical of the funding mechanisms and the burden they placed on the federal budget (*Public Papers*, Eisenhower 1956:135, 260, 648).

Eisenhower's vetoes of annual appropriations bills (as opposed to the authorization bills cited earlier) were much more threatening to the water iron triangle and, as a result, less successful. Throughout his first term he tried to reduce funding for water development, but Congress kept adding projects that were not in the president's recommended budget. He signed the Public Works Appropriation Bill for 1956 "with great reluctance" because it contained 107 new starts that were not approved by the Bureau of the Budget (*Public Papers*, Eisenhower 1956:696). Growing increasingly frustrated, Eisenhower adopted a "no new starts"[3] policy in his budget for fiscal year 1959, pointing out,

> For the fiscal years 1956, 1957, and 1958, a total of $210 million was provided as the first-year appropriations for starting 407 new projects having an estimated total cost of $4.5 billion. As a result, expenditures for these two agencies [the corps and the Bureau of Reclamation] in 1959 will be higher than in any of the 5 preceding years and will increase further in 1960. (*Public Papers*, Eisenhower 1958:68–69)

Congress reacted by adding 118 new project starts to the appropriations bill. Eventually the president signed it because it contained several projects he wanted, but the stage was set for another confrontation the following year.

For fiscal year 1960 Eisenhower again attempted to pursue a "no new starts" policy and again Congress added a long list of new construction starts, this time 67 new corps and Bureau of Reclamation projects. Eisenhower immediately vetoed the bill, claiming that it "ignore[d] the necessity for an orderly development of America's water resources within the Nation's fiscal ability" (*Public Papers*, Eisenhower 1959:618–620). He stated that he would approve the bill if Congress removed the 67 new starts.

Most members of Congress reacted angrily to the veto, claiming they were "appalled at the flippancy" (*Congressional Record* 2 September 1959:17756) of the veto, which reflected the administration's "shrill demands" (*Congressional Record* 1959:17752) for reduced expenditures. A vocal minority, led by Everett Dirksen in the Senate and John Tabor in the House, supported the president. The attempt to override failed by one vote. One congressman warned of "political suffering" in the next election for those who voted against the override (*Congressional Record* 1959:18608). Senator Dirksen acknowledged the political value of the projects and noted that it took courage to veto the bill "knowing the diffusions of these projects in so many areas" (*Congressional Record* 1959:18925). After extensive debate Congress passed a second public works appropriations bill that was identical to the first one, including the 67 new starts, except that it pared 2.5 percent off each project. Again Eisenhower vetoed the bill and suggested that Congress enact a continuing resolution to fund ongoing construction (*Public Papers*, Eisenhower 1959:647). This time Congress voted to override, the first time it had garnered sufficient votes to defy the president since he took office (he had issued 144 previous vetoes).

Eisenhower also tried to change the decision-making process that selected projects for authorization and appropriation. He attempted four reforms. First, he emphasized comprehensive planning, as had all of his predecessors. Second, he tried to institute tougher standards for projects, relying principally on the Budget Bureau to establish new criteria and then apply them to water projects. The Budget Bureau responded by producing what became known as "Budget Circular A-47," which was considerably stricter than previous standards. As the previous discussion indicated, however, Congress simply ignored the Budget Bureau and funded new starts regardless of whether they met the stricter criteria.

The third reform espoused by the Eisenhower administration concerned cost-sharing and project reimbursement. The president wanted states and project beneficiaries to pay a greater portion of project costs. In his 1954 budget message Eisenhower noted that "special attention is being given to requirements for the sharing of costs among private beneficiaries, State and local groups, and the Federal Government" (*Public Papers*, Eisenhower 1954:166). He continued to stress this theme throughout his tenure in office and often referred to "partnership water development" (*Public Papers*, Eisenhower 1955:158), which today is known as cost-sharing.

A final effort to reform the decision-making process involved the creation of a new administrative body to review project proposals independently. Again this idea was not new, as the previous discussion makes clear. In 1954, Eisenhower created the Cabinet Committee on Water Resources Policy to "undertake an extensive review of all aspects of water resources policy" (*Public Papers,* Eisenhower 1954:509). That same year he also established the Inter-Agency Committee on Water Resources to improve planning and coordination (*Public Papers,* Eisenhower 1954:510). Later, when it became evident that Congress would simply ignore these new units, he relied increasingly on the Budget Bureau for an independent review. This provoked much congressional criticism of the "pencil-and-paper boys down at the Bureau of the Budget" who "had never seen a flood in their lives" (*Congressional Record* 1959:18595–18596).

Despite Eisenhower's concerted efforts, his impact on federal water policy was temporary at best. He managed to slow the authorization of new projects, and spending increased at a slower rate for a few years, but the basic decision-making process remained intact. Congress did not accept his proposals for cost-sharing; they ignored his new standards and review process; and log-rolling rather than comprehensive planning remained the principal mode of project selection.

President Eisenhower's incursion into the usually autonomous domain of water development policy-making was not unprecedented, but it was an unusually concerted effort to accomplish a politically risky goal. Subsequent presidents have also become involved in water policy, but until Jimmy Carter none of them made an effort equal to Eisenhower's. Kennedy was favorably disposed toward increased funding for federal water projects (Caulfield 1984:220) and replaced the restrictive criteria of Budget Circular A-47 with the more lenient Senate Document 97. Lyndon Johnson initially supported Kennedy's emphasis on water development, but as the war in Vietnam became increasingly costly he began to resist funding for projects. In 1967 he asked for only 7 new starts, but Congress budgeted 36. The following year the president insisted on a maximum of 11 new starts. The usual response would have been for Congress to ignore his plea and add more new starts, but Johnson was unusually adept at handling the legislature and succeeded in holding the number of new starts to his original request.

Nixon also tried to hold down the number of new construction starts, asking for 37 new starts in 1970. Congress responded in classic fashion this time, adding 102. This provoked an equally classic response from Nixon that was reminiscent of at least a dozen chief executives since President Polk (who was quoted in chapter 2): "Many of these added starts are for projects which would benefit some particularly interested group but would be of little value to the people generally. There is too much pork in this barrel" (*Public Papers*, Nixon 1970:824–825). Despite this sentiment, the budgets of both the Corps of Engineers and the Bureau of Reclamation grew considerably during Nixon's tenure in the White House. This trend continued for the most part with Gerald Ford.

In sum, during the period 1910–1975 the water development iron triangle enjoyed an unusual level of autonomy, but by no means was it immune from presidential influence. A long list of presidents challenged traditional water policy-making, some more success-fully than others. For the most part their impact was only tempo-rary. The political costs of such a challenge were considerable, and this tended to minimize the time and effort that the president was willing to invest in water policy reform. Only President Eisen-hower, in his second term, was willing to commit himself to a full-fledged battle with the water development iron triangle. Perhaps only a lame-duck president, especially a personally popular one, can afford the risk.

IMPLEMENTABILITY

The fourth element in the general policy environment concerns the implementability of the iron triangle's output. This requires clear political goals, program legitimacy, and a high level of generalized support. In terms of political goals, the output of the iron triangle was consistently clear to the principal participants throughout the first seventy years of this century. Agreement on these goals was threatened by two factors: political conflict over the values and priorities of water development (the subject of chapter 6) and changes in the general political environment (which is the topic of chapter 7). As long as conflict could be minimized, however, and the general environment remained supportive, then it was relatively easy for the iron triangle participants to agree on a course of action.

Program legitimacy was established through bold congressional initiative that delegated enormous power—and money—to the fed-eral water development program. Although there have been dis-agreements as to Congress' priorities in water development, there were seldom any doubts as to Congress' devotion to water de-velopment as a legitimate goal of government. The programs of the Bureau of Reclamation and the Corps of Engineers have a clear statutory base with significant judicial and administrative decisions to buttress the goals established by Congress.

The third requirement is a supportive political, social, and economic climate. Until the 1970s this condition was met with gusto as a result of several widely popular norms that were fueled by an insistence that a massive water crisis was just around the corner. This perception has been promulgated by numerous government reports and no fewer than five books with titles containing the phrase "water crisis" (Halacy 1966; Nikolaieff 1967; Moss 1967; Anderson 1983; Welsh 1985). The First National Water Assessment found that every major river basin in the country had either "major" or "severe" water management problems (U.S. Water Resources Council 1968:I-29). The Second Assessment concluded that "there is now no water crisis" but without "special efforts" there would be by the turn of the century (U.S. Water Resources Council 1975:I, 80). These studies and reports have been used to justify increased water development and have helped to create a supportive political atmosphere for at least some elements of the water development iron triangle.

Despite repeated warnings of an impending water crisis, a contradictory notion has also had an impact on water development, and that is what Maurice Kelso called the "water-is-different syndrome" (1967; also see Senator Moynihan's foreword in Andrews and Sansone 1983:1, and Conservation Foundation 1984:37). This refers to the refusal to recognize water as a finite resource and has led to the belief that more and more water (and hence water projects) should be made available to everyone simply because it is perceived as free and abundant. Paradoxically, this attitude has also resulted in a supportive atmosphere for water development, though for reasons quite different from the crisis rationale cited previously.

Several generalized norms also go hand in hand with the "more water development is better" approach. The traditional notion of conservation stressed the diversion and use of water. Any water that escaped to the sea was considered wasted; hence the primary emphasis was "on full development and use and not on efficiency in the economic sense" (Mann 1982:12). Only recently has the notion of conservation been expanded to include efficiency.

Another popular notion that has spurred water development is the public's fascination and respect for engineering achievements. Giant dams were viewed as a source of national pride and evidence of our technological prowess. This, coupled with a persistent faith in technology, created a very favorable atmosphere for the dam builders. Perhaps the epitome of this "technological fix" approach to water problems was the proposal in the 1960s to divert 36 trillion gallons of water from the Yukon River in Alaska to thirty-three states, seven Canadian provinces, and northern Mexico. This proposal was called the North American Water and Power Alliance (NAWAPA), and *Newsweek* called it the "greatest, the most titanic, colossal, stupendous, supersplendificent public-works project in history" (22 February 1965:53). The fact that this proposal was even discussed and encouraged by high-ranking officials (Secretary of Interior Stewart Udall said of the project: "I'm for this type of thinking. I'm glad the engineers talk so much about it"; *Newsweek* 22 February 1965:53) indicates an atmosphere conducive to massive water development programs. According to some sources, NAWAPA is again being touted as the solution to the West's water problems (see Welsh 1985:105–108, and Reisner 1986:506–513).

Finally, water development is congruent with the basic notion that development is intrinsically good. A mixture of the Protestant work ethic, capitalism, and a profound respect for material wealth, this belief system (Worster called it an "unrelenting American cultural imperative," 1985:188) found a responsive outlet in the government's water development program. This mix of values can clearly be seen in the Bureau of Reclamation's description of its Salt River Project: "Horatio Alger's Thesis on a magnificent scale . . . is found in the story of the irrigation development of the Salt River Valley" (quoted in Mann 1963). Clearly the federal water development program flourished in a generally friendly and supportive social, economic, and political atmosphere.

By no means has water development been immune from criticism, however. Maass's 1951 study of the corps (*Muddy Waters*) was something of a pioneering effort in that it offered a full frontal attack on some of the water development practices of the Corps of Engineers (also see Peterson 1954). Many other academic studies followed that criticized both the corps and/or the Bureau of Reclamation.[4] With the advent of the environmental movement these attacks intensified.[5] The media also criticized alleged pork barrel water projects; during the congressional debate over the Eisenhower vetoes one congressman complained, "We hear so much of pork barrel and fat in this bill from the press of the country" (*Congressional Record* 1959:18607). Indeed, papers as diverse as the *New York Times* (12 September 1959:20) and the *Wall Street Journal* (23 July 1959:6, 2 September 1959:6) editorialized in favor of the vetoes.

Beginning in the 1960s criticism of the federal water development program reached unprecedented levels. The quiet anonymity of water development iron triangles began to be plagued by incessant calls for reform. It appeared that a major change in the general policy environment was taking place. In the early 1970s several scholars of water policy argued that a new policy environment was emerging that was much less supportive of classic distributive water policy. Ingram argued that the traditional "decision rules" of distributive water policy were changing (1972:11). This was primarily a result of the increasing influence of environmentalism, which heightened conflict, diminished local support for projects, and made it more difficult for policymakers to engage in logrolling (Ingram 1972:1187). Mann pointed out that federal water development was increasingly becoming regulatory in nature and no longer limited merely to distributive policy-making (1973, 1975). But the boldest statement of the "new era" hypothesis was Henry Caulfield's presentation at the 1975 National Conference on Water. Caulfield, a past director of the Water Resources Council, argued,

> The Federal water-development program is politically dying, if not already dead. In recent years, Federal development programs have doubled (not even keeping pace with inflation in construction costs) while federally-assisted state and local programs, largely for waste water management, have increased sixteenfold. Clearly, national value priorities have changed. (1976:181)

Caulfield attributed the decline of the federal water development program to five factors: opposition from the Office of Management and Budget, the environmental movement, the decreasing role of federal involvement in western development, the completion of major water development programs for nearly every river system in America, and the emergence of a national urban majority that eclipsed the dominant position of agriculture in the water policy-making process (1976:181–182).

Support for this view came from other sources as well. Environmentalists began to predict the demise of pork barrel water projects (Carlin 1971:221–227). They had been successful in the 1950s in stopping the Echo Park Dam, proposed by the Bureau of Reclamation to be built within the Dinosaur National Monument (Stratton and Sorotkin 1959), and they stopped two dams from being built in or near the Grand Canyon in the 1960s (Mann 1975:101–104). Environmentalists also succeeded in convincing Congress to pass several important laws designed to protect the environment and to curb water development that had significant negative environmental impacts. Examples are the 1964 Wilderness Act, the Wild and Scenic Rivers Act of 1968, and the National Environmental

Policy Act of 1969. By the early 1970s the environmentalists had
become a powerful force in federal natural resource policy.

The promise of change also found its way into political circles.
Presidential candidate Jimmy Carter, who had successfully fought
a corps dam in Georgia, promised a new approach to water policy
if he were elected to office. Upon his election he immediately acted
upon his promise with a move so forceful it stunned even his
supporters. The impact of that action is discussed in chapter 7.

Conclusion

The water development iron triangle has been remarkably successful. An enormous amount of money has been
spent by the federal government to develop the nation's water
resources. In this chapter I examined this iron triangle with respect
to factors outlined in chapter 1 and found that most of them were
present, sometimes to an extraordinary degree.

There have always been important exceptions, however. In Congress there was always an element that opposed distributive water
projects. This faction was quite evident in the debate over the 1902
Reclamation Act. It also prevented Congress from overriding some
presidential vetoes. And it has resisted packing some subcommittees, especially those concerning appropriations.

Interest group support also has a conditional element. The primary source of organized support for water projects comes from
local beneficiaries. In a sense these are fair-weather friends, for
their support is based not on an abstract notion of loyalty or ideology but on the delivery of the requested benefits. They have
been quick to criticize federal decision makers who threaten these
benefits. Most of the groups active in the water development iron
triangle were not public interest groups; they participated because
they hoped to receive direct, specific benefits. If an agency fails to
deliver these benefits, it may break the feedback loop that funnels
political support back into the iron triangle.

And the agencies themselves have sometimes worked against
the interests of the triangle as a whole. The Reclamation Service
resisted relaxed repayment requirements, and the Corps of Engineers sometimes favored reforms not popular with Congress and
has on numerous occasions issued negative project recommendations even though the project obviously had support in Congress.
And the agencies involved in federal water resource development

have done a poor job of controlling interagency rivalry and conflict, even though it reduced the political harmony of the iron triangle.

The policy environment, though generally supportive, also presented some exceptions. A long list of presidents injected a measure of influence into water policy. At times this compromised the autonomy of the triangle, upset its stability, increased visibility, and reduced available funding. This in turn made logrolling more difficult, increased conflict, and made the allocation of benefits to potential opponents a less effective strategy. It is also clear that the iron triangle was not immune from the impact of exogenous variables. For example, both the Korean War and the Vietnam War diverted funds from water development to the military. A very different example is the Progressive Movement's emphasis on planning, which pointed out the illogic of piecemeal water development.

In short, when Jimmy Carter issued his famous "hit list" of water projects in 1977, his actions were not unprecedented. Other changes in the political environment convinced many observers that the old style of water policy via pork barreling iron triangles was fast becoming a thing of the past. Although resistance to the water development iron triangle was not new, *successful* resistance was, and it began to appear that a sea-change had finally occurred. Was the iron triangle dying? If so, what would take its place? And what impact would these changes have on Indians? Chapters 7 and 8 attempt to answer these questions, but first we must see how the BIA's water development program was faring while the events described in this chapter were taking place.

CHAPTER FIVE

The BIA Water Development Program

We began our first irrigation project in 1867 and we've never finished one yet.

—An old saying in the BIA

Introduction

Forty-one years before the *Winters* decision, the BIA began its water development program with a small canal on the Colorado River Reservation. This project set a bad precedent; the work was carried out "in a desultory manner" (Schmeckebier 1927:238) and after a few years the project was abandoned. The BIA initiated several other small projects before the turn of the century but hired no professional irrigation engineers, and as a result the work "proved so unsatisfactory and in some cases even disastrous that the necessity of having some trained employee . . . became apparent" (memorandum entitled "Irrigation," n.d., BIA Irrigation Division, about 1919). By the time the Reclamation Act became law the BIA water development program had made little progress. Chief Engineer Newell of the Reclamation Service warned in 1903 that there was a "great danger" that the Indians would lose their water because it was not being put to beneficial use and would inevitably be appropriated by others (Reclamation Service Annual Report 1903–1904:268).

By 1908 the BIA program was in serious trouble and in need of outside support, and the *Winters* decision had the potential to provide such support. It recognized that Indian water development lagged behind both private development and that sponsored by the Reclamation Service. If implemented, the decision would reserve water for the Indians until the BIA had time to develop its projects. In this chapter I will examine how the BIA responded to this opportunity.

Two basic questions will be addressed. First, how did the BIA attempt to implement the newly created doctrine of reserved rights? Second, how did the politics of the Indian iron triangle affect this implementation? As pointed out in the first chapter, water rights in the West are often meaningless without a method of diverting and using the water. Therefore we must examine Indian water development in a political context in order to understand the impact of the Winters Doctrine. This political context consists of the BIA as a whole, its irrigation division, and the iron triangle in which the agency operates. It also includes the agencies that develop non-Indian water—the Reclamation Service and the Corps of Engineers—which were discussed in the previous chapter.

The BIA's Official Water Rights Policy

It is clear that in the aftermath of the *Winters* case the BIA began to develop a growing appreciation of problems caused by water rights conflicts, although the agency seemed to waiver between near panic and lackadaisical awareness. In 1911 the commissioner of Indian Affairs reported a "general alertness" to the problem of Indian water rights (Annual Report 1911:16) and three years later noted casually that those rights "seem to be more or less in jeopardy" (Annual Report 1914:39). The chief of irrigation expressed much more concern that year, however, noting that BIA projects all over the West were being threatened with water rights litigation and outright confiscation by nearby whites. He reminded the commissioner that "it must be borne in mind that the valuable water resources which we are attempting to confirm to the Indians are frequently much desired by white interests" (Chief Engineer Annual Report 1914:10).

Although it finally became clear there was a serious problem with rights, it was not at all clear what the BIA was going to do about it. Basically the agency developed a somewhat incongruous amalgam of Winters Doctrine rights, and claims under the Prior Appropriation Doctrine of state law. These doctrines are diametrically opposed, and therefore this approach became problematic. In an effort to resolve this inherent conflict, the BIA developed its own procrustean approach to each doctrine.

THE BIA AND THE WINTERS DOCTRINE

Until the 1908 decision the BIA had no choice but to follow the precepts of the Prior Appropriation Doctrine, which had become the law of the land in arid states. The *Winters* decision potentially opened new doors, but the ambiguity of the decision, coupled with the Court's silence on how the new doctrine might be implemented within the framework of existing law, left the BIA with considerable discretion as to how to interpret the doctrine's range and applicability.

The BIA did not quickly formulate an official policy statement on the new doctrine, and as a result there was much confusion (see Pisani 1986:166). In 1909 the superintendent for the Southern Utes wrote to BIA headquarters asking if the Indians on that reservation had riparian rights or only rights of beneficial use (Robinson to Code 25 September 1909). In an attempt to answer the question, the superintendent for irrigation wrote a rambling, ten-page review of water law that said, in essence, he was not sure and that local laws requiring prior appropriation should be followed just to be safe (Robinson to Code 25 September 1909). The following year the superintendent tried again, this time producing a twenty-six-page document that concluded it was not necessary to buy water rights for the Indians because they "have all the rights necessary under their treaty, and the higher courts" (Robinson to Code 8 November 1910).

The superintendent of irrigation's attempt to formulate a rudimentary policy on reserved rights left many questions unanswered. That same year U.S. Attorney John McCourt, who was litigating a water rights case on behalf of the Umatilla Reservation, produced a fairly precise conceptualization of the Winters Doctrine. He noted that beneficial use is not necessary to protect the right, the uses to which the water can be put are not limited to irrigation, the right is open ended, and it cannot be controlled by state law (McCourt to Attorney General 1 October 1910). This formulation is nearly identical to that espoused by Indian claimants today. It is a broad interpretation of the doctrine but anchored in the Court's decision.

The BIA did not officially adopt McCourt's interpretation. In fact, it did not formulate an official policy on the doctrine until 1913. In the five years that had passed since the *Winters* decision the agency essentially used an ad hoc approach without any real policy direction. And when an official position was finally announced in 1913, it was significantly different from that formulated by McCourt. The commissioner of Indian Affairs included a paragraph on water rights in his annual report for 1913. The language, which was lifted verbatim from the Annual Report of the Chief Engineer (1913:5), is instructive because it provided the basis for BIA water rights policy for half a century:

The legal rights to the use of water is of primary importance in the work of the irrigation branch of the Indian Service. The water right for Indian lands rests upon common law riparian rights in some cases, and in others it would appear that beneficial use of water must be made before title can be acquired. The United States Supreme Court has decided in the case of *Winters v. U.S.* that prior appropriation by the United States and beneficial use by the Indians is not necessary, because of an implied reservation of water with and at the time of the reservation of the land sufficient for the irrigation thereof. However, the land in question had not been allotted, and the case did not involve the rights of any individual Indian but settled the right of the United States on behalf of unallotted Indians. (1913:19)

This paragraph indicates that the BIA took a narrow view of the doctrine; it assumed that the Winters Doctrine applied only to unallotted land (i.e., tribal land that had not been parceled out to individual Indians) and that the right belonged to the federal government, not the Indians. The BIA viewed the doctrine as a temporary government strategy that was to be used only until allotments were made and Indians began farming. An internal BIA memorandum, circulated late in 1913, explained that reserved rights would automatically be dissolved when the individual Indian became the owner of an allotment (memorandum entitled "Indian Water Rights" 16 October 1913). Nowhere is there any evidence that the BIA thought of reserved rights as belonging to the tribes themselves; it was a government right to aid in the allotment program and was to be applied only for farming purposes for a temporary period.

The BIA's narrow view of the Winters Doctrine may be explained by the agency's obvious misunderstanding of the case. The commissioner's statement, the annual report of the chief of engineers, and the internal memorandum cited earlier all refer to the doctrine as being "based upon riparian rights in government ownership" (memorandum entitled "Indian Water Rights" 16 October 1913). U.S. Attorney Rasch based some of his claims in the *Winters* case on riparian rights, but the courts rejected that argument and instead based the doctrine on treaty rights.

The BIA also failed to recognize the depth of the threat to Indian water rights. Another memorandum from 1913 stated that "there appears to be no danger of immediate loss of water rights" (memorandum entitled "Superintendent to Pass upon Water Rights" 20 June 1913). This statement was incorporated into the BIA's budget proposal submitted to Congress for fiscal year 1914, and Congressman Mondell quoted it as justification for his claim that a statute reserving Indian water rights was not needed because the rights were not in danger (*Congressional Record* 14 February 1914:3661). This damaged the BIA's attempt to pass a reserved water rights bill in 1914.

In short, the BIA chose to minimize the Winters Doctrine and the impact it might have on Indian water rights. As a result the doctrine was not considered important at the time; a survey of the annual reports of the National Irrigation Congress from 1905 to 1911 reveals not a single reference to the case or the doctrine. These Congresses discussed almost everything of relevance to irrigation, from canals in Brazil to the role of women in irrigation, but apparently never believed the *Winters* case warranted their attention. In 1908 the BIA even sent a representative to the Irrigation Congress to show slides of Indian projects, but there was no mention of the "landmark" decision (National Irrigation Congress 1908:17). Chandler's book, *Elements of Western Water Law* (1913), does not mention the Winters Doctrine either. The BIA's chief engineer, at the request of the secretary of interior, attended an irrigation convention held in 1914 and reported that "nothing was brought up in this convention that in any way directly affects the interest of the Indians" (Reed to Sells 13 April 1914). Apparently the Winters Doctrine was not a major concern to those people either.[1] Samuel Weil did mention the doctrine in his highly regarded 1911 treatise on water, and in so doing undoubtedly summed up the view of the doctrine prevailing at the time:

> The law of reserved public land, and of water and rights of way thereon, is now in the making, and but little can be done further than to state the meager authority which exists regarding it, premising that any conclusions drawn are tentative and that the field is more one of new governmental policy than of established law. . . . Confining ourselves to a statement of the authorities, we find divergent theories regarding the laws of waters on . . . Indian reservations. (1911:236, 138)

To a great extent this view of the Winters Doctrine helps to explain the BIA's position. Basically the agency did not trust it; the doctrine was much too vague, it contradicted prevailing policies, and it was based on case law rather than statutory law and hence difficult to implement. This attitude is evident in Assistant Commissioner Merritt's 1914 statement in support of the proposed reserved water rights bill, which was deemed necessary "to establish more certainly and securely water rights of Indians" (*Congres-*

sional Record 20 June 1914:10787). In short, the Winters Doctrine lacked political legitimacy, and the BIA knew it.

Still the agency occasionally relied upon the doctrine. In 1916 the BIA asked the Justice Department to file suit on behalf of the Uintah Reservation, claiming that "under the doctrine of reserved water rights the Indian's land is entitled to sufficient water to properly irrigate the crops produced" (Commissioner of Indian Affairs Annual Report 1916:41). In the 1923 annual report of the chief engineer he stated that on the Moapa Reservation the "Indian Office has always held that the Government is entitled to use whatever amount of water is necessary to irrigate the cultivated lands" (1923:9). The chief engineer also noted that "it is believed that the State of Utah is without jurisdiction over these inalienable [water] rights" of the Uintah Indians (1923:13). The commissioner of Indian Affairs' annual report for 1926 notes that the case of *Winters v. U.S.* protects the water rights of "the several Indians" (1926:24). In that same year Secretary of Interior Hubert Work wrote to Senator Charles McNary, chairman of the Committee on Irrigation and Reclamation, and explained that because of the *Winters* case the rights of Indians did not have to comply with state law (Work to McNary 12 February 1926:4).

The BIA also demonstrated a willingness to use the Reserved Rights Doctrine in court if a claim could not be made on the basis of beneficial use. During the half-century after the *Winters* decision nearly every major BIA irrigation project experienced legal problems in regard to water rights. Encroaching development constantly threatened the Indians' supply of water. Many of the resulting court cases were simply declarative in nature; the BIA hoped to clarify the water rights situation, arguing that "the value of this vast investment [in Indian irrigation projects] depends almost wholly on the legal rights to use of water on the land, and even though title to some of it may rest on the laws of appropriation and beneficial use, the only 'good' title to water for irrigation under such laws is a decree of a court" (BIA memorandum entitled "Superintendent to Pass on Water Rights" 20 June 1913).

Thus some of these declarative cases were clearly based on state prior appropriation laws. A number of cases, however, argued in favor of reserved rights and provided an opportunity for the courts to clarify the scope and applicability of the Winters Doctrine (*In re Conrad Investment Company v. U.S.* 1908; *Skeem v. U.S.* 1921; *U.S. v. Walker River Irrigation District* 1939; *U.S. v. Powers* 1939; *U.S. v. Ahtanum Irrigation District* 1956; *Arizona v. California* 1963). These and other cases kept the Winters Doctrine alive in the courts and helped to clarify and amplify the meaning of the doctrine. Not all courts were responsive to the doctrine, however; the federal district court for Nevada declared that it was "not moved to give a decree destroying the rights of the white pioneers" (*U.S. v. Walker River Irrigation District* 1936; also see *U.S. v. Wrightman* 1916; *Byers v. Wa-Wa-Ne* 1917).

Although these court cases helped to clarify the Winters Doctrine, they did nothing to solve the problems of implementation that had long plagued reserved rights; the lack of strong congressional support and the political resistance from other federal agencies such as the Bureau of Reclamation and its allies still robbed the doctrine of its political legitimacy. So the BIA faced political reality and turned to the only alternative scheme for protecting water rights: the Prior Appropriation Doctrine. From the time of the *Winters* case to the decision of *Arizona v. California* in 1963 (discussed in a subsequent section) the BIA utilized an incongruous combination of these two contradictory doctrines.

THE BIA AND THE
PRIOR APPROPRIATION DOCTRINE

Although the BIA was willing to use the Reserved Rights Doctrine in some cases as a matter of policy, it attempted to rely on state prior appropriation law when possible. A survey of the annual reports of the commissioner of Indian Affairs and the BIA's chief engineer indicate a persistent deference to state law and the doctrine of prior appropriation. The main thrust of BIA policy through these years was not to expand Indian claims via the Winters Doctrine but to protect water rights through beneficial use. There are several dozen references to this protect-through-use policy, perhaps best exemplified by a statement made by the chief of irrigation in 1915:

> The desirability of a large increase in the area being irrigated on several of the reservations is not only apparent on account of the larger self-support thus afforded the Indians, but also for the preservation of undisputed legal rights to the water needed for irrigation. The laws under which irrigation appropriations are made especially require such use of the water upon several reservations, and in addition to this it is the accepted custom and practice, and usually the law in arid states, that title to water for individuals can only accrue to him who needs and uses it, and while the application of this principle to the United States

is not admitted, cooperation with State officials is encouraged by acting in harmony with this plan. (Annual Report 1915:1)

Thus the BIA generally bowed to the political necessity of following state water law. According to one BIA official, state law was followed "to avoid criticism by white landowners" (quoted in Fradkin 1981:145). During the two decades after *Winters* the annual reports for the agency and its irrigation division contain references to at least eight reservations where water rights were considered subject to state prior appropriation water law.[2] There were also references to five other reservations where the stated policy was the protect-through-use approach.[3] Even Fort Belknap was included on the latter list (Chief Engineer Annual Report 1909:20). In 1932 the chief engineer was still referring to this strategy and used it as one of the criteria for allocating water development funds (Annual Report 1932:46).

The BIA's reliance on prior appropriation and the protect-through-use strategy had three important dysfunctions: it created even more confusion, it led to a widespread policy of leasing Indian lands, and it meant that water rights protection became a function of project funding levels. Each of these will be discussed.

The BIA's attempt to rely on both prior appropriation and reserved water rights was bound to create confusion.[4] They are completely contradictory doctrines, and recognition of one constitutes a denial of the other. One of the reasons the Winters Doctrine was important was because it would serve notice to non-Indians that they should not develop water sources that would be needed in the future by Indians. By relying on the Prior Appropriation Doctrine part of the time, however, the BIA gave the impression that water would not be claimed under the Reserved Rights Doctrine. This encouraged farmers to develop sources of water of potential use to Indians. In addition, the employees of the BIA were unsure of the agency's policy. When the BIA irrigation program was investigated in 1928, the investigators "fail[ed] to see any consistency in the application or practical working out by the Indian Bureau, of the principle involved in the *Winters* decision" (Preston and Engle 1928:2232). In effect the BIA's reluctance to use the Winters Doctrine as a matter of policy compromised the effectiveness of the doctrine. When the agency did attempt to rely on it, the effort looked hypocritical after the agency had filed for prior appropriation rights in state court.

The second problem triggered by reliance on prior appropriation was that it created a need to develop irrigated farming as rapidly

as possible. Because the Indians themselves were slow in making
the quantum leap from their traditional life-style to that of farmer,
the BIA adopted an aggressive policy of leasing Indian lands to
non-Indian farmers in order to put the water to beneficial use and
thereby to protect the right. In 1910 the BIA chief engineer suggested that a "plan of colonization" be formulated to encourage
non-Indians to lease Indian lands (Annual Report 1910:25, 27). In
1918 the chief engineer called the leasing policy "a wise one" and
predicted that the lessees would prepare the land for farming and
then at the end of the lease period would return the land to the
Indians "in a condition that will allow the Indian to take up the
occupation of farming with prospects of making a success" (Annual
Report 1918:3).

The leasing program generated a number of long-term problems
for Indians, however. First, the lessees did not take care of the
land. In 1923, just five years after the chief engineer issued the
optimistic statement quoted above, another annual report stated
that the leasing program "prompted the lessees to rob the soil—
'while the going was good'—by non-rotation of crops and lack of
fertilization" (Chief Engineer Annual Report 1923:8). Second, much
of the best land was leased to non-Indians, making the transition
from hunter to farmer even more difficult for the Indians. The
Meriam Report, a 1927 investigation of Indian conditions, found
that "the better sections of land have fallen into the hands of the
whites" (Meriam and Associates 1928:5). Because non-Indians had
the best land and are more experienced farmers, their per acre
production has been much higher than that from the land farmed
by Indians (Brophy and Aberle 1966:79; Sorkin 1971:66). Furthermore these lands were leased at extremely low rates. Levitan and
Hetrick found that in 1969 non-Indians grossed $109.3 million from
farming activity on Indian land but paid only $13.8 million in rent,
which was well below market prices (1971:134). Another study
concluded that Indians received only one-third of the gross earn-
ings from agricultural production on Indian lands; the other two-
thirds went to non-Indian lessees (U.S. Commission on Civil Rights
Staff Report No. 2 1972:19).

The third and most obvious problem generated by the BIA leasing program concerns the loss of land. This condition was exacerbated by the sale of Indian lands within the BIA irrigation projects. By 1929 only 32 percent of the land was actually irrigated
by Indians. Another 31 percent was leased to non-Indians and
37 percent was owned by non-Indians (Commissioner of Indian
Affairs Annual Report 1929:15). A 1915 investigation of Indian

irrigation by the Board of Indian Commissioners (a quasi-official regulatory agency for Indian Affairs) claimed that many projects were actually operated for the benefit of whites, not Indians (Abbott 1915:7). Another investigation, completed in 1928 by Preston and Engle, concluded that

> based on the acreage of land being used, many of the so-called Indian irrigation projects are in reality white projects. The acreage farmed by Indians is small in comparison with that farmed by whites and is continually decreasing, and under present condition will continue to decrease. . . . The continual decrease in the acreage farmed by Indians is the natural and logical result of the leasing system (1928:2220).

The leasing of Indian land, originally conceived as a way to protect Indian water rights under the Prior Appropriation Doctrine, created a permanent Anglo presence on many reservations. By 1974 non-Indians were farming 71 percent of all irrigated Indian land (1974 BIA 50–1 form, Part 1). Table 9 contains a breakdown of Indian/non-Indian farming on a selection of "Indian" irrigation projects. They range from 100 percent Indian to 100 percent non-

TABLE 9

IRRIGATED ACREAGE ON INDIAN RESERVATIONS
FARMED BY INDIANS AND NON-INDIANS

Reservation	Indian Operator		Non-Indian Operator	
Crow Creek	150	(55%)	121	(45%)
Crow	2,754	(9%)	27,533	(91%)
Standing Rock	300	(100%)	0	
Fort Hall	10,780	(16%)	56,033	(83%)
Umatilla	0		360	(100%)
Duck Valley	6,455	(99%)	78	(1%)
Fort McDermitt	2,853	(100%)	0	
Moapa	500	(100%)	0	
Total	20,888	(20%)	84,125	(80%)

Source: Adapted from the Report on Reservation and Resource Development and Protection, Task Force Seven, the Final Report of the American Indian Policy Review Commission, 1976.

Indian, but the largest percentage of non-Indian holdings are in the largest irrigation projects.

Thus far I have discussed two dysfunctions of the BIA policy of protecting Indian water rights through beneficial use. The first was increased confusion; the second was the emphasis on leasing. A third problem of this strategy was the enormous amount of pressure on the BIA to increase funding and hence construction so that project acreage and water use would increase. In essence the BIA entered a race with private irrigators and the Bureau of Reclamation to see who could divert the water first. This was precisely the kind of situation the *Winters* decision was designed to prevent. Nevertheless, funding for the Indian irrigation project became a principal determinant of the scope of Indian water rights. And funding was not the BIA's forte.

As I pointed out previously, the BIA did not develop an active orientation toward the water rights problem until about 1913, at which time the agency formulated a position on reserved water rights, albeit a very conditional position. The following year the agency and its friends in Congress pushed for a water rights bill that would recognize reserved rights. This period of time was acutely important for Indian water rights: the West was being developed quite rapidly, the Bureau of Reclamation program was expanding, and as a consequence the amount of unappropriated water was dwindling fast. It was the last chance for the BIA to obtain large quantities of water that were not already allocated to non-Indians. Therefore speed was essential; it was of paramount importance that the BIA obtain increased funding for projects that divert water to Indian reservations.

They got off to a bad start. The Indian appropriations bill for fiscal year 1916 failed to pass Congress because of a last-minute filibuster in the Senate over funding for enrollees of the Five Civilized Tribes in Oklahoma (*Appendix to the Congressional Record* 4 March 1915:928–929). As a result no new work was undertaken on any irrigation projects. For years after that the BIA, especially the irrigation division, continued to experience funding difficulties, prompting the chief of irrigation in 1920 to complain that "the work of the Indian Irrigation Service has been seriously handicapped by lack of sufficient funds to carry on the work contemplated" (Annual Report 1920:2).

The long-term rate of budgetary growth of the BIA's water development program can be discerned from the data presented in table 10, which provides budget totals, in five-year increments, for all BIA expenditures related to water development. The budget

TABLE 10

BIA APPROPRIATIONS FOR INDIAN WATER DEVELOPMENT, 1905–1975

Year	Appropriation		Line Item
1905	$ 185,000 90,000	—	Irrigation: small projects; Crow Reservation Project
	$ 275,000	Total	
1910	$ 200,000 6,000 1,003,000		Irrigation: small projects; water engineers; 9 individual projects
	$ 1,209,000	Total	
1915	$ 345,700 669,740		Irrigation: small projects; 16 individual projects
	$ 1,015,440	Total	
1920	$ 253,750 2,392,565		Irrigation: small projects; 21 individual projects
	$ 2,646,315	Total	
1925	$ 192,000 82,000 1,415,000		Irrigation: small projects; water supply; 23 individual projects
	$ 1,689,000	Total	
1930	$ 160,000 45,100 797,761		Irrigation: small projects; water supply for stock; 21 individual projects
	$ 1,002,861	Total	
1935	$ 130,000 52,810 256,435		Irrigation and drainage: small projects; water supply: Arizona and New Mexico; 16 individual projects
	$ 439,435	Total	
1940	$ 208,500 100,000 1,214,073		Irrigation and drainage: small projects; water supply: Arizona, New Mexico, and Utah; 18 individual projects
	$ 1,522,573	Total	
1945	$ 1,508,901 100,000		Irrigation and drainage; water supply: Arizona, New Mexico, and Utah
	$ 1,608,901	Total	
1950	$ 469,800 3,598,351		Maintenance, operation, and repair: irrigation systems; construction: irrigation systems
	$ 4,068,151	Total	
1955	$ 515,302 3,512,415		Maintenance, operation, and repair: irrigation systems; construction: irrigation systems
	$ 4,327,717	Total	

TABLE 10 (Continued)

BIA APPROPRIATIONS FOR INDIAN WATER DEVELOPMENT, 1905–1975

Year	Appropriation		Line Item
1960	$ 791,000 3,956,000 $ 4,747,000	 Total	Maintenance, operation, and re- pair: irrigation construction, extension, and rehabilitation; irrigation systems
1965	$ 1,246,000 8,275,000 $ 9,512,000	 Total	Maintenance, operation, and re- pair: irrigation systems; con- struction extension, and re- habilitation irrigation systems
1970	$ 1,461,000 4,231,000 $ 5,692,000	 Total	Maintenance, operation, and re- pair: irrigation systems; con- struction extension, and re- habilitation: irrigation systems
1975	$ 6,790,000 25,160,000 $31,950,000	 Total	Revenues derived from charges for operation and maintenance; construction, extension, and re- habilitation: irrigation systems (includes the Navajo Indian Irrigation Project)

Source: Appropriation bills, the Federal Budget, and the Annual Reports of the Commissioner of Indian Affairs

figures in table 10 are not entirely comparable over time because of inflation and changes in budget computation. To help identify the changes in computation, the table provides the titles of the line items that correspond to the figures in the column labeled "appropriation." This gives the reader an idea of when and how the BIA budget for water development changed from 1905 to 1975. The data in table 10 should be interpreted in light of the previous discussion; a large percentage of the irrigated land is farmed by non-Indians. In addition, not all expenditures are for irrigation; the BIA program also provided wells and delivery systems for domestic use and livestock.

The budget totals indicate a classic pattern of incremental budget increases. The *Winters* decision certainly did not precipitate a rush to develop Indian water; the appropriation for 1908 was $810,000 (Commissioner of Indian Affairs Annual Report 1908:54), whereas the sum for the following year was actually smaller (Commissioner

of Indian Affairs Annual Report 1909:49). In the long run appropriations have increased, but this increase has been painfully slow;
the funding for 1945 was only $400,000 more than the funding for
1910. In recent years funding grew as a result of inflation. Only in
1975, when a large sum was included for the Navajo Indian Irrigation Project, did the budget grow rapidly.

Figure 1 provides another look at BIA funding for irrigation by
graphing the amount of money allocated for construction, rehabilitation, engineering, and surveys and investigation (which includes
water rights protection after 1970). It is quite clear that except for
the Navajo Indian Irrigation Project, which was authorized in 1962,
the funding for irrigation construction has been erratic and remained at a relatively low level of funding from 1955 to 1976.

It is clear from figure 1 that the BIA had very little money for
project rehabilitation, which is also important to the effort to divert
water for beneficial use. In the hearings for the 1977 BIA budget
the commissioner of Indian Affairs explained, "Very candidly, a
lot of the existing projects that we have were authorized and were
never completed. So what we do is we try to keep the projects
operational with what we have, and it is kind of giving enough
money so that the project doesn't completely collapse" (U.S. Congress 1976b:106). In other words, funding is so inadequate that the
BIA cannot maintain its present facilities, much less expand. A
1975 BIA report to Congress pointed out that the lack of adequate
maintenance dramatically increased rehabilitation costs:

> Construction of most Indian irrigation projects began many years ago,
> and deterioration now requires a large portion of the construction fund
> ing received to be used for rehabilitation. This tends to slow construction
> progress. Also the past level of appropriated funds to pay the O&M
> assessments for indigent Indians has resulted in deferred maintenance
> which eventually causes deterioration to the point where rehabilitation
> is necessary. (BIA Report to the Senate, mimeograph, 1975, 38 pp.)

Considered together, table 10 and figure 1 provide convincing
evidence that a policy of protecting Indian water rights through
beneficial use was not a viable approach. The agency simply did
not receive sufficient funding for irrigation construction to divert
large amounts of water for beneficial applications.

Another measure of the success of the BIA's race to irrigate
Indian reservations is total irrigated acreage. This is somewhat
problematic, however, because of considerable disagreement over
the data. The BIA often included acreage figures in its budget

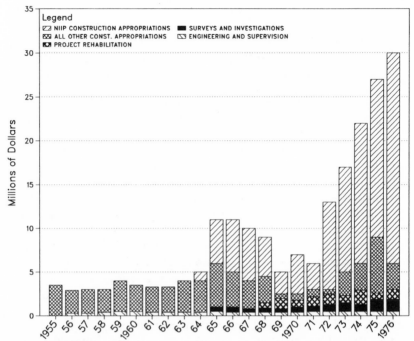

Source: Report to the U.S. Senate, Committee on Interior and Insular Affairs, by the BIA, 1975.

Fig. 1. BIA Irrigation Appropriations by Function, 1955–1976

justifications which indicated the number of acres that would be irrigated if all projects were completed and fully utilized. This has never happened. In 1928 the Preston-Engle Report claimed that "much of the data relating to the utilization of land, crop production, and other activities in the reports and justifications from some of the reservations is so exaggerated as to be worse than useless" (1928:2240). My own survey of numerous and diverse sources indicates substantial disagreement and inconsistencies in the data, even among the BIA's own figures. Hence any conclusions based on irrigated acreage must necessarily be suspect. Nevertheless I will attempt to estimate the acreage increase for BIA projects.

Apparently at the time of the *Winters* decision, the BIA irrigation program was watering about 160,000 acres, with a fourth of that amount being farmed by non-Indian lessees and owners (Commissioner of Indian Affairs Annual Report 1910:21). In 1930 it was reported that 361,708 acres were irrigated, one-third by non-Indians (Commissioner of Indian Affairs Annual Report 1930:21).

This would indicate a nearly threefold increase in acreage during those critical years when the BIA had an opportunity to divert large amounts of unappropriated water. Other sources disagree with these figures, however. Preston and Engle concluded "the acreage utilized by Indians has been rapidly decreasing for some years" (1928:2240). Leonard Carlson reviewed the available data for the same period and reached a similar conclusion: "After 1910 Indian farming declined in every state except Montana. . . . By 1930 the decline was universal" (1981:149–150). The BIA has had a little more success in recent years; according to the National Indian Water Policy Review of 1977, Indians were irrigating 370,000 acres (Gerard et al. 1978:17). Thus although there have been some gains in recent years, the BIA made little progress during the critical years when unappropriated waters were still relatively plentiful.

In sum, the BIA's strategy of protection through use was damaging in three respects: it created even more confusion about the applicability of the Winters Doctrine; it encouraged the leasing of the best Indian lands to non-Indians, often at very low rates; and it put the BIA in a race to divert water before it was appropriated by others, thereby making the BIA budget the determining factor in Indian water rights acquisition. The agency's reliance on the Prior Appropriation Doctrine was born out of desperation; they were well aware of the difficulty in implementing a court-mandated water right in the face of a hostile political environment. Still the BIA occasionally resorted to reserved rights in an attempt to preserve a water supply for its projects. As in the past, support for reserved rights came primarily from the courts, but it was not until the 1960s that the policy environment changed sufficiently to permit a change in the BIA's water rights strategy.

A NEW APPROACH TO
RESERVED RIGHTS

The Winters Doctrine of reserved Indian water rights remained an obscure case in Indian law throughout the first half of the twentieth century and had little substantive impact on western water development. This began to change slowly during the 1950s and more rapidly in the 1960s.

The first harbinger of an expanded approach to reserved rights came in 1955 when the U.S. Supreme Court handed down *Federal Power Commission v. Oregon*, known as the Pelton Dam case. In that decision the Supreme Court held that the U.S. government did not have to comply with state water law when it constructed a dam on a nonnavigable stream bordered by federal lands. The suit involved a proposed federal power dam that was to be constructed with one abutment on an Indian reservation and one on federally held public lands. Hence it involved more than just Indian land and a reservation of water for a BIA water project. The case is important because it marks the first time that a federal reserved right to water was extended to non-Indian federal uses. Prior to Pelton Dam it was easy to ignore reserved rights because they applied only to a small, relatively powerless minority. Suddenly, however, reserved rights were potentially applicable to other uses on other federal reservations. Western advocates of state prior appropriation laws had always been uneasy about the Winters Doctrine, but their fears of massive Indian water claims were muted by the political realities of western water policy. They knew that the BIA and its pro-Indian allies in Congress did not have the political clout necessary to give widespread substance to reserved Indian water rights. But the Pelton case applied the doctrine of reserved rights to other federal activities that were more viable politically. As a result many westerners and their allies in Congress reacted in horror. One commentator wrote that the case established an "overriding government right, never before known or believed to exist" (Davis 1960:21). An article in the *Oregon Law Review* accused the court of creating "a new doctrine of riparianism" (Munro 1956–1957:222), despite the fact that the decision was based on principles established in the *Rio Grande* case (1898) and *Winters* (1908). This reaction is not surprising, however, given the obscurity and minimal impact that the Winters Doctrine had up to that time. It was not a new doctrine at all, but its potential application to non-Indian federal purposes was an important expansion of its application. A group of western congressmen quickly attempted to neutralize the case's impact by introducing a series of "water rights settlement acts" that would have virtually abolished federal reserved water rights (Morreale 1966). The congressional reaction to these bills is instructive because it mirrors the events in Congress in 1914 and subsequent years when both the BIA and its opponents tried to persuade Congress to recognize their view of western water rights. As in these previous instances Congress adopted an essentially passive posture. Neither side had the votes to overwhelm the other. The Justice Department lobbied against the settlement acts, arguing that they would emasculate federal efforts to protect water rights for its reserved lands. And not all westerners supported such legislation; some feared that it might interfere with the flow of federal money to western water projects that produced power and stored water for irrigation. Congress was responsive to this plea but at the same time would not statutorily recognize the Reserved Rights Doctrine. In short, they left it up to the courts and federal administrators.

With Congress predisposed to do nothing about reserved water rights, the actual substantive impact of the Pelton decision was minimal, despite westerners' fears. There was no wholesale takeover of western water by federal bureaucrats (see Morreale 1966: 466, 504). The federal government's long-standing deference to state water law continued unabated for the most part, with the Pelton decision serving as an important but relatively isolated exception. However, the Pelton decision planted the seed of expanded federal water rights, and that seed took root eight years later when the Supreme Court again expanded reserved rights in the case of *Arizona v. California* (1963).

In that landmark case the high court strongly reaffirmed the Reserved Rights Doctrine and applied it to all federal reservations. In addition, the Court determined that the date of priority of reserved claims should be the date on which the federal reservation was established. And in a ruling that affected five tribes along the Colorado River, the Court stated that irrigable acreage would be used to determine the quantity of the reserved right. The case marked a definitive watershed in the development of federal reserved rights, including Indian rights. The Winters Doctrine was no longer an obscure case in Indian law; now it applied to half a dozen federal agencies with a cumulative power base that dwarfed the previous bureaucratic proponents of reserved rights. Together these agencies control one-third of the nation's land; 60 percent of the surface water in the West originates on these federal holdings.

For the first time the BIA began to pursue reserved Indian water rights aggressively. Hirshleifer, De Haven, and Milliman make this point clear:

> The fact is that the historical use of water by the Indian tribes has never been large, with the result that most western water has already been put to use by other persons under appropriative rights granted by state laws.
>
> Until a few years ago the legality of non-Indian water use on streams adjacent to Indian reservations was not in question, as open-ended Indian water rights had never been claimed. The whole issue came to light, however, in the *Arizona v. California* suit. (1969:251)

The new-found faith in reserved rights cannot be attributed entirely to the Arizona case. That decision certainly helped to legitimize the Reserved Rights Doctrine and expand its applicability, but a court decision—even one from the highest court in the land—suffers from the numerous implementation difficulties already discussed. It took more than a judicial reaffirmation of *Winters* to make a significant difference in the federal government's policy toward Indians. The additional impetus for an expanded approach to Indian rights came from the widespread rise of concern for minority rights in the 1960s. For the first time since the Civil War the populace as a whole became cognizant of the problems and the oppression of racial minorities. The black civil rights movement initiated and nurtured this growing awareness, but the recognition of Indian rights soon became enmeshed in the struggle for change in this issue area. By the mid-1960s there was an unprecedented public awareness of Indian problems, so much so that it became something of a "pop" issue that resulted in considerable cultural misunderstanding. Nevertheless it provided increased political support for a more aggressive stance on Indian claims to water.

The civil rights movement was accompanied by the environmental movement, which also had an impact on reserved rights. The Arizona decision applied reserved rights to all federal reservations, such as national forests, parks, and wildlife refuges. Federal agencies responsible for administering these lands developed an interest in reserved rights as a way of protecting stream flows and other water-related resources. This considerably enlarged the federal interest in reserved rights. It also increased western fears and opposition and introduced another set of competitors for federal reserved water.

By the beginning of the 1970s the "modern" era of Indian water rights was in full swing. By that I mean that the BIA and the Justice Department—and the tribes themselves—were making widespread claims for open-ended water rights. This approach to Indian reserved rights marked a new era in the BIA's policy on water rights, but with the exception of a few cases it still did not result in a significant and direct increase in water for Indians. The primary legacy of this new policy has been litigation, not water. Indians complain that they have plenty of "paper" water, meaning court-recognized reserved rights, but they are grievously short on "wet" water—that is, utilizable, deliverable water. To a great extent the BIA's effort simply came too late. In 1957, Charles Corker wrote that "the time for an orderly procedure which will end the Indian water right chaos has long passed" (1957:627). The BIA's new approach to Indian water rights came a decade after that, sixty years after the *Winters* decision, and many years after much of the unappropriated waters in the West had already been put to use on non-Indian lands. As a result, a striking continuity appears in remarks regarding the BIA's efforts to protect Indian water rights:

1914: Where was the Indian Service, with their reclamation bureau, that they were not on the job to see to it that the Indians got their [water] rights? (*Congressional Record* 29 July 1914:12950)

1922: Indians were a forgotten people in the Colorado Basin, as well as in the country at large; and their water needs, when not ignored, were considered negligible. (Hundley 1975:80)

1956: High standards for fair dealing required of the United States in controlling Indian affairs . . . are but a demonstration of a gross national hypocrisy. (*U.S. v. Ahtanum Irrigation District* 1956:338)

1973: In the history of the United States Government's treatment of Indian tribes, its failure to protect Indian water rights for use on the Reservations it set aside for them is one of the sorrier chapters. (National Water Commission Final Report 1973:475)

1973: It appears that the United States Government, which has the obligation to preserve and protect Indian property rights including water rights, has been grossly derelict in its duties and, as a consequence, Indian water rights are gravely threatened. (The Southwest Indian Report of the U.S. Commission on Civil Rights 1973:131)

1976: It is hard to find a single incident when the Department of Interior or Bureau of Indian Affairs took positive, aggressive action to protect Indian water rights against the taking of their water by non-Indians. . . . [Indians] have won these water rights but still there was not an advocate part taken by the Bureau to protect the water rights. (U.S. Congress, Senate 1976a:17)

1984: Paiute [water rights] had only the dubious protection of the Bureau of Indian Affairs. (Knack and Stewart 1984:346)

1985: And there was another community in the West who were ignored, closed out, . . . the Indians. Outside a few of its judges, the government did not acknowledge that the Indians might need or want water too. (Worster 1985:297)

In short, the BIA did an inadequate job of protecting Indian water rights, and the agency's more aggressive efforts in the past fifteen years offered too little, too late.

Why did the BIA fail? Attempts to answer this question generally fall into two categories. The first school of thought maintains that the BIA itself is to blame; it is inept and incapable of performing its duties. The second approach claims that the BIA is simply a scapegoat for the failure of the American public, Congress, and other policymakers to deal with Indians in an honorable fashion. According to this view the BIA has done an admirable job under extremely difficult conditions. Using the iron triangle as our frame of reference, we can evaluate these arguments by examining the three "corners" involved in Indian policy as well as the general policy environment.

The Indian Iron Triangle

CONGRESS

The Committee on Indian Affairs was created in 1821, making it one of the oldest continuous standing committees in Congress. Age does not necessarily breed success, however, at least as far as iron triangles are concerned. The reason committee members become involved in an iron triangle is so they can "bring home the bacon," which, it is assumed, helps them get reelected. In other words, there must be some kind of payoff. In this respect the Indian iron triangle presented a conditional and often conflictual possibility for a payoff.

There are two rationales for serving on an Indian Affairs committee. The first is based on sympathy for Indians and is primarily moralistic in intent and approach. The second is much more pragmatic; it serves the interests of non-Indians who are either threatened by the actions of the first group—the moralists—or who simply seek to obtain Indian resources, especially land or water. This, of course, compromises the highly cohesive, low-conflict environment in which iron triangles most effectively operate. There is considerable evidence that both of these factions have long coexisted on the Indian Affairs committees, and as the following discussion will make clear, they have adopted a rather unique approach to distributing—and obtaining—benefits.

The Committee on Indian Affairs has done more than merely minister to the needs of Indians. In 1910, Francis Leupp, a past commissioner of Indian Affairs, wrote about an "unwritten law" he called "the courtesy of the Senate":

> Any Senator who is a member of the Indian Affairs Committee may have practically whatever he asks for in his own State, if within the power of the committee to grant. Thus it sometimes happens that a dubious item finds its way into an Indian bill while it is in committee, and is reported to the Senate with the rest. (1910:212)

The "dubious item" he refers to concerns instances in which non-Indians want something of value from Indians. In essence this is a form of pork barrel, the source of the goods being Indian reservations rather than the federal treasury, but it serves the congressman in much the same way. In 1912 the commissioner of Indian Affairs complained that Indian appropriations "should be put on a budget basis and the present logrolling and personal aggrandizement of members of Congress and others should be made as difficult as possible" (Putney 1979:236). Twenty years later the commissioner of Indian Affairs complained about "the usual deluge of bills affecting Indians" which were mostly claims by Indians or non-Indians for some personal benefit (Commissioner of Indian Affairs Annual Report 1932:21). In short, the Indian committees in Congress have done more than allocate government funds to Indians; they have also allocated Indian resources to non-Indians.

Demands by non-Indians for Indian resources often were successful. I already established the fact that Indian water was transferred to non-Indian use in many cases. Congress also permitted the large-scale transfer of Indian land to non-Indians. In 1875, Indian reservations encompassed 166 million acres of land. By 1934, when the disastrous allotment program was ended, Indian landholdings were down to 52 million acres. After 1934 the federal government occasionally purchased land for Indians but at the same time took another 1.8 million acres, mostly for water projects being built by the Corps of Engineers and the Bureau of Reclamation. Clearly there has long been an element in Congress, well represented on the Indian Affairs committees, that engaged in a type of distributive policy whereby Indian resources were transferred to non-Indians. In this case the benefits are concentrated, but so are the costs. This latter fact is not typical of distributive policy, but the bearers of these costs—the Indians—were not sufficiently powerful to do much about it. Those in Congress who did object to these transfers were not sufficiently numerous to stop them, but they did have the power to obtain government benefits for Indians. In other words, in classic distributive fashion they were indulged through the allocation of government funds to the BIA, albeit an insufficient amount. In essence these allocations were compensatory; they replaced the loss of Indian resources with government welfare programs (see Barsh and Diaz-Knauf 1984). As a result both factions in Congress got something, which fits quite nicely into the distributive framework.

There is an important exception to the classic iron triangle, however, which limited the political usefulness of the Indian triangle. With the presence of both factions on the committee conflict remained high, and this interferes with the operation of a triangle. The presence of the anti-Indian/anti-BIA element on the Indian Affairs committees is well established. As pointed out in chapter 3, most of these legislators came from western states with small Indian minorities but strong, organized Anglo constituencies. Table 11 provides a breakdown of regional representation of the House and Senate Indian Affairs committees from 1904 to 1915, roughly the period when it was critical for the BIA to obtain unallocated water before it was diverted by others. The table clearly shows that the West was overrepresented in proportion to its population but that the other sections of the country were also represented in significant numbers. It should be noted that the Sixty-second and Sixty-third Congresses had the opportunity either to repudiate or statutorily to recognize the Winters Doctrine, and they chose to do neither. The regional breakdown of the legislators may help to explain this. In all of the Congresses represented in the table except one (the Sixtieth), westerners held a majority on the Senate committee; but in the House the West held a majority only twice (the Sixtieth and Sixty-second Congresses). As a result the House committee was generally more amenable to pro-Indian legislation.

Freeman examined a more recent sample of Indian committees (1933 to 1946) and reached the following conclusion:

> Regardless of party, the membership of the Committees in both houses was drawn overwhelmingly from Western or Indian-minority-populated states. . . . In view of their saturation with members elected by white majorities from Indian-minority-populated constituencies, one can better understand the Committees' frequent tendencies to work counter to a Bureau that promoted the interests of Indian minorities in the face of objections by local whites. The same applies for the Committees' greater accessibility to local, non-Indian interest groups. And one

TABLE 11

MEMBERSHIP OF HOUSE AND SENATE INDIAN AFFAIRS COMMITTEES,
BY REGION, 1904–1915

.	West	North	South
1904–1905 (58th Congress)			
House	8	9	1
Senate	9	4	2
1906–1907 (59th Congress)			
House	9	7	3
Senate	8	5	1
1907–1908 (60th Congress)			
House	10	6	3
Senate	7	5	3
1909–1910 (61st Congress)			
House	8	9	2
Senate	9	4	1
1911–1913 (62d Congress)			
House	12	6	2
Senate	9	5	1
1913–1915 (63d Congress)			
House	10	9	3
Senate	8	6	1

is not surprised to find that sectional, ethnic, and socio-economic interests tend to overshadow differences in party label among the members. (1965:100)

Tyler studied the Indian committees for about the same period of time, reached the same conclusion, and pointed out the importance of the committee chairman:

Party politics has tended to have little significance in the vote on Indian bills. The chairmen and senior members of Indian affairs and appropriations committees have usually wielded a strong influence regardless of party, with the vote on controversial bills tending to line up along regional rather than party lines. Indian bills often come up on the consent calendar where a single dissenting vote will kill the bill. (1973:8)

A more comprehensive and up-to-date regional breakdown of the Indian affairs subcommittees is provided in tables 12 (the House) and 13 (the Senate). From 1956 to 1978 western legislators clearly dominated the House Indian Affairs Subcommittee; they enjoyed a wide majority in every Congress. In the Senate the term "regional overrepresentation" is something of an understatement. From 1956 to 1976 only one nonwesterner served on the Senate Subcommittee on Indian Affairs. Of course, not all of these western legislators were anti-Indian, but many of them were. The eastern moralist who traditionally led the fight for Indian rights is conspicuously absent. The lone easterner on the subcommittee was Senator James Buckley, an arch-conservative from New York not known for his support of Indian rights.

When the BIA launched a more aggressive Indian rights cam-

TABLE 12

HOUSE INDIAN AFFAIRS SUBCOMMITTEE, BY REGION, 1956–1978

Year	West	North	South
1956	12	4	2
1958	12	3	2
1960	12	4	1
1962	10	2	2
1964	7	4	4
1966	8	5	2
1968	8	1	3
1970	9	1	3
1972	9	1	4
1974	9	2	2
1976	5	1	1
1978*	11	2	1
1980, 1981, 1983	Transferred to the Subcommittee on Water Power and Resources		

*Indian Affairs and Public Lands.

TABLE 13

SENATE INDIAN AFFAIRS SUBCOMMITTEES, BY REGION, 1956–1984

Year	West	North	South
Subcommittee on Indian Affairs, 1956–1976			
1956	5	—	—
1958	5	—	—
1960	6	—	—
1962	6	—	—
1964	8	—	—
1966	9	—	—
1968	9	—	—
1970	10	—	—
1972	10	1	—
1974	7	—	—
1976	7	—	—
Select Committee, 1978–1984			
1978	4	1	—
1980	3	1	1
1982	5	1	1
1984	4	—	2

paign in the early 1970s, the anti-Indian westerners on the subcommittee engineered a backlash. Congressman Lloyd Meeds from Washington was a leader of the backlash and also chairman of the House Indian Affairs Subcommittee. Meeds was replaced as chairman by Teno Roncalio, also from Washington and also a leader of the backlash (*National Journal* 26 August 1978; Bee 1982:135–137).

The power of the anti-Indian members of the Indian Affairs committees has been held in check by a long tradition of legislators who have been supportive of Indian rights. Congressman John Stephens of Texas, cited previously, is a prime example. Robert La Follette of Wisconsin was a member of the Senate Indian Affairs Committee and also an advocate of Indian rights. More recently, Congressman James Haley of Florida, who was chairman of the House Indian Affairs Subcommittee, was described by Secretary of Interior Udall in 1968 as "a staunch champion of Indian rights and of justice for them" (U.S. Congress, House 1968:834). In the Senate James Abourezk, chair of the Subcommittee on Indian Affairs in the Ninety-third Congress, was an "outspoken Indian advocate" (Bee 1982:81), one of the few from a western state (he retired after one term).

Because of the ideological split on the Indian Affairs subcommittees the subcommittee chair assumed unusual importance. To a certain extent he could orient the subcommittee in an anti-Indian or pro-Indian direction. Table 14 lists the chairmen for both House and Senate Indian Affairs committees and subcommittees from 1956 to 1984. Until 1974 Congressman Haley in the House helped to offset the anti-Indian sentiment in the Senate, where men such as Frank Church and Lee Metcalf, who favored termination, chaired the Indian subcommittee. In later years the situation was reversed: the House became more hostile to Indian rights under the leadership of Meeds and Roncalio, but in the Senate Abourezk, the sponsor of the American Indian Policy Review Commission bill, protected Indian interests, sometimes fighting alone. The political orientation of these chairmen helps to explain why conflict and stalemate occurred so often. From about 1956 to 1980 the chair of the subcommittee in one house was opposed to the orientation of the chair of the subcommittee in the other.

Because of the inherent and persistent conflict between the factions on the Indian committees, the opportunity to claim credit for constituency benefits in an atmosphere of low conflict was severely compromised. As a result the Indian committees are less attractive than the truly distributive committees such as public works and defense. Deloria and Lytle explain how this affected the committee's makeup:

> Traditionally the two Indian committees of Congress were not popular assignments. Careers could not be built on minor legislation that affected a small racial minority, and many members of Congress studiously avoided being assigned to these committees. As a consequence, they were generally filled with people from the western states, particularly those people whose supporters had business with the Bureau of Indian Affairs. There was unquestionably conflict of interest in these committees, and it meant that often a major piece of legislation would be shelved because of a minor and trivial complaint on another matter voiced by one of the members. (1984:81)

The unattractiveness of Indian committee assignments has persisted. In the Ninety-fifth Congress no one wanted to chair the House Subcommittee on Indian Affairs, so it was merged with

TABLE 14

CHAIRMEN FOR HOUSE AND SENATE INDIAN AFFAIRS
COMMITTEES AND SUBCOMMITTEES, 1956–1984

Year	Senate	House
	Subcommittee on Indian Affairs (Committee on Interior and Insular Affairs), 1956–1976	
1956	Joseph C. O'Mahoney (Wyoming)	James A. Haley (Florida)
1958	Richard L. Neuberger (Oregon)	James A. Haley (Florida)
1960	Richard L. Neuberger (Oregon)	James A. Haley (Florida)
1962	Frank Church (Idaho)	James A. Haley (Florida)
1964	Frank Church (Idaho)	James A. Haley (Florida)
1966	Lee Metcalf (Montana)	James A. Haley (Florida)
1968	George McGovern (South Dakota)	James A. Haley (Florida)
1970	George McGovern (South Dakota)	James A. Haley (Florida)
1972	George McGovern (South Dakota)	James A. Haley (Florida)
1974	James Abourezk (South Dakota)	Lloyd Meeds (Washington)
1976	James Abourezk (South Dakota)	Lloyd Meeds (Washington)
	Select Committee on Indian Affairs, 1978–1984	New Subcommittee—Indian Affairs and Public Lands, 1978–1984
1978	James Abourezk (South Dakota)	Teno Roncalio (Wyoming)
		New Subcommittee—Water Power and Resources with Office of Indian Affairs
1980	John Melcher (Montana)	Abraham Kazen, Jr. (Texas)
1982	William S. Cohen (Maine)	Abraham Kazen, Jr. (Texas)
1984	Mark Andrews (North Dakota)	Abraham Kazen, Jr. (Texas)

another committee. The same thing happened in the Ninety-sixth Congress, so the subcommittee was abandoned altogether and Indian affairs were handled by the whole committee (Bee 1982:74; also see Taylor 1984:120).

The BIA's problems in Congress were particularly acute when they concerned water development, because it interfered with the ability of Congress to allocate resources to both factions on the Indian committees. The anti-Indian faction has been rewarded with allocations of Indian resources, principally water and land, but the BIA water development program threatened to reverse this. James Officer, a past associate commissioner of Indian Affairs, personally experienced the congressional resistance to Indian water development:

> I found getting appropriations for Indian irrigation projects to be the most difficult task I had to face. The appropriations committees, as well as the representatives of the Budget Bureau [now Office of Management and Budget], could find dozens of reasons for denying money to the BIA for Indian irrigation projects, while endorsing gigantic sums to finance reclamation projects with much worse cost-benefit ratios in the districts of influential congressmen. (Officer, personal correspondence 28 December 1983)

One method used to overcome the opposition to funding for Indian irrigation was the so-called Indian blanket approach. This involved building projects that had both Indian and Anglo beneficiaries and therefore could be supported by both factions in Congress. In this way the distributive goals of the iron triangle could be met by allocating benefits to both Indians and Anglos. For example, most of the larger BIA irrigation projects also provide water for non-Indian lands, including the Indian land sold to settlers after reservation allotment. This explains in part why such a large percentage of Indian irrigation projects are farmed by non-Indians. The resistance to Indian projects was so intense that authorization was often possible only if non-Indian recipients were included. As water became more scarce this approach became more necessary politically. In the last forty years the only Indian water projects that have been authorized are two that are combination Anglo-Indian projects. In 1956 the Fort Hall-Michaud project was authorized as part of a larger Bureau of Reclamation project. The Navajo Indian Irrigation Project was authorized in 1962 simultaneously with the San Juan-Chama Project, which was to serve the City of Albuquerque and other non-Indians.

The Indian blanket approach helped to get these projects authorized, but it was not so helpful in obtaining appropriations for the Indian portion. The San Juan-Chama (i.e., Anglo) segment of the 1962 dual authorization was completed ahead of schedule, but the Navajo portion was only 17 percent complete eighteen years after the project was authorized (Price and Weatherford 1976:129), and by 1975 not a single acre of Navajo land was irrigated (BIA Report to the Senate 1975). The Navajos grew so frustrated with the BIA's funding problems they requested that the funding be funneled directly to the Bureau of Reclamation, bypassing the Indian agency (the request was denied; see Lawson 1976:22).

Given the difficulty in authorizing Indian projects, it is somewhat remarkable that even these two projects were accepted. They would never have survived without the Indian blanket strategy of tying Indian needs to Anglo development. Table 15, a list of the sixteen "major" BIA Indian water projects as of 1975, makes it evident that congressional authorizations are relatively scarce, especially in recent decades. Half of the projects were authorized before the *Winters* decision was handed down, and three of these "major" projects (as defined by the BIA) irrigated no land in 1975.

TABLE 15

SIXTEEN MAJOR INDIAN IRRIGATION PROJECTS, 1975

Reservation	Authorized	(1975) Irrigated Acreage
Crow	1891	39,893
Fort Hall	1894	37,208
Flathead	1904	122,063
Yakima: Wapato	1904	110,806
Wind River	1905	39,893
Uintah	1906	53,506
Blackfeet	1907	38,463
Fort Peck	1908	17,791
San Carlos	1924	13,213
Middle Rio Grande Pueblos	1928	11,000 (est.)
Colorado River	1935	60,329
Coachella Valley	1950	151
Fort Hall–Michaud	1954 (Bur. Rec.)	12,671
Navajo	1962 (Bur. Rec.)	0
Papago: Vaivo Vo	1965 (Corps)	0
Soboda	1970	0

The Navajo Indian Irrigation Project is really the only significant project to be initiated in the past half-century.

Thus although the BIA as a whole experienced trouble in Congress, the BIA's irrigation program was even more vulnerable. When the agency adopted a more aggressive approach to water rights in the 1970s, it destroyed the delicate balance between the two factions in Congress; it was no longer possible to coopt the BIA's opponents by allocating Indian resources to them. The Indian blanket strategy temporarily alleviated this problem, but because of the growing scarcity of water that approach is limited. Furthermore, budget reductions diminished the ability of the BIA to allocate government resources to the Indians. This greatly increased conflict and interfered with the *raison d'être* of the Indian iron triangle: to distribute benefits. As in the past, both factions in Congress had sufficient political clout to veto the major plans of the other and, in effect, create a stalemate on certain issues, especially water rights. This happened in 1914 when both sides attempted to legislate their view of western water rights. It happened again in the mid-1950s following the Pelton decision, when Congress refused to pass any of the proposed water settlement bills that would have destroyed federal reserved water rights but also refused statutorily to recognize the Winters Doctrine. By the early 1970s it appeared that once again Congress might reach a stalemate over the problem of Indian water rights and water development. I will return to this in chapter 8 when I discuss the contemporary period of water policy.

INTEREST GROUPS

When the *Winters* decision was handed down, there were no Indian interest groups. Rather, there were several organizations of concerned white citizens who lobbied for what they viewed as the interests of the Indians. Many of these groups were composed of eastern intellectuals, social reformers, or religious proselytizers. Examples are the American Indian Defense Association, the Indian Rights Association, and the Association of American Indian Affairs. All of these groups were active in Indian affairs by the late 1920s or early 1930s, and all were primarily Anglo groups that favored Indian assimilation. Thus their mission was not to protect traditional Indian life but to promote government aid in helping Indians adopt the Anglo life-style. They were interested in protecting Indian resources only to the extent that these resources were necessary to the process of assimilation. Freeman calls these organizations "non-clientele" groups and points out that they often disagreed with one another as to the best methods of promoting assimilation and helping Indians (1965:92).

Indians themselves have been slow to develop their own interest groups, partly because of the cultural differences between Indians and Anglos (it's a long way from traditional Indian culture to pressure group politics in Washington). As Indians have been exposed to Anglo culture, however, they have realized the necessity of providing their own political spokesmen. The first truly Indian interest group was the Society of American Indians, established in 1918 (Deloria and Lytle 1984:39). Not until 1944 was an effective pan-Indian group formed. In that year the National Congress of American Indians (NCAI) was established to lobby Congress on all issues affecting Indians. Because different tribes often disagree with one another, it is difficult for an organization such as the NCAI to represent all Indians. There simply is no such thing as the "Indian position" on many issues.

Despite the hardships, the NCAI survived. For many years it stood virtually alone, and has developed into one of "the most durable of the national all-Indian advocacy groups" (Bee 1982:87). On most issues NCAI received support from sympathetic Anglo groups such as those cited earlier, but unfortunately these groups often interpreted Indian needs from their own perspective; their assimilationist views in the 1920s and 1930s would be considered distinctly anti-Indian by current standards. Thus their well-meaning but often misguided efforts were sometimes a handicap to Indian causes in Congress.

Not until the 1970s did Indian interest groups begin to blossom. Spurred on by the civil rights movement and increased public support for Indian rights, a number of new Indian organizations were formed. The National Tribal Chairmen's Association (NTCA) was established in 1970 to coordinate the various needs of tribal governments, the Council of Energy Resource Tribes (CERT) was formed in 1975, and the Native American Rights Fund (NARF) came into existence in 1970. There are also at least sixteen regional tribal organizations that can have an important impact on policy (Taylor 1983:141). One can see how interest groups that affect Indian policy have changed over time by examining a list of groups from 1918 and comparing it to a list from 1972. In 1918 the following groups testified concerning the use of peyote by the Native American Church, a controversial issue in Indian policy at the time:

—Indian Rights Association
—National Women's Christian Temperance Union
—National Congress of Mothers and Parent-Teachers Associations
—Bureau of Catholic Missions
—Anti-Saloon League of America

All of these groups were composed of non-Indians and all opposed the use of peyote. The only group to testify in favor of peyote was the Society of American Indians, the only Indian interest group in existence at the time (Deloria and Lytle 1984:39). In contrast, the following Indian organizations endorsed the 1972 Trail of Broken Treaties:

—National Council on Indian Work
—National Congress of American Indians
—American Indian Movement
—National Indian Leadership Training
—Native American Legal Defense and Education Fund
—National Indian Lutheran Board
—National Indian Brotherhood
—National Indian Youth Council
—Native American Rights Fund
—National American Indian Council
—American Indian Commission on Alcohol and Drug Abuse
—Americans for Indian Opportunity
—Native American Women's Action Council
—United Native Americans
—Coalition of Indian Controlled School Boards

Obviously the extent of organized Indian participation in politics changed a great deal between 1918 and 1972. The impact these new groups have had on contemporary water rights and water development is detailed in a subsequent chapter.

These Indian groups and their non-Indian allies have been countered by organized anti-Indian interests. The American Indian Federation was organized in 1934 to fight the proposed Indian Reorganization Act. It was composed of a few pro-assimilationist Indians and a core group of extreme right-wing Anglos who believed the reservation system was communistic and the BIA was a conscious agent of communist subversion (Freeman 1965:108; Deloria and Lytle 1984:173). Despite this group's fanaticism, it received a sympathetic hearing by the Senate Committee on Indian

Affairs. In recent years the anti-Indian backlash provoked by increased interest in Indian rights expressed itself in a number of organizations. In 1974, Montanans Opposed to Discrimination was formed to resist Indian claims. Two years later the Interstate Congress for Equal Rights and Responsibilities was established to provide a broader base for anti-Indian organized activity (Taylor 1983: 155). According to Bee, this group "provided a good example of a well-managed lobby" during hearings on various backlash bills in 1978 (1982:140). In regard to Indian water development the organized opposition has been primarily from the non-Indian water development lobby.

Although the anti-Indian groups were never many in number, they have managed periodically to "gain the upper hand in determining federal [Indian] policy" (Bee 1982:135). Freeman calls these groups "anti-protection," meaning they resisted the protection of Indian resources, and explains how they established their legitimacy in Congress:

> The local, anti-protection groups were usually less amenable to the [BIA] Commissioner's views and were more likely to oppose him before the legislative committees as long as his major efforts were to guard energetically the economic interests of his clientele and to promote extensively their security through government aid. Frequently it was possible for the leaders of these groups to convince committee members that they carried great weight in Western constituencies, since their memberships included more non-Indians of the West. . . . The result . . . was basically to reduce congressional and public confidence in the Bureau's policies and personnel. To some extent this made it easier to assert local non-Indian interests over against those of Indians. (1965:93–94)

These anti-Indian groups also have an advantage in terms of group resources. Indians are the poorest segment in American society, and this poverty is reflected in their interest groups. The NCAI has never had a large budget. Similarly, another Indian group called the United Effort Trust, organized to fight the anti-Indian backlash in 1978, simply did not have the money to do the job:

> The effort under the auspices of UET barely managed to get off the ground. Using the contributions from tribes, it assembled a staff and began to build an information file. Those involved realized the magnitude of their undertaking and knew that it would take time for their effort to have an impact. But the effort lacked the money to buy the time it needed. Within a few months it was bankrupt. (Bee 1982:148–149)

The poverty of Indian interest groups forced them to seek support from the federal government, and as a result most of them "have been heavily dependent on Federal grants and contracts" (Taylor 1983:132). For example, the federal government was a major source of income for the National Congress of American Indians, the National Tribal Chairmen's Association (sometimes called "the puppet of the BIA"; see Officer 1984:90), the Council of Energy Resource Tribes, and the Native American Rights Fund (Taylor 1983:136–154). Dependency on the federal government for funding deprived these groups of their independence and made them vulnerable to budget cuts. (Indeed, the Reagan administration eliminated federal funding for all of these groups.)

In sum, the interest groups that are actively involved in the Indian iron triangle are of three types: pro-Indian Anglo groups, Indian groups, and anti-Indian groups. In the area of water development this latter classification can be extended to include the very powerful lobbies that oppose any interference from Indians with non-Indian water development. The divisions in the relevant interest groups help to explain why the Indian iron triangle has really served two different conflicting constituencies. The anti-Indian groups were fairly successful, at least until recently, at convincing the federal government to transfer Indian resources, particularly land and water, to non-Indians. At the same time, the Indians were served by allocations of government benefits. These benefits have stressed welfare programs rather than land and water development programs because the latter would have interfered with the transfer of Indian resources to non-Indians. It was only in the last fifteen or so years that a new, more aggressive policy of protecting Indian resources evolved. This upset the traditional operation of the Indian iron triangle and created a showdown between the Indian groups and their allies on one hand and the anti-Indian groups and the water development lobby on the other. Thus the contemporary era presents a new chapter in the operation of the Indian iron triangle.

THE BIA AS ADMINISTRATIVE AGENCY

At the beginning of this section I outlined two possible explanations as to why the BIA was not able to protect and develop Indian water resources effectively. One school of thought argues that the BIA was saddled with a nearly impossible task without the political support necessary for success but made an admirable attempt to achieve its mission and overcome the hostility of other policymakers. The foregoing discussion of Congress and interest groups lends credence to the claim that the BIA has operated in a hostile and unsupportive political and social environment, but did the BIA perform well under these adverse conditions? A second school of thought blames the agency for failing to avail itself of the limited opportunity to aid Indians, especially in the area of resource development. In this section I will evaluate the BIA as an administrative agency and attempt to assess its efforts to aid Indians, focusing on the BIA water development program. As outlined in the first chapter, the discussion will concentrate on agency mission, organization, scientific and political expertise, and organizational image.

An agency operates best in an iron triangle if it distributes divisible goods and services. The BIA is hindered from functioning in such a manner for a number of reasons. First, the BIA does not function exclusively as a service agency. In many ways the agency serves more of a management/regulatory function. For the first 100 years of its existence the BIA sought mostly to control Indians, and this managerial/regulatory function has tended to linger, often resulting in accusations of paternalism and domination. The final report of the 1977 American Indian Policy Review Commission recommended "modernization of the Bureau of Indian Affairs in order to change it from a management to a service Agency" (1977:23). The BIA also tended to operate as a welfare agency rather than a construction and development agency. This was necessary in order to make the trade-offs in Congress between the anti-Indian and pro-Indian factions; resource development programs militated against the transfer of Indian resources to non-Indians, but welfare programs provided an acceptable (to Congress, at least) compensation for the loss of these resources. Hence the agency was able to obtain funding for welfare programs much easier than for water development projects. The goods and services distributed to Indians have tended to emphasize items such as health care, education, and income support rather than water resource development. The demands for Indian water rights thus constitute a major reordering of BIA priorities that threatens to upset the fragile balance of powers within the Indian iron triangle.

The BIA also has a fairly obvious problem expanding its programs. Indians constitute .4 percent of the American populace and their remaining landholdings are only about 4 percent (including Alaska) of the total land mass of the United States. This makes it difficult to engage in logrolling in Congress. Murphy points out that partisan cooperation over distributive issues is highest when they concern "national allocation issues" that provide something for everyone (1974:170). He cites expenditures for the District of Columbia as an example of poor cooperation, and hence lower funding, because it represents a localized allocation to an isolated set of recipients. Obviously the same can be said for Indian reservations.

The second area of importance to an agency serving in an iron triangle is organizational stability. An organizational scheme that maximizes stability is the best possible condition. However, numerous reorganizations have prevented the bureau from achieving a high level of bureaucratic stability. A statement by Theodore Taylor, a career BIA employee, indicates how these constant reorganizations made it difficult for the agency to operate within the confines of an iron triangle: "Frequent reorganizations, one every time a new political head arrives to supervise the BIA, have had the effect of slowing things down, disrupting work processes, and breaking up the informal systems and relationships that often are the best way of achieving expeditious action" (1984:128–129).

The BIA's Irrigation Division also experienced serious problems with organizational stability. The following litany of reorganizations makes it evident that the irrigation program had problems finding a suitable niche in the bureaucratic structure:

1907:   Irrigation handled by the Land Division.
1907:   Field Work Division established. Responsibilities include irrigation.
1908:   Field Work Division reduced to a section in the Office of Chief Clerk.
1909:   Field Work Section abolished. Irrigation activities transferred to Uses Section of the Land Division.
1910:   Separate Irrigation Section established within the Land Division. Later in year combined with the Forestry Section to form the Field Section.
1912:   Field Section divided into Irrigation and Forestry Section and removed from Land Division.
1924:   Irrigation Division established.
1954:   Irrigation activities moved to the Branch of Land Operations in the Division of Resources.
1970:   Irrigation activities handled by the Division of Land and Water Resources.

The BIA also experienced some organizational shifts in the personnel who handle water rights. The agency was first authorized by Congress to hire an employee versed in irrigation law in 1915. By 1932 the agency had one "chief field counsel" and three district counsels in the Irrigation Division to handle water rights problems (Chief Engineer Annual Report 1932:6). Not until 1972—105 years after the BIA water development program began—did the agency establish a separate section to deal with water rights. And within two years this Office of Indian Water Rights was absorbed by the Office of Rights Protection. In short, the BIA's water development program has been less than stable in terms of bureaucratic organization.

The internal organization of the irrigation program has also been criticized. The Preston-Engle Report concluded that the "organization of the Indian Irrigation Service is entirely inadequate" (1928: 2222). Another author wrote of organizational problems "of almost stifling proportions" (Stuart 1985:142–143). Recently the entire BIA structure has been subjected to a Management Improvement Program "to end the long-standing management problems" (Bee 1982:193).

In terms of agency expertise the BIA's ability in regard to water development has always been challenged. In 1907 the four largest BIA irrigation projects were transferred to the Reclamation Service because of that agency's superior expertise (they were transferred back to the BIA in 1924). The 1928 Preston-Engle Report found that the BIA generally lacked the expertise necessary to build and operate irrigation facilities and concluded,

> Failure apparently on the part of the Indian Bureau to comprehend the importance, the magnitude, and the difficulties of the irrigation activities is the principal cause of the trouble, and is what might be expected as a result of the present system whereby this work is directed by a bureau primarily interested in education and welfare work. (1928:2229)

Four years later the BIA director of irrigation (i.e., chief engineer) admitted that his program was "impaired somewhat by the lack of the specialists originally intended" (Annual Report 1932:10). The BIA's inability to handle the legal problems generated by water rights disputes has already been cited.

The lack of expertise in irrigation and water rights contributed to the BIA's problems in generating information. The BIA seemed never to have sufficient data on its irrigation program. Table 16 is a reproduction of a table that appeared in the 1932 Annual Report of the BIA Director of Irrigation. The responses to the questions are quite revealing. Question 7 asks if the water used for irrigation is measured, and the answer is no for nine of the ten major reservations listed. On all ten of the reservation projects there is no determination of the water loss (question 9). These are incredible responses for an agency that based many of its water rights claims on beneficial use, bringing into question the agency's generally positive response to question 19: "Is [sic] water rights data up to date or complete?" It would even be difficult to make a claim based upon the Winters Doctrine with these data because on all ten reservations the BIA does not know the consumer demand for water (question 13). In all, the table contains 66 "yes" responses and 120 "no" responses. In other words, nearly two-thirds of the requisite data are missing.

The BIA's inability to generate reliable and complete data has clearly hurt the agency in the appropriations process. Preston and Engle criticized the BIA for its "incomplete and unreliable data in justifications for appropriations" (1928:2239) and concluded that it damaged the agency's credibility in Congress. In hearings held in response to the Preston-Engle Report, John Collier, speaking as an officer of the American Indian Defense Association, explained that his group had done its own investigation of BIA data used in the appropriations process:

> The Interior Department, the Indian Office, prior to 1929 requested appropriations from Congress without giving Congress adequate information on which Congress could decide either project or appropriation items in irrigation; that not only was the information not furnished Congress, but that expressly incorrect information and inconsistent information was furnished Congress through these years by the [BIA] Irrigation and Reclamation Service. (Preston and Engle 1928:2715)

More recently Bee (1982:190–192) and Taylor (1983:2) have made similar statements regarding the quality of BIA information.

Another important factor that affects an agency is image, which has both an internal and an external component. Thus far the problems of the BIA could be blamed for the most part on exogenous variables: the narrow mission, the hostile political environment, and the lack of expertise and data. To a great extent these problems are cumulative; the constricted mission limits the development of a strong political base, which makes it nearly impossible to generate sufficient funding to hire the expert professionals needed to generate data and develop professional expertise in specific programmatic areas. As such it supports the first school of thought discussed at the beginning of this section—that the BIA has been the hapless victim of an uncaring people, a "whipping boy" (Deloria and Lytle 1984:85). A review of the agency's external image, however, leads to the conclusion that the BIA itself is responsible for at least some of its problems. The reputation of the agency as reflected in reports, reviews, and investigations over the last 120 years indicates a continuous and intense lack of faith in the BIA. Rather than attempt to summarize these, a selection of illustrative quotes from a wide variety of sources is provided:

1869: I am compelled to say that no branch of the national government is so spotted with fraud, so tainted with corruption, so utterly unworthy of a free and enlightened government, as this Indian department. (Congressman and later Secretary of Interior James Garfield, quoted in Schmeckebier 1927:49)

1912: The Graham committee [investigating the BIA] recommended that the Indian Bureau be either drastically overhauled or abolished. (Putney 1979:239)

1922: By 1922 the forces of reform were attacking the bureau on almost every front. (Deloria and Lytle 1984:40)

1928: Under the poorest administration, there is little evidence of anything which could be termed an economic program. (Meriam and Associates 1928:25)

1928: The Indian Bureau, almost from the date of its organization, had been almost constantly under criticism. (Preston and Engle 1928:2253)

1959: The Bureau is at present ill-prepared to conduct a program of economic development. If it cannot organize a staff and adopt the requisite philosophy for carrying out such a task, the possibility of transferring this function to another agency should be considered. (Dorner 1959:228)

1969: The Bureau has done a terrible job. (Cahn 1969:14)

1977: The impression I have is that BIA is nowhere near the kind of agency it should be. (Statement by Congressman Yates, U.S. Congress, House 1977:935)

1982: There are several facets to BIA's incompetence. (Bee 1982:214)

1984: There is no evidence that the BIA's large administrative structure contributes to either effective or efficient program management. (Government report quoted in Barsh and Diaz-Knauf 1984:5)

TABLE 16

STATUS OF HYDROGRAPHIC WORK AND WATER SUPPLY DATA ON ACTIVE MAJOR PROJECTS, 1932

	Fort Hall	Uintah	Wapato	Black-feet	Crow	Flat-head	Wind River	Colorado River	San Carlos	Pine River
1. Is hydraulic data fully maintained?	No	No[a]	No	No	No	No	No	Yes	Yes	No
2. Has it been reviewed by hydrographic engr.?	Yes	Yes	Yes	No	Yes	Yes	No	No	Yes	Yes
3. Has plan of measurement been approved?	No	No	Yes	No	No	Yes	No	No	Yes	No
4. Are records in standard U.S.G.S. form?	Yes	Yes	Yes	No	—	No	—	Yes	Yes	—[a]
5. Are duplicate annual records filed in F.O.?	Yes	No	Yes	No	—	Yes	—	No	Yes	—[a]
6. Is entire available support measured?	Yes	No	Yes	No	No	No	No	Yes	Yes	Yes
7. Are all deliveries from source measured?	Yes	No	Yes	No	No	No	No	?	Yes	No
8. Is water used for irrigation purposes?	No	No[a]	No	No	No	No	No	?	Yes	No
9. Are principal losses determined?	No	No	No	No	No	No	No	?	No	No
10. Is actual irrigated acreage kept?	Yes	Yes	Yes	Yes	Yes	Yes	Yes	Yes	Yes	?

11. Is actual diversion duty determined?	Yes	No[a]	Yes	No	No	No	?	?	?
12. Is headgate duty determined?	No	No	Yes	No	No	No	No	No	No
13. Is consumers annual demand known?	No	No	No	No	No	No	No	No	No
14. Is percent of full service known?	No	No	No	No	No	No	No	No	No
15. Is over-year storage involved?	Yes	No	No	Yes	No	Yes	No	Yes	No
16. Is regulative storage involved?	No	No	No	Yes	No	Yes	No	Yes	No
17. Is behavior of reservoirs determined?	No	—	—	—	—	No	—	Yes	—
18. Has safe yield of project been determined?	Yes	No	No	No	No	No	Yes	Yes	No
19. Is water rights data up to date or complete?	Yes	No[b]	No	Yes	Yes	Yes	Yes	Yes	Yes
20. Are there any U.S.G.S. stations?	Yes	Yes	No	No	Yes	Yes	Yes	Yes	Yes

Source: Annual Report of the BIA Director of Irrigation for 1932.

Notes: Uintah: [a]yes as to Federal ditches; [b]lake investigations and proposed Dechesne to Provo diversion pending. Pine River: [a]State—yes.

It is evident that the professional image of the BIA as viewed by members of Congress, other policymakers, and academicians is not favorable. The agency's irrigation program has received less attention but has on occasion been the subject of scrutiny. The most comprehensive investigation of the Indian water development program was the 1928 Preston-Engle Report, which was exceedingly critical of the program. It recommended that the largest projects, and all legal work, be transferred to the Bureau of Reclamation, and that three projects—Blackfeet, Northern Cheyenne, and Fort Peck—be abandoned altogether. The latter project was referred to as "a monument to futility" (1928:2528). The report also criticized the agency for its lack of reliable data and its inability to handle the Indians' legal problems. The idea of transferring the program to the Bureau of Reclamation was not new. Indeed, the Bureau of Reclamation had built and managed four Indian projects from 1907 to 1924. Preston and Engle wanted them to take over the entire program. This suggestion was made again by the secretary of interior the following year (Deloria and Lytle 1984:58) and again in a Senate report issued in 1943 (Fey and McNickle 1970:149). The BIA irrigation program was again criticized in 1959 by Dorner, an economist who examined the BIA's economic development program, including Indian irrigation, and found that "there are no plans to speed up the development of irrigable land. There is no program to get Indians established on sufficient-sized units. There is no program to solve the problems of land, management, and inadequate credit for undertaking development. Nor are such programs being planned!" (1959:179). Similar accusations were made by the American Indian Policy Review Commission (1977:337) and Carlson (1981:140).

Not surprisingly, this negative image has had a deleterious impact on agency morale. The agency was involved in so many scandals during the first part of the century (the critical time for appropriating water for Indians) that by 1913 "the Indian Office was badly demoralized" (Kelly 1979a:243). Preston and Engle noted that the field employees had an "attitude of hopelessness and discontent" (1928:2240). This attitude was undoubtedly exacerbated by the existence of the Senate's "temporary" investigative Subcommittee on Indian Affairs, which lasted for sixteen years (1928–1944) and "became a sounding board and a collection agency for all manner of charges against the Bureau" (Freeman 1965:45).

Some of the agency's problems may be attributable to its leadership. In a number of cases a political appointee was forced on the agency who had little experience in the bureau. The most notorious case is probably the infamous Secretary of Interior Albert Fall, who "acted as his own Indian Commissioner" (Kelly 1979*a*:252). No agency can thrive under such conditions. The most innovative and dynamic commissioner of Indian Affairs was John Collier, who served from 1933 to 1944, but he lacked certain diplomatic and political skills and "left the Bureau in a shambles" (Officer 1984:77).

It could still be argued, however, that the agency's poor image is a result of inadequate funding and a hostile and uncooperative political environment. Thus a close look at the personnel of the agency is necessary if we are to judge the sincerity of their effort. Again, however, we find that funding levels have an impact; there are numerous references to the poor quality of BIA personnel, especially in the past, which are attributable to low pay. In 1902, Hamlin Garland wrote that "the pay is too small [in the BIA] to secure the services of a really capable man" (1902:481). The Meriam Report and the Preston-Engle Report also noted the low pay and difficult conditions of BIA work, but Preston and Engle observed that the agency had many dedicated and efficient employees in spite of the bad pay (1928:2240).

In recent years the most common charge against BIA personnel is that they are self-serving (Cahn 1969; Nelson and Sheley 1982). Indeed there is a substantial bureaucratic overhead for Indian programs. For the ten-year period from 1965 to 1975, $4.08 billion was allocated to the BIA, but a significant portion of that funding went to Anglo administrators (Barsh and Diaz-Knauf 1984). Self-preservation as a bureaucratic ethos is certainly not unique to the BIA, and there is almost no support among Indians for abolishing the agency. What can we conclude, then, about the quality of BIA personnel? My own experience and research have led me to believe that many recent and current employees of the agency are conscientious and devoted professionals. When the BIA began its more aggressive posture in the late 1960s it provided in essence a test by fire for its employees: those who were not serious about Indian rights no longer fit in, and those who were serious found a supportive environment—for a change. Unfortunately their hands have been tied to a great extent by funding limitations and the other factors that have been discussed in this chapter.

In sum, the BIA does not meet the requirements of an able participant in an iron triangle. In terms of mission, organization, expertise, and image the agency does not fit the archetypal administrative agency that operates well within such a political environment. And political support from Congress and interest groups has always been weak. The situation in Congress for many years was based on a distribution of benefits that is no longer tenable in an era of Indian resource development. In terms of interest groups the BIA has been opposed by strong groups (especially on the issue of water development) and supported by weak ones, and even its supporters have often been critical. In fact, Indians are often the agency's most vocal critics. This leads us back to the original question concerning the two schools of thought as to why the agency has done so poorly. One more set of factors needs to be brought to light, however: the general policy environment in which the BIA must operate.

THE GENERAL POLICY ENVIRONMENT

As explained in the first chapter, the policy environment consists of four factors: the potential for distributive policy, the potential for logrolling, the level of autonomy, and implementability. The first three were discussed within the context of the three "corners" of the Indian triangle. The problems of implementability, however, are important and deserve some discussion.

The first factor affecting implementability concerns the clarity of political goals. This requires a clear and consistent view of what is to be accomplished, and Indian policy, perhaps more than any other policy area, exemplifies the opposite of this. A 1924 review of Indian policy noted, "It is often said that the Government has no Indian policy or that its Indian policy is vague, inconsistent, a mere patchwork of expediencies" (U.S. Congress, House Document No. 149, 1924:18). President Nixon said that Indian policy oscillated between "harsh and unacceptable extremes" (*Public Papers,* Nixon 1970:565). The government's official policy toward Indians has gone from one of extermination, to allotment and assimilation, to self-government and tolerance, back to assimilation and the termination of government services, to one of self-determination and, currently, a period of unpredictable budget cuts. These wild swings in policy goals and the political ramifications that accompanied them have made it almost impossible to develop rational, long-term solutions to the "Indian problem."[5]

The second factor affecting implementability concerns program legitimacy. The conspicuous absence of congressional approval hindered the Winters Doctrine from its inception. The doctrine so obviously lacked legitimacy that the BIA was afraid to base its water development program on it. There was always too great a chance that rights claimed under the doctrine would simply be ignored, and indeed in the few cases in which it was relied upon enforcement became a critical problem. Federal reserved water rights for Indians is a classic example of how case law can lack authoritative legitimacy. This creates enormous problems during the implementation and enforcement stages of policy-making.

The final factor that affects implementability is the level of support and/or opposition. I have already discussed the specifics of interest group activity, but in the case of Indian policy there is a more general context that is of relevance. Perhaps more than anything else the BIA and its water development program have been hampered by racism. Remember that the critical period for water development came during the first decade or two of this century. It is important that we familiarize ourselves with the attitudes of whites toward Indians at that time. By the time of the *Winters* decision the government's policy of dealing with Indians with military force had not been entirely abandoned. *Winters* was handed down only six years after Geronimo surrendered, so the Indian wars were still fresh in memory. During the years that the *Winters* case was in the courts federal troops were used on the Uintah, Hopi, and Navajo reservations to ensure that the Indians conformed to official policy directives (Parman 1979:225–227).

During that same period of time expressions of racism were commonplace.[6] Theodore Roosevelt, president when the *Winters* decision was in the courts and the father of western reclamation, declared, "I don't go so far as to think that the only good Indians are the dead Indians, but I believe nine out of every ten are, and I shouldn't inquire too closely into the case of the tenth" (Hagerdorn 1921:335). A speaker at the 1907 National Irrigation Congress declared that the American West was "destined by the Almighty for a white man's country" (1907:119; also see Townley 1978:21). At the 1911 National Irrigation Congress C. J. Blanchard of the U.S. Reclamation Service offered the thought that "in the West there is to be a coalescing of all the Aryan races into a final race-type. In time that type will dominate the world" (1911:58). Such Hitlerian sentiments sound extreme today, but in 1911 they represented the prevailing ethos of Manifest Destiny. Indians were viewed as inferior human beings by many Anglos.[7]

In recent years such sentiment is expressed in a subtler manner, yet it still persists. The governor of Arizona declared in 1963 that "Indian claims [to water are] a nuisance and excess baggage" (quoted in Fradkin 1981:158). In 1977 Congressman Cunningham introduced a bill to abrogate all treaties with Indian tribes (H.R. 9054: "The American Indian Equal Opportunity Act"). It is arguable as to whether these sentiments are based on prejudice or simply differences in policy, but the point is that anti-Indian attitudes persist in the West, and they continue to have an impact on the BIA's water development program. And the more blatant statements still appear; an Idaho deputy prosecutor stated in 1979, "When the Indians talk about rights, they should remember it's like a master-servant relationship. . . . This is the white man's case: there are more of us than there are of them" (quoted in Josephy 1984:75). There is probably only a small percentage of people who view race relations in such stark terms. Still, the absence of overt racism does not translate into political support. A survey of four western states completed in 1976 revealed that most respondents felt that the Indian already had enough water; in terms of water development priorities both state legislators and the public at large ranked Indians near the bottom of a list of fifteen possible alternatives (Ingram, Laney, and McCain 1980:124–127). It is clear that if Indians are going to succeed in the political arena, they must do it primarily on their own.

Postscript: Fort Belknap

Before concluding this chapter it is worthwhile to return to the Fort Belknap Reservation to see if they made any progress since Hawk Feather and Eyes-in-the-Water spoke to government officials in 1910. By 1914 the Indians were irrigating 7,670 acres (Abbott 1914), although about 34,000 acres were irrigable. The Preston-Engle Report found Indians irrigating 9,699 acres, but 80 percent of this was for noncultivated wild hay and alfalfa (1928:2302). In regard to water rights they wrote, "It is believed by the advisors that in order to hold this water even under the *Winters* decision it will be necessary to make beneficial use of it to a much greater extent than is now being done" (1928:2307). The report also cited the Fort Belknap project as one of the worst examples of misleading and unreliable data. The American Indian Defense Association called the project an "irrigation fiasco" (Preston and Engle 1928:2735). By 1975 the project was still not finished (BIA Report to the Senate 1975). And a 1977 BIA report noted that "many areas of the [irrigation] project are in need of rehabilitation. Laterals, drains, and old concrete structures are badly deteriorated" (U.S. Congress, House 1977:130).

Conclusion

In 1910 the commissioner of Indian Affairs stated that "there are millions of acres of irrigable lands in Indian reservations" and declared an intention to irrigate them (Annual Report 1910:21). Seventy-five years later, however, only about 7 percent of that irrigable land was irrigated (Western States Water Council 1984:93). Clearly the BIA water development program failed to meet its objective. This failure can be attributed to the agency itself or to exogenous variables over which the agency has no control. In fact, it appears to be a combination of the two, which points out the inherent weakness of the Indian iron triangle. This triangle is unique in several respects.

First, it developed a unique form of benefit distribution that resulted in the transfer of much Indian land and water to non-Indians while also providing government welfare services to Indians. The former was necessary to reduce the political opposition of powerful non-Indian interests, and the latter functioned as compensation for the loss of these resources. This delicate balance worked for many years but became untenable when the BIA began to pursue more aggressively the development of Indian resources. The growing political power of Indian tribes, as evidenced by increased interest group activity, also helped to stem the loss of Indian resources. The principal result was stalemate; each side was strong enough to veto the major proposals of the other but not sufficiently strong to coax a decisive solution out of Congress. The old Indian iron triangle is now in the process of changing, a process that is more fully discussed in chapter 8.

Another unique facet of the Indian iron triangle concerns the level of conflict. The classic iron triangle controls conflict by distributing benefits to all interested parties. In the case of Indian policy this was accomplished as described earlier. The inevitable clash of interests of Indians and non-Indians made it impossible to "distribute away" all of their differences, however. Consequently the payoff for serving on an Indian subcommittee has been low, unlike truly distributive subcommittees. This became even more pronounced when the concerted push for Indian rights began in the 1960s. As a result, "Indian policy is a no-win situation" for congressmen (Bee 1982:81). This obviously interferes with the function of the iron triangle.

A third unique characteristic of the Indian iron triangle concerns its autonomy. As Freeman (1965) points out, it is one of the more autonomous and isolated triangles in Washington, but the agency's water development program is an exception to this. Indian water development brings the BIA into direct conflict with the powerful non-Indian water iron triangle. Anti-Indian interest groups and the non-Indian water development lobby have often joined forces to resist Indian resource development. This creates formidable opposition. And without the requisite autonomy the iron triangle has difficulty functioning in this policy area.

A final unique facet of the Indian iron triangle concerns implementability. Indian water development has been greatly affected by larger issues that involve the BIA as a whole and its position in the overall political and social environment. The current debate over Indian water development cannot be understood without a thorough comprehension of this larger context. The BIA and its water development program must coexist with the water development programs of the Bureau of Reclamation and the Corps of Engineers. It was inevitable that these programs would come into conflict. That conflict is the subject of the next chapter.

CHAPTER SIX

Conflict Among Programs
and Priorities

The basic element is survival. No matter what color you are, you get thirsty.

—Cecil Williams, Papago Tribal
Chairman, 1979 (Quoted in the *Arizona Daily Star*
21 February 1979:20)

Introduction

Conflict is the nemesis of iron triangles. It makes them vulnerable to outside interference and reduces their ability to distribute benefits. There are a number of ways an iron triangle can mute internal conflict (Ripley and Franklin 1986:104–105), but conflict from external sources—especially other iron triangles—presents more of a problem. Distributive policy works best when the allocation of benefits to one group is not perceived as a loss to others. Under conditions of scarcity this quickly breaks down, and the result is competition and conflict. In the issue area of water development a number of finite limits can potentially create conflict. First, there is the finite supply of water, a condition that is especially applicable to the West. Second, a finite amount of government funding can be made available for water resource development. Third, there is a finite amount of control over the decision-making process that allocates this water and money. Hence it was inevitable that conflict would arise over the development of water resources.

This conflict is multidimensional. It involves interagency conflicts, interdepartmental conflicts, and intergovernmental conflicts. And because iron triangles are composed of interest groups and their allies in Congress, these conflicts sometimes pit one group of beneficiaries against another, a struggle that is often reflected in Congress when the elected spokesmen for each side join the fray.

161

In this chapter I will examine some of these conflicts because of their critical impact on water policy and because of the important theoretical questions raised by such extensive conflict in an issue area characterized by the presence of iron triangles. According to the accepted view, iron triangles operate in an environment of low conflict. If this is true, then how has the water development iron triangle managed to thrive amid these various conflicts? By examining these clashes we can investigate how iron triangles respond to conflict and how they resolve such dilemmas, if they do indeed resolve them.

Indians, the BIA, and the Bureau of Reclamation

Conflict between these two agencies was inevitable and not long in coming. Not only did the Bureau of Reclamation seek waters that were potential sources for Indian projects, but the agency also coveted the enlargement of its mandate—and control—that would result if the irrigation functions of the BIA were transferred to the new agency. The Bureau of Reclamation offered a convincing rationale for its proposition to take over all irrigation work: the agency's superior expertise in irrigation engineering would improve the Indian irrigation program. It would also improve coordination and planning. Both of these claims were potentially valid, and by 1907 the secretary of interior was convinced that the Bureau of Reclamation should be responsible for both non-Indian and Indian irrigation projects. He ordered the agencies to prepare a plan for "the closest cooperation" between the two bureaus (Garfield to Newell 7 March 1907). Director Newell then drew up a plan that gave the BIA responsibility to "indicate the localities where irrigation is to be conducted and the conditions to be met as regards future allotments of lands, treaty obligations, and fiscal relations." He conditioned this power, however, with a further stipulation that "the character and general location of the structures should be recommended by the Director of the Reclamation Service, and all broad questions of policy settled in advance by the Secretary of Interior" (Newell memorandum 27 March 1907).

Indian Commissioner Leupp also supported the takeover of Indian irrigation projects by the Reclamation Service. In fact, in his annual report for 1908 he took credit for originating the idea, explaining that duplication of programs was "so grave a source of waste" that it was a mistake for the BIA to maintain "a little reclamation service . . . and several other minor organizations for work along lines commonly cared for, and presumptively better cared for, by special bureaus established by law for the benefit of the American people at large" (Annual Report 1908:2). The two agencies quickly worked out an agreement:

> Plans and estimates for proposed work are prepared by engineers of the Reclamation Service and transmitted to the Office of Indian Affairs for review. If the plans and estimates are concurred in by the Office of Indian Affairs and are afterwards approved and authorized by the Secretary of the Interior, the work is prosecuted by the Reclamation Service in accordance therewith, and the cost is eventually returned to the reclamation fund from the authorized Indian appropriations. (Reclamation Service Annual Report 1908–1909:19)

In practice this meant that the BIA lost control over its largest projects. Three of them (Blackfeet, Crow, and Flathead) were immediately transferred to the Reclamation Service, and a fourth (Fort Peck) was transferred the following year. In addition, parts of the Indian projects on the Yakima and Pima reservations were handled by the Reclamation Service (the Crow project soon reverted back to the BIA because of the lack of construction activity). The "closest cooperation" originally envisaged never developed, however. The *Winters* case had left a host of bad feelings, followed closely by the bitter controversies on the Yakima and Pima reservations described in chapter 3. The basic view of the Reclamation Service was that reserved water rights were dangerous and should not be recognized. When U.S. Attorney McCourt wrote to the attorney general in 1910, he noted that "the reclamation officers [of the Reclamation Service] are inclined to take the view that the Indians have no rights under (their) treaty" (McCourt to Attorney General 1 October 1910:3). Thus any time the BIA claimed water under the Winters Doctrine there was bound to be conflict between the two agencies.

Another point of contention that had its origins in that period concerns the taking of Indian lands for reclamation projects. The Act of June 25, 1910 gave the secretary of interior the power to reserve lands within Indian reservations for power and reservoir sites. This would ultimately lead to the transfer of a considerable amount of land from Indian to non-Indian ownership.

As the relationship between the two agencies degenerated, they began to squabble over a number of issues. In 1912 Director Newell wrote a six-page letter to Indian Commissioner Valentine complaining that the BIA's cost per acre estimates for the projects it still controlled were ridiculously low. Because of this, "unfavorable comparisons have been drawn with the work of the Reclamation Service" (Newell to Commissioner of Indian Affairs 9 May 1912:2). As an example Newell used the Fort Belknap Reservation (did he choose Fort Belknap because it had caused the Reclamation Service so much grief?), where the BIA claimed a cost per acre of $4.61 for its irrigation project. Newell said that his men investigated this "startling statement" and found that the true cost per acre was "probably over $50.00, and may have reached nearly $80.00" (1912:3). Not to be outdone, the BIA occasionally made critical references to the Reclamation Service. In 1913 an agency memo subtly noted that "other irrigation development contemplating the use of water from the same sources as that required for the Indians is proceeding" (memorandum entitled "Superintendent to Pass upon Water Rights" 20 June 1913). The following year the BIA chief engineer stated (or, more accurately, understated) that "there has been some misunderstanding as to the proper functions of the two bureaus" on the Yuma Reservation (Annual Report 1914:202). In fact the "misunderstanding" was quite severe and eventually required the intervention of outside parties.

It is tempting to dismiss these exchanges as petty bureaucratic rivalry, and that certainly played a role, but many of the complaints definitely were not trivial matters. Eventually these differences helped to poison the atmosphere between two agencies that were mandated to work closely together. In 1915 the BIA's mistrust of the Reclamation Service was made public in no uncertain terms. In his annual report to the secretary of interior the Indian commissioner explained,

> Careful consideration of the rights of the Flathead, Blackfeet, and Fort Peck Indians has convinced me that the conditions under which the cooperative irrigation work on these reservations has been done in the past is not for their best interest, and that its continuance would be a great injustice to the Indians. (Annual Report 1915:47)

The commissioner was disgruntled over the amount of land that was being transferred to whites and the charges that were being levied against the Indians for projects that were increasingly benefiting non-Indians. Similar accusations were made on the Yuma Reservation, where construction of an irrigation project had been taken over by the Reclamation Service in 1914, and problems immediately developed over project repayment and water rights.

During this entire period the Reclamation Service initiated only one new Indian project, and the fate of that project did not instill confidence in the agency's approach. The Riverton Project was begun in 1918, but within two years so much land had passed to whites that it was no longer tenable to call it an "Indian" project, so the project became a regular item on the Reclamation Service list of projects (Reclamation Service Annual Report 1919–1920:460). The BIA assumed responsibility for a small project on the remaining Indian lands. Today there is a stark contrast between the poorly funded Indian project and the well-maintained Riverton Unit (Ambler 1986:23–24).

Throughout the latter half of the teens the BIA tried to regain control over the three Montana projects being built by the Reclamation Service. The agency was unsuccessful until the early 1920s, at which time both bureaus were investigated by special commissions. (For the BIA it was The Committee of One Hundred; for the Reclamation Service it was the Committee of Special Advisors on Reclamation.) Neither of these investigations made recommendations regarding control over the disputed projects, but the committee that investigated the Reclamation Service recommended the agency be streamlined and reorganized along functional lines (U.S. Congress, Senate Document No. 92, 1924b). As a result of these recommendations the agency was reorganized and renamed the Bureau of Reclamation. Soon thereafter the secretary of interior ordered all three Indian projects being constructed by the agency returned to the BIA. The two agencies' explanations as to why the secretary did this are wildly contradictory. The Bureau of Reclamation told its constituency the following:

> For a number of years the Bureau of Reclamation has acted in the capacity of an agent for the Bureau of Indian Affairs in the construction and operation of certain of the Indian irrigation projects. . . . This was a natural consequence of the conditions then existing in that the Bureau of Reclamation was engaged in constructing and operating large irrigation projects under the provisions of the reclamation act and had the necessary force and equipment to handle this work for the Bureau of Indian Affairs. In recent years the amount of construction to be done on these Indian projects has been reduced, with the result that there is no necessity for the Bureau of Reclamation handling them. (*Reclamation Record* February 1924:31)

The BIA offered a completely different story. Soon after the secretary of interior issued the transfer order he was deluged with criticism from western legislators who wanted the Bureau of Reclamation to administer the Indian projects. Apparently having second thoughts, he sent a letter to the Indian commissioner instructing him to justify why the BIA, and not the Bureau of Reclamation, should have control over Indian water projects. The commissioner's response lists several reasons why the BIA should control the projects:

> A Bureau not conceived for the purpose of looking after the welfare of the Indians would not and could not render this invaluable service to the Indians that they are receiving under the present management of handling their irrigation work. . . . The cost of constructing, operating and maintaining the Indian irrigation projects will show by comparison that this Bureau has been successful in accomplishing the same at considerably less cost than the Bureau of Reclamation. . . . The cost of these projects, coupled with general conditions, resulted in your issuing orders under the date of January 12 and 15, 1924, turning over the administration of these three projects to this bureau. (Commissioner of Indian Affairs, "Memorandum for the Secretary," 6 December 1924)

These were powerful charges and indicate that the BIA was on the defensive and that the relationship between the two agencies had deteriorated to a point of open hostility. To make sure the secretary got the message, the Indian Affairs commissioner noted in his annual report for that year that two of the transferred projects— Fort Peck and Blackfeet—were in bad shape and "their prospects are not very encouraging" (Annual Report 1924:19). In short, the Indian commissioner had accused the Bureau of Reclamation of incompetence, inefficiency, and poor treatment of the Indians.

As in their past disputes over water rights, the two agencies turned to Congress when they were unable to work out their problems through legal and administrative machinery. Both agencies found sponsors in Congress for bills that would mandate their control over the three Indian projects. In most instances a direct confrontation between the BIA and the more powerful Bureau of Reclamation would result in disaster for the former. But in this case it turned out differently, primarily because the secretary of interior, who had already committed himself to BIA control of the projects, supported the bill to retain control with the BIA. In a letter to Congressman Leavitt the acting secretary of interior explained again why the BIA should administer Indian irrigation projects: "As to the Indians on these and other projects, their conditions and problems are such as to require very careful consideration. They cannot as a whole succeed in their irrigation pursuits if placed on a parity with the white farmer" (Acting Secretary to

Leavitt about December 1924:2). This, of course, was the same reasoning developed by the courts in the *Winters* family of cases.

In 1925 a bill was passed forbidding the BIA to relinquish control of any of its irrigation projects to the Bureau of Reclamation. The BIA's takeover of the projects provoked fear among reclamation people that the agency would try to claim reserved rights on the newly reacquired projects. Miffed at their defeat in Congress in 1925, they returned the following year with a bill that would have nullified all federal reserved rights. This bill was similar to those proposed in 1914 but went even further by outlawing all proceedings on behalf of the federal government which might affect appropriative state water rights (the bill was also an early forerunner to the water rights settlement acts that were introduced in the 1950s). This time the secretary of interior himself lobbied against the bill, arguing that the "manifest injustice against the Indians and their rights that would be wrought by the passage of the resolution is . . . apparent" (Work to McNary 12 February 1926:6).

This bill failed to pass, but the controversy over control of the three Montana Indian projects continued. Westerners who supported the Bureau of Reclamation's takeover of the projects were frustrated with Congress' unwillingness to pass anti-reserved rights legislation and essentially were attempting a "back door" method of limiting reserved water rights. It was well known that the Bureau of Reclamation did not support the concept of reserved rights, and it was assumed there would be less likelihood of reserved claims if Reclamation, rather than the BIA, was in control of the Montana projects. This approach received a boost in 1928 when both the secretary of interior and the Preston-Engle Report recommended that all major Indian irrigation projects be turned over to the Bureau of Reclamation. (The secretary changed his mind again two years later, deciding that the BIA was not so bad after all.) The persistence of the pro-Indian faction in Congress and opposition from the Indian commissioner prevented the transfer of the projects back to the Reclamation Service. (According to an anonymous source, the Reagan administration is considering plans to transfer Indian water projects *back* to the Bureau of Reclamation.)

The internecine struggles over water rights, and the controversy over administrative control of the Montana Indian projects, created a legacy of bitterness and distrust between the two agencies. This hostility is quite evident in correspondence from the period. An excellent example comes from the Fort Belknap Project, where ongoing conflicts over water rights reached a boiling point in the late 1920s. An exchange of letters between Director Mead of the

Bureau of Reclamation and Indian Commissioner Burke reflected the mutual hostility that characterized the relationship between the two agencies. On 5 July 1927, Commissioner Burke wrote to Mead complaining about the theft of the Indians' water by the people on the Milk River Reclamation Project. He based his claims for Indian water on *Winters* (Burke to Mead 5 July 1927). Mead immediately responded with a letter of his own, explaining that the citations to *Winters* in Burke's letter were to the case syllabus, not the decision, and therefore inapplicable (Mead to Burke 9 July 1927). Burke shot back a reply stating that the section of the syllabus quoted in his previous letter was nearly identical in language to the actual court decision (Burke to Mead 11 August 1927).

The fact that the top men in two federal agencies were quibbling over semantics is illustrative of the polarization of the two camps. At issue was whether the Bureau of Reclamation was taking more than its share of the water. The BIA viewed it as a legal problem, and the Bureau of Reclamation insisted it was simply a question of measurement. Two reclamation field employees wrote to headquarters complaining that the "Office of the Commissioner of Indian Affairs seems to cling to the idea that the case of United States against Winters is important in connection with the administration of affairs connected with the Belknap Reservation and the Milk River Irrigation Project, but this legal phase is not important" (Johnson and Roddis to Chief Engineer 17 August 1927). The impasse was finally resolved by requiring that both the Bureau of Reclamation and the BIA check all water flows, thereby making sure the other side did not cheat.

Another example comes from the Wapato Project on the Yakima Reservation, where the BIA field cost accountant wrote a memo explaining that "a difference of opinion exists between this Bureau and the Reclamation Service" (Walker to Wathen 16 March 1933:1). The memo minces no words, calling the rival agency's method for calculating water charges "inequitable and unfair" and resulting in "an annual quarrel that has increased in gravity with each year since about 1918" (Walker to Wathen 16 March 1933:5). He accused the local project manager for the Bureau of Reclamation of being a "dictator" and concluded that "there is much prejudice in the local Reclamation office against the claims of the Wapato" Indian project (1933:8).

Throughout this period Indian lands continued to be sold to incoming settlers or acquired by the government for Bureau of Reclamation projects. This effort was facilitated by a massive publicity campaign to attract settlers to reclamation projects. An example of this publicity is presented as figure 2, which announces the sale of lands on the Riverton Project—the one that started out as an Indian project on the Wind River Reservation but was transformed into a reclamation project because so much land was diverted to whites. The poster notes that public lands were free and Indian lands were $1.50 an acre.

In many instances the agencies' quarrels wound up in court. Most of the momentous Indian water rights cases involved a conflict with the Bureau of Reclamation. The 1935 case of *U.S. v. Gila Valley Irrigation District* (the Globe Decree) involved both the Gila River and San Carlos tribes as well as the reclamation project associated with the Coolidge Dam. The long and bitter struggle over water for Pyramid Lake pitted the Paiute Indians against the Newlands and Washoe Reclamation projects (*U.S. v. Orr Water Ditch Co.* 1944; *U.S. v. Alpine Land and Reservoir Co.* 1950; *U.S. v. Alpine Land and Reservoir Co.* 1970; *U.S. v. Alpine Land and Reservoir Co.* 1971; *Pyramid Lake Paiute Tribe of Indians v. Morton* 1973; *U.S. v. Nevada and California* 1973; *Nevada v. U.S.* 1983; also see Knack and Stewart 1984). The 1956 case of *U.S. v. Ahtanum*, which forcefully restated the premise of the Winters Doctrine, also involved a reclamation project next to the Yakima Indian Reservation. And the landmark case of *Arizona v. California* (1963) concerned the water rights of five Indian reservations and had an impact on numerous reclamation projects, including the Central Arizona Project.

In the 1950s conflict between the two agencies diminished somewhat because of the termination policy that attempted to end the federal commitment to Indians. With the development of a more aggressive Indian water rights policy in the 1960s, however, the conflict reached new heights. Indians and their allies blamed the Bureau of Reclamation for many of their water problems. A selection of quotations will demonstrate this point:

> The Bureau of Reclamation has taken and continues to take from the American Indians throughout the western United States rights to the use of water for the projects which it builds. (Veeder 1969:492)

> But to the Indian people, Reclamation might just as well be the cavalry all over again. . . . Whenever Indian interests in land and water resources collide with other interests . . . the Indians lose. . . . Almost always a single Federal agency seems to lurk behind these losses—the Bureau of Reclamation. (U.S. Congress, Senate 1971:1598, remarks by Senator Edward Kennedy)

> The Bureau of Reclamation . . . sits in a hopeless conflict of interest with the Indian rights supposedly protected by the Department [of

DEPARTMENT OF THE INTERIOR
HUBERT WORK, *Secretary*

INFORMATION FOR HOMESEEKERS

THE BUREAU OF RECLAMATION of the United States Department of the Interior offers irrigable farms to qualified settlers on the following four reclamation projects:

> Tule Lake Division of Klamath Project, Oregon—California.
> Willwood Division of Shoshone Project, Wyoming.
> Pavillion Division of Riverton Project, Wyoming.
> Interstate, Fort Laramie, and Northport Divisions of North Platte Project, Nebraska—Wyoming.

These farms are subject to entry under the Homestead and Reclamation laws. The public lands under these projects are free except for the payment of filing fees. Indian lands on the Riverton project are sold for $1.50 an acre. In addition these farms will be subject to the payment of irrigation charges fixed by the Secretary of the Interior.

Applicants must have had at least two years of farming experience and must possess, free of encumbrances, not less than $2,000 capital, in cash or in farm equipment, livestock, or other assets as useful in developing a farm as cash, and give satisfactory evidence of character and industry, health and vigor in order to be approved. They must be at least 21 years of age and possess their homestead rights.

In addition to the public lands the Bureau offers over 150 irrigated farms on the Belle Fourche Project, South Dakota, and the Lower Yellowstone Project, Montana— North Dakota, which have been placed under its control for sale. Prices of these farms have been fixed by independent appraisal and vary from $12 to $110 an acre depending on improvements. The terms of purchase are as follows: Payment of 10 per cent at the time of purchase and the remainder to be paid in amortized payments extending over 20 years with 6 per cent interest.

Applications for these farms will be received by the Bureau of Reclamation, Department of the Interior. Further information regarding how to obtain these farms or regarding the kind of crops grown, markets, and other matters which affect the success of settlers will be furnished by the Commissioner, Bureau of Reclamation, Washington, D. C.

ELWOOD MEAD,
Commissioner of Reclamation.

Approved, June 30, 1927.

JOHN H. EDWARDS,
Assistant Secretary of the Interior.

POSTMASTERS PLEASE POST
HARRY S. NEW,
Postmaster General.

Fig. 2.

Interior]. The entire history of the events of this conflict of interest is one of narrow, strict interpretation of Indian water rights. (Dellwo 1971:227)

The Bureau [of Reclamation], as might be expected, defines the Winters doctrine as narrowly as possible. (Berkman and Viscusi 1973:157)

When the two bureaus are in conflict—and they often are—the prior and paramount water rights of the Indian give way to the Anglo's need for more land, water, and power. (U.S. Congress, Senate 1974:80, remarks by Paul Eckstein, general counsel of the Navajo Tribe)

The federal government for many years has appropriated and spent billions of taxpayer dollars to fund massive irrigation projects, taking Indian water and delivering it to the non-Indian farmers. This is something that has not only happened in the past; it is happening today and will continue to happen in the future. (Indian Water Policy Symposium 1982, remarks by John Narcho, Papago Water Commission)

These sentiments could be dismissed as the biased opinions of partisans involved in a political controversy, but a similar point of view has also been voiced by more neutral sources. The 1973 National Water Commission concluded that the Bureau of Reclamation's water development policy "was pursued with little or no regard for Indian water rights and the Winters Doctrine. . . . With few exceptions the projects were planned and built by the Federal Government without any attempt to define, let alone protect, prior rights that Indian tribes might have had in the water used for the projects" (National Water Commission Final Report 1973:474–475). Frederick and Hanson, in their book *Water for Western Agriculture*, state that "virtually all western surface water has been put to use without regard for Indian rights" (1982:98). Charles Wilkinson recently noted that "the reclamation program proceeded on the backs of Indian people" (1985:323). Others have voiced similar opinions (Chambers 1971:7; Young 1972; U.S. Congress, Senate 1974:112, remarks by Brent Blackwelder; Indian Water Policy Symposium 1982:84–86, remarks by Richard Collins; Knack and Stewart 1984: 320; Upite 1984:194; Pisani 1986).

The Bureau of Reclamation has always denied these allegations, arguing that its work aided Indians on a number of reservations. In James's 1917 panegyric to the Reclamation Service he reviews the four projects then being built by the service for the BIA. He argues that there were a "few far-seeing men in the Indian Service" who recognized the need for extensive irrigation projects, realized their agency did not have the expertise to build them, and called upon the Reclamation Service for help (1917:366–367). He quotes a report from Reclamation Service field personnel that states, "the efficiency of the Indian has improved greatly during the period of years in which he has worked for the Reclamation Service" (1917:371). Critics of the Reclamation Service argue that its principal impact has been to transfer land and water from Indians to non-Indians, but James argued that the needs of the Indians always came first, and only then were Anglo settlers permitted to absorb Indian resources: "In due time when the Indians are fully settled on their irrigated lands, the unused lands are opened up to settlement, and water is supplied to the homesteaders outside of the reservation" (1917:373).

In the 1970s the Bureau of Reclamation was still arguing the same point. In an increasingly hostile atmosphere the bureau repeatedly pointed to the work it had done for Indians. During hearings to investigate the Indians' difficulties in securing water rights, officials from the Bureau of Reclamation recited the list of benefits the agency had provided for Indian tribes:

> Reclamation has been responsible for a significant portion of the Federal works that make a dependable water supply available for Indian land irrigation, water-oriented outdoor recreation, development of Indian coal reserves, domestic water, and other Indian uses. For example, more than 500,000 acres of irrigated Indian lands in the 17 western States are being supplied water as a result of the construction of storage, conveyence, and other facilities by Reclamation. (U.S. Congress, Senate 1971:1600)

In a 1976 report the agency stated: "In developing and studying water and land resources relative to Bureau of Reclamation projects . . . the prior rights of Indians have been consistently recognized. Benefits from these projects to land and water owned and utilized by Indians have been substantial" (Bureau of Reclamation 4 November 1976:cover letter). The report lists and describes thirty operating projects that provide benefits to Indian reservations. These benefits include the direct delivery of water to a substantial amount of irrigated Indian land and water for recreation, fish, and wildlife. The report also lists a number of studies and investigations the agency was completing at the request of the BIA or various tribes. The report quotes the chairman of the Irrigation Committee of the Middle Rio Grande Pueblos: "Our priorities have been honored and respected by the . . . Reclamation Bureau" (1976:SW-1). And, it should be noted, the agency's Fresno Dam, completed in

1939, provides some water for the Fort Belknap Reservation (the BIA paid for one-seventh of the project). In the conclusion to its 1976 report the Bureau of Reclamation provided a definitive statement in regard to its policy on Indian water development:

> Having followed the precepts that irrigation potentials should be formulated without regard to land ownership, that the Indian water rights are senior to others, that our policy recognized the Indian need to develop its irrigable land, and that our planning studies show a preempted water use for that purpose, we have endeavored to avoid any conflicts over Indian water requirements. (1976:UM-8)

Indeed, Taylor argues that the Bureau of Reclamation's work on Indian reservations "may help support Indian claims to water" (1984:72).

Currently the two most visible reclamation projects that benefit Indians are the Central Arizona Project (CAP) and the Navajo Indian Irrigation Project (NIIP). The former will deliver water to several central Arizona tribes and the Papago Tribe in the southern part of the state. The latter is the largest Indian water development authorized to date and is being funded through the BIA but built by the Bureau of Reclamation, an arrangement very similar to the one that existed from 1907 to 1924. The Indian benefits that will accrue from these projects, however, are not necessarily the result of an active effort by the Bureau of Reclamation to help Indians. In the case of CAP, Indian participation is a result of the Supreme Court's decision in *Arizona v. California* (1963) and subsequent litigation and negotiation. In essence the Arizona Indian tribes used the threat of lengthy litigation based on open-ended Winters Doctrine rights to gain concessions. It should also be noted that the Orme Dam component of the CAP would have inundated the Fort McDowell Reservation (see Welsh 1985:147–151). In the case of the NIIP the Indians had to give up their Winters Doctrine claims, and there has been considerable conflict between the Navajo Tribe and the Bureau of Reclamation. The lack of progress on the project has already been noted. The most recent clash involves an effort by the Bureau of Reclamation to reduce the water flow to the NIIP, claiming that more efficient irrigation methods make it permissible to lower the Navajo's water allocation from 508,000 acre-feet to 370,000 acre-feet.

In addition, the 1976 Bureau of Reclamation report that cited thirty projects that helped Indians also discussed sixteen projects under a section entitled "areas of possible controversy." A more recent report by the agency found twenty-three "major cases" in which there was conflict between Indians and the Bureau of Reclamation. Nearly 75 percent of those cases "were judged to be moderately to very serious" (Bureau of Reclamation 27 April 1984). These reports also contained references to twelve reservations that lost Indian land to Bureau of Reclamation projects.

In addition, the Bureau of Reclamation takes a view of the Winters Doctrine that, compared to the Indian interpretation, would be considered restrictive. In an interview in 1970 Assistant Commissioner of Reclamation (later commissioner) Gilbert Stamm was asked if his agency respected the Winters Doctrine. He replied: "You're talking about a doctrine as compared to a law. . . . We are obligated to carry out the laws as passed by Congress" (quoted in Berkman and Viscusi 1973:158). During congressional hearings in 1971 Commissioner Stamm made it clear that the Bureau of Reclamation considered the Winters Doctrine applicable only to agricultural uses, and therefore only irrigable acreage should be used as a measure of Indian water rights (U.S. Congress, Senate 1971:1606–1608). This was the measure adopted by the Supreme Court for the five Colorado River tribes in *Arizona v. California* (1963). Indians argue that reserved rights can be applied to any purpose for which the reservation was created, including nonagricultural applications. They cite language in the *Winters* case that the water was reserved "for irrigation, as well as for other purposes" (*Winters v. U.S.* 1908:745). They also point out that the special master in the *Arizona* case specifically noted that reserved rights were not necessarily restricted to irrigable acreage (*Arizona v. California* Special Master's Report 1963:266).

In sum, the Bureau of Reclamation provided substantial benefits to Indian reservations but also imposed substantial costs in terms of the loss of land and water. The bureau's willingness to provide benefits to Indians is, in many cases, an example of the so-called Indian blanket. This has helped reduce conflict, which is so inimical to the operation of an iron triangle. But this strategy is limited by the scarcity of water in the region; every acre-foot of water diverted to Indians is an acre-foot that cannot be diverted to the Bureau of Reclamation's traditional constituency. Hence it is in the best interests of the bureau to minimize Indian claims and divert Indian water to other uses, and we have seen some evidence of this. Open conflict between the Bureau of Reclamation and the BIA was not so problematic for the former when the Indian Bureau pursued an unenthusiastic policy of developing Indian resources. But when this policy began to change in the 1960s and the Indians themselves developed some political clout, the conflict intensified. The Bureau of Reclamation was not alone, however, in the conflict over Indian water development; the Corps of Engineers also played a role.

Indians, the BIA, and the Army Corps of Engineers

The 1950s was a bad decade for American Indians. The drive for termination was in full swing and the "relocation" program was moving thousands of Indians away from their tribal homelands. Within this context two large water development projects brought the Corps of Engineers and the Indians and their allies into direct conflict: the Kinzua Dam in New York and the Pick-Sloan Plan for the Upper Missouri River.

The Kinzua Dam involved the Seneca Indians' Allegany Reservation, which was ultimately flooded by the project. The Senecas resisted the loss of their reservation, which was guaranteed to them in the Pickering Treaty of 1794. The Indians, with the help of several pro-Indian Anglo groups, initially tried political means to stop the dam. When it was obvious that Congress was not going to respond, they took their case to court but lost there also (*Seneca Nation of Indians v. Brucker* 1958). Finally, accepting defeat, the tribe lobbied Congress for an acceptable level of compensation, but even this question became bogged down in politics. Ultimately a compromise amount of compensation was agreed to with the additional stipulation that the tribe would be "terminated." This raised the specter that "the construction of dams was to be a new means for alienating Indian land" (Levine and Lurie 1965:68).

The conflict over Kinzua Dam was important for two reasons. First, it demonstrated how unimportant the Indian iron triangle was compared to the Corps of Engineers. According to Arthur Morgan, a vociferous critic of the corps, there was significant disagreement among engineers as to whether Kinzua Dam was the best option. He argued that an alternative reservoir site would have been better from an engineering point of view and would have avoided the destruction of the Indian reservation (1971:338–367). Even under these qualified conditions the Indian lobby was unable to deter the strong congressional/corps drive for the dam. According to Senator Paul Douglas, the corps "was determined to ride roughshod" over the Seneca Indians (foreword to Morgan 1971:x).

The second reason this project is important concerns the precedent it set. It soured relations between the corps and the Indian tribes and became something of a standard as to how bad the federal water development program could be for Indians. For example, when Congress was debating Orme Dam, a Bureau of Reclamation project that would have flooded nearly the entire Fort McDowell Reservation in Arizona, the Kinzua Dam was used as a reference point. The following exchange between Interior Secretary Stewart Udall and Congressman Haley, a supporter of Indian rights, makes this clear:

Secretary Udall: If we are going to wipe out an Indian reservation without doing what this committee has done so generously with Indian tribes previously, I think you present me then with some very serious choices. . . .

Mr. Haley: Mr. Secretary, you say that is not a wipeout of an Indian reservation in this project?

Secretary Udall: It is not as bad as the Seneca Indian problem, where the reservation was eliminated entirely. . . .

Mr. Haley: Well, the Secretary does not propose to allow the Bureau of Reclamation to take the devious methods that were being taken by the Corps of Engineers in the Seneca situation, do you?

Secretary Udall: Congressman, I do not propose that by any means. We can use a newer method and new approach. . . . I propose . . . to make the small but fine little reservoir we are creating here into an Indian recreational development. (U.S. Congress, House 1968:833)

The fact that the "fine little reservoir" and Orme Dam were defeated in the 1980s demonstrates how much Indian political power grew since the days of the Kinzua Dam controversy.

The 1950s also witnessed the development of numerous water projects on the Upper Missouri River that involved Indians. These projects were part of the 1944 Pick-Sloan Plan, which authorized a total of 107 dams (officially known as the Missouri River Basin Development Program). Nearly all of these dams were small tributary structures to be built by the Bureau of Reclamation, but five dams were to be massive mainstream dams constructed by the Army Corps of Engineers.

The Pick-Sloan Plan was the result of what one critic called "a shameless, loveless shotgun wedding" (Terral 1947:230). Both the Bureau of Reclamation and the corps wanted to develop the upper Missouri River, and there was bitter rivalry between the two agencies as to which would get the job. This rivalry suddenly melted into cooperation, however, when a proposal for a Missouri Valley Authority, modeled after the Tennessee Valley Authority, developed political momentum. If this proposal were adopted it would mean that neither the bureau nor the corps would get the job. So in a hastily arranged marriage of convenience, the two agencies combined their respective plans (Worster called it "a paste-up job": 1985:268) into one massive omnibus that included nearly all the projects originally conceived by the two agencies (Hart 1957:127–135; Shanks 1981:111–113). The Pick-Sloan legislation made no mention of Winters Doctrine rights (Lawson 1982:45).

The dams to be built by the Bureau of Reclamation did not pose a serious threat to the Indian land. In fact, the original plan was to irrigate 216,000 acres of Indian land (this was never accomplished), but the five corps dams inundated thousands of acres of Indian lands. The Fort Berthold Reservation was hardest hit by the land losses. One-fourth of the reservation was flooded, including the most valuable and productive land on the reservation—the bottom lands along the river where most of the people lived. The termination mentality played a role in the decision to displace the Indians from their traditional lands. This can be seen in Richard Baumhoff's book, *The Dammed Missouri Valley*, which celebrates the work of the corps and the Bureau of Reclamation. He opines that "it is possible that the projects for dams and reservoirs may be of real service in *forcing* a long step toward assimilation of the Indians into *normal* society" (1951:115, emphasis added). The displacement of the Indians and their land was justified with the same kind of reasoning that Secretary Udall displayed in the discussion of Orme Dam quoted earlier. The governor of North Dakota explained why the Indians should welcome the dam: "It is true that the bottomland to be inundated is the timber land, the better hay land, and the pleasant area in which the Indians like to dwell. The reservoir, however, will offer advantages in sport and recreation and economic value that do not now exist" (quoted in Baumhoff 1951:118).

As in the case of the Senecas, the Indians of Fort Berthold initially resisted but quickly realized that it was hopeless and began to negotiate for the best deal possible. Ultimately the Indians sold

155,000 acres of their best land on the condition that the Corps of
Engineers relocate them, pay for their land, and provide for certain
structural improvements on the reservation. George Gillette, chairman of the Fort Berthold Indian Tribal Business Council, noted at
the bill-signing ceremony that "the members of the tribal council
sign this contract with heavy hearts. . . . Right now the future
does not look good for us" (quoted in Morgan 1971:48). Cahn
described the land sale as a "final, bitter defeat" for the Fort Berthold Indians (1969:69–70). The Indians "intensely feel that they were
not justly compensated" and to this day they are still battling the
government over the alleged discrepancy (Final Report of the Garrison Unit Joint Tribal Advisory Committee 1986:2).

Fort Berthold was not the only reservation to be flooded by the
Corps of Engineers on the Missouri River. Five different Sioux
reservations also lost land. Again, the impact was quite severe:
over one-third of the members of five Sioux reservations were
relocated. The dams destroyed nearly 90 percent of the tribes'
timberland, 75 percent of the wild game, and the best agricultural
lands (Lawson 1982:45–67). According to author Vine Deloria, a
member of one of the affected Sioux tribes, the corps was "ap-
pallingly insensitive to the Indians' rights and needs" (Deloria
1982).

Although total acreage figures vary, the Missouri River Basin
Development Program cost the Indian tribes approximately 350,000
acres of their best tribal lands, as well as the intangible costs of
cultural and emotional impact (Shanks 1974:576; Lawson 1982:46–
56). According to Michael Lawson's well-documented case study
of the program's impact on Indians, these costs far outweighed the
benefits derived by the Indians (1982:179–194). Shanks writes that
the program "replaced the subsistence economy of the Missouri
River Indians . . . with a welfare economy. . . . As a result of the
project, the Indians bore a disproportionate share of the social
costs of water development, while having no share in the benefits"
(1981:116). And, water-related problems persist; a recent congressional report notes that the water systems on the affected reservations "do not meet minimal public health standards" and laments
the fact that "funding for Indian water projects . . . is given very
low priority in comparison to non-Indian irrigation projects" (U.S.
Congress, House 1986:29).

The five corps dams also left a legacy of bitterness. Recently a
tribal chairman voiced an opinion of the corps that is undoubtedly
the result of this legacy: "Every time the Corps of Engineers thinks

of something, they create another problem for us Indians. These are the kinds of things going on back home in relation to water" (Indian Water Policy Symposium 1982:73, remarks by Reuben Snake, Chairman, Winnebago Tribe). Mr. Snake's opinion may have also been influenced by the corps' acquisition—against the Winnebago Tribe's wishes—of tribal land for a water project (see *U.S. v. 697.30 Acres of Land* 1970).

There have been other conflicts as well. A situation developed on the Papago Reservation in the early 1960s that bore some similarity to the relocation controversy on the Fort Berthold Reservation. A corps dam required the removal of a Papago village. The tribe claimed that the corps failed to live up to its promises regarding reimbursement for the relocation (Morgan 1971:57–61). In another case the Umatilla Tribe successfully convinced a federal district court that the Corps of Engineers had illegally impaired their fishing rights guaranteed by treaty (*Confederated Tribes of the Umatilla Indian Reservation v. Alexander* 1977). And the Colville Tribe claims that the corps-built Chief Joseph Dam seriously damaged their traditional fishing areas (Bureau of Reclamation 4 November 1976). The corps' Catherine Creek Lake Project in Oregon also provoked conflict with Indians (U.S. Congress, Senate 1974:112). And, the Cherokee Nation is fighting the corps in court over compensation regarding the McClellen-Kerr Project (*Cherokee Nation v. U.S.* in progress).

However, as in the case of the Bureau of Reclamation, there is another interpretation. Charles Flachbarth, assistant chief counsel for the corps, recently stated: "Our role has been one of being very supportive of Indians. I know they won't believe that" (interview 13 June 1984). Taylor writes, "The Corps of Engineers often has projects benefiting Indians" (1983:96). He cites a small boat harbor, a proposal to build an Amerind Center in Ohio, and three harbor revetment projects where Indians were "incidentally benefited" (1983:96).

In sum, the Corps of Engineers, like the Bureau of Reclamation, has provided benefits to Indian tribes but has also imposed costs, and in the case of the Senecas and the upper Missouri River tribes, substantial costs. In the latter case it appears that the corps was sufficiently strong politically that only a diminutive "Indian blanket" was needed to get the project through Congress. On the whole the corps has experienced less conflict with Indian tribes than the Bureau of Reclamation because many of its projects actually consume small amounts of water; navigation improvements

and most flood control projects retain water more than they consume water. Hence there is somewhat less potential for conflict
with potential Indian consumptive uses.

Indians, the Departments of Interior and Justice, and Conflict of Interest

In chapter 3 I discussed the untenable position of the
Department of Justice in regard to Indian water rights. Burdened
with the responsibility of representing all federal interests in court,
even when they are in conflict, the Justice Department had problems litigating Indian water rights since the first brief was filed in
the *Winters* case. This inherent conflict of interest has been a point
of contention between Indians and the department on many occasions. The usual charge against the Justice Department is that it
has failed in some cases to carry out the federal government's
fiduciary duty as trustee for Indian interests and property. The
Justice Department, however, shares responsibility for this duty
with the Interior Department and the BIA; thus if there have been
failures to represent the Indians adequately in court, it could be
attributable to any or all of these government agencies. Justice
argues that the Interior Department is its client, and it is in the
latter department that policy decisions are made, which are then
merely implemented by the Justice Department. But the politics/
administration dichotomy died a long time ago, so culpability for
past failures must be borne by all parties charged with the fiduciary
responsibility, if indeed there have been failures on the part of the
federal guardian.

Accusations of such failures are numerous and often include
reference to the Department of Interior as well as the Department
of Justice:

> No self-respecting law firm would ever allow itself to represent two
> opposing clients in one dispute; yet the federal government has fre-
> quently found itself in precisely that position. There is considerable
> evidence that the Indians are the losers when such situations arise.
> (*Public Papers*, Richard Nixon 1970:573)

> The Justice Department would not allow certain lawyers . . . to come
> out there and do the work or help the Indians get ready for a suit. (U.S.
> Commission on Civil Rights, Southwest Indian Report May 1973:137,
> remarks by Dominga Montoya, Sandia Pueblo Reservation)

We could cite you example after example of where we are either told not to help the tribe or pull off after a certain amount of work has been done. (U.S. Commission on Civil Rights, Southwest Indian Report May 1973:140, remarks by Lafollette Butler, assistant to the Phoenix area BIA director)

Our suits are usually not knocked down in the Supreme Court. They are usually knocked back by the Department of Justice and the Department of Interior. (U.S. Congress, Senate 1974:67, remarks by Ernest Stevens, Vice President of the National Congress of American Indians)

A formidable body of case law protects the Indians' water rights, and proper enforcement and application of the law should preserve these rights. However, as evidenced by the following cases, the Interior and Justice Departments have often in the past been lax in enforcement of these rights and have not infrequently adopted adverse positions, contributing to the erosion of the Indian water rights. (American Indian Policy Review Commission Final Report 1977:331)

A substantial literature exists that attempts to prove these accusations by examining cases in which the federal government allegedly failed in its capacity as trustee (see, for example, Chambers 1971; Young 1972; Pisani 1986). Many examples are cited, but three in particular stand out: Pyramid Lake, *Arizona v. California*, and the negotiations with the Navajos for the Navajo Generating Station and the Navajo Indian Irrigation Project.

Pyramid Lake, on the Pyramid Lake Indian Reservation in Nevada, has been a *cause celebre* among Indians and their allies for fifty years (see Veeder 1969:497–512; Josephy 1984:153–173; Knack and Stewart 1984). The level of water in the lake has been declining since the Newlands Reclamation Project began diverting the Truckee River, the principal source of water for the lake. In 1944 the Departments of Interior and Justice reached an agreement that awarded the Pyramid Lake Paiutes a meager amount of water and claimed no *Winters* rights for the tribe (*U.S. v. Orr Water Ditch Co.* 1944). Subsequent government activity made the situation worse. Another reclamation project that eventually threatened the lake, the Washoe Project, was authorized in 1956. Throughout this period the water level in the lake declined and the Indians were continually asking the government for relief. Knack and Stewart's detailed history of the Pyramid Lake Paiutes discusses repeated instances in which the Justice Department was less than enthusiastic about protecting Indian water rights (1984:287, 291, 315, 319).

Finally, in 1970 the tribe hired its own lawyers and sued the government, charging a breach of fiduciary responsibility. A federal district court agreed and reminded the government that the "conduct of the U.S. when representing Indians should be judged by the most exacting fiduciary standards" (*Pyramid Lake Paiute Tribe of Indians v. Morton* 1973:252). The significance of this victory for the Indians has been muted by a recent Supreme Court decision that denied the claims of the tribe and declared the 1944 decree to be *res judicata*, meaning it is the established law of the land and cannot be altered by subsequent litigation (*Nevada v. U.S.* 1983). This case also established a much more lenient concept of the fiduciary responsibility: "The Government cannot follow the fastidious standards of a private fiduciary" (1983:4979). In the same case the high court blamed the BIA for the Indians' poor showing in the 1944 agreement. The Court quoted an assistant U.S. attorney who argued at the time of the agreement that Indian water rights were based on *Winters* and should be "established to the fullest extent" (1983:4981). According to the Court the BIA chose not to pursue an aggressive course, "for reasons which hindsight may render questionable" (1983:4981).

The second celebrated case involving the Justice Department and potential conflict of interest grew out of the government's case in *Arizona v. California* (1963). This conflict was a result of a clash of personalities, parties, and politics as well as questions of law. The *Arizona* case was something of an epic: it took ten years to resolve; filled forty-three volumes of hearings, testimony, and decisions; and involved conflicts between states, between the federal government and western states, and between Indians and non-Indians.

The original petition to intervene filed by the United States in 1953 declared that "the United States of America asserts that the rights of the use of water claimed on behalf of the Indians and Indian tribes as set forth in this petition are *prior and superior* to the rights to the use of water claimed by the parties to this cause in the Colorado River" (*Arizona v. California* Petition of Intervention, 2 November 1953:23, emphasis added). The author of this passage was William Veeder, a Justice Department attorney and "an intransigent, zealous protector of Indian water rights" (Fradkin 1981:160). Officials from western states reacted angrily to such a bold assertion of Indian rights. They immediately arranged a meeting with the U.S. attorney-general and "in no uncertain terms objected to the assertion . . . that the federal government intended to claim 'prior and superior' water rights for 30 Indian tribes"

(Johnson 1977:94). Responding to this political pressure, the Justice Department recalled the petition, which had already been filed with the clerk of the Supreme Court, and removed the "prior and superior" language. According to one author's opinion, this was done so "the government could minimize present and future Indian water rights" (Young 1972:320).

The Navajo tribe believed the alteration of the petition was clear evidence that the Justice Department was not properly representing the Indians. They hired their own lawyer, who argued before the special master of the case that the government had violated its fiduciary duty. This argument was not accepted by the Court, but the issue remained alive for many years. A rehearing of the case in 1983 confirmed the original holding on this point, stating that "there is no demonstration that the United States, as a fiduciary, was involved in an actual conflict of interest" (*Arizona v. California* 1983:4331). The Court noted that just because the government "was slow to press Indian claims" it could not be held that the Justice Department violated its duty to Indians (1983:4331).

A third case that has received considerable attention as a result of charges of conflict of interest concerns the Navajos. In two different sets of negotiations Department of Interior officials convinced the Navajos to give up all claims to Winters Doctrine water rights in return for development projects. The first case concerned the Navajo Generating Station. The tribe agreed to limit its claim strictly to Colorado River water in exchange for the construction of a power plant on the reservation that would create jobs and provide a market for Navajo coal. During the negotiations over the agreement there was very little discussion of *Winters* rights, and the tribe had to rely on data supplied by the Bureau of Reclamation and other private participants who had a vested interest in minimizing Indian water claims. Furthermore, it is questionable whether the BIA had sufficient expertise to advise the tribe adequately. There are also claims that the BIA, because of political considerations, pressured the tribe into entering an agreement that may not have been in their best interest. Price and Weatherford argue that the Department of Interior "played conflicting roles" in the negotiations (1976:116), and the agreement was presented to the tribe as a *fait accompli* without their full participation and understanding of the consequences.

A somewhat similar scenario took place in regard to the Navajo Indian Irrigation Project (NIIP). Again the Navajos agreed to limit their claim to water in return for the government-built project. Several years after the agreement was signed the Navajos began to have doubts. The tribe's potential claim to five million acre-feet of San Juan River water was sacrificed for the assurance that the government would build the project, which would require 508,000 acre-feet of water. The Interior Department maintains that the Navajos anxiously and willingly entered into the agreement, but in ensuing years the tribe claimed it was put under intense pressure, and BIA and other officials in the Department of Interior failed to protect the Indians' interests fully (Price and Weatherford 1976:119–131; Lawson 1976:19–29; Fradkin 1981:165–178; Sombrero 1982:1–10). Given the extremely slow pace of funding for the Navajo project and the early completion of the San Juan-Chama Project, the Navajos have begun to question the legitimacy of the original agreement. The Bureau of Reclamation's recent attempts to reduce the Navajo's appropriation of water has made the tribe even more suspicious.

The three cases just reviewed all involved accusations that the Departments of Interior and Justice, because of a conflict of interest, did not fulfill their responsibility to protect and defend Indian rights and property fully.[1] The Department of Justice has been cognizant of these charges and has made attempts to improve the situation. In the 1960s, when the "modern" era of Indian water rights began to emerge, the department increased the number of lawyers in the Indian rights division. In the early 1970s a separate section—the Indian Resources Section—was set up in the department's Land and Natural Resources Division to isolate Indian rights litigation from other departmental activities and therefore to decrease the potential for conflict of interest. From that time until the Reagan administration began cutting domestic spending the department spent an increasing amount of time and manpower on Indian water rights cases. It could also be argued that criticizing the Justice Department is simply "killing the messenger." The department's mission, which was established by Congress, inevitably leads it into litigation where a governmental interest is present on both sides. Furthermore, in conflicts between Indians and the Bureau of Reclamation the different levels of legitimacy for court-created rights and statutorily created rights become readily apparent. The Winters Doctrine is case law and has never been blessed by explicit congressional approval. In contrast, the appropriative rights under which the Bureau of Reclamation operates have been repeatedly recognized by state legislatures and the U.S. Congress. This difference in program legitimacy is bound to affect all participants, including the Justice Department.

Federal-State Conflict

A great deal has been written about the conflict over water rights between the national government and various state governments, mostly in the West. Considerable animosity has been generated over this subject, but much of what is viewed as federal-state conflict could be categorized more accurately as intrafederal conflict. The preceding sections in this chapter, and indeed much of the rest of this book, are concerned with conflict between federal water development programs. Rather than viewing these controversies as straightforward problems of federalism, I think a more accurate interpretation is as follows.

The federal government espoused two conflicting water doctrines: the Winters Doctrine and the Prior Appropriation Doctrine. Because of political and statutory considerations some elements in the federal government rely upon and promulgate the latter and some the former. This inherently leads to conflict. It is not an equal contest, however. Those at the federal level who favor state control over water rights are much more powerful than those who rely on the Winters Doctrine. As a result the federal government has spent literally billions of dollars and has stored, diverted, and delivered millions of acre-feet of water under the aegis of state water law. In contrast relatively little water has been diverted under the aegis of the Winters Doctrine. Hence "the conflict, uncertainty, bad feelings, jealousy and bitterness" (Trelease 1971:11) that many westerners feel toward the federal government is actually directed at the policies of only a small portion of that government. Historically state-level policymakers have had more allies than enemies among federal water policymakers.

If the federal government was truly intent on imposing a federal water code on states, it would have made all federally funded water development contingent upon acceptance of federal control, but it has not. Bien and Newell tried that approach but found the political resistance too great and abandoned it. Rather, the policy of the federal government has been to defer to state law, with the important exception of the doctrine of reserved rights. Hence it is really more accurate to discuss "federal policies" than "federal policy" because the government endorsed two mutually contradictory water doctrines, albeit unequally.

The potential for conflict under such a bifurcated policy was enormous, and because conflict is inimical to iron triangles it was in the interest of most parties at the federal level to minimize the clash between the two doctrines. This explains why the BIA faced so much opposition to an aggressive campaign for *Winters* rights; as long as Indian water claims could be minimized, federal and state policymakers could proceed in relative harmony to develop the West's water resources. Western states have always jealously guarded their control over water rights, and interference with that right disrupts the iron triangle. Thus an important goal of federal water policymakers involved in the iron triangle was to encourage federal-state harmony. In previous chapters I discussed how these federal policymakers repeatedly deferred to state water law, including section 8 of the 1902 Reclamation Act. This helped to maintain federal-state harmony. In the 1950s, in an effort to ensure closer relations, Congress passed the McCarran Amendment, which waived the federal government's rights to sovereign immunity in water rights cases. In practical terms this meant that federal water rights could be adjudicated in state courts. Because the federal courts were the primary source of support for the federal Reserved Rights Doctrine, this law gave the states—through their own courts—an opportunity to minimize federal claims. The law did not have a significant impact at the time because federal claims to reserved water were insubstantial in the early 1950s. Later, however, the law would assume enormous importance.

While Congress was attempting to ensure federal-state harmony, the Supreme Court was heading in a different policy direction. The landmark cases of *Federal Power Commission v. Oregon* (1955) and *Arizona v. California* (1963) dramatically increased the power of the federal government to control the allocation of western waters. These cases, and the rising support for Indian rights, helped to usher in the "modern" era of Indian water rights referred to in the previous chapter. But this potential increase in federal control was of little use to the two principal water development agencies—the corps and the Bureau of Reclamation. Dependent upon local political support, they were reluctant to antagonize local interests by recognizing federal reserved water rights. Warne writes that the Bureau of Reclamation "has not become embroiled in the federal-state water rights controversy that has embittered the western states during the past two decades. It has never asserted a superior right, has not imposed its projects on communities, and is therefore not suspected of ambitions to arrogate states' rights" (1973:176). A similar policy has been followed by the Army Corps of Engineers, which places the water allocation process "in the hands of the state water rights administration" (Clyde 1982:529).

This long-standing deference to state law creates a problem for

Indians; traditionally they have been subject only to federal law. Federal Indian policy has long recognized the need to insulate Indian tribes from local or state law. In 1885 the Supreme Court explained why: "[Indians] owe no allegiance to the states and receive from them no protection. Because of local ill feelings, the people of the states where they are found are often their deadliest enemies" (*U.S. v. Kagama* 1886:383–384). To protect Indians from this local animosity the federal government created an exclusive Indian-federal relationship that placed Indians beyond the reach of state law and state judicial systems. In response to political pressure, however, Congress has permitted a number of exceptions to this previously exclusive relationship, an example being the McCarran Amendment discussed earlier.

In regard to water, this exclusive federal-Indian relationship was challenged in the early 1970s when state courts, relying upon the McCarran Amendment, began adjudicating water rights cases that involved federal reserved lands (see McCallister 1976:303–310; Wallace 1985). In the early 1950s, when the McCarran Amendment was passed, the courts narrowly defined its scope and limited its utility to the states (Palma 1978:312–313). But in 1971, two Supreme Court cases reinterpreted the amendment and held that it permitted in some instances concurrent state court adjudication of federal reserved water rights (*U.S. v. District Court in and for Eagle County* 1971; *U.S. v. District Court in and for Water Division No. 5* 1971).

Although the 1971 cases involved only non-Indian federal lands, the tribes feared that the decision would ultimately lead to state court adjudication of Indian water rights. Indeed, in 1976 the high court ruled that all reserved water rights, including Indian rights, could be adjudicated in state courts if the state had established a comprehensive, basinwide plan for allocating water (*Colorado River Water Conservation District v. U.S.* 1976, also known as the Akin Case). This decision was an important exception to the long-standing doctrine of Indian immunity from state law. Proponents of state control over water rights were pleased with the decision, but the tribes and their allies in the federal government vigorously denounced it. In congressional hearings held shortly after the decision was handed down, spokesmen for the Bureau of Indian Affairs pointed out that numerous state court decisions had been invalidated in recent years by the Supreme Court because state courts "ignored the federal principles and protections of federal Indian law" (U.S. Congress, Senate 1976:14).

The *Colorado River* decision precipitated a "rush to the courthouse" (Dellwo 1980:113) as states attempted to try as many Indian water rights cases in state courts as possible. At the same time Indian tribes sought relief in federal courts. The tribes hoped to narrow the impact of the decision by arguing it did not apply to states that disclaimed control over Indian lands in their constitutions or the enabling act that admitted the state into the union (this would include nearly every western state where Indian water rights are an issue). In 1983, however, the Supreme Court ruled against the tribes and permitted concurrent state court adjudication in all western states (*Arizona et al. v. San Carlos Apache Tribe of Arizona et al.* 1983; *Montana et al. v. Northern Cheyenne Tribe of the Northern Cheyenne Indian Reservation et al.* 1983).

At the present time there are numerous Indian water rights cases in both federal and state courts. It is too early to determine whether the state court proceedings will minimize Winters Doctrine rights, as the Indian tribes predict, or merely result in "wise judicial administration," as the proponents of state control have argued (*Colorado River Water Conservation District v. U.S.* 1976:810–811). Of course, state court adjudication does not eliminate the possibility of appeal to the U.S. Supreme Court. If state court adjudication fails to protect Winters Doctrine rights, the tribes can be expected to appeal.

The Indian tribes and the BIA are not the only federal interests that can claim water under the Reserved Rights Doctrine. The *Arizona v. California* case (1963) applied the Reserved Rights Doctrine to all federal reservations, not merely those for Indians. This would include national parks, forests, and wildlife refuges, and military bases (see Ranquist 1975). However, claims of reserved water rights by the agencies responsible for these areas have been modest, for three reasons. First, there are numerous statutory limitations on agencies that require them to honor state water law. In a recent case the Supreme Court cited thirty-six such laws that are similar in content to section 8 of the Reclamation Act and apply to federal resource management agencies (*Sporhase v. Nebraska* 1982:3461). Second, recent court cases have limited somewhat the ability of non-Indian federal agencies to make claims under the Winters Doctrine (*U.S. v. New Mexico* 1978; *Sierra Club v. Watt* 1981; *U.S. v. City and County of Denver* 1983. But see *Sierra Club v. Block* 1985 for an application of the Reserved Water Rights Doctrine to wilderness areas). Third, most federal resource management agencies are subject to the same political pressures that have influenced the Bureau of Reclamation and the Corps of Engineers; they are reluctant in some situations to antagonize local interests.

In sum, the predominant theme of federal water resource development has been to defer to state water allocation law. The Winters Doctrine represents a critically important exception to this. To pursue both water rights doctrines is to incite intense conflict, however, which in turn disrupts the smooth functioning of both the non-Indian water iron triangle and the traditional Indian iron triangle. To minimize such conflict the government has generally acceded to the requirements of state law. Still, state-level water policymakers have fiercely resisted efforts by the BIA, the Justice Department, and occasionally other federal agencies to claim reserved rights. This clash is usually characterized as a dichotomous state-federal conflict, but in reality it involves three parties: the states, the dominant element in the federal government that honors state water law and is tied politically to state-level interests, and the minority of federal policymakers who actively support reserved rights. Hence much of what is characterized as federal-state conflict is actually the clash of two contradictory and mutually exclusive federal water policies.

Those elements in the federal government espousing reserved water rights are hindered by the lack of program legitimacy of reserved rights, and also lack the solid political foundation of a strong iron triangle. As a result they must operate within a policy context that militates against their claims: "Given the conflicting indications over the last hundred years . . . the better policy is to follow state law in acquiring federal water rights to the greatest practicable extent" (Krulitz 1979:577). Prior to the advent of the "modern" era of Indian water rights (i.e., before the 1960s) the proponents of reserved water rights were so weak politically, and hence so unsuccessful, that a deputy attorney general could argue with some accuracy that

> for all the outcry arising from the Federal-State water rights controversy, not one State, not one county, not one municipality, not one irrigation district, not one corporation, not one individual has come forward to plead and prove that the United States, exercising alleged proprietary rights in the unappropriated waters of the public domain, has destroyed any private property right or rendered ineffective any State or local government regulation. (U.S. Congress, Senate 1964:39)

In actuality there are some exceptions to this. Settlers across the river from the Fort Belknap Reservation would testify to that. But overall, in terms of water actually diverted and consumed, the Reserved Rights Doctrine remains a relatively minor exception to the federal policy of deferring to state water law. As Richard Collins recently stated, "There have been extravagant claims of the 'threat' posed by Indian water claims, but actual conflict has been almost entirely a war of words, paper, and lawyers. Indian calls [for water] are not shutting anyone's headgates" (1985:482).

Conclusion

Accepted theory postulates that iron triangles operate in an environment of low conflict, yet the water development iron triangle, the "classic" iron triangle, has been subjected to an atmosphere of multifaceted conflict. In this chapter I reviewed the elements of this conflict that directly affect Indian water development, but there are other sources of conflict as well. The Bureau of Reclamation and the Corps of Engineers have engaged in "noisy combat" (Warne 1973:174) since the former agency was established. There has been conflict between the Bureau of Reclamation and agencies in the Department of Agriculture, and water development agencies have clashed with other federal agencies with preservationist missions such as the National Park Service and the U.S. Fish and Wildlife Service.

The non-Indian water development iron triangle has managed to thrive amid this conflict by engaging in a kind of damage control that ameliorated the political repercussions of the conflict. There appear to be four responses to conflict that have been used by policymakers involved with federal water development.

The most typical response has been to extend the range of benefits to potential adversaries. Politically this is the easiest and fits quite nicely into the distributive mode of policy-making. This method works only when there are sufficient resources to meet all demands, however. In the realm of water policy there are finite amounts of water, funding, and authority over allocation (i.e., power). In such a situation another response must be activated, and that is some form of mutually beneficial agreement that in some cases amounts to a truce. Three examples can be drawn from the material covered in this chapter. The first two concern the threat of an outside party: first, the Pick-Sloan Plan, in which the threat of a Missouri Valley Authority quickly convinced the Bureau of Reclamation and the Corps of Engineers to forget their differences and work together for mutual benefit. A second example comes from the *Arizona v. California* case, in which these two states were bitter rivals for many years (at one point the governor of

Arizona called out the Arizona National Guard to prevent construction of a dam on the Colorado). Even this level of hostility could be momentarily overcome by an outside threat—in this case Indian claims that threatened the water supply of both states. At one point an attorney with the Salt River Valley Water User's Association counseled, "It might well be that Arizona and California will be required, to some extent, to forget their differences in order to jointly defend against Indian claims" (quoted in Mann 1963:15). In short, an outside threat creates an inducement to settle conflict through a mutually beneficial agreement or truce.

Another case of a mutually beneficial agreement concerns the conflict between state governments and Washington. This dates from the original proposal for a federally sponsored reclamation program. Political realities were such that a federal program could not succeed without local support. To remain politically viable, the water development iron triangle essentially called a truce, agreed to abide by state law, and for the most part has lived up to that. The resulting combination of federal money and state water law has proven beneficial to both local and federal participants.

A third response to conflict works only when there is great inequality in political strength among the contestants. In such a situation the stronger of the two parties can afford to ignore, to a certain extent, the conflict. For it is not conflict per se that impedes the iron triangle; rather, it is the political fallout from the conflict. If one of the contesting parties is quite weak and the other quite strong, the political costs of the conflict may be of such small consequence that the stronger party can afford to ignore it. That is perhaps the best description of the response of the non-Indian iron triangle to Indian water rights, at least until the advent of the modern era defined in the previous chapter. The former could afford to ignore the latter. When there was some political cost involved, the non-Indian triangle would try the "Indian blanket" approach to ameliorate these costs. But the dimensions of the Indian blanket were usually quite small, which made good political logic given that the threat posed by Indian interests was also fairly modest. Hence the size of the allocation matched the size of the potential political costs of conflict.

A fourth response to conflict is to do nothing to ameliorate it, an option that is not appealing to an iron triangle. For other participants, however, this may be an option. For example, the Justice Department, not part of an iron triangle, has lived with serious conflict of interest problems since its inception. Attempts to mitigate this in the early 1970s were unsuccessful, primarily because the Justice Department may actually benefit from some forms of conflict; the agency has more power and funding when it is responsible for *all* federal litigation. This is not to say that the agency operates in a political vacuum; there is evidence that it favored the claims of non-Indians for many years. And later, when Indian political power began to increase, the Justice Department responded with more aggressive action on behalf of Indians. This latter action increased conflict, but for an agency not a part of a triangle, that is not necessarily life-threatening.

In sum, water development agencies have used the selective allocation of benefits and mutual agreement as conflict-mitigating strategies in situations in which such conflict created serious potential political costs. When the political costs of conflict were low, iron triangles could afford a token allocation, or no allocation, to a weaker party. And policy-making entities not part of an iron triangle can sometimes afford to ignore a high level of conflict because it does not necessarily pose a threat to their political basis of support. In short, the theoretical assumption that iron triangles function most effectively in an atmosphere of low conflict appears to be well founded. Hence they developed several strategies for ameliorating such conflict when it is potentially costly. These strategies did not eliminate conflict entirely, however, so it appears that iron triangles can continue to function under less than ideal circumstances. Policy-making entities that are not part of an iron triangle may not have the same powerful incentive to reduce conflict. In fact, conflict may even be useful in some cases.

As far as Indian and non-Indian water development are concerned, a recurrent theme in this chapter is the unequal status of these two conflicting programs. To a great extent the success of a program depends on the competitive environment in which it must operate, and the Indian water development program faced a formidable opponent: the federal water development iron triangle. To reiterate a critical point made in the first chapter, it is impossible to understand Indian water without a thorough knowledge of the larger political context—in which the federal water development iron triangle looms large. The following chapter discusses that iron triangle and how it has adjusted to the political realities of the contemporary period of water policy, which began with the announcement of Jimmy Carter's "hit list" in 1977.

CHAPTER SEVEN

Contemporary Federal Water Development: The Battle Over Water Projects

> If you think I'm going to walk up to the Hill with another hit list and go through the agony and heartburn I went through last year, I can only say, "I'm not stupid."
> —Secretary of Interior Cecil Andrus, 1978
> (quoted in *Weekly Report*
> 4 March 1978:565)

Introduction

When President Carter announced his famous "hit list" in 1977, the water development iron triangle was already experiencing difficulties in adjusting to a changing political environment. After the announcement of Carter's new water policy, the argument that the era of the federal water pork barrel was coming to a close suddenly became much more popular. And when Ronald Reagan began making unprecedented cuts in domestic spending, his action generated even more support for the proposition that water project pork barrel was a thing of the past. Robert Gottlieb concluded that "the era of the pork barrel seems to be ending" (*Wall Street Journal* 2 March 1983:22). Lawrence Mosher argues that we are at the "end of federal largesse" as far as water development is concerned (1986:14). Robert Dawson, the new head of the corps, recently claimed that "The old epithet of pork barrel, which was justifiably, at times, hung around our neck, just won't be available to a critic anymore" (*National Journal* 22

November 1986:2824. Also see Howe 1980:16; Schooler and Ingram 1981; Caulfield 1984; Edgmon and De Young 1984; Smith 1984:1–3; *National Journal* 17 August 1985:1876–1887; *Wall Street Journal* 3 May 1985:44).

Several students of water policy trace this diminution of support for federal water projects to Congress, the traditional champion of federal funding for water development. Congressman Morris Udall stated in 1977 that although "the old water lobby is still powerful . . . a new breed of suburban congressman is saying we're at the end of the federal dam-building period" (*New York Times* 19 December 1977:4). Henry Caulfield wrote that "majority votes in the Congress for water projects East and West, which were increasingly hard to put together before the Carter Administration, have been much more so since 1977" (1982:10). The recent passage of the 1986 Water Resources Development Act, which represents a sharp break with past omnibus bills, reflects many of the reformist sentiments of Congress.

This chapter will examine these developments by taking a close look at the water development iron triangle during the Carter and Reagan years. There are three reasons why this period deserves careful inspection. First, it is important to focus on the political health of the water policy iron triangle because it has important ramifications for Indian water development. The question is, can Indians compete effectively against the traditional political dominance of the water policy iron triangle? To answer that question, we must assess the political strength of both Indian and non-Indian interests.

Second, this period offers a somewhat unique analytical opportunity. The reforms promulgated by the Carter and Reagan administrations permit us to examine a powerful iron triangle under extreme duress. How do iron triangles respond to such a challenge? How flexible are they in their attempts to deal with the crisis? How far can they bend before breaking? And if crisis demands change, is such change permanent or merely an ad hoc response to a temporary political situation?

Third, the condition of the water development iron triangle after ten years of attack may indicate what to expect in this field over the next few decades. If the federal water development iron triangle is crumbling, what will take its place? What impact will it have on the relevant federal agencies, their constituents, and members of Congress? And what are the implications for other iron triangles currently in existence?

Attempted Reforms in the Water Policy Decision-Making Process

Both Presidents Carter and Reagan have attempted to change the decision-making process that determines which projects are authorized and how they are funded (specific authorization and appropriation bills are the topic of the following section). These proposed changes were designed to increase presidential control over water project expenditures and reduce the ability of Congress to use water projects as a form of pork barrel. In this section I will review the reforms proposed by Presidents Carter and Reagan, which can be divided into three categories: changes in project criteria, bureaucratic reorganization, and budgeting reform (the latter category includes two items: user fees and cost-sharing).

CHANGES IN PROJECT CRITERIA

The foundation of Carter's water policy was his call for more stringent criteria for project authorization and funding. He wanted to emphasize a more "realistic assessment of both economic and environmental costs and benefits" (*Presidential Documents:* 18 April 1977:558). Specifically, this meant a shift in three basic aspects of water project authorizations and appropriations. First, Carter wanted to adopt a nonstructural approach to water development, a proposal that struck at the very heart of traditional federal water policy. Second, he wanted to emphasize environmental protection and conservation. This goal could be partially accomplished simply by adopting a nonstructural approach. The third change in project criteria concerned the interest rate used to compute project costs and benefits.[1] By law project costs must be equal to or less than the benefits. An important variable in the cost-benefit ratio is the interest rate. Federal water development agencies followed the long-established practice of computing these rates according to the rate extant when the project was authorized, which often occurs many years prior to when funds are actually appropriated. To ensure that this practice continued, Congress made it mandatory in 1974 (P.L. 93–251, Sec. 80(b)). Carter proposed that these rates be computed when funds are actually appropriated, not when the project was authorized. In his view this would provide a more realistic, up-to-date total of actual project costs (*National Journal* 9 April 1977:546). Simply by changing the interest rate from the date of authorization to the date of appropriation, many projects lose their positive cost-benefit ratio. When Carter took office the project interest rate was limited by law to incremental increases, which kept the rate far below market value. But Carter's call for significantly higher rates "ran into powerful opposition on Capitol Hill" (Andrews and Sansone 1983:114) and failed to become law (a realistic interest rate was finally adopted in the 1986 Water Act).

In June 1978, Carter reiterated his intention to establish new project criteria based on nonstructural alternatives, environmental considerations, and conservation (U.S. Congress, Senate 1979, 3–7). To ensure compliance his administration developed a new "standardized water project planning manual" that detailed the new criteria and mandated that all federal agencies adhere to them (*Federal Register* July 1979:72, 892).

Carter's attempt to revamp a century of water policy tradition was "an audacious and ultimately disastrous move" (Wiley and Gottlieb 1982:57). Despite a concerted effort, he was unable to overcome the water development iron triangle (see Miller 1985). Many politicians from western states were particularly incensed because of the region's long-term reliance on federally funded structural solutions to water problems. For example, Governor Lamm of Colorado called the new policy "a tragedy" that would result in "the complete strangulation of the West" (Lamm and McCarthy 1982:192). What was needed, in their eyes, was a pro-development president, and they thought they had their man with the election of Ronald Reagan.

President Reagan's view of project criteria contrasted sharply with Jimmy Carter's. Reagan supported a structural approach to water problems, and he, along with Interior Secretary James Watt, were willing to minimize environmental considerations. Upon assuming office Reagan replaced Carter's mandatory project planning standards with optional guidelines. And the new administration made it clear that it was "pro-water development in the West" (*New York Times* 12 September 1981:1). It looked as though the "big water projects were back on track" (Wiley and Gottlieb 1982:307).

But there was a big "if" attached to President Reagan's willingness to promulgate structural water resource development; he would gladly support big projects, but only if local beneficiaries paid for a significant portion of the project. This policy, called cost-sharing, has had an important impact on recent water policy and is dealt with in depth in the subsequent section on budgetary reforms.

In sum, Carter's plan to reorient basic federal policy on water development toward nonstructural alternatives, environmental considerations, conservation, and realistic interest rates met with intense resistance. Ultimately he failed to alter basic policy substantially. In contrast, President Reagan has been supportive of structural solutions and less interested in environmental and conservation factors. But Reagan pushed hard for new budgetary criteria that would force local beneficiaries to bear a larger percentage of project costs.

BUREAUCRATIC REORGANIZATION

Both Carter and Reagan wanted to increase presidential control over water resources planning by reorganizing lines of authority. This would reduce the traditional autonomy of the water development iron triangle. Carter tried to increase presidential control by enlarging the review function of the Water Resources Council. This would have standardized project criteria and interjected a measure of presidential control between the agencies and Congress. Carter hoped to route all project recommendations through the Water Resources Council so that agency could cull the projects that did not meet his new criteria (*Public Papers of the Presidents* 6 June 1978:1044–1051).

The House, recognizing that this would severely curtail the autonomy of the water iron triangle, voted to abolish the Water Resources Council. The Senate did not demand outright abolition but refused to fund the council for fiscal year 1979. Carter vetoed the 1979 appropriations bill, and part of the resulting compromise was a continuation of funding for the council for one more year (*Weekly Report* 14 October 1978). However, Congress refused to authorize an expanded review function for the Council.

In 1979, Carter proposed that a new Department of Natural Resources be established. As indicated in chapter 4, this was not the first time a president attempted to place all water resources functions in one closely supervised department. One southern senator remarked to Carter: "Look, you're going to get your nose bloodied on this one—why take on one you're sure to lose?" (*New York Times* 12 February 1979:A-18). Carter's proposal for a Department of Natural Resources was quietly put to rest.

Carter was willing to accept the defeat of his proposed department, but he was unwilling to give up his quest for "independent" (i.e., presidential) project review. In 1979 he issued an executive order that required all water project plans to be submitted to the Water Resources Council before being submitted to the agency heads (Executive Order 12113, 4 January 1979).

Congress nullified this executive order by refusing to allocate funds for the council's project review function. Carter, in turn, tried to maneuver around this by issuing another executive order stating that "before any agency submits to the Congress, or to any committee or member thereof, a report relating to . . . public works . . . such report or plan shall be submitted to the Office of Management and Budget for advice as to its relationship to the program of the President." The council, however, retained its "impartial technical review" (Executive Order 12141, 5 June 1979). Under this plan the president ostensibly had two potential opportunities to review projects: the Office of Management and Budget and the Water Resources Council. However, Congress found ways to circumvent these checkpoints.

Carter continued to battle Congress over the lines of bureaucratic authority for the remainder of his term but without much success. President Reagan has also tried to inject a greater measure of executive review into the water policy decision-making process, but unlike Carter, he did not want to rely on the Water Resources Council. He revoked Carter's executive order establishing a review function for the council and convinced Congress to eliminate the agency's funding (they gladly consented). In its stead the president planned a number of alternative means to control the selection of projects. First, he issued an executive order requiring all agencies to submit project plans to OMB *before* they are presented to Congress (Executive Order 12322, 17 September 1981). This was the fourth time an executive order of that nature was issued (his predecessors were Franklin Roosevelt, Eisenhower, and Carter). The fact that Reagan believed this was necessary attests to the failure of earlier efforts to produce the desired effect. The role of OMB in water policy-making has expanded during the Reagan presidency. However, Congress has proven quite adept at maneuvering around the agency *if* there is sufficient political incentive to do so.

In addition to OMB the president has relied upon two other bureaucratic entities of his own making. He created a Cabinet Council on Natural Resources and Environment, which is not a new agency but simply an official collection of cabinet personnel who are active in that policy area. The Council initially played an important role, but after the departure of James Watt its influence waned considerably. Reagan also set up an Office of Water Policy in the Interior Department, but it proved ineffectual and was soon abandoned.

Most members of Congress have resented these intrusions into traditional congressional domain. In an effort to counter the president's proposals, Congress has attempted to establish its own version of a review function that primarily would be responsive to input from Congress and the states. Nearly all of the water project authorization bills that have been proposed annually but not passed during the Reagan years included an authorization for one or more policy review agencies. With names such as the National Board on Water Policy, the State Water Resources Advisory Commission, and the Waterway Users Board, these proposed review bodies would help Congress and its allies in the states to maintain control over water policy. Not surprisingly, Reagan promised to veto any bill authorizing such an agency. The House version of the 1986 Water Resources Development Act called for a National Board on Water Policy, but at Reagan's insistence it was eliminated in conference. A waterway user board was authorized by the Act, but it has only an advisory function.

The Reagan administration's attempt to alter the bureaucratic structure dealing with water policy has not been limited to the project review process. OMB, under the leadership of David Stockman, pressed for a reorganization of water agencies that would combine the Bureau of Reclamation and the Army Corps of Engineers. The resurrection of this timeless proposal once again generated fierce resistance, as it always has. Not only Congress but many members of Reagan's own administration opposed the plan. Secretary of Interior William Clark argued that the Bureau of Reclamation should remain independent because the agency's work "is closely integrated with state and local governments" (*Washington Post* 18 December 1984:A15), and a merger would destroy that close relationship. The *New York Times* editorialized in favor of the proposal but predicted it would never be accepted because the bureau is "a sacred cow," and even if the water agencies would merge it probably "wouldn't shut down the Washington porkbarrel. Both agencies know how to accommodate Congress" (13 February 1985:26). The Stockman proposal became the latest in a "half-century of failed attempts" (Conservation Foundation 1984:52) to unify federal water development agencies.

Both Carter and Reagan have made repeated attempts to alter bureaucratic lines of authority so that the president could exert more control over water policy formulation. Carter relied primarily on the Water Resources Council, and Reagan has utilized the Office of Management and Budget. For the most part these efforts have failed. Congress has tenaciously resisted presidential incursions that would compromise their ability to maintain control over water development policy. As a result, "neither OMB nor the Council [WRC] has played a critical role in the review and formulation of project plans" (Andrews and Sansone 1983:246).

BUDGETING REFORM

A third area in which both Carter and Reagan have attempted to reform the water policy decision-making structure concerns budgeting procedure—how projects are budgeted and who pays for them. The two most important reforms concern user fees and cost-sharing.

User fees affect primarily the U.S. Army Corps of Engineers because they apply to navigational waterways. The corps, unlike the Bureau of Reclamation, is not limited by payback requirements for most projects; for many years project beneficiaries, such as barge operators, contributed nothing to the construction and maintenance of the rivers and channels they use. Carter intended to change that.

In 1977 the Carter administration began working on a bill that would recover 100 percent of maintenance costs and 50 percent of new waterway construction costs through the imposition of a barge fuel tax. Although there was support for Carter's proposal in the Senate, it bogged down when the bill was attached to a massive authorization bill. When this strategy appeared doomed, the Senate changed strategies and tied a weak waterway user fee to the authorization of the controversial Lock and Dam 26. The proposed fee recovered 20 percent of maintenance costs and 1 percent of construction costs, a drastic reduction in the Carter proposal (*Weekly Report* 6 May 1978:1091–1092). This "watered-down" (Reid 1980:83) bill ultimately became law, placing a four-cent a gallon tax on barge fuel in 1978, rising to ten cents a gallon in 1985 (P.L. 95–502). Although the 1978 Inland Waterway Revenue Act was little more than a symbolic nod toward Carter's objectives, he was never able to impose a higher tax. It is noteworthy that many western legislators opposed the barge tax, even though there are no waterways in their districts or states. This indicates the continuing importance of reciprocity and logrolling: the westerners feared a reprisal against their projects if they supported the barge tax increase (see Reid 1980:61).

President Reagan continued the struggle for increased waterway user fees. He proposed an increase immediately after assuming office but Congress ignored his request, even though it came at a time when the president was enjoying unprecedented success in passing his legislative policy goals. Not deterred, Reagan continued to press for significant increases in the barge fuel tax and a new tax on cargoes handled by federally financed port facilities. The waterway lobby, still a powerful political force (see *Wall Street Journal* 5 October 1984:2; *Washington Post* 22 June 1985:A-4; *New York Times* 22 June 1985:I32), managed to resist the drive for higher fees for nearly a decade. However, their desire for new projects, and Reagan's insistence on a fee increase, ultimately convinced the waterway lobby that a higher fee was the price for more construction projects. Hence the 1986 Water Resources Development Act doubles the current fee over a period of ten years.

Cost-sharing, the second budgeting reform, is related to the idea of a user fee, but cost-sharing requires local and state governments to share a portion of project costs rather than tax individual users. Cost-sharing was an integral part of Carter's revised water policy. His statement of 18 April 1977 on water projects recommended "comprehensive reforms" concerning cost-sharing formulas that are "essential to genuine water program reforms" (*Presidential Documents* 18 April, 1977:557–559). When Carter announced his proposed cost-sharing formula, however, it was not very comprehensive. He proposed that states pay a modest 10 percent of costs for a vendible project (one that produces salable resources such as electricity and irrigation water), 5 percent for nonvendible projects, and 20 percent for flood control projects (*Public Papers of the Presidents* 6 June 1978:1044–1051). Carter explained that under the cost-sharing plan states would be given a greater role in the decision-making process. He reasoned that if states had to pay part of the costs of projects, they would be much more selective. This would weaken congressional control over the process and reduce the value of water projects as a "gift" to the home district of congressmen. Secretary of Interior Andrus predicted that cost-sharing legislation would be supported by states that have "good projects and are willing to put their money where their mouth is" (*New York Times* 17 May 1979:16). Secretary Andrus was wrong, however. States with a large number of projects, especially western and southern states, allied themselves with Congress in opposition to any form of cost-sharing. None of Carter's cost-sharing proposals was passed by Congress.

Cost-sharing has been the centerpiece of the Reagan administration's efforts toward water policy reform, and provoked an epic battle between the president and proponents of traditional pork barrel water policy. Reagan began his drive for cost-sharing soon after taking office, but it was unclear for some time how large the nonfederal contribution would be. Secretary of Interior James Watt suggested in 1981 that state and local sponsors should pay at minimum 15 to 25 percent of project costs (U.S. Congress, House 1981c:20). As Reagan's reelection approached, his commitment to cost-sharing waned considerably. Senator Paul Laxalt and other western senators warned the president that cost-sharing was perceived as "anti-West" and "anti-water" (*Weekly Report* 30 July 1983:1553). By 1983 cost-sharing had "become as popular on Capitol Hill and in the ranks of the Reagan Administration as an outbreak of the mumps" (*National Journal* 23 July 1983:1559). With the dawn of the election year, Reagan, in "a major policy swing" (*Washington Post* 25 January 1984), reversed many of his demands for cost-sharing. He promised that the federal government would bear all costs for dam repairs and that cost-sharing would be determined on a project-by-project basis based on ability to pay. Reagan's retreat particularly pleased his western supporters, but those legislators in Congress who had supported his more stringent proposals were incensed. Congressman Bruce Vento of Minnesota complained that "cost-sharing is a difficult legislative initiative even with presidential support. Without strong White House backing, it's near impossible" (*Weekly Report* 28 January 1984:143). Randall Ripley called the president's retreat "a symbol of the potency" of the traditional water policy iron triangle (1985:116).

After Reagan's landslide reelection he once again began a concerted effort to impose a cost-sharing policy. In essence, he held appropriations for new construction starts and new authorizations hostage until cost-sharing was accepted by Congress. His support for this type of legislation was not unprecedented; nearly every modern president has striven for the same goal. But the tenacity and scope of Reagan's efforts set a new standard. He expended enormous political capital in the fight over cost-sharing. His lame-duck status and personal popularity helped make this possible. In 1985 the Senate and OMB worked out an agreement on cost-sharing that broke the deadlock over project authorizations (*Weekly*

Report 22 June 1985:1240). However, the House, where resistance to cost-sharing has always been greatest, resisted these provisions.

The differences between the House and Senate approaches to cost-sharing were reflected in the authorization bills passed by both houses in 1985 and 1986. The Senate version of H.R. 6 (which became the 1986 Water Act) closely followed the precepts formulated by the Reagan administration in regard to cost-sharing and a host of other policy reforms. The House version offered a much more lenient approach which would have resulted in a significantly greater federal investment. For example, the House bill contained a cost-sharing exemption for the entire Mississippi River and Tributaries (MR&T), which was strongly supported by Congressman Jamie Whitten and other legislators from the basin. The Mississippi River Valley and tributaries covers about 41 percent of the continental United States so the issue was not a minor point. Another source of conflict concerned "up-front" funding; Reagan insisted that the non-federal share be paid before and during project construction. Such a funding arrangement would make it difficult for Congress to grant payment amnesty to states or communities that put political pressure on legislators to cancel debts incurred under the cost-sharing arrangement (such a scenario would be reminiscent of the numerous exemptions granted by Congress for the reclamation payback provisions).

H.R. 6 languished in conference for over five months, primarily because of the cost-sharing issue. Finally, acting under threat of veto if a rigid cost-sharing standard was not applied, the House members of the conference committee relented and accepted the Senate's version. The cost-sharing provisions of the 1986 Water Resources Development Act represent a truly significant shift in federal water policy. Senator Stafford remarked that, "The key to this bill—and possibly the single most important reform ever crafted onto the Nation's water resources development policy—is cost-sharing" (*Congressional Record* 1986:16982). The bill requires nonfederal sponsors to pay between 25 and 100 percent of the costs of construction, depending on the purpose of the project. It also requires that a significant share of funds be paid up-front. Because of these requirements the federal share of the $16.5 billion pricetag is only $9.5 billion.

The new cost-sharing provisions will certainly have an impact on the ability of legislators to make pork barrel water policy; in the past the key to such policymaking was the combination of concentrated benefits and dispersed costs. The latter half of that formula is now more difficult to achieve. It may be a mistake, however, to conclude that the age of federal water pork barrel is over. There are three reasons for this.

First, the federal share of local water development costs has been reduced but not eliminated. As one congressman pointed out, the "primary responsibility for funding and planning remains with the Federal Government" (*Congressional Record* 1986:11547. Remarks by James Howard). The cost-sharing policy—if fully implemented—will probably eliminate the most egregiously wasteful projects, but there is still a significant amount of federal money to be allocated, and therefore, there is still considerable advantage in spending it on projects with a political payoff. Constituents will still be pleased that the federal government will pay up to 75 percent of the costs of local water development.

A second point that may indicate pork barrel is not just a thing of the past concerns the continued political opposition to cost-sharing. A significant number of legislators voted for the 1986 Water Act—despite their opposition to cost-sharing—with the intention of revising that section of the act at a later date. A number of legislators from the Mississippi River Basin promised they would continue their battle against cost-sharing:

> The cost-sharing provisions of this bill as they relate to the MR&T are not only unfair to the localities in the Lower Mississippi Valley, but they preclude the completion of the project on the basis of ground rules long established. I want to assure my colleagues that they have not heard the last of this change-in-the-rules travesty. My colleagues and I from the Lower Mississippi will be back, urging future Congresses in every way we can, to see that this burden is shifted from our constituents and spread evenly among all of those who have responsibility to this national resource—the Mississippi River and its tributaries. (*Congressional Record* 1986:11551. Remarks by Congressman Emerson of Missouri)

The fight against cost-sharing may be aided by the fact that Congressman Jamie Whitten and Senator John Stennis chair the House and Senate Appropriations Committees. Both are from Mississippi, and both fought hard to exempt the entire MR&T from cost-sharing. And they may have an ally in Senator Byrd, once again the Majority Leader in the Senate. He was opposed to applying cost-sharing to Mississippi River tributaries, especially the Tug Fork Project in his home state of West Virginia. With Byrd in command, the Senate's approach to cost-sharing may be different than that of Robert Dole, who was Majority Leader in the 99th Congress when the 1986 Water Act was passed.

Although the 1986 Act does not provide exemptions for the tributaries of the Mississippi River, it does include an "ability-to-pay" clause. This section permits the secretary of the army to cancel the cost-sharing requirements for any flood control or agricultural water supply project if the non-federal sponsor can demonstrate an inability to pay their share (Title I-Sec. 103m). The Act gives the secretary complete discretion as to how to implement the provision. The current secretary is expected to formulate fairly restrictive criteria in order to minimize exemptions under this provision. A future secretary, appointed by a different president with different spending priorities, could formulate an entirely different set of criteria.

A third reason why water pork barrel may still be a possibility concerns the limited application of the new cost-sharing law. There are two significant areas of water development that are not affected. The first is the main stem of the Mississippi River. The Senate insisted that tributaries of the Mississippi be covered by the provision (the "separable elements"), but agreed to exempt about 86 percent of main stem project construction. The second arena of water development not affected by the cost-sharing law is the programs of the Bureau of Reclamation; the 1986 Act applies only to the corps. The original omnibus bill introduced in 1985 included the bureau in the cost-sharing provision, but opposition from powerful westerners—many of them allies of the Reagan administration—convinced the managers of the bill that it had no chance of success unless the bureau was exempted from the provision. In short, even if the cost-sharing law is fully implemented, there will still be significant areas of federal water development policy that remain unaffected.

In summary, there have been a number of significant changes in the decision-making process that controls federal water development policy. After a long battle President Reagan succeeded in many areas where Carter had failed; the 1986 Water Act imposed cost-sharing, increased user fees, and adopted a more realistic method for computing project costs and benefits. In the area of bureaucratic reorganization, however, neither president experienced much success. The intensity and duration of the conflict over water policy indicates that the reformers have been gaining momentum over the last decade, but the traditional water iron triangle is still a potent political force.

Conflict over Appropriation and Authorization Bills

Jimmy Carter's battle with Congress over the so-called hit list is now something of a legend (see Fradkin 1981:3–14; Wiley and Gottlieb 1982:61–68; Miller 1985; Clarke and McCool 1985:19–27, 99–102). Soon after taking office Carter naively announced a tentative list of ongoing water projects that were to be studied for possible exclusion from that year's appropriation bill. The response from Congress was remarkably hostile; one western congressman said the hit list was based on "ignorance, intransigence, and obduracy" (quoted in Lamm and McCarthy 1982:189). Despite this resistance, Carter continued his efforts to curb spending for what he considered wasteful projects. In 1977 he issued a revised list of projects that recommended deleting funds for 18 projects, modifying 5 projects, and continuing 9 projects on his original list. It is important to note that the projects on Carter's list were a tiny proportion of the 292 ongoing Corps of Engineer projects and the 75 ongoing Bureau of Reclamation projects. Specifically, he attempted to delete funding for 4.9 percent of all ongoing projects and reduce funding for 1.4 percent of those projects. Yet even this modest decrease incited intense opposition from Congress, western and southern politicians (especially western governors), and interest groups that profit from the traditional approach to water development.

A revealing portrait of many legislators' attitude toward water project funding was provided by the conference report that accompanied the 1978 appropriations bill:

> The conferees are agreed that the Congress retains the right to select water resource projects for funding. All authorized water resource projects will be considered on their merits, and each and every authorized project will be considered by the committees in the deliberations on the 1979 appropriations bill. (H.R. 7553, 1977)

The Carter hit list was the beginning of a heated battle between the president and Congress over both appropriation and authorization bills for water projects. This struggle included Carter's veto of the Energy and Water Development Appropriations Act for fiscal year 1979. This cost the president so much politically that by 1979 he was retreating rapidly from his previously bellicose stance. In fact, Carter's proposed fiscal year 1980 budget offered a 13 percent increase in the combined budgets of the corps and the Bureau of

Reclamation, including funding for 10 new corps projects and 6 new bureau projects (U.S. Congress, House 1979: 8, 795). Environmentalists, who had vigorously supported his efforts to cut project spending, complained that Carter was trying to curry favor with Congress by offering a "whopping increase in pork for 1980" (Hubbard 1979:4). In short, after a three-year internecine struggle Carter achieved only "minuscule savings" on water projects (Fitzgerald and Lipson 1984:1).

Carter was more persistent in his opposition to new construction starts and authorization bills, however. When a water resource development act was introduced in 1979, the president noted that the new projects were scattered throughout 70 percent of the congressional districts in the nation, evidence that the norm of reciprocity still shaped water policy. At one point members of the House became so infuriated that they amended the authorization bill to include a monument to the Corps of Engineers—and 61 more projects.

Carter's efforts to decrease sharply annual expenditures for water projects was largely ineffectual, but his adamant promise of a veto won him a victory over Congress' attempts to pass an omnibus authorization bill. Like Eisenhower, he worked with a small but dedicated group of legislators to limit support for new authorizations. Opponents appeared to have sufficient votes to pass an omnibus bill but not enough for an override. The futility of the effort prevented most of these measures from coming to a floor vote. The failure of these bills to become law did not stop the corps' construction program because a $60 billion backlog of authorized but as yet unfunded projects had built up. This backlog permitted the corps to continue operations until new projects could be authorized (*GAO Report to the Congress* 26 January 1983).

President Reagan's approach to water resources funding and authorization has been something of a contradiction. His drive for reduced federal spending often clashed with his pro-development philosophy and his desire to aid southern and western allies, many of whom are involved in the water development iron triangle. For example, when Reagan took office he promised he would challenge entrenched iron triangles (see *National Journal* 3 March 1981:516–518; Ripley and Franklin 1984:102), but the rhetoric of his administration appeared to support continued water development, especially in the West. During appropriations hearings Secretary of Interior Watt stated that "billions of dollars" will be needed to stave off "the largest, biggest crisis that will confront America . . . a water shortage in the 1990's" (U.S. Congress, House 1981c: 1–2).

The commissioner of reclamation assured concerned westerners that the Reagan administration is "a pro-water policy administration" that foresees a serious water crisis if there is not a major effort to develop water resources (*Tucson Citizen* 20 January 1982:3-A).

Conflict over these divergent goals, budget problems, and the partisan split in Congress during the Reagan years spawned a nearly continuous struggle over a complex array of regular appropriation bills, supplemental appropriations, and authorization proposals. A review of recent appropriations bills, followed by a discussion of the authorization proposals and the 1986 Water Resources Development Act, will demonstrate how these conflicting goals have affected federal water development policy.

Reagan has often been relatively supportive of regular appropriations bills for water development. During Reagan's first year in office he got nearly everything he wanted from Congress in terms of budget priorities. But in the case of funding for water projects, Congress balked when Reagan wanted to "stretch out" expenditures (U.S. Congress, House 1981a, Part 1:560). The president ultimately agreed to sign an appropriations bill that was $375 million over his request (*Weekly Report* 12 December 1981:2433). His willingness to compromise on water projects but not social programs prompted angry reactions from some legislators. Senator Howard Metzenbaum, upset by the Senate's support for the president's budget, exclaimed:

> We're not going to worry about people who will go hungry and people who will be starving. We're not going to worry about senior citizens going cold this winter. But don't lay a hand on those water projects. What's so sacred about water projects? (*New York Times* 12 May 1981:IV-22)

Senator William Proxmire called the water project expenditures the "most bloated part of the budget proposed for 1982" (*New York Times* 12 May 1981:IV-22).

The following year Reagan again demonstrated a willingness to fund water projects; his budget proposal for fiscal year 1983 included a 23 percent increase for the Bureau of Reclamation. The largest part of that increase was for construction (U.S. Congress, House 1982, Part 3:57). Proposed funding for the corps was reduced slightly, but Congress later increased the amount substantially (from $2.7 to $3.4 billion). The president's proposals provoked a headline in the *Washington Post* that read, "Water Projects Sail On, Despite Budget Cuts" (24 February 1982:AP21).

The president's budget proposals for fiscal years 1984 and 1985 were again generous to the Bureau of Reclamation, raising the agency's proposed budget from $966 million to $1.079 billion for the latter year. The "lion's share" of the increase was for construction (*Weekly Report* 4 February 1984:199). The president's sensitivity to preelection politics was plainly evident. After the election, however, Reagan reversed the trend and offered a proposed budget for fiscal year 1986 that slashed spending for water development. Congress reacted by substantially increasing the funding for both the Corps of Engineers and the Bureau of Reclamation (*Weekly Report* 19 October 1985:2122). For fiscal year 1987 Reagan again softened his opposition to water project funding and proposed substantial increases for the corps ($3.1 billion, up from $2.8 billion) and the Bureau of Reclamation ($853 million, up from $744 million). Yet even these increases were not enough to please the House. By a lopsided margin of 329 to 82 the full House voted to spend an additional $169 million for water development. Most of the increase was for new project construction. The vote for more funding occurred despite "extraordinary budget pressure" to reduce such expenditures (*Weekly Report* 21 June 1986:1423, and 26 July 1986:1715). Of course it is impossible to estimate the outcome of the budget process given the uncertainties brought about by the Balanced Budget Act (the Gramm-Rudman bill) and the Supreme Court decision invalidating portions of the Act. It is clear, however, that many members of Congress, especially in the House, still like to spend money on water projects. As one disgruntled congressional opponent to the traditional water pork barrel noted recently, "from what we've seen so far, the pork barrel continues. Appropriators bury favors for members in bills, and if they took them out they'd lose a lot of votes" (*Weekly Report* 7 June 1986:1261).

Reagan's willingness to support regular appropriations for the water development agencies contrasts sharply with his opposition to the supplemental bills that have been pursued by Congress every year since Reagan took office. This is primarily a result of the congressional strategy of using the supplemental as a vehicle to fund projects that were sufficiently unpopular with the president that inclusion in the regular appropriations bills endangered all water project spending. Again, the principal issue was cost-sharing. Congress has repeatedly used the supplemental bill to push new construction starts without a cost-sharing proviso and to maneuver around Reagan's blockage of authorization bills by providing funds for numerous projects that had yet to be authorized. For example, the supplemental bill for 1983 provided funding for forty-three new projects—half of which were unauthorized. Reagan countered by offering his own list of new projects, all of which required cost-sharing. Both the 1983 and 1984 supplementals died at the end of their respective sessions because of the promise of a veto.

In 1985, Congress tried once again to pass a substantial supplemental appropriations bill. By this time there had been no new construction starts in five years. Again the bill contained numerous projects that were unauthorized. The *New York Times* editorialized against the bill: "One of the most durable instincts on Capitol Hill is the irresistible lure of the pork barrel. In particular, legislators can whip themselves into a feeding frenzy at the first whiff of a bill providing money for water projects" (3 June 1985:I-16). Reagan made it clear that he would veto the supplemental bill unless it contained cost-sharing language. This placed Congress in a predicament; it could continue the stalemate on new construction starts and new project authorizations, or it could accept the bitter pill of cost-sharing and get its new projects. In a crucial test of these opposing approaches, an amendment deleting nearly $100 million for unauthorized corps projects passed—by one vote. Then, in an additional compromise, the House agreed with the Senate to a revised bill that provided $48.8 million for forty-one corps projects and $14.3 million for four Bureau of Reclamation projects (scattered throughout thirty states) with the proviso that no projects could begin until an authorization bill stipulating a cost-sharing requirement passed, or an OMB-imposed cost-sharing plan is accepted for each project (*Weekly Report* 28 December 1985:2736). Because this "fencing" language guaranteed cost-sharing, the president signed the bill. The 1986 Water Act provided the requisite authorization.

This brings us to the discussion of authorization bills. Omnibus authorization bills used to be presented—and passed—biennially, but presidential opposition since 1976 prevented the passage of a major omnibus water project authorization bill for the Corps of Engineers until 1986. President Reagan steadfastly refused to sign such a bill without cost-sharing. Many of these bills had the look of the traditional pork barrel omnibus, with a panoply of projects in nearly every district and state. And they were often top-heavy with projects in states and districts that were represented by members of the authorization subcommittees in Congress. For example, the House version of the bill (HR6) that ultimately became the 1986 Water Act was fairly traditional in its approach to water development. It called for the authorization of 350 projects costing $20 billion. The bill passed the House easily with bipartisan support from every region of the country. It contained a limited cost-sharing requirement but fell far short of President Reagan's demands. For that reason and others Reagan promised a veto, arguing that 80 percent of the projects in the bill "are of dubious economic or environmental benefit or have been incompletely studied" (*Wall Street Journal* 14 November 1985:58). Brent Blackwelder of the Environmental Policy Institute, a persistent critic of water development policy, claimed that "every cat and dog imaginable is found in this bill" (*U.S. Water News* January 1986:7). The Senate version of HR 6 contained nearly all of the reforms demanded by the Reagan administration, and authorized fewer projects at less federal cost. As the 99th Congress drew to a close, and President Reagan maintained his veto threat, it became obvious to the proponents of federal water development that they would have to accept reform or face yet another year without new project authorizations. Reluctantly the House agreed to nearly all of the language in the Senate version. In the final moments of the session Congress passed the first omnibus water act in over a decade. In the House the vote was 329 to 11. The Senate vote was also lopsided: 84 to 2. Even long-time environmental critics such as the Sierra Club supported the conference bill. The *National Journal* declared that a "new era" had begun for the corps (22 November 1986:2822).

The 1986 Water Resources Development Act was indeed a landmark bill. One legislator hailed it as "the most significant water resources development bill in over 50 years" (*Congressional Record* 1986:16991. Remarks by Senator Abdnor). The Act authorized over 270 projects with a total estimated cost of $16.5 billion. Perhaps even more important are the substantive reforms that may affect water policy for many years. In addition to the new policies discussed in the previous section of this chapter, the Act also provided for automatic de-authorization of unfunded projects, put a limit on cost over-runs (the corps once received Senator Proxmire's Golden Fleece Award for cost over-runs), and set a ceiling on annual construction spending. In a nod to environmentalists the Act requires that fish and wildlife mitigation occur concurrently with construction. The bill also eliminated the use of "regional benefits" in calculating legally mandated cost-benefit analyses. Such benefits were often used in the past to justify projects that were not economically viable.

The passage of the 1986 Water Act was the culmination of a long

and bitter struggle between the traditionalists in the water development iron triangle, and President Reagan and his congressional
allies. To a great extent Reagan's success can be attributed to the
strategy of tying substantive policy reforms to project authorization. This "hostage" approach had been used before by proponents of reform; in the late seventies they tied re-authorization of
Lock and Dam 26 to an increase in the barge fuel tax (see Reid
1980). Similarly, President Reagan made it clear that he would
veto any omnibus corps authorization bill that did not meet his
new standards. In essence, the president played a waiting game;
after his landslide reelection it was obvious to his opponents that
they would have to wait a long time indeed. Ultimately, Reagan
"achieved what Mr. Carter could not with the trade of further
projects for structural reform" (*Washington Post* 7 October 1986:
A26). One commentator noted dryly that Carter should have been
invited to the bill signing ceremony.

In addition to the 1986 Water Act, two other notable authorization bills were passed in recent years. First, the president signed
a dam safety authorization bill that approved funding for the repair
of sixty western dams. President Carter signed a dam safety bill in
1978, but it was inadequate. Initially Reagan insisted on cost-sharing for dam repair as well as all other authorizations, but he
abandoned that stance at the behest of his western friends. However, eastern opposition in Congress, led by Senator Metzenbaum,
forced Reagan and his allies to compromise. The bill that ultimately
became law requires beneficiaries to repay 15 percent of costs at
market interests, with the exception of irrigation users, who will
be subject to the payback proviso only if they have the ability to
pay, and they will not be charged interest (*Weekly Report* 27 October
1984:2799). Although this bill received little publicity outside the
West, it represented a significant authorization of additional federal
largess and provides an indication of the continuing political power
of traditional western water interests.

The second water authorization bill to become law in recent
years concerned federal support for water research. Congress
passed—over Reagan's veto—legislation authorizing $36 million
annually to fund water resources research institutes at land grant
colleges for the next five years. Reagan argued that such research
was "not an appropriate federal activity" (*Presidential Documents* 21
February 1984:250), but Congress overwhelmingly disagreed. It
should also be noted that several relatively small authorizations
have been made for the Bureau of Reclamation.

A Contemporary Water Policy Iron Triangle?

The events of the last ten years make it abundantly evident that the politics of water has changed. Does this mean that an iron triangle, distributing pork barrel, is no longer the major force in determining water policy? In order to answer that question it is necessary to examine the contemporary situation with respect to the variables affecting iron triangles that were outlined in chapter 1. A number of those variables appear especially relevant to today's water policy.

First, logrolling and the norm of reciprocity still appear to be popular in Congress, at least with most legislators. An explicit demonstration of that approach came during the House debate over a 1984 omnibus authorization bill. Leaders of the House Public Works Committee circulated a list of legislators whose districts contained a project authorized in the bill. A black spot appeared beside the names of those who had opposed the committee on a crucial vote on the bill earlier in the week (*New York Times* 30 June 1984:8). The implicit message was that those legislators who voted against their colleagues' projects would have their own project removed from the bill: "The Black Spot list . . . made manifest a fundamental rule of procedure governing water projects, highways, and other public-works measures in Congress. The rule is that members are expected to vote for colleagues' projects, regardless of merit, and then expect similar favors in return" (*Washington Post* 30 June 1984:A3).

The following year Congressman Robert Roe, a leading proponent of the omnibus water authorization bills, once again spelled out the importance of reciprocity. When Congressman Robert Edgar, a persistent critic of water pork barrel, offered an amendment to the authorization bill that would delete certain benefits, Roe derided his efforts: "Everybody comes up and they tinker. Do you know what that tinkering does? It does somebody else in. It is not fair. . . . It is all very well to go and try to grab something out of the pot, but it is fundamentally wrong if we deny somebody else" (*Weekly Report* 6 November 1985:2384). The Edgar amendment was voted down by a substantial majority.

Another indication of the reciprocal nature of recent congressional activity in regard to water is the scope of recently proposed authorization bills; they included a wide variety of projects spread throughout dozens of states and congressional districts. In distributive policy the classic response to potential opposition is to coopt those opponents by offering them benefits. This reduces conflict and expands the number of parties who are involved in the logrolling process. For example, the 1985 House bill (H.R. 6) included all the traditional activities as well as funds for municipal water supply, environmental mitigation, fish and wildlife, groundwater research, soil conservation, farmers, and tidal power. There was even money to help communities break up river ice (*Federal Bill Digest 1985*:A-45). Most of these projects also appeared in the 1986 Water Act. In classic reciprocal fashion, there is something for everyone, including both the traditional recipients of the water pork barrel as well as their inveterate opponents such as environmentalists and legislators from eastern cities. The net of reciprocity was cast wide indeed.

A second important element affecting contemporary water policy concerns congressional personnel. A recent article in the *Wall Street Journal* declared that "the great water czars are gone from Congress (3 May 1985:44), but that appears to be an overstatement. There are numerous proponents of federal water development in the 100th Congress, and some of them hold important leadership positions. In the House, Congressman Whitten, chairman of the House Appropriations Committee, is a zealous supporter of traditional water policy. (He recently celebrated the opening of the Tennessee-Tombigbee Waterway, which is the largest civil works project ever undertaken by the Corps of Engineers, by floating down the canal on a flower-bedecked barge; see *Wall Street Journal* 31 May 1985:1.) Congressman Edgar complained that "Whitten never loses. He may lose on the merits; he may lose on procedure. . . . But his committee will stay up all night to figure out how to get those projects funded" (*Weekly Report* 8 June 1985:1124. Also see *National Journal* 12 June 1986:1708–1712). James Howard, chairman of the Public Works and Transportation Committee, is one of "the foremost proponents of federal aid for water projects" (*Weekly Report* 8 June 1985:1125). Tom Bevill, chairman of the Appropriations Subcommittee on Energy and Water Development, is also a longtime supporter of massive federal funding for water development (*Washington Post* 26 July 1985:E-10). Thus in the House three of the six committees and subcommittees that have the greatest impact on the federal water development program are chaired by longtime advocates of that program.

In the Senate the Appropriations Committee is chaired by John Stennis of Mississippi, who replaced Republican Mark Hatfield when the Democrats won control of the 100th Congress. According to one commentator, the switch from Hatfield to Stennis will make only a marginal difference, "but those margins matter alot because they often determine who gets which water project" (*National Journal* 15 November 1986:2777). Senator Stennis was generally opposed to the new cost-sharing provisions, especially when they were applied to portions of the Lower Mississippi River. Senator J. Bennet Johnston of Louisiana also plays a leading role in water policy. Characterized by an environmentalist as "no great friend of the environment," (*National Journal* 15 November 1986:2784), Johnston also fought for the cost-sharing exemption for the Mississippi River and Tributaries, and is a longtime supporter of federal water development. He is chair of both the Committee on Energy and Natural Resources and the Appropriations Subcommittee on Energy and Water Development.

To be sure, there are vociferous congressional critics of pork barrel water projects. There always have been, but a few contemporary legislators stand out. Senator Daniel Moynihan, now chair of the Environment and Public Works Subcommittee on Water Resources, has tried on numerous occasions to pass legislation altering the traditional water policy decision-making process. In the House, Silvio Conte (who wore a pig mask on a day the House voted on water projects), George Miller (chair of Interior's Subcommittee on Water and Power Resources), and Robert Edgar have fought vigorously against what they perceived to be water pork barrel. Their crusade, however, was often a lonely one. The case of Edgar, a member of the Public Works and Transportation Committee's Water Resources Subcommittee for four years, is instructive. He was routinely chastised by his colleagues, one of whom suggested he be given a "Pinocchio Award" because he kept violating the norm of reciprocity by sticking his nose into other legislators' business (Arnold 1981:259). Reisner called Edgar "a virtual pariah among his colleagues" (1986:322). Smith and Deering argue that "the fact that Edgar stands out among his committee colleagues indicates Public Works' continuing district orientation" (1984:108). In 1986 Edgar was defeated in his bid for a Senate seat.

A final element that is having an impact on contemporary water policy concerns the changing role of interest groups. In recent years much of the opposition to the water iron triangle came from environmental groups. Development-oriented interests have responded to this challenge with new organizations of their own. Wiley and Gottlieb note that in response to the environmental lobby, "corporations active in the West threw together a number of powerful new lobbying organizations" (1982:65). One of the best examples of this corporate lobbying activity is the Western Regional Council, which has been quite active in promoting the developmentalist perspective. The Mountain States Legal Foundation, once represented by James Watt, has pursued similar objectives.

The corporate effort to organize has been matched by similar efforts at the state and local government level, especially in the West. Organizations such as the Western Governors' Association (created in 1984 by the merger of the Western Governors' Policy Office and the Western Governors' Conference), the Western States Water Council, and the Conference of State Legislators have pushed for more federal spending for water development. Reisner called the Colorado Water Conservation Board "a chamber of commerce for dams" (1986:433). In addition, it is now common for local governing entities, including irrigation districts, to hire professional lobbyists to promote their interests in Washington. For example, lobby registrations for just one month—April 1986—listed seven such governments that hired lobbyists to promote their interests in water development legislation. Three of these (Provo, Utah; Redondo Beach, California; and the Oceanside Redevelopment Corporation of California) cited the omnibus water bill (H.R. 6) as their primary legislative interest (*Weekly Report* 6 September 1986:2093–2094). Others are even more specific in terms of their interests; Tucson, Arizona, lobbies for more appropriations for the Central Arizona Project; the port of Wilmington, Delaware, relies upon its lobby to influence user fees; and Westlands Water District lists its legislative interests as "Oppose legislation regarding *Westlands Water District v. U.S.*" (*Weekly Report* 12 July 1986: 1588). Some water districts have been fortunate enough to hire former congressmen to promote their interests on Capitol Hill; John Rhodes, past Minority Leader, represents the Central Arizona Water Conservation District, and former U.S. Representative Raymond Kogovsek is an agent for two water conservancy districts in Colorado.

Some of the long-standing interest groups in the water policy iron triangle have maintained their strength. When Senator Domenici tried to raise waterway user fees in the late 1970s, he was opposed by "the Association for the Improvement of the Mississippi River, the Upper Mississippi River Valley Association, and a passel of former Congressmen, Senators, and executive branch officials" (Reid 1980:49). Five years later, when Reagan again wanted to raise the waterway user fee, he had to make "significant compromises" with the powerful barge industry (*New*

York Times 22 June 1985:I-32). Still other traditional interest groups have adapted to changing conditions. For example, the National Water Resources Association, whose influence has been waning because of declining interest in irrigation, joined forces with the Groundwater Management Districts Association (*U.S. Water News* February 1986:2).

The discussion thus far indicates that the water policy iron triangle is still a force to be reckoned with, albeit in modified form. If this is true, then why were no new omnibus authorization bills passed in ten years, why have there been so few new construction starts, and why did Congress accept the reforms embodied in the 1986 Water Act? A number of scholars, cited in the introduction to this chapter, attribute this failure to the demise of the water policy iron triangle and its penchant for classic distributive politics. There is no doubt that the iron triangle's role in water policy decision making has changed; the carte blanche of previous years is gone. But I think the iron triangle, in its contemporary form, still has an enormous impact on water policy. Thus the failure of recent water bills can be attributed to a number of other factors.

First, the most important development was the intrusion of the president. Both Carter and Reagan expended considerable political capital in their battles against what they perceived as water pork barrel. Of course, Reagan was much more successful in this endeavor. His role in the formulation of the 1986 water bill was decisive. Senator Abdnor, who helped write the Senate version of H.R. 6, noted that "the administration has been kept abreast all during the conference negotiations" (*Congressional Record* 1986: 16992). The House, which was much more hostile to the president's demands, still had to acknowledge his omnipresent influence: "[H.R. 6] was crafted under the watchful care of the Reagan administration" (*Congressional Record* 1986:11554). During the five months the bill was in conference the conferees repeatedly excised sections of the bill that drew the threat of a veto: a water supply loan program, the proposed National Water Policy Board, and the cost-sharing exemption for Mississippi River tributaries are examples of deleted policies. The total cost of the bill was pared by nearly a third.

Reagan's influence over the bill was enhanced by two political factors. First, the Senate was controlled by his own party. This gave Reagan more leverage over the legislation and made it more difficult for committee and subcommittee chairmen to vote against the president. This helped create significant differences between the Senate and House versions of all the omnibus bills introduced in the last five years; in every case the Senate version provided less federal money and more water policy reforms. The differences were especially notable on the cost-sharing issue. One House member, incensed that the final version of H.R. 6 abandoned the cost-sharing exemption for Mississippi River tributaries, argued that "with the insistence of the current presidential administration and the assistance of the Republican-controlled Senate, this conference report is going to stop flood control progress in the Mississippi River and Tributaries Project" (*Congressional Record* 1986:11571).

The other factor that enhanced Reagan's influence was his status as a personally popular lame-duck president. He could afford to expend the political capital necessary to keep authorization bills in line with his policy reforms. His strategy of holding project authorizations hostage until substantive reforms were accepted would not have worked if he had lacked the political latitude that accompanies popularity in the second term. The point is, the president played a lead role in the move for substantive reform. Presidential intervention does not guarantee policy reform, however. If the conference report had been written after the Iran-Contra affair, and after the Democrats took over the Senate, the final bill might have looked different. And to speculate further, if the president had been supportive of the traditional approach to water development, there might not have been any reforms at all. Indeed, one congressional staffer offered the opinion recently that Congress "would go along in a heartbeat" if the White House supported more federal water development.

Another factor that greatly affected the debate over H.R. 6 was the deficit crisis. Nearly all forms of domestic spending have been cut, but funds for water development have actually fared quite well relative to other programs. If and when the deficit problem is solved, or a different set of spending priorities is adopted (say, a shift of funds from defense to domestic infrastructure), funding for project construction may increase significantly.

And finally, many of the votes against recent water bills should not be construed as opposition to water pork barrel. Indeed, quite the opposite is true; many of the diehard traditionalists voted against new starts and omnibus authorizations because they did not want to authorize cost-sharing. Their strategy was to outlast the president and wait until they could have new projects without cost-sharing, but the president has definitely won the first round of the waiting game.

In summary, there still appears to be considerable congressional and interest group support for the federal water development program. Despite this support, President Reagan successfully stalled major new authorization bills and new construction starts until Congress accepted cost-sharing.

Much of this discussion can be verified by examining budget data for the contemporary period. Table 17 contains two columns of data. The "Request" column indicates the total amount of funding for the Corps of Engineers and the Bureau of Reclamation requested by the president in his annual budget. It demonstrates how much the president wants to spend on federal water development. The second column, marked "Appropriation," indicates the amount of funding actually appropriated by statute. This provides an indication of the influence of Congress on the president's budget proposal.

Two general trends are evident in the data. First, funding for water projects has been fairly consistent, even in the years when the Reagan administration slashed domestic spending. To quote the *Congressional Quarterly Weekly Report*, "Annual appropriations for the corps and the bureau . . . have proven pretty reliable over

TABLE 17

PRESIDENTIAL REQUESTS AND ACTUAL APPROPRIATIONS FOR
FEDERAL WATER DEVELOPMENT, 1977–1986
(in billions of dollars, rounded)

Year	Request	Appropriation
1977	2.9	3.4
1978	3.1	3.5
1979	3.0	3.4
1980	3.2	3.9
1981	3.8	3.9
1982*	3.5	3.7
1983	3.2	4.3
1984	3.1	3.6
1985	3.6	4.0
1986	3.3	3.5 (est.)

Source: U.S. Annual Budget, 1977–1987 fiscal years

Note: These figures represent the combined total budgets of the U.S. Army Corps of Engineers and the Bureau of Reclamation.

*Reagan's revised request.

the years—flowing more steadily than rivers themselves" (27 October 1984:2797). Overall the budget appropriations look supportive of water development. There are two caveats to this conclusion, however. First, a growing proportion of these budgets is for operation and maintenance rather than construction. Traditionally it was the latter that provided the substance of the pork barrel. As "O&M" becomes more dominant, it may be subjected to a more politicized allocation process. In addition, the fairly constant budgets of the last decade contrast sharply with the rapid budget growth of earlier decades. The potential for pork barrel water funding is still extant, but there is less money for expansion and for bringing in new beneficiaries.

Another basic trend in the data is Congress' persistent efforts to spend more than the president on water development. In every year of the sample Congress spent more on water development than the president wanted. Obviously Congress is still willing to expend considerable effort to increase funding over the president's request. In light of these data it is difficult to conclude that Congress is no longer supportive of water development. That support has diminished somewhat in recent years, but it is still quite impressive. An article in the *Washington Post* succinctly made this point: "No one is ready to say that Congress is breaking its dam habit, but there are signs that the traditional porkbarrel is filling less readily than in the past. . . . Feelings thus still run high, and if Congress has changed on the surface, it may not have changed underneath" (22 June 1983:A-2).

Of course, this may change if some form of a balanced budget act is ever implemented; the potential reductions are substantial. The ultimate impact on federal water development is difficult to predict, however. A balanced budget does not preclude the generous expenditure of water development funds according to political criteria. In fact, the glory years of the big dam era—the 1950s and 1960s—were characterized by minute deficits (by current standards). For example, in 1970 the federal budget deficit was only $2.8 billion, but it was a good year for the water development iron triangle. Also, it is important to remember that only about .2 percent of the federal budget is allocated to water project construction.

Conclusion

In recent years the water development iron triangle has been subjected to severe challenge. The rise of the environmental movement, Jimmy Carter's new water policy, and Reagan's budget austerity have put the triangle to the test. Did these challenges destroy the political effectiveness of the water development iron triangle? I think there is a two-part answer to that question.

First, I do not believe the water development iron triangle is politically moribund. If this were true a reform bill would have passed without a prolonged and bitter political struggle. After ten years of arduous effort the reformers found the right combination of circumstance, timing, and political advantage to break the stalemate. This victory did not eliminate the demand for water pork barrel, but the impact of the ten-year effort for reform has been sobering for the traditional water policy establishment. The failure to override Carter's veto of the 1978 appropriations bill and the inability to overcome Reagan's insistence on cost-sharing indicate that traditional pork barrel is no longer approved in a knee-jerk fashion on Capitol Hill. As a result, I think Congress will assess the political viability of water projects more carefully in the future. But here again there are caveats. Political viability is not the same as economic viability. Pork barrel expenditures will still occur, but a greater effort will have to be made to line up political support. This may mean that the iron triangle will need to expand its logrolling efforts, compromise on some issues, and share government largess with an expanding pool of beneficiaries. Ultimately this could lead to a greater number, and a greater variety, of water expenditures.

Another area in which Carter and Reagan met with some success concerns public attitudes. The long and bitter struggle over project funding raised public consciousness about the issue, making it more difficult for the water development iron triangle to operate under conditions of low visibility. However, this achievement may be short-lived at best. The public has a short attention span, and as a result the movement for reform may fall prey to the "issue attention cycle" (Downs 1972) that has plagued so many other issues. This may be occurring already; for example, a leading interest group in Utah opposed to water development is in danger of demise due to lack of public support (*High Country News* 4 August 1986:4).

A final point, which may help to answer the question of whether the water iron triangle is still politically effective, concerns the potential for confusing situation characteristics with systemic characteristics. Some of what is attributed to a changing political system may in fact be attributable to ad hoc circumstance. The basic policy-making process can undergo considerable situational variation without altering the fundamental process.[2] In the case of water policy it may be that the problems experienced in recent years by the traditional iron triangle may be a function of the times rather than a function of a new mode of policy-making that is fundamentally hostile to the iron triangle's goals. Ronald Reagan will not be president forever, and domestic budget cuts are not an automatic output of the existing system; just the opposite may be true. Indeed, one budget expert argues that recent domestic budget cuts have created "a lot of pent-up desire to spend money" for "infrastructure" and other basic programs (*Wall Street Journal* 19 January 1987:1). In short, what may be perceived as a typical systemic output may in fact be an aberration in the system that is attributable to temporary situational factors. As Rene Dubos pointed out, "trend is not destiny" (1972:191).

If this is true, then a new set of situational variables would produce a water policy at variance with that pursued by Carter and Reagan. The "environmental crisis" had a powerful impact on water policy. So has the "deficit crisis." A water supply crisis may also have a profound impact, but with dramatically different results as far as water projects are concerned. For example, Trelease notes that the severe problems facing farmers dependent on the Ogalalla Aquifer will inevitably lead to calls for rescue (1984:78). Indeed, it has: the 1986 Water Act provides funding to study the problems of the Ogalalla. And the cries of impending water crises are still very much in evidence (see Andrews and Sansone 1983:225; Conservation Foundation 1984:xi; Lamm 1985:159–162; Grigg 1985:4–6; *National Journal* 17 August 1985:1876–1887; Welsh 1985; Frederick 1986:1–3). One writer recently commented, "It has become a cliché for news writers and speechmakers to identify water as the 'next resource crisis'" (*Weekly Report* 30 July 1983:1558). The desire for reelection in Congress, the demands of constituents, and the bureaucrat's drive for security and power are still very much a part of the American political system. When new demands for water projects arise, the water iron triangle will probably respond.

This leads us to the second part of the answer to the question, Is the water development iron triangle still politically effective? If the answer is yes, and I think it is, then it is only because the triangle has been willing to adapt to changing political circumstances. But these adaptations have not eliminated the potential for pork barrel water projects or destroyed the water development iron triangle. Rather, the triangle has sought new outlets to accommodate these changing political circumstances. I see six areas of policy-making activity that may provide such outlets in the future.

First, the demand for energy will create new demands for water development. The current energy "glut" is based on a finite resource that will inevitably decline. In the future, hydropower, coal slurry, oil shale, pumped storage facilities, and the need for more energy-efficient water delivery systems will make water and energy policy more interrelated. The drive for small hydropower has already begun. It is basically true that the era of enormous dams is drawing to a close; nearly all practicable sites have been developed.[3] There is still a potential, however, for many small dams with hydroelectric capability. A 1977 study by the Corps of Engineers concluded that the nation's hydropower capacity could be more than doubled simply by rehabilitating or retrofitting existing dam sites (*National Journal* 26 April 1980). Environmentalists generally favor this approach because it minimizes the need for new dams and other environmentally questionable energy-producing activity. The 1986 Water Act authorized funding to study the feasibility of small-dam hydropower.

A second area of potential growth concerns conservation and increased efficiency, an issue particularly relevant to the West. Conservation creates an enlarged role for regulation and water management, which has been pointed out by numerous students of water policy. There is also a potential for continued development, however, especially as specific areas such as the Ogalalla Aquifer reach a crisis stage. The Bureau of Reclamation is currently searching for an expanded mission, and anything from lining existing irrigation systems to installing sprinklers, could provide an outlet for the agency and compensate for the reduced need for additional irrigated acreage.[4] There may also be a role for the Bureau of Reclamation in the burgeoning business of water marketing, which is simply another way of achieving increased water efficiency. This is accomplished by allocating water to the highest bidder (see Anderson 1983, and *U.S. Water News* July 1986). In a true open market the buyer would purchase the water at market value and also cover the cost of transporting the water to its new use. In actuality, there will be incessant political demands for government subsidies to aid in the construction of such transportation facilities.

A third area of future activity is the urgent need to rehabilitate and expand urban water delivery systems. Many older cities, especially in the East and Midwest, are in dire need of new water systems. Some of the pipelines in New York City, for example, are made of wood. To rehabilitate these systems will be an expensive proposition, one sure to create a demand for federal largess. And the cities of the Sunbelt are searching for new sources of water and the means to deliver that water.

Fourth, the water quality issue may ultimately involve agencies such as the Bureau of Reclamation and the Corps of Engineers, whose traditional work has usually focused on problems of water quantity rather than quality. This is a lucrative field for federal construction—$39 billion has already been spent—and is certain to draw interest from these agencies (see GAO Report to the Congress 1986). The Corps of Engineers is already authorized to build water treatment plants. In the West problems associated with ground-water quality and contaminated irrigation runoff create potential new activities for the Bureau of Reclamation.

Fifth, many irrigation projects are plagued by two incessant problems: salinity (one expert called it "the monkey on irrigation's back," quoted in Reisner 1986:479) and siltation. Proposed solutions to these problems include the construction of massive drainage systems, desalination plants (like the $300 million Yuma plant on the Lower Colorado), and siltation reservoirs. The capital investment required for such structural solutions may exceed the original construction costs of the troubled projects.

Finally, interbasin transfer projects are a potential form of future water development. Today, the states that stand to lose water in an interbasin transfer fiercely resist such schemes. The 1986 Water Act forbids the federal government from even studying transfers from the Columbia River Basin and the Great Lakes region without the approval of the affected states' governors. Politicians from these areas see only the loss of water. If the price is right, however, I think they will change their minds. It is ironic that the current trend toward water marketing may increase the political and economic feasibility of interbasin transfers by allowing the price of water to rise to market levels. When regions such as the Pacific Northwest or the Great Lakes can sell their water the same way Texas sells oil or Wyoming sells coal, then their resistance may give way to active encouragement of massive transfer projects.

I do not think these new issues will come totally at the expense of the traditional iron triangle; rather, they may even enhance its position through increased potential for cross-program logrolling: the easterner and northerner who traditionally opposed water projects can be "bought" with a program to renew urban water systems in that area. Environmentalists will favor government construction projects that solve water pollution problems, increase the efficiency of water systems, produce clean energy, or aid fish and wildlife (an environmental pork barrel??). Urbanites in the West will favor conservation projects that increase the availability of water for municipal, industrial, and recreational uses. Thus there is tremendous potential for vote-trading across these programs; in short, a classic distributive solution may occur.

These new areas of endeavor will require the water development iron triangle to adapt to changing circumstances. If the past is an indicator, the triangle has proven to be flexible and resilient in the face of opposition (this is especially true for the Corps of Engineers; see Clarke and McCool 1985; Mosher 1986:14). Many attempts have been made through the years to emasculate this triangle. There have been times when presidents interfered, the press and the public took notice, and conflicts flared. But the iron triangle has so far managed to survive, driven by the political dialectic of concentrated benefits and dispersed costs.

A final point concerns the Indians. What impact will this expansion of water-related activities have on Indian tribes? Is it possible that tribes could become another participant in the web of reciprocity? In the past this did not happen because of the Indians' lack of political power; there was no incentive, beyond the occasional "Indian blanket," to include them. By the mid 1970s, however, the political equation in regard to Indians had changed somewhat. The old political imbalance of power appeared to be yielding to new imperatives, which are the focus of the next chapter.

CHAPTER EIGHT

The Politics of Contemporary Indian Water Rights

My boy is 8 years old; he walks around saying Winters Doctrine. We understand that.

—Ernest Stevens, Vice President,
National Congress of American
Indians, 1974 (U.S. Congress, Senate 1974:67)

Introduction

In the previous chapter I argued that the non-Indian water development iron triangle still retains much of its political influence. However, water policy is changing, and if the triangle is to survive it must also change. This will mean that new missions and an expanded list of priorities will have to compete in this political environment. This has important implications for Indian water development. Can they compete in this new environment? Can Indian water development become one of the new priorities? Can Indian tribes become part of an expanded network of logrolling that encompasses diverse types of water development? To a certain extent this depends on whether Indian tribes can develop their political power.

In the past the predominant political force in Indian policy was a weak iron triangle that attempted to accommodate the interests of both Indians and non-Indians through a two-stage system of allocation. Indian resources, principally land and water, were allocated to non-Indians. At the same time, the Indians were compensated with expensive government welfare programs. This uneasy peace broke down when the "modern" era of Indian rights began to have an impact in the early 1960s. It became increasingly difficult to separate Indians from their land and water as a result of the growing political power of Indian rights. At the same time, prob-

226

lems with water scarcity in the West and attacks on the water development establishment in Washington created a crisis atmosphere among many non-Indians. In short, the stakes were high and competition and conflict intensified. Both sides grew adamant in their demands.

In this chapter I will examine the politics of Indian water in this context of increased demands and increasing conflict. The emphasis on politics underlines the shift from solely a litigious strategy, which had been the predominant arena of Indian water rights for seventy years, to an expanded effort involving negotiation, bargaining, and trade-offs. Negotiation is not a new idea. Chapter 6 described the Navajo experience with negotiations concerning the Navajo Generating Station and the Navajo Indian Irrigation Project. At about the same time the Utes of the Uintah and Ouray reservations also negotiated a deal with the federal government. In return for the promise of a water project in the future the Utes signed an agreement in 1965 that deferred their water rights until after 2010. This agreement was necessary to establish sufficient water rights for the Central Utah Project. In both the Navajo and Ute cases the Indians later claimed that the government failed to fulfill its promises. Nevertheless both Carter and Reagan adopted negotiation as an official strategy.

Some things did change by the mid-1970s. The government's new policy of self-determination gave Indian tribes more control over their own affairs. New Indian interest groups—ones that were not composed of only pro-Indian Anglos—began to develop political clout. Several congressional hearings held in the early 1970s brought increased attention to the Indians' water problems. And water policy in general was undergoing changes as well. To some observers and participants it looked as though there might finally be concerted, definitive action on Indian water rights and Indian water development.

Indian Water Rights and the Carter Administration

When Jimmy Carter assumed the presidency, one of his first acts in office was to challenge the firmly entrenched water policy establishment. The president had high hopes of dramatically reforming nearly every aspect of federal water policy. One aspect of that policy was the increasingly intense controversy surrounding western water rights. Widely conflicting claims by Indian tribes, the federal government, and western states were provoking acrimonious political discussion as well as numerous lawsuits and counter suits.

In response to these problems President Carter attempted to institute several reforms in regard to Indian water rights. These proposals were part of the larger program of reforms discussed in the previous chapter which tried to redirect the decision-making process that allocated water and water project expenditures. Thus Indian water rights policy under the Carter administration was inextricably tied to the administration's efforts to modify the entirety of the federal government's water resource development policy. His zeal for new policies diminished over time as he encountered bitter opposition, but there were still several significant developments.

When President Carter began developing a list of projects he wanted to delete or deauthorize, Indian claims were a factor in his decision as to which projects to cut. Four of the projects placed on the original cut list in early February 1977 were recommended for cuts because of, among other problems, conflict with Indian water rights.

For many years two of these projects—the Garrison Unit in North Dakota and the Oahe Unit in South Dakota—have had an impact on Indian reservations in the area. When the Garrison Dam was built in 1953 it flooded one-fourth of the Fort Berthold Indian Reservation. The Bureau of Reclamation wanted to enlarge the project with additional dams and canals that would, according to the Bureau of Reclamation, "entice outdoor recreation enthusiasts from a wide area providing for the Indians an excellent opportunity for concession and other visitor-use services and facilities" (Bureau of Reclamation 4 November 1976:UM–3). The Oahe Reservoir, when first built, flooded 160,889 acres of Indian lands (Lawson 1982:50). Additions called for over 100 miles of canals and more reservoirs that "might provide significant area redevelopment benefits to four nearby Sioux Indian Reservations" (Bureau of Reclamation 4 November 1976:UM–7).

Both of these projects, however, diverted water away from Indian reservations for non-Indian use. The Garrison Unit would irrigate an additional 250,000 acres and the Oahe would add another 190,000 acres, little of it Indian land. For this reason and because of potential environmental disruption, Carter recommended in his 18 April 1977 policy statement that the Oahe be deleted and the Garrison Project be significantly modified (*Presidential Documents* 18 April 1977:557).

The Carter administration viewed the conflict over water rights as an integral part of the larger problems confronting contemporary water policy. As part of his reform efforts Carter authorized a comprehensive study of various water problems to improve "economic efficiency, safety, environmental protection, and fair distribution of project benefits" (*Federal Register* 15 July 1977:36788). The latter item included problems concerning federal and Indian reserved water rights. The issue promised to be as divisive and acrimonious as the fight over project expenditures. An Omaha, Nebraska, newspaper headline read, "Water Rights for Indians Near a Boil" (*Omaha World Herald* 19 May 1977).

It was within this context, and the more widespread furor over the "hit list," that Carter announced his plan to create a Policy Committee that would produce issue papers on various aspects of water policy. The day after the president's announcement, Secretary of Interior Cecil Andrus outlined nine actions that he claimed would lead "toward a comprehensive and realistic national water policy." Among them was a call for the "quantification of Indian water rights and federal reserved water rights" (*Federal Register* 6 July 1977:34564).

Both Indian and non-Indian interests immediately began to apply pressure on the administration, hoping their views would be reflected in the upcoming issue papers (Veeder 1978:6). The tribes worried that their interests would be lumped together with all other federal reservations. In order to appease Indian interests, the secretary of interior appointed the first assistant secretary for Indian Affairs, Forrest Gerard. Non-Indian water users also viewed the Carter proposals with considerable skepticism. They feared that the new policies would increase federal control over water policy at the expense of the states. Secretary Andrus and Policy Committee chairman Guy Martin tried to persuade them that the states would retain control over water (Simms 1980b:11). Carter met with several governors and reiterated his commitment to state control over water: "I want to make clear from the very beginning that there absolutely will be no preemption of state or private prerogatives in the use or management of water. This is not the purpose of the policy at all" (*Presidential Documents* 22 October 1977:1615).

While Carter was assuring the governors that state control over water was in no danger, Assistant Secretary for Indian Affairs Gerard was meeting with Indian leaders, trying to explain that legal principles must always be considered within the context of the political reality of water development:

This situation is a political fact of life which represents the most serious threat to the tribes' ability to secure the water supply to which they are legally entitled. While legally these considerations are irrelevant to the tribe's rights, as a practical matter these competing interests cannot be ignored. They represent the most formidable obstacle against any effort to apply Indian water to beneficial uses for the Indian owners. (Quoted in Fradkin 1981:163)

In essence Gerard was talking about program legitimacy and how it affects implementation. Court-created rights nearly always encounter "formidable obstacles" when they confront statutorily recognized rights.

In 1978 the Carter administration issued a report on Indian water policy. Written by Gerard and others in the Indian Affairs Division of the Department of Interior, the "National Indian Water Policy Review" emphasized three basic objectives: Indian rights protection, inventory and quantification of Indian water, and the development of Indian water resources. This report was one of several "task force option papers" submitted to the president in late 1977 and early 1978. Predictably, expressions of cynicism and concern came from all quarters. Western states voiced fears that Carter was trying to usurp state control despite statements that the administration would not change the existing deference to state water law (*Weekly Report* 4 March 1978:565). The National Governors' Association proposed that federal water rights be adjudicated and administered by state governments to "insure that there is equity and that procedures are prompt and orderly" (*GAO Report to the Congress* 16 November 1978:48–149).

In contrast to the National Governors' Association, the National Congress of American Indians (NCAI) and the National Tribal Chairmen's Association (NTCA) issued a press release calling for an entirely different approach. They took issue with a number of statements that appeared in the task force reports. The most important point, however, was the Indians' resistance to quantification—the centerpiece of the Carter proposal. The NCAI/NTCA statement argued, "Quantification of Indian Winters Rights is neither necessary nor desirable at this time. A final determination, made at any given date, is inconsistent with the open-endedness of the right itself" (*GAO Report to the Congress* 16 November 1978:49–50). Obviously the two sides on the issue were still poles apart. After a year of studies, statements, hearings, and reports, very little progress toward a solution had been made.

In 1978 Carter reiterated his support for quantification and negotiation. He directed the Bureau of Indian Affairs to develop a plan to inventory all Indian water within ten years and ordered federal water development agencies to evaluate water projects that would develop Indian water resources once they had been quantified. In an apparent nod to state-vested water rights Carter stated that such development "will be consistent with existing laws, principles, standards and procedures governing water resource development" (*GAO Report to the Congress* 16 November 1978:70–71). The response from some Indian spokesmen was extremely critical. An article appeared in the *Akwesasne Notes,* an Indian newspaper, entitled "Water Negotiations—A New Word for Fraud." Writing in *Wassaja,* Rupert Costo warned that "termination will be the ultimate result of negotiations in which Indians give up their rights piece by piece" (both quoted in an Indian Law Resource Center mimeograph 1981:98). Western states, however, found some solace in the Carter proposals because they did not attack state control. According to the *Congressional Quarterly Weekly Report,* western governors had "scared Carter away from anything but promises for more federal cooperation and assistance in state water management" (10 June 1978:1491).

In 1978 the General Accounting Office examined the problem of Indian and federal water rights and endorsed the president's policy of negotiation and quantification. The Indian response to the report, as expressed by the National Congress of American Indians, urged that the entire report be rejected because it reflected "a process underway in state and federal water policy-making of 'blaming the victim'" (*GAO Report to the Congress* 16 November 1978:99). The NCAI held that the report "place[s] the burden of compromise and loss upon Indian tribes. . . . The conclusions of the report nowhere discuss the fact that the problem has been largely created by federal stimulation and subsidization of non-Indian water use and consumption to the detriment of Indian interests" (p. 101).

Not all tribes were opposed to negotiation, however. In 1978 the Ak-Chin Reservation of Arizona successfully negotiated a settlement that guaranteed the annual delivery of up to 85,000 acre-feet to the reservation in return for a tribal agreement to forfeit all other claims to water under the Winters Doctrine. The Ak-Chin bill and the president's new policy of negotiation/legislation encouraged a number of tribes to consider negotiation as an alternative. The Papago Tribe of Arizona, which had filed suit against all non-Indian water users in the area in 1975, began working with goverrn-ment negotiators in hopes of finding an equitable solution (*Wash-*

ington Post 6 February 1978). In Colorado the Ute Mountain Ute Tribe also expressed an interest in negotiation. Their incentive to negotiate derived in part from their support for the Dolores Project, which was placed on the president's original cut list in February 1977. The tribe supported the project because it would provide water for tribal irrigation (*Denver Post* 2 January 1978).

Successful negotiations over water rights were the exception rather than the rule, however. In most cases the opposing sides were so far apart that negotiation outside of court was nearly impossible. In Montana, for example, the debate over Indian water was particularly bitter. Non-Indians formed two organizations to oppose Indian claims to water, the Citizens Rights Organization (*Billings Gazette* 16 April 1977) and Montanans Opposed to Discrimination (*Billings Gazette* 21 May 1977). Their efforts were supported by the Billings Chamber of Commerce and the town of Hardin, Montana. At the Montana Cattlemen's Association's 1977 convention they passed a resolution calling for the abolition of Indian sovereignty and all Indian water rights (*Billings Gazette* 20 November 1977).

The Indian tribes were also adamant about their rights and formed a coalition to protect them (*Indian Historian* 1979:34). In such an atmosphere the potential for voluntary negotiations was negligible. According to one source, "the Carter Administration hoped to use the Montana situation as a showcase of how their negotiation process would work. However, negotiations broke down, virtually before they had begun, triggering a race to the courthouse" (Indian Law Resource Center 1981:101). Many Indian leaders continued their opposition to legislation and negotiation. One tribal leader summed up the Indian perspective: "We have the President's water policy of quantification and negotiation, the *Akin* case giving the states jurisdiction, the states rushing to their courts. They call this assimilation. I call it annihilation" (quoted in Dellwo 1980:115). Rather than enter into negotiations, most tribes continued to sue for their rights in federal courts. Amid this furor over water rights one small victory was won for the Indians. Congress finally agreed to meet a seventy-three-year-old commitment to transfer 2,640 acres of irrigable land to the Fallon Indian Reservation in Nevada and provide funds for a small irrigation project there (*Indian Affairs* 1979:2).

With few exceptions President Carter failed to resolve the controversy over western water rights. For the most part he did not attain the goals that were proposed at the beginning of his administration. As the new incoming president prepared to take office the situation in regard to Indian water rights had changed very little over the previous four years. A great deal of political maneuvering, planning, and commission studies had taken place, but very few decisions were made that actually allocated water to Indians. The two exceptions were the Ak-Chin bill and the Fallon bill. But both of these reservations are very small (21,840 acres and 8,120 acres, respectively) and the amount of water involved was not large.

Indian Water Rights and the Reagan Administration

Some Indian tribes had high hopes for the new administration. During the 1980 campaign Reagan was asked what he would do about Indian water rights. He responded:

> The best protection of Indian water rights is the perfection of those rights through beneficial usage of the water by Indian people. This can be done with assistance to the tribes and their people for them to develop their energy, agricultural, and other tribal natural resources. (*CERT Report* 21 November 1980)

On the basis of such statements, and because of their disillusionment with Carter, many tribal organizations endorsed Reagan. With the election of Ronald Reagan the search for a solution to western water rights problems intensified. In recent years a number of legislative proposals have been made. These can be classified into two categories: the all-inclusive approach, by which a blanket water rights settlement is applied to all parties in dispute, and the tribe-by-tribe approach, which results in legislation specific to an individual tribe.

ALL-INCLUSIVE SETTLEMENT BILLS

While Reagan and Carter were campaigning for the presidency in 1980 the Western Conference of the Council of State Governments was drafting a legislative proposal entitled the Water Rights Coordination Act. This proposal was similar to previous proposals, such as the 1956 Barrett Bill, that limited federal reserved rights and increased state control over water resources. This bill, like all of its predecessors, never became law. How-

ever, the drive for an all-inclusive legislative settlement act continued. Attention soon shifted to a proposal offered by the Western
Regional Council, a coalition of forty-seven western business interests. The preamble of the bill stated that "comprehensive management by the western states of the limited water resources and an
early quantification of Indian water rights are essential to forestall
a water crisis" (Western Regional Council 1981:1). Indian reaction
to the proposed bill was swift and scathing. Alberta Tippeconnic
of the Intertribal Council of Arizona stated, "It's a racially moti-
vated bill and it's unconscionable in terms of Indian affairs and
Indian people" (*CERT Report* 29 January 1982:11). The executive
committee of the National Congress of American Indians rejected
the bill out of hand, and John Echohawk of the Native American
Rights Fund called it "a confiscation of the Winters Doctrine"
(*CERT Report* 8 February 1982:14).

In response to these attempts to pass water rights settlement
acts, the National Congress of American Indians formulated a
position paper in 1981 entitled "National Resources, Litigation and
Trust Responsibilities." The sections of the position paper that
dealt with water rights made specific recommendations for congressional action. First, NCAI asked Congress to amend the
McCarran Amendment to exempt Indian water rights from state
court adjudication. Second, the paper asked for immediate approval of tribal water codes. Third, it called for a moratorium, if
requested by a tribe, on all non-Indian development that antici-
pates the use of water that may be subject to Winters Doctrine
rights. The paper also called for more funding for Indian irrigation
projects and supported the resolution of water rights conflicts on
a tribe-by-tribe basis rather than the all-inclusive approach expressed in bills such as the one proposed by the Western Regional
Council (National Congress of American Indians, 1981:Sec. 1).

SETTLEMENT BILLS FOR INDIVIDUAL TRIBES

The NCAI's call for tribe-by-tribe negotiation was
taken seriously by the Papago Reservation, the second largest reservation in the United States. Approximately one-third of the
Papago Reservation's nearly three million acres is considered potentially irrigable (Foster 1978:188). The only dependable source of
water in the area is groundwater, which is rapidly being depleted
by off-reservation uses. In 1975 the tribe filed suit against the City
of Tucson and nearby mines and farms, claiming 160,000 acre-feet

as compensation for depleted groundwater (Civ. No. 75–39 TUC, D. Ariz). There were over 17,000 defendants in the case. The legal and technical questions relevant to the case were enormously complex. It was obvious to all parties that a litigated settlement would take years. In 1978 a committee was formed, called the Water Resources Coordination Committee, to attempt to work out a mutually acceptable bill that would settle the water rights question and eliminate years of uncertainty and costly court battles. This committee was an informal discussion group consisting of the tribe, the Corps of Engineers, the Bureau of Reclamation, and representatives of the defendants. Congressman Morris Udall, from the Tucson area, took an active interest in the negotiations and in 1980 drafted a proposed bill (H.R. 7640). In 1981 hearings on the bill were held and a second draft was introduced (H.R. 4363). A final draft was finally introduced in November 1981 (Roop 1982:8).

Not all members of the Papago Tribe were pleased with the final bill. The original draft called for 160,000 acre-feet for the Papagos, the same amount that was claimed in the 1975 lawsuit, but through successive drafts this amount was reduced to 76,000 acre-feet (*Arizona Daily Star* 23 November 1981). Furthermore, the bill specified which districts of the reservation received the water, leaving most of the districts on the reservation without any benefit from the bill. The Papago Tribal Council asked Udall to amend the bill to provide water to an additional reservation district and to supply financing to put the water to use (*Papago Runner* 20 January 1982:8).

The final bill introduced in 1982 did not add more reservation districts, but it did provide funds for development. Titled the Southern Arizona Water Rights Settlement Act, the bill guaranteed annual delivery of 76,000 acre-feet of water to the Papago Reservation from a variety of sources including the Central Arizona Project and underground aquifers. The bill also directed the secretary of the Department of Interior to build a water delivery system and set up a $15 million trust fund to help the tribe develop an efficient water use system. In return the tribe would drop its lawsuit and abandon all future claims to water. The act passed the House by a substantial margin (311–50) and was approved by the Senate by voice vote two months later (*Weekly Report* 12 June 1982:1404).

The Southern Arizona Water Rights Settlement Act was a major step toward the successful negotiation of water rights conflicts. The bill involved a substantial amount of water in an area suffering from a critical water shortage. Through seven years of negotiations both sides had made compromises and adjustments. In addition, the bill contained the very important stipulation that the Papagos would receive not only water rights but a water project to deliver the tribe's water. In other words, the Papagos would receive wet water, not just paper water. The bill was hailed as an important precedent that could become the model for subsequent water rights negotiations.

President Reagan vetoed the Papago settlement bill. Technically the veto was based on what Reagan called a "serious flaw": "The United States Government was never a party to the negotia- tions. . . . The result of this negotiation was that the United States Government . . . would bear almost the entire financial burden of the settlement at a potential initial cost of $112 million and an annual cost of approximately $5 million" (*Weekly Report* 19 June 1982:1498). It was possible for Reagan to claim that the federal government was never a party to the negotiations because the Water Resources Coordination Committee, where most negotia- tions took place, was an informal body with no expressed authori- zation to negotiate for the federal government. The veto gave the president an opportunity to express his disapproval of the cost of the bill and to push for a rewrite that would shift some of the costs of the bill from federal to state and local sources. In other words, Reagan's cost-sharing approach to water projects was applied to the Papago project as well.

Negotiators went back to work on the bill, this time making sure that the federal government's presence was official. A new settle- ment was worked out which shifted some of the costs to local governments and businesses. Under the new arrangement the federal government will pay only $5.25 million of the $15 million trust fund. Local government and businesses will pay an equal amount, and trust fund interest, which will accumulate until 1990 when the project is finished, will provide the rest (*National Journal* 30 October 1982:1843).

CURRENT POLICIES AND STRATEGIES

While debate over the Papago bill, the Western Re- gional Council bill, and other proposed legislation was taking place, the Reagan administration was attempting to establish a general policy on western water rights. During the first year of his presidency Reagan sent his Secretary of Interior James Watt on a "goodwill" trip to western states to reassure them that the admin- istration fully supported state control over water rights. Watt stated that the Reagan water policy would defer to "the historic primacy of state water management" (*New York Times* 12 September 1981:1).[1] The Reagan administration further clarified its position on western water rights with the announcement of a new policy on 14 July 1982. Secretary Watt explained that the administration favored negotiation as the preferred method of resolving the numerous Indian water rights lawsuits: "President Reagan has forcefully indicated his concern that these suits—which have stalled essential economic progress in both Indian and non-Indian areas—be settled quickly through negotiated settlements that are equitable to all parties" (*Decision* 1982:1).

While the Reagan administration was formulating its position on western water rights, the nation's Indian tribes were refining theirs. At a 1981 Symposium on Indian Water Policy sponsored by the American Indian Lawyer Training Program, a variety of tribal spokesmen and interested individuals convened to discuss strategy and approaches. The emphasis of the convention was on the politics of formulating water policy, which reflects the tribes' growing political sophistication and awareness of alternatives to litigation. The announcement for the symposium made this point quite clear: "It is imperative that Indian water rights move from legal abstraction to actual beneficial use. . . . Indians face new problems requiring fresh approaches to formulating tribal water policies" (American Indian Lawyer Training Program 1981). Peter MacDonald, Navajo tribal chairman, spoke on the first day of the conference and argued for an aggressive approach emphasizing resource development and tribal political strength:

> There are alot of lawyers here. You lawyers shouldn't have one-track minds. Don't just sell us rights and lawsuits. We can't drink them. . . . And you water experts. Don't just sell us long-term plans. Because the water won't be there unless we can find a way to use our water now. . . . I am interested in claims awards. I am interested in water. I am interested in survival. (Indian Water Policy Symposium 1982:122)

MacDonald called for the establishment of national or regional tribal water cooperatives that could pool Indian water rights and other bargaining advantages in order to put water to beneficial use. In essence, tribes would become involved in water marketing, which would secure their rights through beneficial use and also provide much-needed tribal revenues (Folk-Williams 1982:25). The American Indian Lawyer Training Program has continued to offer annual forums to discuss Indian water rights. One of the main topics on the agenda in 1982 was "The Politics of Indian Water," which stressed "concerted political action on the part of tribes nationally and regionally to counter non-Indian pressure" (*CERT Report* 23 July 1982:21).

By 1982 the Reagan administration had convinced some tribes that negotiation was the way to go, but other Indians still distrusted the negotiating process. In many cases the two sides in the dispute are still so far apart that negotiation is nearly impossible. Estimates vary as to how many tribes are seriously interested in negotiation. William Horn, deputy undersecretary at the Department of Interior, stated in 1982 that only three of fifty-five lawsuits are "ripe for settlement" (*National Journal* 30 October 1982:1842). Hank Meshorer, chief of the Justice Department's Division of Indian Resources, and Charles Corke, chief of the BIA's Water and Land Resources Division, agreed that only a small percentage of the Indian water rights cases are "ripe" for negotiated settlement (Meshorer interview 15 June 1984; Corke interview 12 June 1984). A more optimistic estimate claims that a dozen water rights disputes are now being seriously negotiated (Clinton 1985:4).

The Indians' reluctance to negotiate can probably be traced to their fears that legislation will be passed that forces the tribes to negotiate within certain restrictions. Two possible scenarios could occur, depending upon the order in which negotiation and legislation take place. In one scenario, negotiations would precede legislation; each side would participate in an effort to protect its own interests while seeking a mutually acceptable accommodation. Once an agreement is made, legislation would be passed that formally recognized the agreement and made it binding. The Papago negotiations are an example of this scenario. Most tribes would probably not object to negotiations in that kind of situation in which all decisions, including the timetable and ground rules of the negotiating process, are determined by mutual consent.

In the second possible scenario legislation would precede negotiation. The legislation would set up time limits and restraints on negotiations and force tribes to reach negotiated settlements or accept a government-imposed quantification of Indian water. This approach is evident in a statement by the Western Regional Council:

> Indian interests have suggested that water rights conflicts can be resolved through negotiation and settlement. The Western Regional Council believes it would be a serious mistake to expect that nego-

tiated settlements are realistically possible in very many situations. . . . The impracticality of successfully negotiating conflicting claims between thousands of claimants (state, Indian, and non-Indian) is evident. . . . The Western Regional Council believes that the most practical and most sensible way to resolve the water rights controversy in the West is through comprehensive legislation. (*Decision* 1982)

Some of the concern voiced by Indian leaders appears to be the result of fears that the second scenario is what policymakers have in mind when they talk of legislation and negotiation.

All-inclusive legislation is not the only form of potential coercion that Indians fear. There is also concern that funding will be administered in such a way as to reward those tribes that negotiate and punish those that prefer litigation. An internal memo from the Department of Interior candidly discusses this approach:

If . . . a tribe is involved in litigation but is not interested in negotiation, then that tribe would not be rated as a high priority for water planning funding. . . . Thus, even though we maintain that negotiation is voluntary, the fact that we fund those tribes that are interested in negotiations earlier than those that are not could be viewed as blackmail by those who are not interested in negotiations. (Undated, about 1982, "Water Resource . . .")

The Reagan administration has made it clear that tribes willing to negotiate will receive additional funding. This policy prompted a spokesperson for the NCAI to complain that Indian tribes were being forced into "a box canyon of negotiation" (U.S. Congress, Senate 1985a:44). Hence an important factor in any negotiations is the extent to which participants are "under the gun" of time or funding constraints, or potential confiscation of their rights, if the negotiations fail.

The need for strictly voluntary negotiation has become increasingly evident. When the bill proposed by the Western Regional Council failed to get introduced in Congress and met fierce Indian resistance, the council proposed that both sides sit down and discuss acceptable alternatives. As a result the council met with representatives from the Western Governors' Policy Office and three major Indian groups. In an unprecedented show of agreement these groups wrote a letter to then Secretary of Interior James Watt outlining a strategy based on "consensual negotiated settlements" while at the same time recognizing that "some parties may seek to resolve their differences by litigation or legislation and we do not preclude those choices" (Western Regional Council 1982).

The Reagan administration now uses the term "consensus negotiations" to describe its approach (Clinton 1985:1).

The continuing interest in negotiated settlements has generated a great deal of activity on the part of interest groups and state governments. The Western Governors' Policy Office officially endorsed negotiation. The State of Montana established a Reserved Water Rights Compact Commission, which recently negotiated a settlement with the Fort Peck Reservation. Other western states have begun keeping active files on ongoing negotiations and lawsuits. And the Western States Water Council recently completed an extensive report on Indian water rights for the Western Governors' Association (1984). The report deals at length with the relative costs of litigation as opposed to negotiation.

At present the Reagan administration, through its Federal Water Policy Advisory Group, is vigorously pursuing the negotiation strategy. The effort is proceeding slowly, but at least Indians and non-Indians are discussing issues in a context other than the adversarial confrontation of the courtroom. If negotiation is to succeed, it appears that three factors will play an important role.

First, Indian tribes may be more willing to negotiate if they perceive the courts—especially the Supreme Court—to be hostile to their claims. For many years the high court was supportive of Indian claims, but some recent cases have been critical of an expansive Winters Doctrine and were clearly setbacks for Indian tribes. This trend began with the Akin decision in 1976 (*Colorado River Water Conservation District v. U.S.*), which permitted state court adjudication of Indian water rights. In *U.S. v. New Mexico* (1978) the court ruled that reserved rights could not be applied to "secondary uses." In 1983 the Supreme Court heard three Indian water rights cases, and decided all three against the Indians (*Arizona v. California, Arizona et al. v. San Carlos Apache Tribe*, and *Nevada v. U.S.*). It is difficult to overestimate the importance of these cases; they signal a new, more restrictive approach to the Winters Doctrine. The 1984 report by the Western States Water Council noted that these opinions may "signify a flat rejection of the theory that Indian water rights were open-ended and susceptible to expansion at any time" (1984:15). It is apparent that the contemporary Court is demonstrating a greater concern for state water law and the need for certainty and finality in the determination of water rights (see Coursen 1984:699–701). Not all recent court decisions have been hostile to Indian claims (see *U.S. v. Adair* 1983 and *Colville Confederated Tribes v. Walton* 1981), and no one expects a wholesale reversal of the principle of federal reserved water rights, but Indian tribes may be less inclined to use litigation as the *only* method of obtaining water rights.

The effectiveness of the negotiation strategy will also be influenced by how well existing negotiated settlements are implemented. The Ak-Chin settlement appeared destined for trouble when the Reagan administration tried to cut funding for implementation. Kenneth Smith, Assistant Secretary for Indian Affairs, stated that failure "to pursue the timely funding of the Ak-Chin project would cause a breach of the May 20, 1980 contract and would seriously damage our ability to negotiate with the tribal leadership in the future" (*CERT Report* 7 October 1981:9–11). When it became apparent that insufficient funding for Ak-Chin could endanger the administration's negotiation strategy, the necessary funds began to flow and all contractual obligations were met. Similarly, funding for the Papago settlement has allowed the project to proceed ahead of schedule.

Quite the opposite situation has occurred with the Navajo Indian Irrigation Project (NIIP). Despite this project's status as the first negotiated settlement, it has been consistently underfunded. Although it was authorized concurrently with the San Juan-Chama, a non-Indian project, the Navajo Project has never received commensurate appropriations (blunt testimony to the BIA's inability to compete for water project funding). The San Juan-Chama was completed ahead of schedule and began diverting water in 1972. In contrast, by 1979, the year the Navajo Project was supposed to be finished, only three of eleven irrigation blocks were ready, and the completion date was moved back to 1987 (Sombrero 1982:9–12). By 1986 the project was still only half-done, and President Reagan has made a concerted effort to defer funding altogether. The administration claimed that the Navajo Agricultural Products Industry (NAPI), which is responsible for operating the project, is not sufficiently competent to handle the job. A study of NAPI concluded that it was indeed competent, but the administration still deferred funding in its 1986 and 1987 budget requests (see U.S. Congress, Senate 1985:15).

The Ute Tribe of Utah, which signed a negotiated settlement in 1965, has also complained of problems. Recently the tribe asked that negotiations be reopened because the 1965 agreement "has failed to provide those significant benefits to the Ute Tribe which were the cornerstone of the tribe's agreement to relinquish 60,000 acre feet of water annually to the CUP" (Wopsock to Clark 14 December 1983).

In short, the track record for existing negotiated settlements is mixed. The Reagan administration has showcased the Ak-Chin and Papago settlements, but the Navajos and Utes appear to be less than satisfied with the results of their respective settlements. Other tribes are keenly interested in the outcome of these cases. As Assistant Secretary Broadbent recently noted, "Tribal leaders are likely to be distrustful. . . . The commitment of Federal resources and money will be real proof to the Indian community of Administration sincerity" (Broadbent memo 18 May 1984).[2]

The third factor that will influence the potential for successful negotiations concerns the willingness of non-Indians to give as well as take. Interior Department officials have noted that "frequently the non-Indian competing water users are not interested in reasonable negotiations" (undated memorandum, about 1982, "Water Resources . . . "). If Indians give up their open-ended claims to water, what will they receive in return? To some tribes the negotiations over water bear a distinct resemblance to the nineteenth-century negotiations over Indian land. To them it appears to be another case of the Anglo disingenuously scheming to get something for nothing. It will be difficult to induce Indians to negotiate without specific guarantees that there is something to be gained—and not just lost—from the process.

An Indian Iron Triangle?

Chapter 5 noted that the BIA, especially its water development program, was experiencing a number of problems that prevented the agency from functioning effectively in an iron triangle. These problems have persisted and some have intensified.

First of all, the BIA's image as an ineffective agency persists. In 1978 the Senate Appropriations Committee attempted to cut the BIA's budget, citing "poor program management" and a "continuing failure to deliver adequate services to the Indian people despite increased funding" (*Weekly Report* 19 August 1978:2185). The following year the committee again complained about "slipshod management" (*Weekly Report* 3 November 1979:2478). The General Accounting Office, Congress' investigative arm, has also been quite critical of the BIA (see *GAO Report to the Congress* 15 February 1978, 1 March 1978, 8 September 1982, and 11 July 1984).

In addition, the agency still suffers from a lack of expertise in the area of water development and water rights. The BIA's ability to do water inventories has been hampered by the agency's "very limited professional water resources staff" (Department of Interior memorandum November 1981:1). Charles Corke, head of the agency's Water and Land Resources Division, noted that in clashes with the Bureau of Reclamation, the BIA is at a disadvantage because of the lack of personnel with expertise in irrigation: "They out-expert us," he explained (Corke interview 12 June 1984).

The second corner of the triangle—interest groups—has also experienced problems in recent years. The Reagan administration eliminated federal funding for Indian advocacy groups that had come to depend on government support. Indians are the poorest subgroup in America, so there is little possibility that they can provide much more financial support. The mood of the general public has also militated against Indian interest groups and their efforts to promote the BIA water development program. Concern for minorities is no longer *de rigueur* among the population at large. And federal programs are viewed more often as problems than as panaceas.

Perhaps most important, the congressional corner of the triangle today is weak to nonexistent. Evidence for this can be seen by examining the relationship between the president's budget requests and the congressional response to it. In an iron triangle the expectation is that if the president tries to cut funding, Congress will respond by passing an appropriation bill substantially larger than the president's request. This is typical of what has happened in recent years to the federal water development program. In the case of the BIA, however, this relationship is markedly different. During Carter's term every presidential request was *higher* than the amount actually passed by Congress. In other words, the president, not Congress, was the primary source of support for BIA spending. And Carter was not overly generous, especially in regard to water; his last budget provided so little money for the operation and maintenance of Indian irrigation projects that the BIA's budget justification admitted that "proper maintenance will be delayed resulting in deteriorating systems" (U.S. Congress, House 1981b:299). In the case of President Reagan, the requests have been low and there has been limited effort on the part of Congress to raise them.

These problems are reflected in the agency's recent budgets. Table 18 provides an overview of recent funding for the BIA as a whole, its rights protection activities, and its water development program. These data indicate several important trends. First, spending for Indian rights protection (which includes all Indian rights issues, including water) has not increased in recent years despite "the explosive growth in conflicts involving Indian water

TABLE 18

BUREAU OF INDIAN AFFAIRS APPROPRIATIONS, 1975–1986
(in thousands of dollars, rounded)

Year	Rights Protection[1]	Irrigation[2]	Total BIA[3]
1975	3,177	32,680	795,456
1976	4,265	38,760	747,088
1977	9,021	36,003	804,648
1978	12,556	36,727	919,508
1979	15,184	38,718	1,053,690
1980	19,783	65,061	1,022,807
1981	16,039	41,929	1,233,125
1982	18,516 (est.)	49,076	1,004,737
1983	18,248 (est.)	32,219	1,186,833
1984		34,668	1,014,325
1985	19,384	43,660	1,086,849
1986	18,237 (est.)	30,346	1,049,403

Source: U.S. Budget, 1977–1986

[1] Litigation support, attorney's fees, and unresolved rights issues.

[2] Operation and maintenance, and construction.

[3] Total funding for the BIA; rights protection and irrigation are subsumed under this, in addition to all other BIA activities.

claims" (U.S. Congress, House 1985:476). Second, funds for irrigation construction, operation, and maintenance grew during the Carter years but have declined steadily under the Reagan administration. For the past two years the president proposed that *no* money be spent on Indian water development. Congress increased this amount, but only to half what it was in 1980. If the success of negotiations depends on the ability of the government to offer Indians water projects as an inducement to give up Winters Doctrine rights, then spending patterns will have to change.

Conclusion

The last nine years have witnessed a number of important developments in the area of Indian water rights and water

politics. The events described in this chapter culminate in two
trends that I believe will play significant roles in the future. The
first concerns the changing concept of federal reserved rights and
how it is handled by policymakers. The decision-making environment for Indian water rights has been expanded to include a political context in addition to the traditional judicial context. It is
important to note that the conflict over Indian water rights has not
moved *from* the courthouse *to* the bargaining table; there is a record
number of lawsuits being litigated at the present time. Rather, the
search for solutions has been expanded to include both of these
avenues. Future willingness to rely on political negotiations will
depend upon perceptions of the relative advantages of these two
avenues.

Despite all this activity, the ambiguity of the reserved rights
concept has managed to survive. The Winters Doctrine, after eighty
years, hundreds of law review articles, and thousands of cases,
still "abounds with unanswered questions" (Meyers and Tarlock
1980:233). This creates something of a paradox. The great value of
the Winters Doctrine to Indians today is its open-endedness. It is
so vague that a nearly limitless variety of claims can be filed under
it. In that sense uncertainty is the tribes' greatest weapon. But the
nebulous quality of the doctrine may also be its Achilles' heel. The
doctrine lacks definitive substance. Therefore one can often argue
that it does not apply, and no one can point to a specific clause or
requirement that proves, beyond doubt, otherwise. This gives the
doctrine an ethereal quality and permits detractors to claim, for
example, that it is "rooted in legal fiction" (Simms 1980a:72). Similarly, the National Water Users Association talks of "Indian
claims," refusing to call them rights recognized under law. Justice
Brennan described Indian water rights as "ubiquitous" (*Colorado
River Water Conservation District v. U.S.* 1976:811), but if they are
everywhere, it can be argued that they are nowhere.

This is not to argue that the Winters Doctrine is meaningless or
without impact. On the contrary, it has functioned effectively as a
core around which Indian claims, hopes, and activity have re-
volved. In recent years, as some tribes moved into the political
arena of negotiation and legislation, the Winters Doctrine became
an important political tool. Indian tribes have always been at a
disadvantage in terms of political resources, but the Winters Doctrine helped to change this imbalance. The vague, open-ended
nature of Winters Doctrine rights, the threat of endless litigation,
and the uncertainty created by the doctrine are political bargaining
chips that can be used by Indian tribes in negotiations over water

and water projects. But this "massively destabilizing" (Bloom 1986:142) uncertainty carries a price. If the Court is truly becoming hostile to reserved water rights, the nebulous nature of the doctrine will provide many opportunities to narrow its applicability without necessitating a wholesale reversal and repudiation.

Another factor that will play an important role in the future is funding for Indian water development and water rights. Hank Meshorer, chief of the Indian Resources Division of the Justice Department, made this point recently: "It really comes down to a matter of money; the federal government is going to have to spend a lot of money" (interview 15 June 1984). Kneese and Brown phrase the problem more generally but arrive at the same conclusion: "Since society created the dispute [between Indian and non-Indian water users], society will have to pay at least part of the cost of settlement" (1981:86). It is unclear what kind of solutions will finally be worked out, but every conceivable avenue looks expensive. If negotiation becomes more common, it may require the construction of more Indian water projects. Frank Ducheneaux, aide to Congressman Morris Udall, stated that "the issue is development. Indians don't have the money and the government won't spend it" (interview 14 June 1984).

Even if litigation remains the primary mode of conflict resolution, the costs could be staggering (see Western States Water Council 1984:98–99). The average cost of an Indian water rights suit to the BIA was recently estimated at $3 million. One of the greatest limitations to state court adjudication is cost: the states simply cannot afford the prolonged and complex trials. Some states have spent so much on state court adjudication (Wyoming spent $10 million) that they may have to return to federal court just to cut expenses. The tribes are also suffering funding problems because of the cost of lawyers. Unwilling in some cases to trust the Justice Department, some tribes have hired their own attorneys, but this has proven to be very expensive.

These new developments have important political implications for the role of iron triangles. To an increasing extent the politics of Indian water rights is redistributive (Lowi 1964) in nature. There is a high degree of conflict; the outcome is perceived to be zero-sum; and the costs in terms of lost water are quite concentrated. Furthermore, there is a very real sense of "class" conflict that pits an impoverished racial minority against a dominant socioeconomic majority. Iron triangles are most adept at making distributive policy, so in this case the possibility of the formation of a new iron triangle including Indians is remote. This does not mean iron triangles will not be involved. Quite the contrary; the non-Indian water development iron triangle is a principal participant. But it will be extremely difficult to solve the Indian/non-Indian conflict over water simply by including Indians in an expanded network of cross-program logrolling.

Although the political environment has changed considerably in the last decade, some recurrent themes from an earlier era remain. Congress is still unable to pass a law recognizing the existence of federal reserved water rights. As a result, the Winters Doctrine still lacks the program legitimacy of a statutory law. Yet Congress has also steadfastly refused to emasculate the doctrine through legislation. In Congress both sides still apparently have the political strength to veto each other's more radical proposals. This mutual veto situation developed soon after the *Winters* decision was handed down, and it played an important role in the debates of 1914, the attempts in the 1950s to pass a "water rights settlement act," and the recent rash of bills of a similar nature. Many critical questions are still being left to the courts and administrative agencies. Senator Malcolm Wallop recently complained that "an almost complete lack of national legislation on Indian water rights has hampered the search for a solution" (*New York Times* 20 June 1984:23).

In addition, the century-old deference to state water law remains a powerful factor in the struggle over Indian water rights. This deference continues to dominate the federal government's policy in regard to water allocation, even at times when sincere efforts were made to solve some of the Indians' water problems. It appears that to be politically viable any proposed solution will have to take this into account.

Despite ten years of effort to resolve the conflict, "the cloud of Indian water claims hangs heavy over much of the American West" (Governor Bruce Babbitt of Arizona, quoted in *The New York Times* 8 December 1982:16). According to one estimate, Indian claims may total as much as 45.9 million acre-feet (Western States Water Council 1984:93). In some watersheds, such as the Lower Colorado, these claims are larger than the total amount of water available. But these are *claims*; the reality is that only about 7 percent of the irrigable land on Indian reservations is irrigated, and existing western water supplies are "nearly fully utilized" (Bredehoeft 1984:17). Clearly there will be no easy solutions.

CHAPTER NINE

Conclusion

Great Nations like great men should keep their word.
——Dissenting opinion, Justice Hugo Black,
F.P.C. v. Tuscarora Indian Nation
(1960)

Introduction

This book has examined the tripartite alliances known as iron triangles. Two competing and unequal triangles were investigated, along with an important participant in the policy-making process that was not involved in an iron triangle. This provided both a longitudinal and a latitudinal comparison of how these three policy-making entities reacted to change, conflict, and one another.

Chapter 1 listed four ways that iron triangles can respond to change:

1. The iron triangle temporarily changes in response to ad hoc input from an outside source. When the outside source ceases to apply pressure for change, the iron triangle reverts to its original behavior.
2. New demands that threaten the iron triangle are absorbed into the triangle, usually by offering benefits to potential opponents. The enlarged triangle then meets the needs of the new participants as well as the needs of the original participants. This is similar to what Ripley and Franklin call "major subgovernment adaption" (1984:106).
3. New demands may ultimately result in new iron triangles. These may compete with existing triangles or they may form around a relatively new area of government activity and thus create their own turf. Another possibility is that a new triangle and an established one agree to a truce that demarcates respective territories in order to reduce conflict.

4. Changes in the policy environment and among triangle participants are so great that they destroy the ability of the triangle to
   function, and it ceases to operate.

Relying upon this typology of triangle change, we can discuss how
the Indian triangle, the non-Indian water development iron triangle, and the theoretical concept of iron triangles have changed
in recent years.

The Indian Iron Triangle

The Indian iron triangle, first described by Freeman
in 1956, has disappeared. The relationship between the participants
in this triangle was, even in its heyday, tenuous, potentially conflictual, and often politically ineffectual. An uneasy peace among
various participants broke down when Indians and their allies
began to assert tribal rights to land and water resources. This
effectively dismantled the traditional iron triangle. The general
policy environment and contemporary relations among Indian interest groups, the BIA, and the relevant congressional committees
do not reflect the characteristics outlined in chapter 1. Currently
Indian policy is made through a circular bureau-client relationship
with the following characteristics:

1. There are two principal participants: Indians and their interest
   groups and the BIA. They are bound together through mutual
   dependency.
2. There is a high potential for conflict because the two participants
   compete for control over resources and policy.
3. The policy-making context of this relationship is isolated except
   when it competes with other policy-making entities for scarce
   resources. The issue then becomes a "resource issue," not an
   "Indian issue."
4. Support in Congress is based on individuals, not committees or
   subcommittees, and therefore is sporadic, nonsystematic, and
   dispersed. This creates what is essentially a veto power; it is
   usually strong enough to stop legislation that would do great
   damage to the bureau-client relationship but often too weak to
   push through decisive, innovative legislation. As a result policy
   goals are often based on short-run needs and reflect the temporary alignment of votes at a particular time.
5. Support from outside the primary relationship is diffuse and

conditional. This protects the primary relationship but does not create sufficient political support to compete with organized interests with specific, intense support.

This client-bureau relationship lacks the congressional intimacy and support that typifies the iron triangle, and the issue is too restrictive in scope to use logrolling effectively.

In sum, the story of the Indian triangle is not the saga of the rise and fall of a great and powerful iron triangle. Rather, a weak iron triangle operated with a great deal of difficulty for 120 years. Then, beginning in the 1960s, changes in the Indian community and political goals caused a gradual metamorphosis of the iron triangle into the bipolar relationship just described.

The Non-Indian Water Development Iron Triangle

The non-Indian water development iron triangle has displayed a remarkable degree of tenacity and resiliency. It has responded to change by employing a variety of stratagems to maintain its political influence. Of the four responses outlined earlier, I think the first three apply to this iron triangle.

First, the water iron triangle responded to outside threats and interference in an ad hoc fashion. In some cases the strategy was to "weather the storm" with the assumption that political costs were too great for any president, or his agents, to long resist the demand for distributive policy. This worked with President Eisenhower and many of his predecessors, such as President Cleveland; after a period of presidential interference the politics of water simply returned to business as usual. In other cases the water iron triangle made temporary adjustments during periods of intense scrutiny but after a short time returned to traditional habits. There is evidence of this response during the Carter administration: during the first two years of his presidency Carter fought fiercely with the water iron triangle, forcing it to accept some budget cuts and forgo more project authorizations. But during the latter half of Carter's presidency, when the political costs of his battle against the projects began to weigh heavily against him, he retreated considerably. As a result, the "no new starts" policy was abandoned, and funding again began to rise.

The Reagan administration and the accompanying deficit problems have presented the most severe and sustained test of the water iron triangle's ability to survive. His tenacious opposition to the traditional dependence on federal funding for water projects forced the triangle to accept his reforms, but only after a bitter conflict. It is too early to tell whether his opponents on the issue can once again ride out the storm. In any case, it promises to be a long, hard ride.

A second response to change that has also been employed by the water development iron triangle is the strategy of coopting potential opposition by making it part of the pool of beneficiaries. Both the Corps of Engineers and the Bureau of Reclamation have proven adept at "buying" the opposition. The Bureau of Reclamation, when faced with resistance from project farmers, ultimately agreed to a large subsidy. When easterners resisted, reclamation supporters agreed to support eastern corps projects. When private landowners resisted government water subsidies to settlers on the public domain, the reclamation program was extended to include private land as well. In more recent years the bureau has built wildlife sanctuaries and recreation facilities. The corps has also embraced potential enemies, building fish ladders to assuage the fishing industry, and initiating an environmental mitigation program to ameliorate criticism from that quarter (the 1986 Water Act set up an Office of Environmental Policy within the corps). These are just a few examples, but they demonstrate an ability to accommodate potential adversaries and adapt to changing circumstances.

The third response to change involves the creation of new iron triangles to accommodate new demands. Initially this is what happened when the Reclamation Service was created. The Corps of Engineers was viewed as an agent of primarily southern and eastern development, and westerners wanted a program for arid states. But the fortunes of these two agencies have been so intermixed politically that it is now difficult to conceptualize them as completely separate iron triangles. Their union of political necessity was born with the debate over the original Reclamation Act, and a web of mutually beneficial logrolling has enveloped both of them ever since. Their fortunes coalesced even further when they expanded their missions into overlapping areas and were funded in the same appropriations bill.

These responses to change indicate that the water iron triangle is not a static organization. Such triangles thrive on stability, but in some situations stability can best be preserved by accepting a modicum of change. Whether the water iron triangle can survive the present challenge remains to be seen. I have argued that it is still politically strong, although others have offered persuasive arguments to the contrary. In an era of unprecedented budgetary change it is difficult to tell whether a systemic change has occurred or whether the water iron triangle is simply riding out another storm. If it is the former, then the fourth response to change—the demise of the triangle—may occur.

The Changing Concept of Iron Triangles

This study of both a strong and a weak iron triangle offers a number of insights that may be generalized to triangles operating in other policy arenas. First, there are no "ideal" iron triangles, meaning that none of them always possesses all the characteristics that typify such alliances. The federal water development program is a classic example of a strong, long-lasting iron triangle, but it has never been totally autonomous, it has at times been unstable, it has experienced considerable conflict, and the general policy environment is occasionally less than cordial. Clearly the iron triangle concept is only an approximation of reality.

Second, iron triangles have an impressive capacity to adapt to changing circumstances. The mutually beneficial nature of the triangular relationship creates an inducement for participants to do whatever is necessary in order to continue deriving benefits. In this sense an iron triangle is driven by a fundamentally pragmatic, not ideological, dialectic. However, the case of the Indian iron triangle makes it clear that there are limits to the flexibility of such triangles. There *is* a breaking point at which the inducements to participate in the triangle are no longer sufficiently attractive to maintain a harmonious, close-knit relationship.

Third, in an age of budget austerity, Gramm-Rudman, and changing public attitudes about the role of government, it is legitimate to ask whether the iron triangle and its principal output—distributive policy—are still relevant. Is the age of pork barrel over? For many years scholars have tried to discover why such policies and their supportive alliances exist. Several scholars have concluded that democracies based on local representation will inefficiently overspend when it comes to allocating government largess to specific locales (Buchanan and Tullock 1962:709; Weingast, Shepsle, and Johnsen 1981:658). Brian Barry argued that pork barrel was the result of a need for unanimity and agreement among elected representatives (1965:250–256, 317–318). Others hold that the proliferation of iron triangles and the popularity of distributive

policy are the result of a variety of system characteristics, rang-
ing from the sheer size and growth of government (Clark 1981:
516), the dichotomy of authorization and appropriation processes
(Peters 1984:232), the fragmentation of power (Long 1962; Meier
1985:10) to the "routine functioning of a pluralist system" (Bender
and Moe 1985:772). It appears that as long as our democratic form
of government is responsive to local pressures, even when they
conflict with national goals, there will be an inducement to form
iron triangles and give people what they want. As Shepsle and
Weingast point out, "pork, in various forms, will always serve as
part of the legislator's response to his voter's retrospective question, 'What have you done for me lately?'" (1981:110).

Water Politics, Water Rights, and the Future

The foregoing discussion is concerned with the con-
ceptual utility of the iron triangle configuration. It is not a question
that is lost in theory and abstraction; iron triangles have a very real
and direct impact on water politics and water rights.

In the case of the federal water development program, the future
offers a critical challenge to the makers of water policy. Indeed,
one senator argues that "our nation is in a water crisis right now"
(*U.S. News and World Report* 18 March 1985:67). By one estimate
the nation's water infrastructure is in need of construction and
rehabilitation that will cost $274 billion (see Grigg 1985:55). It is not
surprising, then, that a congressman would conclude that "at the
core of all these problems is money" (*U.S. News and World Report*
18 March 1985:67). Yet it is a mistake to dismiss water development
problems simply as a function of the pork barrel ethic; numerous
federal water projects clearly are not, and there is still widespread
disagreement as to what constitutes pork barrel and whether it is
actually counterproductive. In the meantime federal water law
remains "cumbersome, archaic, confused, filled with contradic-
tions, awkward, uncertain, and on rare occasions, inspired toward
reform" (Andrews and Sansone 1983:130).

Because of the laws of nature, future water policy will have its
greatest impact on the arid West. Richard Lamm, past governor of
Colorado, has written, "In the future of the West, nothing . . . will
be as critical as the nature and direction of federal water policy"
(Lamm and McCarthy 1982:202). Paul Bloom writes that "many of
the western states . . . have priority lists of water resource projects

for which federal construction assistance is considered indispensable" (1986:145).

The future of water in the West is more than just a question of funding, however. The conflict between the Winters Doctrine and the Prior Appropriation Doctrine raises questions of equity and justice. In the words of the Krulitz Opinion, "federal water rights are somewhat at war with each other" (1979:554). The roots of these policies are buried deep in past government decisions. In effect the government has given the water away twice: once through the states and once through the federal courts. More water has been legally allocated than is available.

The Winters Doctrine, based only on case law and promulgated by a politically weak iron triangle, has had limited impact in terms of the amount of water actually diverted. In contrast, deference to state prior appropriation law has been the predominant policy of the federal government. The inequality of these two doctrines was exacerbated by the need for diversion and storage of water; in an arid land the right to water is usually meaningless unless the water can be delivered and applied. This requires water development. In essence the Prior Appropriation Doctrine was applied to Indian reservations in a de facto manner. For the most part water rights in the West have been determined not by abstract legal principles but by diversion, possession, and use.

For Indians, justice on this issue involves more than just the economic value of contested water. Water has become a symbol to Indians of their determination to remain Indian and preserve their traditional homelands. There is also a compensatory notion involved: Indians have often been mistreated (that is a truism), and the water issue presents an opportunity for the white man finally to live up to his promises—in this case the promise of *Winters.* By helping Indians obtain water the government can assuage some of the bitterness caused by past injustice.

The Indians' complaints of past injustices are well founded, and water development is one way to ameliorate past wrongs. But justice for a few is not justice. Whatever the outcome of the conflict over water, it will have a pervasive impact on many non-Indians. The government promised Indians that the small remnants of their traditional lands—reservations—would not be taken from them, including the water that gave them life and value. The government also encouraged millions of settlers to move West and to take up residence, and it clearly sanctioned their water rights. A solution that confiscates water from Anglos in order to meet the government's obligation to Indians simply creates a new set of victims.

The brief for the appellants in the *Winters* case makes this point succinctly:

> In the case at bar, the controversy is between the Government and the Indians on one side, and the settlers on the other: settlers who, in good faith, accepted the grant of the Government, settled upon and reclaimed these lands, at a great expense, and established their homes and civilized communities in that country. The Courts should not construe that agreement [the treaty with the Indians] by extending or limiting the meaning of the language used, to deprive these pioneer citizens of the fruits of their labor, destroy their homes and make their farms barren wastes. (*Winters v. U.S.*, brief for appellants 1908:125)

In short, to bring justice to all concerned the government must provide water or somehow compensate those who have been injured by the lack of water. This returns us to a previous point; the solution will be expensive. It will require more than just pork barrel water policies. And it will test our commitment to justice.

Epilogue: Fort Belknap

Many of the problems and conflicts discussed throughout this book continue to plague the Assiniboine and Gros Ventre Tribes of the Fort Belknap Indian Reservation. Their irrigation project, begun in 1903, is still not finished. And according to a recent draft report by the Interior Department's inspector general, the portion of the project that *was* constructed is "in an advanced state of deterioration" (Inspector General 1985:1). Although the project is supposed to irrigate over 10,000 acres, only about 5,000 are actually producing a crop. Nine project units have been abandoned altogether.

For years the tribes pressured the BIA to obtain the funding necessary to complete the project, but to no avail. In frustration the tribe went directly to Congress and asked for an appropriation. With the help of Senator Melcher, a bill passed in 1985 that authorized $3 million for additional project construction. But before most of the money could be spent the inspector general filed a draft report that severely criticized the project and recommended freezing the funds until further studies could be completed. The BIA agreed with that recommendation even though the project had been thoroughly reviewed by a BIA-funded study in 1976. The inspector general's draft report, and the resulting interaction between the BIA, the tribes at Fort Belknap, and the Interior Department, pinpoint some basic managerial problems in the Indian irrigation program.

The BIA still has problems producing credible data. The inspector general charged that the tribe's request for funding "was not based upon current or accurate cost data" (Inspector General 1985:2). Although the questionable data were prepared by the BIA, the tribes got the blame because they were the party that presented the funding request to Congress. There are other problems as well. For example, the tribal chairman recently wrote to Senator Melcher and explained that the BIA had "erroneously put forth" incorrect budget totals (G. Snell to J. Melcher 4 November 1985). In a related matter a project employee told me that the acreage figures for the project have not been updated since the 1950s.

The agency also appears to have trouble responding in a timely fashion; the inspector general's draft report asked for a response from the agency by September 1985. A prompt response might have prevented the interruption of funding for the project, but the BIA failed to respond. In May 1986 the assistant secretary for Indian Affairs wrote to the inspector general and noted, "Regretfully, the Bureau failed to supply a formal response to the draft report, and . . . failed to provide a reporting to your office and the Senate Committee [on Interior and Insular Affairs]" (Swimmer to Inspector General 2 May 1986:1). The problem was not entirely the fault of the BIA, however; the position of assistant secretary for Indian Affairs was vacant for much of that time, and as a result no one was available to approve the proper documents.

Recent events have also strained the relationship between the agency and its constituents on the Fort Belknap Reservation. The inspector general noted a "rivalry between the [BIA] agency and the tribes" (1985:7). The tribes and the bureau downplay such problems, but there are other signs of strain. For example, the BIA requested no funds for the Fort Belknap Project for fiscal years 1985, 1986, and 1987. Ostensibly this was because of the problems raised by the inspector general, but according to one source, the agency was incensed by the tribes' decision to go straight to Congress for funding and did not want to recognize that the tribes had succeeded where the bureau had failed. It should be noted that soon after the inspector general's draft report was issued, an on-site review of the Fort Belknap Project by an outside irrigation engineering team concluded that the appropriated funds were being spent properly and work on the project should continue (Swimmer to Inspector General 2 May 1986:1).

The age-old problem of project reimbursement has also continued to plague the Fort Belknap Reservation. When the BIA began construction of the irrigation project, it used the tribes' money, but since passage of the Leavitt Act in 1932 the government's policy has been to reimburse tribes for such expenditures. The Fort Belknap tribes never received their reimbursement and have been trying for years to obtain congressional approval for it.

Finally, in 1985, Congress approved a reimbursement bill totaling nearly $500,000, but the deputy assistant secretary for Indian Affairs testified against it, and ultimately the bill was pocket-vetoed by President Reagan.

Another continuing problem concerns the relationship between the Fort Belknap tribes and the Bureau of Reclamation. In 1946 the BIA and the Bureau of Reclamation signed an agreement providing that one-seventh of the natural flow of the Milk River stored behind Fresno Dam would be allocated to the Fort Belknap Reservation. The tribes were not a party to the agreement and have never accepted the Bureau of Reclamation's interpretation of it. One tribal member called the Fresno pact "the agreement that broke the tribe's back; a conspiracy between the BIA, the Bureau of Reclamation, and the Milk River Project water-users." Another called it "a confiscation of Winters Doctrine rights." In the water-short years of 1983–1985, the interpretation of the Fresno Agreement became critical when, in mid-irrigation season, the Bureau of Reclamation determined that the tribe had received its allotment of water and ordered its floodgates closed. In 1985 the tribes filed suit against the Department of Interior, alleging that the Bureau of Reclamation's accounting procedures were unfair and that the Secretary of Interior had failed to fulfill his trust obligation to protect the tribes' reserved water rights. The case was dropped when heavy rains relieved the water shortage and the tribe ran short of funds for continuing litigation (the BIA refused to provide funds for the suit).

The Bureau of Reclamation maintains that its accounting procedure is based upon an accurate interpretation of the Fresno Agreement. It argues that it has tried to accommodate the Indians, noting that the agency, the tribes, the BIA, and Milk River water users "are continuing to work together to resolve the conflict over the accounting and allocation of water in the Milk River" (Bureau of Reclamation Briefing Paper n.d. about 1986). The bureau also points to its proposed project to augment the flow of the Milk River by building a forty-eight-mile canal from the Missouri River to a point upstream of the Fort Belknap Reservation. It notes that "the Tribes could obtain additional water for future irrigation from the proposed supplemental water supply project if they decide to participate in the project" (Bureau of Reclamation mimeograph "Milk River Water Supply Study," n.d.). The leaders of Fort Belknap are not enthusiastic, however. They point out that after waiting over eighty years, their irrigation project is still not completed. They are doubtful they will ever see water from such a diversion, and if they do, they could not put it to use unless they had a functioning, completed irrigation facility.

Finally, the continuing saga of the Fort Belknap irrigation project reminds us of the frailty of the Winters Doctrine. The inspector general's draft report argued that the cost-benefit ratio of the project was so poor that it was wasteful to complete it. Responding to that recommendation, the assistant secretary rhetorically pondered an alternative approach: "one could philosophically argue a case of breach of faith on the part of the government to let the water right of the birthplace of the Winters Doctrine go by default for failure to use" (Swimmer to Inspector General 2 May 1986:2). The tribes have been encouraged to negotiate, but they remain hostile to the idea: "History tells us that we lose when we negotiate." In the meantime, the tribes await yet another study of their irrigation project to determine if it should be completed.

Appendix

Maps of the Continental United States Showing Federal Indian Reservations* and Major Water Development Projects of the U.S. Bureau of Reclamation and the U.S. Army Corps of Engineers**.

Map 1: Western United States
Map 2: Central United States
Map 3: Eastern United States

Map adapted from two sources: "Surface-Water and Related-Land Resources Development in the United States and Puerto Rico," Geological Survey, U.S. Department of Interior, 1982, and: "Indian Lands and Communities," Bureau of Indian Affairs, U.S. Department of Interior, 1971. Adaptation by Debra Meier, Cartographic Service Lab, Texas A&M University.

Note: Only the larger Indian reservations and water projects have been labeled.

---

*Seneca Lands are shown on the map but they are not federally recognized Indian reservations.

**Levees built by the Army Corps of Engineers are not shown.

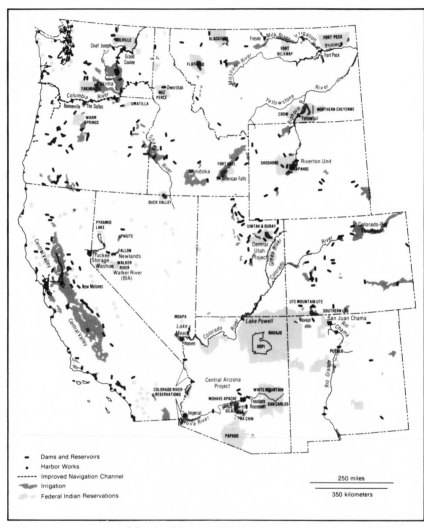

Map 1. Western United States

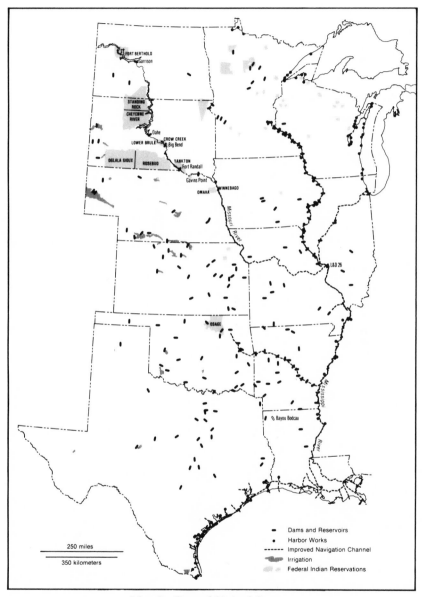

Map 2. Central United States

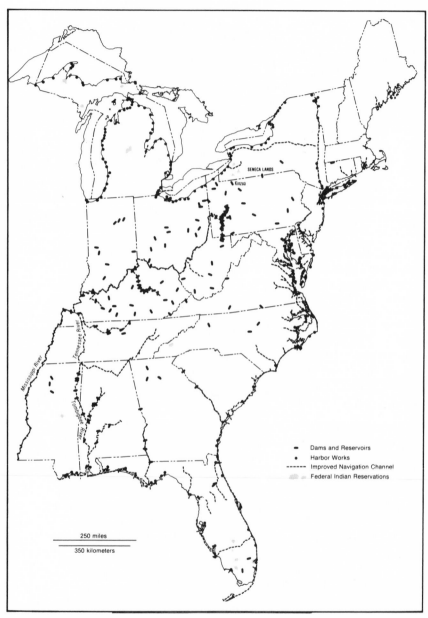

SENECA LANDS

Kinzua

Mississippi River

Tennessee River

Tombigbee River

● Dams and Reservoirs
· Harbor Works
------- Improved Navigation Channel
Federal Indian Reservations

250 miles

350 kilometers

Map 3. Eastern United States

264

Notes

1. Water, Indians, and Iron Triangles

1. It is easy to overemphasize this "meteorological determinism," but it has a large following. Indeed, William H. McNeill's epic history of Western civilization, *The Rise of the West* (1963), credits irrigation for the "breakthrough to civilization." Also see Donald Worster's recent book, *Rivers of Empire* (1985).

2. The term "non-Indian" is awkward. In addition, it is somewhat inaccurate as far as this study is concerned. I will use it to distinguish the Indian beneficiaries of BIA water projects from other people. Considering that a significant portion of western Indians live off-reservation, these "other people" include some Indians as well as Anglos, blacks, Hispanic-Americans, and other ethnic and racial minorities. Despite its awkwardness, "non-Indians" is still the most inclusive term available and hence the most accurate.

3. The erroneous tendency to consider western water development in isolation is part of a larger tendency to consider the West itself as an isolated phenomenon. Bernard DeVoto argued that the West has been consistently misunderstood because of the "tacit classification, the automatic dismissal, of Western as merely sectional, not national, history. No such limitation has been placed on the experience of the American people in New England, the South, or the Middle West. . . . The experience of the West is just as unseparable from the central energies of American history" (introduction to *Beyond the Hundredth Meridian* by Wallace Stegner, 1954).

4. I chose the term "iron triangle" for its dramatic appeal. As a metaphor it can be misleading if one assumes that such alliances are rigid, unchanging, and limited to three discrete participants. One of the principal findings of this study, and other research on iron triangles, is that they are politically malleable and subject to outside influence. Throughout this

book I use the broad term "federal water development iron triangle," or derivatives thereof, to include both the U.S. Army Corps of Engineers and the U.S. Bureau of Reclamation, even though the political environments of these agencies are distinctive in some respects.

5. The term "pork barrel" comes from the days of southern slavery when slaves, after a particularly hard day of work, would be awarded a small portion of salt pork from a barrel. Their usual victuals were entirely inadequate, thus the opening of the barrel was often accompanied by a mad rush to obtain a share of the pork. By 1879 the term was being used to deride members of Congress for their habit of scrambling for a share of public works revenue (see Maxey, 1919; Ashworth, 1981).

6. The term "logrolling" was taken from the pioneer days when neighbors would help each other to build their log homes.

7. I am concerned here only with the implementation of policies made by iron triangles. Much of the recent literature on implementation is intended to apply to all forms of policy, and some studies (for example, Mazmanian and Sabatier, 1983) concentrate on regulatory policy. Hence the focus of this section is different from that of most general studies of implementation.

8. For a much more detailed explanation of the factors that affect iron triangles, see the author's "Subgovernments: Political Viability Under Conditions of Budgetary Retrenchment." Paper presented at the 1986 meeting of the Western Political Science Association, Eugene, Oregon.

9. Ripley and Franklin offer a similar typology of iron triangle response to change (1984:105–107).

2. Federal Water Development at the Turn of the Century

1. Opponents of the reclamation bill claimed that Roosevelt actually favored federal control but publicly went along with his party's position. See *Congressional Record* (1902:6670).

2. The same strategy was used in the House debates. Congressman Ray of New York, an opponent of the bill, was asked by a supporter: "I was going to suggest to the gentleman from New York that we have appropriated millions of dollars for the harbor of New York City. Now, that benefits the city of New York as against Boston, as against Charleston, S.C., and other points, and yet the gentleman has voted for that appropriation, has he not?" (*Congressional Record* 1902:6685).

3. There is a caveat to this point; 13 congressmen voted "present," and 132 did not vote at all. This could mean that for many legislators, the reclamation bill was not critically important.

4. A 1920 civics text with a "good government" slant noted that a large sum of government money had been expended on rivers and canals and

that "some of this has been expended for necessary work, but most of it has been wasted" (Ashley 1920:363).

3. The *Winters* Decision and Its Progeny

1. A miner's inch is a somewhat inexact measure of water flow. According to one source it is the quantity of water that will flow through a one-inch orifice under a specific amount of pressure. The miner's inch has now largely been abandoned in favor of the acre-foot unit, which is the volume of water necessary to cover one acre with one foot of water (see King 1954).

2. Riparian rights developed from English common law and provide the basis for water rights throughout the more humid areas of the country. They provide that riparian property owners (i.e., property adjacent to a water source) have an inalienable right to the water source as long as their diversions from this source do not deprive other riparian properties of water. This approach works well in areas with plentiful water, but settlers and miners moving to the arid regions of the American West quickly discovered that an alternative approach was needed, hence the development of the Prior Appropriation Doctrine.

3. The case at the district court level was known as *U.S. v. Mose Anderson*. Anderson dropped out of the case when the settlers appealed and Henry Winter became the first appellant listed, so the case adopted his name. An errant court clerk added an "s" to his name somewhere along the line. For a detailed explanation of the case see Norris Hundley's two well-researched pieces: "The 'Winters' Decision and Indian Water Rights: A Mystery Reexamined" (1982) and "The Dark and Bloody Ground of Indian Water Rights: Confusion Elevated to Principle" (1978).

4. The language that was proposed for the appropriation bill provided that "the use of so much water that may be necessary to supply for domestic, stock-watering, and irrigation purposes, land allotted or to be allotted to Indians on the Fort Belknap Reservation or set aside for administrative purposes within said reservation, is hereby reserved; and the failure of any individual Indian or Indians to make beneficial use of such water shall not operate in any manner to defeat his or her right thereto while said land is held in trust by the United States. All laws and parts of laws in conflict herewith are hereby repealed" (*Congressional Record* 20 June 1914:10769–70).

5. Senator Robinson's speech in support of the Yakimas ranks as one of the more eloquent indictments of U.S. Indian policy: "Mr. President, there is a stain of shame upon our flag. We have not kept faith with the Indian. Perhaps it was the law of progress that we should conquer him; unavoidable that his hunting grounds should be transformed into fields; inevitable that by war and treaty, by sword and promise, he should be impoverished and despoiled. It is not to our shame, nor to his, that we

have beaten him in battle, for the Indian fights with all the energy of despair. Our disgrace arises from unfulfilled promises, violated treaties. Herein the record is shamefully consistent. It is relieved by few instances of pledges honestly fulfilled" (*Congressional Record* 20 December 1913:1276).

4. Non-Indian Water Development: The Bureau of Reclamation and the Corps of Engineers

1. These proposals included a plan to divert water from the Columbia River to the Colorado River, a nuclear-powered desalinization plant on the coast of California that would provide water for a 400-mile canal to the Colorado River, and a proposal to build an undersea aqueduct from the Klamath River in Northern California to the Los Angeles area.

2. This lack of independence did not prevent the Water Resources Council from making progress on some issues, however. In the late 1960s the council managed to formulate a more realistic discount rate for project benefit/cost analysis. This made it more difficult to meet the criteria of benefit/cost unity. It was a change that was long overdue. This reform was one of the few occasions when the council had a direct and significant impact on politically sensitive reforms.

3. This means no funds are provided to start construction on authorized projects.

4. See, for example, Renshaw (1957), Hart (1957), White (1958), Fesler (1964), Marshall (1964, 1966), Ruttan (1965), Haveman (1965), Young and Martin (1967), Hirshleifer et al. (1969), and Back (1969).

5. For example, books with titles such as these: *The Water Hustlers* (Boyle, Graves, and Watkins 1971); *The River Killers* (Heuvelman 1974); *Dams and Other Disasters* (Morgan 1971); *Damning the West* (Berkman and Viscusi 1973); *Pork Barrel Politics* (Ferejohn 1974); *Killing the Hidden Waters* (Bowden 1977); *A River No More* (Fradkin 1981); *Under the Influence* (Ashworth 1981); *Water: The Nature, Uses, and Future of Our Most Precious and Abused Resource* (Powledge 1982); *Nor Any Drop to Drink* (Ashworth 1982); *How to Create a Water Crisis* (Welsh 1985); *Troubled Waters* (El-Ashry and Gibbons 1986); and *Cadillac Desert* (Reisner 1986). There are also innumerable magazine and newspaper articles bitterly critical of the federal water development program.

5. The BIA Water Development Program

1. This perception of the *Winters* case as unimportant persisted well into the 1950s. For example, three articles concerning water rights in Montana, published in that era, did not mention the Winters Doctrine or any related case. See Heman (1949), Patten (1950), Dunbar (1954). Patten notes that holders of state-granted water rights should not fear proposed

federal development because their water rights "are fixed and immutable, and any use of water will have to avoid disturbing them" (1950:171).

2. Uintah, Pueblo, Taos, Fort Hall, Fort Apache, Kaibab, Wind River, and Yakima.

3. Fort Belknap, Arapaho, Shoshone, Gila River, Salt River.

4. The confusion and complexity of Indian water rights were further exacerbated by additional sources of rights—for example, Pueblo rights dating from the days of Spanish and Mexican sovereignty over the Southwest. See Meyer (1984) and Dumars, O'Leary, and Utton (1984).

5. The inconsistency in policy has affected Indian water development in many ways, but perhaps none is as obvious as the congressional policy on project reimbursement. Until 1914 Indian projects were funded either by the federal government or from general tribal funds, but the Act of August 1, 1914 changed this policy and required that project beneficiaries pay both construction and maintenance costs. Incredibly, the charges were made retroactive (Chief of Irrigation Annual Report 1915:1). This created an enormous financial burden for the Indians who were receiving irrigated water. A year after the new policy was enacted, the commissioner of Indian Affairs argued that it created "a great injustice to the Indians" (Commissioner of Indian Affairs Annual Report 1915:47). By 1917 the reimbursement program had "greatly swelled Indian indebtedness" (Kelly 1979a:247), but nevertheless in 1920 Congress made repayment mandatory (Act of February 14, 1920). It was nearly impossible to assess the charges fairly (Cohen 1942:249), and efforts to collect repayment funds usually proved futile, so in 1924 another law was enacted deferring the charges imposed by the 1920 statute (Kelly 1979b:257).

By 1930 it was clear that the reimbursement policy was a failure; $48 million had been expended but only $5.2 million had been reimbursed, nearly all of it from non-Indians (Commissioner of Indian Affairs Annual Report 1930:22). Finally, the Leavitt Act was passed on 1 July 1932, which permitted the secretary of interior to modify, defer, or cancel the Indians' liability to repay construction charges but maintained the requirement for repayment of maintenance costs, according to ability to pay.

6. The 1902 Reclamation Act contained an expression of this racist sentiment. It provided that "no mongolian labor" could be used on reclamation projects. It was also illegal in some western states for Oriental people to own land irrigated by government projects. To get around this they sometimes leased land from Indians informally. This further reduced the acreage actually farmed by Indians.

7. A popular high school geography book, published in 1916 by Macmillan, explained that there were two kinds of Indians: savages and barbarians. The distinction was based on whether the tribe cultivated crops. The book also explained that the leader among all the races in the world was the white race, and "being more advanced than the other races, the white race has conquered the weaker people and taken their lands from them, so that now they rule almost the whole world" (Tarr and McMurry 1916:12, 215). This same textbook offered a slightly different view of the

work of the Reclamation Service: "So important is irrigation that it is being introduced wherever possible, and every year new irrigation systems are being built, some of them at great expense. Since much of the arid region is public land, the United States government is aiding in this work. There is in fact, a special department of the government in charge of it, and every year millions of dollars are being spent in this way. . . . This is one of the most important works in which our government is engaged" (Tarr and McMurry 1916:120–121).

6. Conflict Among Programs and Priorities

1. Until the BIA adopted a more aggressive approach in the 1960s it often acquiesced to the Justice Department's torpidity regarding Indian water rights. By the late 1960s, however, the agency was becoming frustrated by its dependence on the Justice Department and requested that a legal section be established within the BIA. The secretary of interior denied the request, but a few years later a special section was set up in the Interior Department solicitor's office (Officer 1984:86–89).

7. Contemporary Federal Water Development: The Battle over Water Projects

1. For purposes of clarity and simplicity I have discussed only interest rates. Also important, and closely related, is the discount rate. This means that the costs and benefits of projects that accrue in the future must be discounted against their present value. This assumes that benefits in the distant future are worth less than similar benefits that materialize immediately or in the near future. Obviously the discount rate affects the cost/benefit ratio of a project.

2. Of course, the Balanced Budget Act (Gramm-Rudman) is an obvious systemic change with potentially pervasive impacts. At this time, however, given the constitutional and political uncertainties of the bill, it is impossible to predict its impact.

3. Not all big dams are dead. Denver has plans to build a large dam for its water supply, and a recently approved extension of the CAP would create two new dams and rebuild two existing structures. Some state legislators and administrators in Arizona have revived the idea of a dam in the Grand Canyon. The Animus-La Plata Project, now in progress, will necessitate the construction of a large dam, and the Bureau of Reclamation is studying the proposed Spring Canyon Pumped Storage Project on the Colorado River (estimated cost: $2 billion), which would also require a dam. In addition, several controversial dams are still being considered, including the Narrows Dam in Colorado, the Auburn Dam in California,

and a new Teton Dam to replace the structure that collapsed in 1976. The Corps of Engineers is also planning major projects. In addition to the projects in the 1986 Water Act, the corps is reviewing twenty proposed waterworks. As one congressional staffer noted, "the Corps has alot in the pipeline." And as always, several "mega-projects" are being promoted and discussed, including NAWAPA, a plan to dam James Bay and sell the water to the American Southwest, and a dam across the Bering Strait (*U.S. Water News* September 1986:3); and an Ohio congressman wants to build a canal from Lake Erie to the Ohio River.

4. Not everyone agrees that irrigation should be put on the back burner. Robert Broadbent, past commissioner of reclamation and then assistant secretary of Interior for Water and Science, argued that in twenty years there will be a demand for more irrigation, and considering that reclamation projects take twenty years to complete, these projects should be commenced in the near future (see *New York Times* 19 March 1985:L22).

8. The Politics of Contemporary Indian Water Rights

1. Secretary Watt also announced the reversal of the Krulitz Opinion, a Carter-era solicitor's opinion that created an expansive view of federal water rights for non-Indian federal land reservations. The new opinion, by Solicitor William Coldiron, again demonstrated the Reagan administration's commitment to state control over water rights.

2. The essential element here is trust, but that appears to be in short supply in some cases. Interior Secretary Donald Hodel was recently quoted as saying, "as trustee for the Indians, I wouldn't advise them to trust the state (in this case Colorado and New Mexico). I wouldn't advise them to trust the federal government, either." (Quoted in *High Country News* 13 October 1986:3).

References

Articles, Books, Reports, and Material
from the National Archives

"A Bill to Protect and Conserve the Water Rights of Indians," Memorandum, n.d., about 1913. National Archives, R.G. 75, Irrigation Division, General Correspondence, 1901–1931, Special Topics, Legislation.

Abbott, F. H. "Brief on Indian Irrigation." Prepared under the direction of the Board of Indian Commissioners, n.d., about 1915. National Archives, R.G. 75, Irrigation Division, General Correspondence, 1901–1931. Special Topics, Miscellaneous.

Acting Secretary to Congressman Leavitt, about December 1924. National Archives, R.G. 75, Irrigation Division, General Correspondence, 1901–1931. Special Topics, Legislation.

Allee, David, and Burnham Dodge. "The Role of the U.S. Army Corps of Engineers in Water Quality Management." Institute for Water Resources, Department of the Army, Corps of Engineers, October 1970.

Ambler, Marjane. "A Tale of Two Districts." *High Country News* 18 (27 October 1986):23–24.

American Indian Lawyer Training Program, sponsor of Symposium on Indian Water Policy, 8–10 November 1981, Oakland, Calif.

American Indian Policy Review Commission Final Report, Vol. I. Submitted to Congress 17 May 1977. U.S. Government Printing Office.

Anagnoson, J. Theodore. "Politics in the Distribution of Federal Grants: The Case of the Economic Development Administration." In *Political Benefits*, edited by Barry S. Rundquist, 61–91. Lexington, Mass.: Lexington Books, 1980.

Anderson, Terry L. *Water Crisis: Ending the Policy Drought*. Baltimore: Johns Hopkins University Press, 1983.

Andrews, Barbara T., and Marie Sansone. *Who Runs the Rivers? Dams and Decisions in the New West*. Stanford Environmental Law Society, 1983.

273

Appendix to the Budget for FY 1962.

Appendix to the Budget for FY 1978.

Appendix to the Congressional Record. 4 March 1915. 64th Congress, 1st sess.:928–929.

Arizona Academy. *Arizona Water: The Management of Scarcity.* Prepared for the 31st Arizona Town Hall, 9–12 October 1977.

Arizona Daily Star. 21 February 1979.

———. 18 September 1980.

———. 15 November 1980.

———. 2 December 1980.

———. 23 November 1981.

Arizona Republic. 6 January 1980.

———. 14 October 1980.

Army Corps of Engineers. *Historical Highlights of the United States Army Corps of Engineers.* EP360-1-2, April 1973.

———. *The Corps in Perspective since 1775.* Washington, D.C.: Government Printing Office, December 1976.

Arnold, R. Douglas. *Congress and the Bureaucracy.* New Haven, Conn.: Yale University Press, 1979.

———. "The Local Roots of Domestic Policy." In *The New Congress,* edited by Thomas E. Mann and Norman J. Ornstein, 250–287. Washington, D.C.: American Enterprise Institute, 1981.

Ashley, Roscoe L. *The New Civics.* New York: Macmillan, 1920.

Ashworth, William. *Under the Influence.* New York: Hawthorn/Dutton, 1981.

———. *Nor Any Drop to Drink.* New York: Summit Books, 1982.

Babb, C. to F. Newell, 10 April 1906. National Archives, R.G. 115, General Administrative and Project Records, 1902–1919: Milk River, 548, Settlement of Water Rights.

Babb, C. to M. Bien, 10 April 1906. Subject: "Water Rights Legislation." National Archives, R.G. 115, General Administrative and Project Records, 1902–1919: Milk River, 548, Settlement of Water Rights.

Bachellor, John M. "Lobbyists and the Legislative Process." *American Political Science Review* 71 (June 1977):252–263.

Back, W. S. "Estimating Contributions of Natural Resource Investments to Objectives in Regional Economic Development." *American Journal of Agricultural Economics* 51 (December 1969):1442–1447.

Barry, Brian. *Political Argument.* London: Routledge and Kegan Paul, 1965.

Barsh, Russel L., and Katherine Diaz-Knauf. "The Structure of Federal Aid for Indian Programs in the Decade of Prosperity, 1970–1980." *American Indian Quarterly* 8 (Winter 1984):1–35.

Baum, Lawrence. *The Supreme Court.* Washington, D.C.: Congressional Quarterly Press, 1981.

Baumhoff, Richard G. *The Dammed Missouri Valley.* New York: Alfred A. Knopf, 1951.

Bee, Robert L. *The Politics of American Indian Policy.* Cambridge, Mass.: Schenkman, 1982.

Bender, Jonathan, and Terry Moe. "An Adaptive Model of Bureaucratic Politics." *American Political Science Review* 79 (September 1985):755–774.

Berkman, Richard L., and Kip W. Viscusi. *Damning the West: Ralph Nader's Study Group Report on the Bureau of Reclamation.* New York: Grossman Publishers, 1973.

Bien, Morris. "The Intention of Congress as to State or National Control of Unappropriated Waters Belonging to the Nation, as Disclosed by the Debates Preceding the Passage of the Reclamation Act," n.d. National Archives, R.G. 115, General Administration and Project Files, 1902–1919: General, 762, Legal Discussions, General.

———. "Memorandum Concerning the Origin of the Right of Appropriation on the Water on the Public Domain," 6 February 1904. National Archives, R.G. 115, General Administration and Project Files, 1902–1919: General, 762, Legal Discussions.

———. "Informal Statement Concerning the Right of Appropriation of Water and Riparian Rights in the Arid Region," 1906. National Archives, R.G. 115, General Administration and Project Files, 1902–1919: General, 762, Legal Discussions.

Billings Gazette. 16 April 1977.

———. 21 May 1977.

———. 20 November 1977.

Birkby, Robert H. *The Court and Public Policy.* Washington, D.C.: Congressional Quarterly Press, 1983.

Bloom, Paul L. "Indian 'Paramount' Rights to Water Use." *Rocky Mountain Mineral Law Institute* 16 (1971):669–693.

———. "Law of the River: A Critique of an Extraordinary Legal System." In *New Courses for the Colorado River,* edited by Gary D. Weatherford and F. Lee Brown, 139–154. Albuquerque: University of New Mexico Press, 1986.

Bowden, Charles. *Killing the Hidden Waters.* Austin: University of Texas Press, 1977.

Boyle, Robert, John Graves, and T. H. Watkins. *The Water Hustlers.* San Francisco: Sierra Club Books, 1971.

Bredehoeft, John. "Physical Limitations of Water Resources." In *Water Scarcity,* edited by Ernest A. Engelbert and Ann Foley Scheuring, 17–50. Berkeley, Los Angeles, London: University of California Press, 1984.

Broadbent, Robert, Assistant Secretary for Water and Science, Department of Interior. Memorandum entitled "Federal Reserved Water Rights," 18 May 1984.

Bromley, Daniel, Allen Schmid, and William Lord. *Public Water Resources Project Planning and Evaluation: Impacts, Incidence, and Institutions.* Working Paper No. 1, Center for Resource Policy Studies and Programs, School of Natural Resources. Madison: University of Wisconsin, 1971.

Brophy, William A., and Sophie D. Aberle. *The Indian: America's Unfinished Business.* Norman: University of Oklahoma Press, 1966.

Buchanan, William, and Gordon Tullock. *The Calculus of Consent.* Ann Arbor: University of Michigan Press, 1962.

Bureau of Indian Affairs, U.S. Department of Interior. BIA 50–1 form, Part 1, 1974.

———. "Report to the United States Senate Committee on Interior and Insular Affairs on the Status of Construction of Indian Irrigation Projects." Mimeograph, October 1975.

Bureau of Reclamation. "Information Relating to Indian Water and Land Use Associated with Activities of the Bureau of Reclamation." Mimeograph, 4 November 1976.

———. "Indian Water Rights, Claims, and Related Issues." Secretarial Issue Document. Mimeograph, 27 April 1984.

———. "Milk River Project—Fort Belknap Indians." Briefing Paper, n.d., about 1986.

———. "Milk River Water Supply Study." Mimeograph, n.d., about 1986.

Burke, Charles to Elwood Mead, 5 July 1927. National Archives, R.G. 75, Irrigation Division, General Correspondence, Dist. 3, Fort Belknap, 1907–1931.

Burke, Charles to Elwood Mead, 9 July 1927. National Archives, R.G. 75, Irrigation Division, General Correspondence, Dist. 3, Fort Belknap, 1907–1931.

Burke, Charles to Elwood Mead, 11 August 1927. National Archives, R.G. 75, Irrigation Division, General Correspondence, Dist. 3, Fort Belknap, 1907–1931.

Burness, H. S., R. G. Cummings, W. D. Gorman, and R. R. Lansford. "United States Reclamation Policy and Indian Water Rights." *Natural Resources Journal* 20 (October 1980):808–826.

Campbell, Frank. "The State of Kansas v. The State of Colorado et al., The United States, Intervenor." Memorandum, n.d., about 1907. National Archives, R.G. 115, General Administration and Project Files, 1902–1919: General, 762, Legal Discussions.

Cahn, Edgar S. *Our Brother's Keeper.* New York: World, 1969.

Carlin, A. "Water Resources Development in an Environmentally Conscious Era." *Water Resources Bulletin* (April 1971):221–227.

Carlson, Leonard A. *Indians, Bureaucrats, and Land.* Westport, Conn.: Greenwood Press, 1981.

Cater, Douglass. *Power in Washington.* New York: Random House, 1964.

Caulfield, Henry P. "Let's Dismantle (largely but not fully) the Federal Water Development Establishment, or, the Apostacy of a Longstanding Water Development Federalist." In *Proceedings of the 1975 National Conference on Water.* Washington, D.C.: Government Printing Office, 1976.

———. "U.S. Water Resources Policy: Past, Present, and Future." Paper presented at the annual meeting of the Western Political Science Association, March 1982.

———. "U.S. Water Resources Development Policy and Intergovernmental Relations." In *Western Public Lands,* edited by John G. Francis and Richard Ganzel, 215–232. Totowa, N.J.: Rowman and Allenheld, 1984.

Chambers, Reid P. "Discharge of the Federal Trust Responsibility to Enforce Claims of Indian Tribes: Case Studies of Bureaucratic Conflict of Interest." *American Indian Law Newsletter* 4 (1971):1–20.

Chan, A. H. "The Structure of Federal Water Resource Policy." *American Journal of Economics and Sociology* 40 (April 1981):115–127.

Chandler, A. E. *Elements of Western Water Law.* San Francisco: Technical Publishing Co., 1913.

Chief Engineer, U.S. Indian Irrigation Service Annual Reports to the Commissioner of Indian Affairs, 1908–1923, 1932, Department of the Interior. National Archives, R.G. 75, BIA Irrigation Service, Entry 654, Boxes 30, 68.

The CERT Report. Vol. 2, No. 21 (21 November 1980).

———. Vol. 3, no. 13 (7 October 1981).

———. Vol. 4, no. 1 (29 January 1982).

———. Vol. 4, no. 2 (8 February 1982).

———. Vol. 4, no. 9 (23 July 1982).

Clarenbach, Fred. "Reliability of Estimates of Agricultural Damage from Floods." In U.S. Commission on Organization of the Executive Branch of the Government, Task Force Report on Water Resources and Power, Vol. 3, 1955.

Clarke, Jeanne Nienaber, and Daniel C. McCool. *Staking Out the Terrain: Resource Differentials among Natural Resource Management Agencies.* Albany: State University of New York Press, 1985.

Clinton, Michael J., Special Assistant to the Assistant Secretary for Water and Science. Remarks before the annual meeting of the Colorado River Water Users Association, Las Vegas, Nevada, 17 December 1985.

Clyde, Edward W. "Allocation of Water for Resource Development." *Natural Resource Lawyer* 14, no. 3 (1982):519–540.

Coate, Charles. "'The New School of Thought': Reclamation and the Fair Deal, 1945–53." *Journal of the American West* 22 (April 1983):58–63.

Coates, L. A., to W. S. Hanna, 20 January 1920. National Archives, R.G. 75, BIA Irrigation Division, Dist. 3, Fort Belknap, 1917–1924: Entry 653.

Coggins, George C., and Charles F. Wilkinson. *Federal Public Land and Resources Law.* Mineola, N.Y.: The Foundation Press, 1981.

Cohen, Felix S. *Handbook of Federal Indian Law.* Albuquerque: University of New Mexico Press, 1942.

Collins, Richard B. "The Future Course of the *Winters* Doctrine." *University of Colorado Law Review* 56 (Spring 1985):481–494.

———. "Indian Allotment Water Rights." *Land and Water Law Review* 20 (1985):421–457.

Commissioner of Indian Affairs, Annual Reports. Washington, D.C.: Department of Interior, Government Printing Office, 1908–1920.

———. "Memorandum for the Secretary," 6 December 1924. National Archives, R.G. 75, Irrigation Division, 1901–1931: Special Topics, Miscellaneous.

Commissioner of Reclamation, Annual Reports. Washington, D.C.: Department of Interior, Government Printing Office, 1923–1932.

Congressional Quarterly Almanac, 1968.

Congressional Record. Vol. 20, 50th Cong. 2d sess. (14 February 1889).

————. Vol. 28, 54th Cong. 1st sess. (2–10 June 1896).

————. Vol. 35, 57th Cong. 1st sess. (12–13 June 1902).

————. Vol. 40, 59th Cong. 2d sess. (11 January 1906).

————. Vol. 42, 60th Cong. 1st sess. (17 December 1907).

————. Vol. 45, 61st Cong. 2d sess. (23 June 1910).

————. Vol. 51, 63d Cong. 2d sess. (20 December 1913).

————. Vol. 51, 63d Cong. 2d sess. (19 February 1914).

————. Vol. 51, 63d Cong. 2d sess. (20 June 1914).

————. Vol. 51, 63d Cong. 2d sess. (22, 29 July 1914).

————. Vol. 51, 63d Cong. 2d sess. (7 August 1914).

————. Vol. 105, 86th Cong. 1st sess. (2–10 September 1959).

————. Vol. 108, 87th Cong. 2d sess. (4 October 1962).

————. Vol. 132, 99th Cong. 2d sess. (17 October 1986).

Conservation Foundation. *America's Water: Current Trends and Emerging Issues*. Washington, D.C.: The Conservation Foundation, 1984.

Corker, Charles. "Water Rights and Federalism—The Western Water Rights Settlement Bill of 1957." *California Law Review* 45 (1957):604–637.

Costo, Rupert. "Indian Water Rights: A Survival Issue." *Indian Historian* 5, no. 3 (Fall 1972):4–6.

Coursen, David. "Reserved Rights: Water for Fish Protection and the 1983 Indian Water Rights Decisions." *Oregon Law Review* 63 (1984):699–720.

Culhane, Paul. *Public Lands Politics*. Baltimore: Johns Hopkins University Press/Resources for the Future, 1981.

Dahl, Robert. "The Supreme Court as a National Policy Maker." *Journal of Public Law* 6, no. 2 (1958):279–295.

————. "The Supreme Court's Role in National Policy-Making." In *The Federal Judicial System*, edited by Sheldon Goldman and Charles P. Jahnige. Hinsdale, Ill.: Dryden Press, 1968.

Davidson, Roger H. "Representation and Congressional Committees." *The Annals of the American Academy of Political and Social Science* 411 (January 1974):48–62.

————. "Breaking Up Those 'Cozy Triangles': An Impossible Dream?" In *Legislative Reform and Public Policy*, edited by Susan Welch and John G. Peters. New York: Praeger, 1977.

————. "Subcommittee Government: New Channels for Policy Making." In *The New Congress*, edited by Thomas Mann and Norman Ornstein, 99–133. Washington, D.C.: American Enterprise Institute, 1981.

Davis, Arthur P. "Report on the Irrigation Investigation for the Benefit of the Pima and Other Indians on the Gila River Indian Reservation, Arizona." Senate Document 27, 54th Cong. 2d sess. (Serial 3467), 1897.

Davis, Clarence. "Legal Aspects of Water Use." In *Water and Agriculture*, edited by Roy E. Hockensmith. Washington, D.C.: American Association for the Advancement of Science, 1960.

Deason, J. P., and K. P. White. "Specification of Objectives by Group

Processes in Multiobjective Water Resources Planning." *Water Resources Research* 20 (February 1984):189–196.

Decision. No. 1, 1982 (Copyright by Western Network, Sante Fe, N.M.).

Dellwo, Robert D. "Indian Water Rights—The Winters Doctrine Updated." *Gonzaga Law Review* 6 (Spring 1971):215–240.

———. "Recent Developments in the Northwest Regarding Indian Water Rights." *Natural Resources Journal* 20 (January 1980):101–120.

Deloria, Vine, Jr. "American Indians: Landmarks on the Trail Ahead." *Social Science Journal* 19, no. 3 (July 1982):1–8.

———. Statement on jacket cover of *Dammed Indians* by Michael L. Lawson. Norman: University of Oklahoma Press, 1982.

Deloria, Vine, Jr., and Clifford M. Lytle. *The Nations Within.* New York: Pantheon, 1984.

Denver Post. 2 January 1978.

———. 3 June 1984.

Department of Interior. "President's Water Policy Implementation 10-Year Plan for Review of Indian Water Claims." Mimeograph, August 1980.

———. "Explanation of Ten-Year Plan of Water Inventories and Water Resources Development Planning." Memorandum, November 1981.

———. "Western Indian Water Rights Negotiations." Memorandum, 8 December 1982.

———. "Water Resource Planning Funding Issues." Memorandum, n.d., about 1982.

Dodd, Lawrence C., and Richard L. Schott. *Congress and the Administrative State.* New York: John Wiley, 1979.

Doerksen, Harvey. "Water, Politics, and Ideology: An Overview of Water Resources Management." *Public Administration Review* 37 (September/October 1977):444–448.

Dorner, Peter. "The Economic Position of the American Indians: Their Resources and Potential for Development." Ph.D. diss., Harvard University, 1959.

Douglas, Paul H. (Senator). Introduction. In *Dams and Other Disasters* by Arthur E. Morgan. Boston: Porter Sargent, 1971.

Downs, Anthony. "Up and Down with Ecology: The Issue-Attention Cycle." *Public Interest* 28 (Summer 1972):38–50.

Drew, E. B. "Dam Outrage: The Story of the Army Engineers." *Atlantic* (April 1970):51–62.

Dubos, Rene. *A God Within.* New York: Charles Scribner's Sons, 1972.

DuMars, Charles T., Marilyn O'Leary, and Albert Utton. *Pueblo Indian Water Rights.* Tucson: University of Arizona Press, 1984.

Dunbar, Robert G. "The Search for a Stable Water Right in Montana." *Agricultural History* 28 (October 1954):138–148.

———. *Forging New Rights in Western Water.* Lincoln: University of Nebraska Press, 1983.

Edgmon, Terry D., and Timothy de Young. "Federalism Without the Feds: A Comparative Analysis of State Water Resources, Policy and Administration." Paper presented at the annual meeting of the Western Political Science Association, March 1982.

———. "Categorizing State Models of Water Management." In *Western Public Lands*, edited by John G. Francis and Richard Ganzel, 232–247. Totowa, N.J.: Rowman and Allanheld, 1984.

Edwards, J., to Attorney General, n.d., 1928. National Archives, R.G. 75, BIA Irrigation Division, Dist. 3, Fort Belknap, 1917–1924. Entry 653.

Edwards, George C. III. *Implementing Public Policy*. Washington, D.C.: Congressional Quarterly Press, 1980.

El-Ashry, Mohamed T., and Diana C. Gibbons. *Troubled Waters*. Washington, D.C.: World Resources Institute, 1986.

Executive Order 8455 (June 1940).

———. 9384 (4 October 1943).

———. 12113 (4 January 1979).

———. 12141 (5 June 1979).

———. 12322 (17 September 1981).

Farmline 1, no. 6 (September 1980).

Federal Bill Digest 1985, Vol. 1.

Federal Register. Vol. 42, no. 129 (6 July 1977).

———. Vol. 42, no. 136 (15 July 1977).

———. Vol. 42, no. 142 (25 July 1977).

———. Vol. 42, no. 145 (28 July 1977).

———. Vol. 44, no. 189 (20 July 1979).

———. Vol. 45, no. 239 (10 December 1980).

Fenno, Richard F. *The Power of the Purse*. Boston: Little, Brown, 1966.

Ferejohn, John. *Pork Barrel Politics: Rivers and Harbors Legislation, 1947–1968*. Stanford: Stanford University Press, 1974.

Fesler, James. "National Water Resources Administration." In *Water Resources Development*, edited by Stephen C. Smith and Emery Castle, 368–393. Ames: Iowa State University Press, 1964.

Fey, Harold E., and D'Arcy McNickle. *Indians and Other Americans*. Rev. ed. New York: Harper & Row, 1970.

Final Report of the Garrison Unit Joint Tribal Advisory Committee, Fort Berthold Indian Reservation and Standing Rock Sioux Indian Reservation. 23 May 1986.

Fiorina, Morris. *Congress: Keystone to the Washington Establishment*. New Haven, Conn.: Yale University Press, 1977.

Fitzgerald, Randall, and Gerald Lipson. *Pork Barrel: The Unexpurgated Grace Commission Story of Congressional Profligacy*. Washington, D.C.: CATO Institute, 1984.

Florman, Samuel C. "Hired Scapegoats." *Harper's Magazine* (May 1977):26–29.

Folk-Williams, John A. *What Indian Water Means to the West*. Santa Fe, N.M.: Western Network, 1982.

Foreman, Richard. *Indian Water Rights*. Danville, Ill.: Interstate Printers, 1981.

Foster, Kennith E. "The Winters Doctrine: Historical Perspective and Future Applications of Reserved Water Rights in Arizona." *Groundwater* 16, no. 3 (May-June 1978):186–191.

Fradkin, Phillip L. *A River No More.* New York: Alfred A. Knopf, 1981.

Frederick, Kenneth D. "Overview." In *Scarce Water and Institutional Change,* edited by Kenneth D. Frederick. Washington, D.C.: Resources for the Future, 1986.

Frederick, Kenneth D., and James C. Hanson. *Water for Western Agriculture.* Washington, D.C.: Resources for the Future, 1982.

Freeman, J. Leiper. *The Political Process.* Rev. ed. New York: Random House, 1965.

Froman, Lewis A. *The Congressional Process.* Boston: Little, Brown, 1967.

Gais, Thomas, Mark A. Peterson, and Jack Walker. "Interest Groups, Iron Triangles and Representative Institutions in American National Government." *British Journal of Political Science* 14 (April 1984):161–186.

GAO Report to the Congress. "Tribal Participation in the Bureau of Indian Affairs Budget System Should Be Increased." General Accounting Office Report No. CED-78-62, 15 February 1978.

———. "The Indian Self-Determination Act—Many Obstacles Remain." General Accounting Office Report No. HRD-78-59, 1 March 1978.

———. "Reserved Water Rights for Federal and Indian Reservations: A Growing Controversy in Need of Resolution." General Accounting Office Report No. CED-78-176, 16 November 1978.

———. "Colorado River Basin Water Problems: How to Reduce Their Impact." General Accounting Office Report No. CED-79-11, 4 May 1978.

———. "Federal Charges for Irrigation Projects Reviewed Do Not Cover Costs." General Accounting Office Report No. PAD-81-07, 13 March 1981.

———. "Major Improvements Needed in the Bureau of Indian Affairs Accounting System." General Accounting Office Report No. GOA/AF, MD-82-71, 8 September 1982.

———. "Water Project Construction Backlog—A Serious Problem with No Solution." General Accounting Office Report No. RCED-83-49, 26 January 1983.

———. "Bureau of Indian Affairs' Participation in a Proposed Hydroelectric Facility at Kootenai Fall, Montana." General Accounting Office Report No. RCED-84-126, 11 July 1984.

———. "Additional Information Concerning Irrigation Project Costs and Pricing Federal Power." General Accounting Office Report No. RCED-86-18FS, 10 October 1985.

———. "Issues Concerning Expanded Irrigation in the Columbia Basin Project." General Accounting Office Report No. RCED-86-82BR, 31 January 1986.

———. "Bureau of Reclamation's Bonneville Unit: Future Repayment Arrangements." General Accounting Office Report No. RCED-86-103, 7 March 1986.

———. "The Nation's Water." General Accounting Office Report No. PEMD-86-6, September 1986.

Garfield, James R., to Frederick Newell, 7 March 1907. National Archives, R.G. 75, Irrigation Division General Correspondence, 1901–1931: Special Topics, Miscellaneous.

Garland, Hamlin. "The Red Man's Present Needs." *North American Review* 174 (April 1902):479–482.

Gates, Paul. *History of Public Land Law Development.* Written for the Public Land Law Review Commission. Washington, D.C.: Government Printing Office, 1968.

Gerard, Forrest, et. al. "National Indian Water Policy Review." Department of Interior Mimeograph, 23 January 1978.

———. Memo to all tribal chairmen regarding the "Presidential Directive Regarding National Water Policy." Department of Interior, 24 August 1978.

Getches, David, Daniel Rosenfelt, and Charles Wilkinson. *Cases and Materials on Federal Indian Law.* St. Paul, Minn.: West Publishing, 1979.

———. "Water Rights on Indian Allotments." *South Dakota Law Review* 26 (1981):405–433.

Gist, John R. "Appropriations Politics and Expenditure Control." *Journal of Politics* 40 (February 1978):163–178.

Glass, Mary Ellen. *Water for Nevada: The Reclamation Controversy 1885–1902.* Reno: University of Nevada Press, 1964.

Goss, Carol F. "Military Committee Membership and Defense-Related Benefits in the House of Representatives." *Western Political Quarterly* 25 (June 1972):215–233.

Griffith, Ernest S. *Congress: Its Contemporary Role.* 3d ed. New York: New York University Press, 1961.

Grigg, Neil S. *Water Resources Planning.* New York: McGraw-Hill, 1985.

Hagerdorn, Hermann. *Roosevelt in the Badlands.* New York: G. P. Putnam's Sons, 1921.

Halacy, Daniel S. *The Water Crisis.* New York: E. P. Dutton, 1966.

Hamm, Keith. "U.S. State Legislative Committee Decisions: Similar Results in Different Settings." *Legislative Studies Quarterly* 5 (1980):31–54.

———. "Patterns of Influence Among Committees, Agencies, and Interest Groups." *Legislative Studies Quarterly* 8 (August 1983):379–426.

Hanna, W. S. to W. M. Reed, 31 March 1916. National Archives, R.G. 75, BIA Irrigation Division, Dist. 3, Fort Belknap, Entry 653.

Hanna, W. S. to W. M. Reed, 21 April 1920. National Archives, R.G. 75, BIA Irrigation Division, Dist. 3, Fort Belknap, Entry 653.

Hansen, John M. "The Political Economy of Group Membership." *American Political Science Review* 79 (March 1985):79–96.

Harrison, David, C. *Do We Need a National Water Policy?* Staff Report submitted to the National Academy of Public Administration. Washington, D.C.: National Technical Information Service, U.S. Department of Commerce, December 1981.

Hart, Henry. *The Dark Missouri*. Madison: University of Wisconsin Press, 1957.

———. "Crisis, Community, and Consent in Water Politics." *Law and Contemporary Problems* 21 (Summer 1957):524–536.

Haveman, Robert. *Water Resources Investment and the Public Interest*. Nashville, Tenn.: Vanderbilt University Press, 1965.

Hays, Samuel P. *Conservation and the Gospel of Efficiency*. Cambridge, Mass.: Harvard University Press, 1959.

Heclo, Hugh. "Issue Networks and the Executive Establishment." In *The New American Political System*, edited by Anthony King, 94–105. Washington, D.C.: American Enterprise Institute, 1978.

Heman, Howard W. "Water Rights Under the Law of Montana." *Montana Law Review* 10 (Spring 1949):13–34.

Heuvelman, Martin. *The River Killers*. Harrisburg, Penn.: Stackpole Books, 1974.

Hibbard, Benjamin H. *A History of the Public Land Policies*. Madison: University of Wisconsin Press, 1965.

High Country News. 4 August 1986.

———. 13 October 1986.

Hill, J. J. to Charles Walcott, 20 April 1906. National Archives, R.G. 115, General Administrative and Project Records, 1902–1919: Milk River, 548, Settlement of Water Rights.

Hinckley, Barbara. "Policy Content, Committee Membership, and Behavior." *American Journal of Political Science* 19 (August 1975):543–557.

Hirshleifer, Jack, James De Haven, and Jerome Milliman. *Water Supply*. Chicago: University of Chicago Press, 1969.

Holbrook, Stewart. *The Columbia*. New York: Rinehart and Co., 1956.

Holden, Matthew. "Imperialism in Bureaucracy." *American Political Science Review* 60 (December 1966):943–951.

Holmes, Beatrice H. *A History of Federal Water Resources Programs, 1800–1960*. Economic Research Service, U.S. Department of Agriculture. Washington, D.C.: U.S. Government Printing Office, June 1972.

———. *History of Federal Water Resources Programs and Policies, 1961–1970*. Economic Research Service, U.S. Department of Agriculture. Washington, D.C.: U.S. Government Printing Office, 1979.

Holt, L. M. to W. M. Reed, 17 February 1913. National Archives, R.G. 75, Irrigation Division, General Correspondence, 1901–1931: Special Topics, General (Dist. 1).

Horn, Stephen. *Unused Power*. Washington, D.C.: Brookings Institution, 1970.

Howe, Charles W. "The Coming Conflicts over Water." In *Western Water Resources* (symposium). Boulder, Colo.: Westview Press, 1980.

Hubbard, Henry. "Carter vs. Congress: Another Showdown over Water." *National Wildlife* (April-May 1979).

Hundley, Norris. *Water and the West*. Berkeley, Los Angeles, London: University of California Press, 1975.

————. "The Dark and Bloody Ground of Indian Water Rights: Confusion Elevated to Principle." *Western Historical Quarterly* (October 1978):454–478.

————. "The 'Winters' Decision and Indian Water Rights: A Mystery Reexamined." *Western Historical Quarterly* 13, no. 1 (January 1982):17–42.

Hutchins, Wells A. *Selected Problems in the Law of Water Rights in the West.* Miscellaneous Publication 418 of the Department of Interior. Washington, D.C.: Government Printing Office, 1942.

Indian Affairs. #98 (Fall-Winter 1978–1979).

————. #98 (Spring-Summer 1979).

————. #100 (Fall-Winter 1979).

————. #101 (Spring-Summer 1980).

Indian Historian. "Indian Water Rights . . . the Attack Mounts." *Indian Historian* 12, no. 2 (Summer 1979).

Indian Law Resource Center. "Resolving Indian Conflicts out of Court." Mimeograph, May 1981.

"Indian Reserved Rights: The Winters of Our Discontent." *Yale Law Review* 88 (1979).

Indian Water Policy Symposium. Proceedings published by the American Indian Lawyer Training Program, Oakland, Calif. 1982.

Ingram, Helen. "Patterns of Politics in Water Resource Development: A Case Study of New Mexico's Role in the Colorado River Basin Bill." Publication no. 79. Albuquerque: University of New Mexico, 1969.

————. "The Changing Decision Rules in the Politics of Water Development." *Water Resources Bulletin* 8 (December 1972):1177–1188.

Ingram, Helen, Nancy Laney, and J. R. McCain. *A Policy Approach to Political Representation.* Baltimore: Johns Hopkins University Press, 1980.

Inspector General, Department of Interior. Draft Memorandum Audit Report, "Rehabilitation and Completion of the Fort Belknap Irrigation Project." August 1985.

International Irrigation Congress. *Proceedings,* 1893.

Ippolito, Dennis, and Thomas G. Walker. *Political Parties, Interest Groups, and Public Policy.* Englewood Cliffs, N.J.: Prentice-Hall, 1980.

James, George W. *Reclaiming the Arid West.* New York: Dodd, Mead, 1917.

Johnson, Rich. *The Central Arizona Project, 1918–1968.* Tucson: University of Arizona Press, 1977.

Johnson, Charles A., and Bradley C. Canon. *Judicial Politics.* Washington, D.C.: Congressional Quarterly Press, 1984.

Johnson, H. H. and E. E. Roddis, to Chief Engineer, Bureau of Reclamation, 17 August 1927. National Archives, R.G. 75, Irrigation Division, General Correspondence, 1907–1931: Dist. 3, Fort Belknap.

Josephy, Alvin M., Jr. *Now That the Buffalo's Gone.* Norman: University of Oklahoma Press, 1984.

Justice Department. Memorandum concerning the case of *Winters v. U.S.,* n.d., about 1905. National Archives, R.G. 115, General Administration and Project Files, 1902–1919: General, 762, Legal Discussions.

Kelly, Lawrence C. "Cato Sells (1913–1921)." In *The Commissioners of Indian*

Affairs, 1824–1977, edited by Robert N. Kvasnicka and Herman J. Viola, 243–250. Lincoln: University of Nebraska Press, 1979a.

———. "Charles Henry Burke (1921–29)." In *The Commissioners of Indian Affairs, 1824–1977*, edited by Robert N. Kvasnicka and Herman J. Viola, 251–261. Lincoln: University of Nebraska Press, 1979b.

Kelso, Maurice. "The Water Is Different Syndrome or What is Wrong with the Water Industry." *Proceedings of the Third Annual Conference of the American Water Works Association*, Urbana, Ill., 1967.

King, Anthony. "The American Polity in the Late 1970: Building Coalitions in the Sand." In *The New American Political System*, edited by Anthony King, 391–405. Washington, D.C.: American Enterprise Institute, 1978.

King, Dominic B. "Federal-State Relations in the Control of Water Resources." *University of Detroit Law Journal* 37 (October 1959):1–27.

King, Gary. "Federal Non-Reserved Water Rights: Fact or Fiction?" *Natural Resources Journal* 22, no. 2 (April 1982):424–432.

King, Horace. *Hydraulics*. 5th ed. New York: John Wiley, 1954.

Knack, Martha C., and Omer C. Stewart. *As Long as the River Shall Run*. Berkeley, Los Angeles, London: University of California Press, 1984.

Kneese, Allen V., and F. Lee Brown. *The Southwest Under Stress*. Baltimore: Johns Hopkins University Press/Resources for the Future, 1981.

Kleppe, Thomas. "Report to the Committee on Interior and Insular Affairs." Department of Interior. Mimeograph, 10 March 1976.

Krulitz, Leo (Solicitor of the Department of Interior). "Federal Water Rights of the National Park Service, Fish and Wildlife Service, Bureau of Reclamation and Bureau of Land Management." *Decisions of the U.S. Department of Interior* 86 (25 June 1979).

Lamm, Richard D. *Megatraumas*. New York: Houghton Mifflin, 1985.

Lamm, Richard D., and Michael McCarthy. *The Angry West*. Boston: Houghton Mifflin, 1982.

Lawson, Michael. "The Navajo Indian Project: Muddied Past, Clouded Future." *Indian Historian* 9 (Winter 1976):19–29.

———. *Dammed Indians*. Norman: University of Oklahoma Press, 1982.

Lear, Linda. "Boulder Dam: A Crossroads in Natural Resource Policy." *Journal of the West* 24 (October 1985):82–84.

Lee, Lawrence B. *Reclaiming the American West*. Santa Barbara, Calif.: ABC-Clio Press, 1980.

LeLoup, Lance T. "Agency Policy Actions: Determinants of Nonincremental Change." In *Policy-Making in the Federal Executive Branch*, edited by Randall B. Ripley and Grace A. Franklin, 65–90. New York: Free Press, 1975.

Leupp, Francis E. *The Indian and His Problem*. New York: Charles Scribner's Sons, 1910.

Leveen, E. Phillip. "Reclamation Policy at a Crossroads." *Public Affairs Report* 19 (October 1978):1.

Levine, Stuart, and Nanco O. Lurie, eds. *The American Indian Today*. Deland, Fla.: Everett/Edwards, 1965.

Liebman, Ernst. "The Water Resources Council." PB 211 443. Springfield,

Va.: National Technical Information Service for the National Water Commission, May 1967.

Levitan, Sam A., and Barbara Hetrick. *Big Brothers Indian Programs—With Reservations.* New York: McGraw-Hill, 1971.

Logan W. to F. Leupp, 29 April 1906. National Archives, R.G. 75, BIA Irrigation Division, Dist. 3, Fort Belknap, Entry 653.

Long, Norton. *The Polity.* Chicago: Rand McNally, 1962.

Lowi, Theodore. "American Business, Public Policy, Case Studies and Political Theory." *World Politics* 16 (1964):677–715.

Lowitt, Richard. *The New Deal and the West.* Bloomington: Indiana University Press, 1984.

Maass, Arthur. "Congress and Water Resources." *American Political Science Review* 44 (September 1950):576–593.

———. *Muddy Waters.* Cambridge, Mass.: Harvard University Press, 1951.

Mann, Dean. *The Politics of Water in Arizona.* Tucson: University of Arizona Press, 1963.

———. "Political Incentives in U.S. Water Policy: The Changing Emphasis on Distributive and Regulatory Politics." Paper presented at the annual meeting of the International Political Science Association, August 1973.

———. "Political Incentives in U.S. Water Policy: Relationships Between Distributive and Regulatory Politics." In *What Government Does,* edited by Matthew Holden and Dennis Dresang, 94–123. Beverly Hills, Calif.: Sage Publications, 1975.

———. "Institutional Framework for Agricultural Water Conservation and Reallocation in the West: A Policy Analysis." In *Water and Agriculture in the Western U.S.,* edited by Gary D. Weatherford. Boulder, Colo.: Westview Press, 1982.

Marshall, Hubert. "Rational Choice in Water Resource Planning." In *Water Resource Development,* edited by Stephen Smith and Emery Castle, 403–423. Ames: Iowa State University Press, 1964.

———. "Politics and Efficiency in Water Development." In *Water Research,* edited by Allen Kneese and S. C. Smith, 291–296. Baltimore: Johns Hopkins University/Resources for the Future, 1964.

Matheson, John, to J. J. Hill, 14 April 1906. National Archives, R.G. 115, General Administrative and Project Records, 1902–1919: Milk River, 548, Settlement of Water Rights.

Maxey, Chester C. "A Little History of Pork." *National Municipal Review* 8 (December 1919):691–705.

Mayhew, David R. *Congress: The Electoral Connection.* New Haven, Conn.: Yale University Press, 1974.

Mazmanian, Daniel A., and Jeanne Nienaber. *Can Organizations Change?* Washington, D.C.: Brookings Institution, 1979.

Mazmanian, Daniel A., and Paul A. Sabatier. *Implementation and Public Policy.* Glenview, Ill.: Scott, Foresman, 1983.

McCallister, Elizabeth. "Water Rights: The McCarran Amendment and Indian Tribes' Reserved Water Rights." *American Indian Law Review* 4 (Winter 1976):303–310.

McConnell, Grant. *Private Power and American Democracy.* New York: Vintage Books, 1966.

McCool, Daniel. "Indian Voting." In *American Indian Policy in the Twentieth Century,* edited by Vine Deloria, Jr., 105–134. Norman: University of Oklahoma Press, 1985.

———. "Subgovernments: Political Viability Under Conditions of Budgetary Retrenchment." Paper presented at the 1986 meeting of the Western Political Science Association, Eugene, Oregon.

McCourt, John, to the Attorney General, 1 October 1910. National Archives, R.G. 75, Irrigation Division, 1901–1931: Special Topics, Miscellaneous.

McNeill, William H. *The Rise of the West.* Chicago: University of Chicago Press, 1963.

Mead, Elwood to Charles Burke, 9 July 1927. National Archives, R.G. 75, Irrigation Division, General Correspondence, 1907–1931: Dist. 3, Fort Belknap.

Meier, Kenneth J., and J. R. Van Lohuizen. "Bureaus, Clients and Congress: The Impact of Interest Group Support on Budgeting." *Administration and Society* 9 (February 1978):447–466.

Meier, Kenneth J. *Politics and the Bureaucracy.* North Scituate, Mass.: Duxbury Press, 1979.

———. "Measuring Organizational Power." *Administration and Society* 12 (November 1980):357–375.

———. *Regulation: Politics, Bureaucracy, and Economics.* New York: St. Martin's Press, 1985.

Meriam, Lewis, and Associates. *The Problem of Indian Administration.* Baltimore: Johns Hopkins University Press, 1928.

Meyer, Michael C. *Water in the Hispanic Southwest.* Tucson: University of Arizona Press, 1984.

Meyers, Charles, and A. Dan Tarlock. *Water Resource Management.* 2d ed. Mineola, N.Y.: Foundation Press, 1980.

Mikva, Abner J., and Patti B. Saris. *The American Congress.* New York: Franklin Watts, 1983.

Miller, Arthur, Patricia Gurin, Gerald Gurin, and Oksana Malanchuk. "Group Consciousness and Political Participation." *American Journal of Political Science* 25 (August 1981):494–511.

Miller, Clem. *Member of the House: Letters of a Congressman.* Edited by John W. Baker. New York: Charles Scribner's Sons, 1962.

Miller, Tim. "Recent Trends in Federal Water Resource Management: Are the 'Iron Triangles' in Retreat?" *Policy Studies Review* 5 (November 1985):395–412.

Morgan, Arthur E. *Dams and Other Disasters.* Boston: Porter Sargent, 1971.

Morreale, Eva Hanna. "Federal-State Conflicts Over Western Waters—A Decade of Attempted 'Clarifying Legislation.'" *Rutgers Law Review* 20 (Spring 1966):423–526.

Mosher, Lawrence. "The Corps Adapts, the Bureau Founders." *High Country News* (29 September 1986):14–15, 18.

Moss, Frank. *The Water Crisis*. New York: Praeger, 1967.

Munro, James. "The Pelton Decision: A New Riparianism?" *Oregon Law Review* 36 (1956–1957):221–252.

Murphy, James T. "Political Parties and the Porkbarrel: Party Conflict and Cooperation in House Public Works Committee Decision Making." *American Political Science Review* 68 (March 1974):169–186.

Nakamura, Robert T., and Frank Smallwood. *The Politics of Policy Implementation*. New York: St. Martin's Press, 1980.

National Congress of American Indians. "Natural Resources Litigation and Trust Responsibilities." Statement adopted at the 38th Annual Convention, 11–16 October 1981.

National Irrigation Congress, Proceedings, 1905–1911.

National Journal. 9 April 1977.

———. 26 August 1978.

———. 26 April 1980.

———. 3 March 1981.

———. 30 October 1982.

———. 23 July 1983.

———. 17 August 1985.

———. 12 June 1986.

———. 15 November 1986.

———. 22 November 1986.

National Water Commission. Final Report, 1973. U.S. Government Printing Office.

"Necessity for Legal Assistance." Field Irrigation Memorandum, 25 March 1913. National Archives, R.G. 75, Irrigation Division, General Correspondence, 1901–1931: Special Topics.

Nelson, Robert A., and Joseph F. Sheley. "Current BIA Influence on Indian Self-Determination: A Criminal Justice Planning Illustration." *Social Science Journal* 19, no. 3 (July 1982):73–86.

Newsweek. 22 February 1965.

———. 6 December 1982.

New York Times. 12 September, 1959.

———. 21 February 1977.

———. 7 March 1977.

———. 13 March 1977.

———. 19 December 1977.

———. 12 February 1979.

———. 17 May 1979.

———. 24 June 1979.

———. 2 October 1980.

———. 14 October 1980.

———. 12 May 1981.

———. 12 September 1981.

———. 28 September 1981.

———. 8 December 1982.

———. 20 June 1984.

————. 30 June 1984.

————. 13 February 1985.

————. 17 March 1985.

————. 6 June 1985.

————. 22 June 1985.

Newell, Frederick H. "Irrigation Works on Indian Reservations." Memorandum, 27 March 1907. National Archives, R.G. 75, Irrigation Division, General Correspondence, 1901–1931. Special Topics, Miscellaneous.

Newell, Frederick, to Supervising and Project Engineers, 28 May 1907. National Archives, R.G. 115, General Administration and Project Files, 1902–1919: General, 762.1, Legal Discussions, Constitutionality of Reclamation.

Newell, Frederick, to Commissioner of Indian Affairs, 9 May 1912. R.G. 75, Irrigation Division, General Correspondence, 1901–1931: Special Topics, Miscellaneous.

Nienaber, Jeanne. "Bureaucracy, Policy, and Change: The Impact of Environmentalism in the Corps of Engineers." Report submitted to the Board of Engineers for Rivers and Harbors, Research Paper No. 4, April 1975.

Nikolaieff, George. *The Water Crisis.* Bronx, N.Y., 1967.

Office of Policy Analysis, Department of Interior. *Acreage Limitation.* Washington, D.C., March 1980.

Officer, James. Personal correspondence, 28 December 1983.

————. "The Indian Service and Its Evolution." In *The Aggressions of Civilization,* edited by Sandra Cadwalader and Vine Deloria, Jr., 59–103. Philadelphia, Penn.: Temple University Press, 1984.

Olson, Mancur. *The Logic of Collective Action.* Cambridge, Mass.: Harvard University Press, 1965.

Omaha World Herald. 19 May 1977.

Ornstein, Norman, and Shirley Elder. *Interest Groups, Lobbying and Policymaking.* Washington, D.C.: Congressional Quarterly Press, 1978.

Palma, Jack D. "Indian Water Rights: A State Perspective After *Akin.*" *Nebraska Law Review* 57 (1978):295–318.

The Papago Runner. 20 January 1982.

Parman, Donald L. "Francis Ellington Leupp, 1905–1909." In *The Commissioner of Indian Affairs,* edited by Robert M. Kvasnicka and Herman J. Viola, 221–232. Lincoln: University of Nebraska Press, 1979.

Patten, George Y. "Water Rights in Montana." *Rocky Mountain Law Review* 23 (December 1950):162–171.

Peters, Guy B. *The Politics of Bureaucracy.* 2d ed. New York: Longman, 1984.

Peterson, Elmer T. *Big Dam Foolishness.* Greenwich, Conn.: Devin-Adair Co., 1954.

Pisani, Donald. "State vs. Nation: Federal Reclamation and Water Rights in the Progressive Era." *Pacific Historical Review* 51 (August 1982):265–282.

————. *From the Family Farm to Agribusiness.* Berkeley, Los Angeles, London: University of California Press, 1984.

———. "Irrigation, Water Rights, and the Betrayal of Indian Allotment." *Environmental Review* 10 (Fall 1986):157–176.

Plott, Charles. "Some Organizational Influences on Urban Renewal Decisions." *American Econometric Review* 58 (1968):306–321.

Powledge, Fred. *Water: The Nature, Uses, and Future of Our Most Precious and Abused Resource.* New York: Farrar, Straus and Giroux, 1982.

The President's Water Resources Policy Commission. "A Water Policy for the American People." Final report, 3 vols., 1950.

Presidential Documents. Weekly Compilation, Jimmy Carter. Vol. 13 (18 April 1977).

———. Vol. 13 (22 October 1977).

———. Ronald Reagan. Vol. 20 (21 February 1984).

Pressman, Jeffrey L., and Aaron Wildavsky. *Implementation.* 2d ed. Berkeley, Los Angeles, London: University of California Press, 1979.

Preston, Porter J., and C. A. Engle. "Report of Advisors on Irrigation on Indian Reservations." Submitted 28 June 1928. Reprinted in U.S. Congress, Senate, Committee on Indian Affairs, Subcommittee on Senate Resolution 79, Hearings, "Survey of Conditions of the Indians in the United States." 71st Cong., 2d sess., pt. 6, 21 January 1930.

Price, Monroe, and Gary Weatherford. "Indian Water Rights in Theory and Practice: The Navajo Experience in the Colorado River Basin." In *American Indians and the Law,* edited by Lawrence Rosen, 97–131. New Brunswick, N.J.: Transaction Books, 1976.

"Proposed Legislation: For Insertion in the General Irrigation Item of H.R. 12579." Memorandum, April 1913. National Archives, R.G. 75, Irrigation Division, General Correspondence, 1901–1931: Special Topics, Legislation.

Public Papers of the Presidents, Administration of Dwight D. Eisenhower, 1954.

———. 1955.

———. 1956.

———. 1957.

———. 1958.

———. 1960.

Public Papers of the Presidents, Administration of Richard M. Nixon, 1970.

Public Papers of the Presidents, Administration of Jimmy Carter. Vol. 1, 1978.

Putney, Diane T. "Robert Grosvenor Valentine, 1909–1912." In *The Commissioners of Indian Affairs, 1824–1977,* edited by Robert M. Kvasnicka and Herman J. Viola, 233–242. Lincoln: University of Nebraska Press, 1979.

Ranquist, Harold A. "The Winters Doctrine and How It Grew." *Brigham Young University Law Review* (1975):639–724.

Rasch, C., to M. Bien, 25 November 1905. National Archives, R.G. 115, General Administrative and Project Records, 1902–1919: Milk River, 548, Settlement of Water Rights.

Reclamation Era. 1926.

Reclamation Record. February 1926.

Reclamation Service, *Annual Reports.* Washington, D.C.: Government Printing Office, 1902–1922.

———. "Conflicting Attitude Department of Justice on Irrigation Matters." Memorandum, 8 December 1905. National Archives, R.G. 115, General Administration and Project Files, 1902–1919: General, 762, Legal Discussions.

Redford, Emmette S. *Democracy in the Administrative State.* New York: Oxford University Press, 1969.

Reed, W. M., to the Commissioner of Indian Affairs, 26 March 1913. National Archives, R.G. 75, Irrigation Division, General Correspondence, 1901–1931.

Reed, W. M., to C. Sells, 13 April 1914. National Archives, R.G. 75, Irrigation Division, General Correspondence, 1901–1931, Special Topics.

Reed, W. M. "Memorandum for Commissioner Sells," 9 August 1914. National Archives, R.G. 75, Irrigation Division, General Correspondence, 1901–1931: Special Topics.

Reed, W. M., to M. Conner, 14 July 1915. National Archives, R.G. 75, Irrigation Division, General Correspondence, 1901–1931: Special Topics.

Reed, W. M., to W. S. Hanna, 6 April 1916. National Archives, R.G. 75, BIA Irrigation Division, Dist. 3, Fort Belknap, Entry 653.

Reid, T. R. *Congressional Odyssey.* San Francisco: W. H. Freeman, 1980.

Reisner, Marc. *Cadillac Desert.* New York: Viking, 1986.

Renshaw, Edward. *Toward Responsible Government: An Economic Appraisal of Federal Investment in Water Resource Programs.* Chicago: Llyria Press, 1957.

Report of the Commission on Civil Rights. "The Southwest Indian Report," May 1973.

Rieselbach, Leroy N. *Congressional Politics.* New York: McGraw-Hill, 1973.

———. *Congressional Reform.* Washington, D.C.: Congressional Quarterly Press, 1986.

Ripley, Randall B. *Congress.* 2d ed. New York: W. W. Norton, 1978.

———. *Policy Analysis in Public Policy.* Chicago: Nelson-Hall, 1985.

Ripley, Randall B., and Grace A. Franklin. *Congress, the Bureaucracy, and Public Policy.* 3d ed. Homewood, Ill.: Dorsey Press, 1984.

———. *Policy Implementation and Bureaucracy.* Homewood, Ill.: Dorsey Press, 1986.

Robinson, H. J., to W. H. Code, 25 September 1909. National Archives, R.G. 75, Irrigation Division, General Correspondence, 1901–1931: Special Topics, Power and Reservoirs.

———. 8 November 1910. National Archives, R.G. 75, Irrigation Division, Reports and Related Records, Colorado, Southern Ute.

Robinson, Michael C. *Water for the West: The Bureau of Reclamation, 1902–1977.* Chicago: Public Works Historical Society, 1979.

Rohde, David W., and Kenneth A. Shepsle. "Democratic Committee Assignments in the House of Representatives: Strategic Aspects of a Social Choice Process." *American Political Science Review* 67 (September 1973):889–905.

Roop, Carole Ann. "The Papago Water Bill and the Reagan Veto: Unscrambling the Omelet." *CERT Report* 4, no. 9 (23 July 1982):5–10.

Roosevelt, Theodore. *The Autobiography of Theodore Roosevelt.* New York: Charles Scribner's Sons, 1913.

Rourke, Francis E. "Political and Bureaucratic Elites." In *Bureaucratic Power in National Politics,* edited by Francis E. Rourke, 121–125. Boston: Little, Brown, 1972.

———. *Bureaucracy, Politics, and Public Policy.* 3d ed. Boston: Little, Brown, 1984.

Rucker, Randal R., and Price Fishback. "The Federal Reclamation Program." In *Water Rights,* edited by Terry L. Anderson, 45–81. Cambridge, Mass.: Ballinger, 1983.

Ruttan, Vernon. *The Economic Demand for Irrigated Acreage.* Baltimore: Resources for the Future/Johns Hopkins University Press, 1965.

Salisbury, Robert H. "Interest Representation: The Dominance of Institutions." *American Political Science Review* 78 (March 1984):64–76.

Sander, William. "Federal Water Resources Policy and Decision-Making." *American Journal of Economics and Sociology* 42 (January 1983):1–12.

Savage, H. to M. Bien, 10 March 1906. "Milk River Water Rights Adjudication." National Archives, R.G. 115, General Administrative and Project Records, 1902–1919; Milk River, 548, Settlement of Water Rights.

Savage, H. to F. Newell, 28 April 1908. National Archives, R.G. 115, General Administrative and Project Records, 1902–1919: Milk River, 548, Settlement of Water Rights.

Scheingold, Stuart A. *The Politics of Rights.* New Haven, Conn.: Yale University Press, 1974.

Schlozman, Kay Lehman, and John T. Tierney. *Organized Interests and American Democracy.* New York: Harper & Row, 1986.

Schmeckebier, Laurence F. *The Office of Indian Affairs.* Baltimore: Johns Hopkins University Press, 1927.

Schooler, Dean, and Helen Ingram. "Water Resource Management." *Policy Studies Review* 1 (November 1981):243–254.

Sells, C., to Secretary of Interior, 13 March 1914. National Archives, R.G. 74, Irrigation Division, General Correspondence, 1901–1931: Special Topics, Miscellaneous.

Selznick, Phillip. *TVA and the Grass Roots.* New York: Harper Torchbooks, 1966.

Shanks, Bernard. "The American Indian and Missouri River Water Development." *Water Resources Bulletin* 10 (June 1974):573–579.

———. "Dams and Disasters: The Social Problems of Water Development Policies." In *Bureaucracy vs. Environment,* edited by John Baden and Richard L. Stroup, 108–123. Ann Arbor: University of Michigan Press, 1981.

Shepsle, Kenneth, and Barry Weingast. "Political Preference for the Pork Barrel: A Generalization." *American Journal of Political Science* 25 (February 1981):96–111.

Sherton, Corinne C. "Preserving Instream Flows in Oregon's Rivers and Streams." *Environmental Lawyer* 11 (Spring 1981):381–419.

Simms, Richard A. "Issues in Determining Indian Water Rights." In *Western Water Resources*, symposium sponsored by the Federal Reserve Bank of Kansas City. Boulder, Colo.: Westview Press, 1980a.

———. "National Water Policy in the Wake of *U.S. v. New Mexico.*" *Natural Resources Journal* 20, no. 1 (January 1980b):1–16.

Smith, Karen L. "The Campaign for Water in Central Arizona, 1890–1903." *Arizona and the West* 23, no. 2 (Summer 1981):127–148.

Smith, Rodney. *Troubled Waters.* Washington, D.C.: Council of State Planning Agencies, 1984.

Smith, Steven, and Christopher Deering. *Committees in Congress.* Washington, D.C.: Congressional Quarterly Press, 1984.

Smythe, William E. *The Conquest of Arid America.* New York: Macmillan, 1911.

Solicitor General of the Department of Interior. "Memorandum Relative to Cases Involving Water Rights of Indians in Montana and Washington," n.d., about 6 December 1905. National Archives, R.G. 115, General Administration and Project Files, 1902–1919: General, 762, Legal Discussions.

Sombrero, Albert. "Navajo Indian Irrigation Project: A Status Report." Paper presented at the annual meeting of the Western Political Science Association, March 1982, San Diego, Calif.

Snell, George, to Senator John Melcher, 4 November 1985. Copy in personal files.

Sondheim, Harry B., and John R. Alexander. "Federal Indian Water Rights: A Retrogression to Quasi-Riparianism?" *Southern California Law Review* 34 (Fall 1960):1–61.

Sorkin, Alan L. *American Indians and Federal Aid.* Washington, D.C.: Brookings Institution, 1971.

Starling, Grover. *The Politics and Economics of Public Policy.* Homewood, Ill.: Dorsey Press, 1979.

Stegner, Wallace. *Beyond the Hundredth Meridian.* Boston: Houghton Mifflin, 1954.

Stoevener, Herbert H., and Roger G. Kraynick. "The Changing Perspectives on Benefits and Costs of Irrigation Development." In *Non-Federal Financing of Water Resources Development.* Corvallis: Oregon State University Press, 1978.

Stong, Benton. "The Rivers and Harbors Lobby." *The New Republic* (10 October 1949):13–15.

Stratton, Owen, and Philip Sorotkin. *The Echo Park Controversy.* University, Ala.: University of Alabama Press, 1959.

Strom, Gerald S. "Congressional Policy Making: A Test of a Theory."

Journal of Politics 37 (August 1975):711–735.

Stuart, Paul. "Administrative Reform in Indian Affairs." *Western Historical Quarterly* 16 (April 1985):133–146.

Superintendent of Indian Affairs, "Annual Report for 1872." U.S. Government Printing Office.

"Superintendent to Pass Upon Water Rights." Memorandum of the BIA, 20 June 1913. National Archives, R.G. 75, Irrigation Division, General Correspondence, 1901–1931: Special Topics, Legislation.

Sweeney, B., to T. Gregory (Attorney General), 8 May 1915. National Archives, R.G. 75, BIA Irrigation Division, Dist. 3, Fort Belknap, 1907–1931: Entry 653.

Swimmer, Ross, to Inspector General, Memorandum, "Final Audit Report-Rehabilitation and Completion of the Fort Belknap Irrigation Project." 2 May 1986.

Tarr, Ralph, and Frank McMurry. *New Complete Geography*. New York: Macmillan, 1916.

Taylor, Paul. "The Desert Shall Rejoice, and Blossom as the Rose." In *The Grand Colorado*, edited by T. H. Watkins, 147–202. St. Paul, Minn.: West Publishing, 1969.

Taylor, Theodore W. *American Indian Policy*. Mt. Airy, Mass.: Lomond Pub., 1983.

———. *The Bureau of Indian Affairs*. Boulder, Colo: Westview Press, 1984.

Terral, Rufus. *The Missouri Valley: Land of Drouth, Flood, and Promise*. New Haven, Conn.: Yale University Press, 1947.

Townley, John N. "Reclamation and the Red Man." *The Indian Historian* 11, no. 1 (1978):21–28.

Trelease, Frank. "Federal-State Relations in Water Law." *National Water Commission*, Legal Study No. 5, pt. V, 1971.

———. "Federal-State Relations in Water Law." Accession No. PB203 600. Prepared for the 1973 National Water Commission. Springfield, Va.: National Technical Information Service, 1973.

———. "Discussion: Legal-Institutional Limitations of Water Use." In *Water Scarcity*, edited by Ernest A. Englebert and Ann Foley Scheuring, 77–80. Berkeley, Los Angeles, London: University of California Press, 1984.

Truesdell, John, to W. M. Reed, 9 March 1916. National Archives, R.G. 75, BIA Irrigation Division, Dist. 3, Fort Belknap, Entry 653.

Tucker, Harvey. "Budgeting Strategy: Cross-Sectional Versus Longitudinal Models." *Public Administration Review* 41, no. 6 (November/December 1981):644–648.

Tucson Citizen. 20 January 1982.

Turner, Frederick. *The Frontier in American History*. New York: H. Holt and Co., 1920.

Tyler, S. Lyman. *A History of Indian Policy*. Washington, D.C.: Bureau of Indian Affairs, 1973.

Upite, Daina. "Resolving Indian Reserved Water Rights in the Wake of San Carlos Apache Tribe." *Environmental Law* 15 (Fall 1984):181–200.

U.S. Budget Analysis. FY 1977–1984.

U.S. Budget Appendix. FY 1982–1984.

U.S. Budget in Brief. FY 1982–1983.

U.S. Commission on Civil Rights. The Southwest Indian Report, May 1973.

U.S. Commission on Civil Rights, Staff Report No. 2. "Federal Policies and Programs for American Indians," November 1972.

U.S. Commission on the Organization of the Executive Branch of the Government, Water Resources and Power. Vol. 10, U.S. Government Printing Office, 1955 (usually referred to as the second Hoover Report).

U.S. News and World Report. 18 March 1985.

U.S. Water News. January 1986.

———. February 1986.

———. July 1986.

———. August 1986.

U.S. Water Resources Council. *The Nation's Water Resources: The First National Assessment.* Washington, D.C.: U.S. Government Printing Office, 1968.

———. *The Nation's Water Resources, 1975–2000: The Second National Water Assessment.* Washington, D.C.: U.S. Government Printing Office, 1975.

Van Meter, Donald S., and Carl E. Van Horn. "The Policy Implementation Process." *Administration and Society* 6 (February 1975):445–488.

Veeder, William. "The Pelton Decision: A Symbol—A Guarantee that the Development and Conservation of Our Nation's Resources Will Keep Pace with Our National Demands." *Montana Law Review* 27 (1965):27–45.

———. "Federal Encroachment on Indian Water Rights and the Impairment of Reservation Development." U.S. Congress, Joint Economic Committee, Subcommittee on Economic Government. 91st Cong., 1st sess., 1969.

———. "Indian Water Rights and the Energy Crisis." Mimeograph, October 1978.

Velasquez, Victor. "The San Carlos Irrigation Project." Paper presented at the 1982 annual meeting of the Western Political Science Association.

Vogler, David. *The Politics of Congress.* 2d ed. Boston: Allyn & Bacon, 1977.

Vogler, David, and Sidney Waldman. *Congress and Democracy.* Washington, D.C.: Congressional Quarterly Press, 1985.

Waldo, Dwight. *The Administrative State.* New York: Ronald Press, 1948.

Walker, Jack L. "The Origins and Maintenance of Interest Groups in America." *American Political Science Review* 77 (June 1983):390–406.

Walker, W. A. to (?) Wathen, 16 March 1933. National Archives, R.G. 75, Irrigation Division, General Correspondence, 1901–1931: Special Topics, Legislation.

Wall Street Journal. 23 July 1959.

———. 2 September 1959.

———. 2 March 1983.

———. 5 October 1984.

———. 3 May 1985.

———. 31 May 1985.

———. 14 November 1985.

———. 19 January 1987.

Wallace, Mary. "The Supreme Court and Indian Water Rights." In *American Indian Policy in the Twentieth Century*, edited by Vine Deloria, Jr., 197–220. Norman: University of Oklahoma Press, 1985.

Wanat, John. "Bases of Budgetary Incrementalism." *American Political Science Review* 68 (December 1974):1221–1228.

Warne, William. *The Bureau of Reclamation*. New York: Praeger, 1973.

Wasby, Stephen L. *The Supreme Court in the Federal Judicial System*. New York: Holt, Rinehart & Winston, 1978.

Washburn, Wilcomb. *Red Man's Land/White Man's Law*. New York: Charles Scribner's Sons, 1971.

Washington Post. 19 December 1977.

———. 6 February 1978.

———. 23 January 1980.

———. 22 June 1983.

———. 25 January 1984.

———. 30 June 1984.

———. 18 December 1984.

———. 22 June 1985.

———. 26 July 1985.

———. 7 October 1986.

Washington Times. 26 September 1983.

Water and Power Resources Service, U.S. Department of Interior. "Fact Sheet." Publication No. 853–605. Washington, D.C.: U.S. Government Printing Office, 1979.

"Water Rights." Memorandum n.d., about 1913. National Archives, R.G. 75, Irrigation Division, General Correspondence, 1901–1931: Special Topics.

Waters, Frank. *The Colorado*. New York: Holt, Rinehart & Winston, 1946.

Weekly Report, Congressional Quarterly. 2 July 1977.

———. 30 July 1977.

———. 4 March 1978.

———. 6 May 1978.

———. 12 May 1978.

———. 10 June 1978.

———. 17 June 1978.

———. 24 June 1978.

———. 12 August 1978.

———. 19 August 1978.

———. 14 October 1978.

———. 27 January 1979.

———. 28 July 1979.

———. 3 November 1979.

———. 28 June 1980.

———. 16 May 1981.

———. 18 July 1981.

———. 3 October 1981.

———. 14 November 1981.

———. 28 November 1981.

———. 12 December 1981.

———. 19 December 1981.

———. 24 February 1982.

———. 12 June 1982.

———. 19 June 1982.

———. 28 August 1982.

———. 25 September 1982.

———. 30 July 1983.

———. 28 January 1984.

———. 9 June 1984.

———. 27 October 1984.

———. 1 June 1985.

———. 8 June 1985.

———. 22 June 1985.

———. 19 October 1985.

———. 6 November 1985.

———. 28 December 1985.

———. 7 June 1986.

———. 21 June 1986.

———. 12 July 1986.

———. 26 July 1986.

———. 6 September 1986.

Weingast, Barry, Kenneth Shepsle, and Christopher Johnsen. "The Political Economy of Benefits and Costs: A Neoclassical Approach to Distributive Politics." *Journal of Political Economy* 89 (1981):642–663.

Welsh, Frank. *How to Create a Water Crisis.* Boulder, Colo: Johnson Books, 1985.

Western Regional Council. "Indian Water Rights Act of 1981." Mimeograph, n.d.

———. Letter to James Watt, Secretary of Interior, 31 August 1982.

Western States Water Council. *Indian Water Rights in the West.* Study prepared for the Western Governors' Association, May 1984.

White, Gilbert F. "Broader Bases for Choice: The Next Key Move." In *Perspectives on Conservation,* edited by H. Jarrett, 212–233. Baltimore: Resources for the Future/Johns Hopkins University Press, 1958.

White, William S. *Citadel: The Story of the U.S. Senate.* New York: Harper, 1956.

Wiel, Samuel C. *Water Rights in the Western States.* San Francisco: Bancroft-Whitney, 1911. Reprinted by Arno Press, 1979.

Wiley, Peter, and Robert Gottlieb. *Empires in the Sun.* New York: G. P. Putnam's Sons, 1982.

Wildavsky, Aaron. *The Politics of the Budgetary Process.* 2d ed. Boston: Little, Brown, 1974.

Wilkinson, Charles. "Western Water Law in Transition." *University of Colorado Law Review* 56 (Spring 1985):317–345.

Williams, Maynard Owen. "The Columbia Turns on the Power." *National Geographic* (June 1941):749–792.

Wilson, James Q. "The Rise of the Bureaucratic State." *The Public Interest* 41 (Fall 1975):77–103.

Wilson, Leonard V. *State Water Policy Issues.* Lexington, Ky.: Council of State Governments, 1978.

Wilson, Woodrow. *Congressional Government.* Boston: Houghton Mifflin, 1908.

Wopsock, Floyd, Chairman of the Ute Indian Tribe, to Secretary of Interior William Clark. "Request of the Ute Indian Tribe to Meet with the Secretary of the Interior to Negotiate a Settlement of the Ute Tribal Water Rights." 14 December 1983.

Work, Hubert, to Charles L. McNary, 12 February 1926. National Archives, R.G. 75, General Correspondence, 1901–1931: Special Topics, Legislation.

World's Work. "Reclamation Becomes a Pork Barrel" 51 (February 1926):354.

Worster, Donald. *Rivers of Empire.* New York: Pantheon Books, 1985.

Young, Robert A., and William E. Martin. "The Economics of Arizona's Water Problems." *Arizona Review* 16 (March 1967).

Young, Ronald T. L. "Interagency Conflicts of Interests: The Peril to Indian Water Rights." *Law and Social Order* (1972):313–328.

Congressional Hearings and Documents (chronological order)

HOUSE

U.S. Congress, House Document No. 149. "Resolution of the Committee of One Hundred, Appointed by the Secretary of Interior, and a Review of the Indian Problem." 68th Cong., 1st sess., 1924.

U.S. Congress, House, Committee on Appropriations, Subcommittee on Public Works. "Appropriations for 1958." 85th Cong., 1st sess., 1957.

U.S. Congress, House, Committee on Interior and Insular Affairs, Subcommittee on Irrigation and Reclamation. "Colorado River Basin Project." 90th Cong., 2d sess., 30 January, 1–2 February, Part 2, 1968.

U.S. Congress, House, Committee on Appropriations, Subcommittee on Public Works. "Appropriations for 1971." 91st Cong., 2d sess., Part 3, 1970.

U.S. Congress, House, Committee on Appropriations, Subcommittee on the Department of Interior and Related Agencies. "Appropriations for 1974." 93rd Cong., 1st sess., Part 2, 1973.

U.S. Congress, House, Committee on Appropriations, Subcommittee on Public Works. "Appropriations for 1975." 93rd Cong., 2d sess., Part 3, 1974.

U.S. Congress, House, Committee on Appropriations, Subcommittee on Public Works. "Appropriations for 1976." 94th Cong., 1st sess., Part 4, 1975.

U.S. Congress, House, Committee on Appropriations, Subcommittee on the Department of Interior and Related Agencies. "Appropriations for 1977." 94th Cong., 2d sess., Part 2, 1976.

U.S. Congress, House, Committee on Appropriations, Subcommittee on the Department of Interior and Related Agencies. "Appropriations for 1978." 95th Cong., 1st sess., Parts 2 and 4, 1977.

U.S. Congress, House, Committee on Appropriations, Subcommittee on Public Works. "Appropriations for 1979." 95th Cong., 2d sess., Part 1, 1978.

U.S. Congress, House, Committee on Appropriations, Subcommittee on Public Works. "Appropriations for 1980." 96th Cong., 1st sess., Part 1, 1979.

U.S. Congress, House, Committee on Appropriations, Subcommittee on Energy and Water Development. "Appropriations for 1981." 96th Cong., 2d sess., Part 1, 1980.

U.S. Congress, House, Committee on Appropriations, Subcommittee on Energy and Water Development. "Supplemental Appropriation and Recision Bill, 1981." 97th Cong., 1st sess., Part 1, 1981*a*.

U.S. Congress, House, Committee on Appropriations, Subcommittee on the Department of Interior and Related Agencies. "Appropriations for 1982." 97th Cong., 1st sess., Part 2, 1981*b*.

U.S. Congress, House, Committee on Appropriations, Subcommittee on Energy and Water Development. "Appropriations for 1982." 97th Cong., 1st sess., Part 3, 1981*c*.

U.S. Congress, House, Committee on Appropriations, Subcommittee on the Department of Interior and Related Agencies. "Appropriations for 1983." 97th Cong., 2d sess., Part 9, 1982.

U.S. Congress, House, Committee on Appropriations, Subcommittee on Energy and Water Development. "Appropriations for 1983." 97th Cong., 2d sess., Parts 1 and 3, 1982.

U.S. Congress, Committee on Appropriations, Subcommittee on the Department of Interior and Related Agencies. "Appropriations for 1986." 99th Cong., 1st sess., Part 2, 1985.

U.S. Congress, House. Rept. 99–525, "Garrison Diversion Unit Reformation Act of 1986." 99th Cong., 2d sess., 9 April 1986.

SENATE

U.S. Congress, Senate Document 325, 60th Cong., 1st sess. (the final report of the 1907 Inland Waterways Commission), 1908.

U.S. Congress, Senate Document No. 805, 2 February, 61st Cong., 3d sess., "Letter from the Secretary of Interior" (in response to the Senate Resolution of June 23, 1910), 1911.

U.S. Congress, Senate Document No. 92. "Federal Reclamation by Irrigation." A report submitted by the Committee of Special Advisors on Reclamation. 68th Cong., 1st sess., 1924.

U.S. Congress, Senate, Committee on Interior and Insular Affairs, Subcommittee on Indian Affairs. Hearings on Indian Irrigation. 79th Cong., 2d sess., 1946.

U.S. Congress, Senate Select Committee on National Water Resources Report. "Water Resources Activities in the United States." Senate Report No. 29, 87th Cong., 1st sess., 1961.

U.S. Congress, Senate, Committee on Interior and Insular Affairs, Subcommittee on Irrigation and Reclamation. "Hearings on S. 1275." 88th Cong., 2d sess., 1964.

U.S. Congress, Senate, Committee on the Judiciary, Subcommittee on Administrative Practice and Procedure. Hearings on the Administrative Practices and Procedures Relating to the Protection of Indian Natural Resources. 92d Cong., 1st sess., 1971.

U.S. Congress, Senate, Committee on Interior and Insular Affairs, Subcommittee on Indian Affairs. "Hearings on the Various Social, Economic, and Political Aspects of Indian Water Rights." 93d Cong., 2d sess., 1974.

U.S. Congress, Senate, Commission on Indian Affairs. Meetings of the American Indian Policy Review Commission, 20 February, 8–9 May, vol. 2, 1976.

U.S. Congress, Senate, Committee on the Judiciary. "Selection and Confirmation of Federal Judges." 96th Cong., 1st sess., 13, 18, 19, 23, 27 July, Part 3, 1979.

U.S. Congress, Senate, Select Committee on Indian Affairs. "Fiscal Year 1986 Budget." 99th Cong., 1st sess., 27 February 1985*a*.

U.S. Congress, Senate, Select Committee on Indian Affairs. "Budget Views and Estimates for Fiscal Year 1986." 99th Cong., 1st sess., March 1985*b*.

Court Cases (alphabetical order)

Anderson v. Spear-Morgan Livestock Co., 79 P.2d 667 (Sup. Ct., Mont. 1938).

Arizona v. California, 373 U.S. 546 (1963); 103 S.Ct. 1382 (1983).

Arizona et al. v. San Carlos Apache Tribe of Arizona et al., 103 S. Ct. 3201 (1983).

Babbitt v. Andrus, Civ. No. 80–992 PHX CLH (D. Ariz. 1980).

Byers v. Wa-Wa-Ne, 169 PAC. 121, 86 Or. 635 (1917).

California et al. v. U.S., 438 U.S. 645 (1978).

Cappaert v. U.S., 426 U.S. 128 (1976).

Chaote v. Trapp, 224 U.S. 665 (1912).

Cherokee Nation of Oklahoma v. U.S., Eastern District of Oklahoma, U.S. District Court # 83-306-C (in progress, 1986).

Colorado River Water Conservation District v. U.S., 424 U.S. 800 (1976).

Colville Confederated Tribes v. Walton, 460 F.Supp. 1320 (E.D. Wash. 1978); 647 F.2d 42 (9th Cir. 1981).

Confederated Tribes of the Umatilla Reservation v. Alexander, 440 F.Supp. 553 (Dist. Ct. Ore. 1977).

Confederated Salish and Kootenai Tribes v. Namen, 534 F.2d 1376 (9th Cir. 1974).

Conrad Investment Co. v. U.S., 161 F. 829 (9th Cir. 1908).

Federal Power Commission v. Oregon, 349 U.S. 435 (1955).

Federal Power Commission v. Tuscarora Indian Nation, 362 U.S. 99 (1960).

Johnson v. McIntosh, 8 Wheat. 543 (1823).

Jones v. Meehan, 175 U.S. 1 (1899).

Kansas v. Colorado, 206 U.S. 46 (1907).

Los Angeles v. San Fernando et al., Cir. No. 65D,079 (Super. Ct. Los Angeles County, Calif. 1967).

Merrill v. Bishop, 74 Wyo. 305, 287 P.2d 620 (Sup. Ct. Wyo. 1955).

Montana et al. v. Northern Cheyenne Tribe of the Northern Cheyenne Indian Reservation et al. 103 S. Ct. 3201 (1983).

Nevada v. U.S., 103 S.Ct. 2906 (1983).

Northern Cheyenne Tribe v. Adsit, 668 F.2d 1080 (CA9, 1982).

Northern Cheyenne Tribe v. Tongue River Water Users, 484 F.Supp. 31 (D.C. Mont. 1979).

Phelps v. Hanson, 163 F.2d 973 (9th Cir. 1947).

Pyramid Lake Paiute Tribe of Indians v. Morton, 354 F.Supp. 252 (D.C. Dist. 1973).

San Carlos Apache Tribe v. State of Arizona, 484 F.Supp. 778 (1979).

San Carlos Apache Tribe v. State of Arizona, 668 F.2d 1093 (CA9, 1982).

Scheer v. Moody, 48 F.2d 327 (1931).

Segundo v. U.S., 123 F.Supp. 554 (S.D. Calif., Central Div. 1954).

Seneca Nation of Indians v. Brucker, 162 F.Supp. 580 (D.D.C.), aff'd., 262 F.2d 27 (D.C., Cir. 1958).

Sierra Club v. Block, 622 F.Supp. 842 and 615 F.Supp. 44 (D.C. Colo. 1985).

Sierra Club v. Watt, 659 F. 203 (1981).

Skeem v. U.S., 273 Fed. 93 (9th Cir. 1921).

Sporhase v. Nebraska, 103 S. Ct. 3456 (1982).

Texas v. Valmont Plantations, 346 S.W. 2d 853 (1901).

Tweedy v. Texas Company, 286 F.Supp. 383 (D. Mont. 1968).

U.S. v. Adair, 723 F.2d 1394 (9th Cir. 1983).

U.S. v. Akin 504 F. 2d 115 (10th Cir. 1974).

U.S. v. Alpine Land and Reservoir Co. (The Alpine Decree), Equity No. D-183 (D. Nev., March 1950).

U.S. v. Alpine Land and Reservoir Co., 431 F.2d 763 (9th Cir. 1970).

U.S. v. Alpine Land and Reservoir Co., 401 U.S. 520 (1971).

United States and the Papago Tribe v. City of Tucson, Civ. No. 75–39 Tuc. (D. Ariz. 1978).

U.S. v. Ahtanum Irrigation District, 236 F.2d 321 (9th Cir. 1956).

U.S. v. Alexander, 131 F.2d 359 (9th Cir. 1942).

U.S. v. City and County of Denver, 656 P.2d 1 (Colo. 1983).

U.S. v. District Court in and for Eagle County, 401 U.S. 520 (1971).
U.S. v. District Court in and for Water Division No. 5, 401 U.S. 527 (1971).
U.S. v. Gila Valley Irrigation District, Globe Equity No. 59 (D. Ariz. 1935).
U.S. v. Kagama, 118 U.S. 375 (1886).
U.S. v. McIntire, 101 F.2d 650 (9th Cir. 1939).
U.S. v. Mose Anderson et al., Memorandum Order (December 1905).
U.S. v. Nevada and California, 412 U.S. 534 (1973).
U.S. v. New Mexico, 438 U.S. 697 (1978).
U.S. v. Orr Water Ditch Co., Equity No. A-3 (D. Nev., September 1944).
U.S. v. Parkins, 18 F.2d (D. Wyo., 1926).
U.S. v. Powers, 305 U.S. 527 (1939).
U.S. v. Preston, 352 F.2d 352 (9th Cir. 1965).
U.S. v. Rio Grande, 174 U.S. 690 (1898).
U.S. v. 687.30 Acres of Land, 319 F.Supp. 128 (D. Neb. 1970).
U.S. v. Walker River Irrigation District 14 F. Supp. (D. Nev. 1936).
U.S. v. Walker River Irrigation District, 104 F.2d 334 (9th Cir. 1939).
U.S. v. Winans, 198 U.S. 371 (1905).
U.S. v. Wrightman, 230 Fed. 277 (D. Ariz. 1916).
Winters v. U.S., 207 U.S. 564 (1908).
Worcester v. Georgia, G. Pet. 515 (1832).

Statutes (chronological order)

Rivers and Harbors Bill of May 24, 1824 (18th Cong., 1st sess., Ch. 140, 1824, p. 32).
U.S. Statutes at Large (4, Sec 9:735–738, 1834).
Homestead Act of May 29, 1862 (12 Stat. 392).
Mining Law of July 26, 1866 (14 Stat. 253).
Act of March 2, 1867 (14 Stat. 492).
Act of July 9, 1870 (16 Stat. 377).
The Desert Land Act of 1877 (19 Stat. 377).
The General Allotment or Dawes Act of 1887 (25 U.S.C. Sec. 331).
Act of February 8, 1887 (24 Stat. 390).
Act of March 3, 1891 (26 Stat. 989).
Act of February 26, 1897 (29 Stat. 598).
Act of March 2, 1897 (29 Stat. 603).
Act of June 4, 1897 (30 Stat. 11).
The Reclamation Act of 1902 (43 U.S. C. 391).
Act of April 24, 1904 (33 Stat. 189).
Act of April 27, 1904 (33 Stat. 352).
Act of March 3, 1905 (33 Stat. 1016).
Act of June 21, 1906 (34 Stat. 325).
Act of April 30, 1908 (35 Stat. 70).
Act of June 25, 1910 (36 Stat. 855).
The Reclamation Extension Act of 1914 (38 Stat. 686).

Act of February 14, 1920 (41 Stat. 408).
The Boulder Canyon Project Act of December 21, 1928 (45 Stat. 1057).
Act of July 1, 1932 (47 Stat. 564).
The Flood Control Act of 1936 (49 Stat. 1570).
Act of August 31, 1937 (50 Stat. 737).
The Reclamation Project Act of August 4, 1939 (53 Stat. 1187).
The Barret Bill (also known as the Water Rights Settlement Act of 1956;
    S. 863, 84th Cong. 2d sess., 1956).
Water Resources Development Act of 1974 (P.L. 93–251. 88 Stat. 34).
Indian Self-Determination and Education Assistance Act of 1975 (P.L. 93
    680. 88 Stat. 2203).
Continuing Appropriations, FY 1979 (1978) (P.L. 95–482. 92 Stat. 1603).
Inland Waterways Revenue Act of 1978 (P.L. 95–502. 92 Stat. 1696).
Reclamation Safety of Dams Act of 1978 (P.L. 95–587. 92 Stat. 2470).
Water Resources Development Act of 1986 (reprinted in the *Congressional
    Record* 1986:H11478–11534).

Bills, Resolutions, House and Senate Reports (chronological order)

H.R. 2164, 1896
H.R. 9054, 1977
H.R. 7553, 1977
S. 905, 1977
H.R. 8099, 1978
H.R. 8309, 1978
H.R. 11655, 1978
H.R. 12928, 1978
H.J. Res. 1139
S. 1582, 1978
H.R. 4788, 1980
H.R. 7640, 1980
H.R. 3432, 1981
H.R. 4363, 1981
H.R. 5118, 1982
H.R. 7145, 1982
H.R. 6, 1985

Interviews

Anderson, John. Division of Planning, Bureau of Reclamation. Inter-
    viewed by phone 16 September 1986.
Baird, Paul. Associate Solicitor for Indian Affairs, Department of Interior.
    Interviewed 12 June 1984.

Bigby, Delmar. Planner, Fort Belknap Indian Reservation. Interviewed by phone 9 July 1986 and 26 August 1986.

Boylan, Virginia. Staff Attorney, Senate Select Committee on Indian Affairs. Interviewed by phone 9 July 1986.

Clinton, Michael. Special Assistant to the Assistant Secretary for Water and Science, Department of Interior. Interviewed by phone 6 March 1986.

Cluff, Donald. Chief, Programs Division, Directorate of Civil Works, Department of the Army. Interviewed by phone 28 February 1986.

Corke, Charles P. Chief, Water and Land Resources Division, Bureau of Indian Affairs, Department of Interior. Interviewed 12 June 1984. Interviewed by phone 2 November 1982; 25 January 1983; and 16 April 1986.

Deason, Jonathan. Office of the Assistant Secretary of the Army, Civil Works Division. Interviewed 11 June 1984.

Ducheneaux, Franklin. Counsel on Indian Affairs, Majority Staff, House Committee on Interior and Insular Affairs, Office of Indian Affairs. Interviewed 14 June 1984.

Eacock, Gordon. Billings, Montana, Regional Headquarters of the Bureau of Reclamation. Interviewed by phone 8 July 1986.

Flachbarth, Charles. Assistant Chief Counsel, Office of the Chief of Engineers, Department of the Army. Interviewed 13 June 1984. Interviewed by phone 8 April 1981.

Fleischer, Ruth. Staff, Office of Senator William Proxmire. Interviewed by phone 15 January 1986.

Garrabrant, Ann. Minority Staff, Senate Committee on Environment and Public Works, Subcommittee on Water Resources. Interviewed 28 August 1986.

Hangy, Randall. Programs Division, Directorate of Civil Works, Department of the Army. Interviewed by phone 30 September 1985.

Jones, Proctor. Majority Staff, Senate Committee on Appropriations, Subcommittee on Energy and Water Development. Interviewed by phone 16 January 1986.

Lee, Hayden. Division of Planning, Bureau of Reclamation, Department of Interior. Interviewed 15 June 1984.

Longfox, Charles. Tribal Vice-Chairman, Fort Belknap Indian Reservation. Interviewed by phone 26 August 1986.

Main, William. Tribal Chairman, Fort Belknap Indian Reservation. Interviewed by phone 26 August 1986.

Meshorer, Hank. Chief, Division of Indian Resources, Department of Justice. Interviewed 15 June 1984.

Musgrove, James. Water Resources Specialist, Fort Belknap Indian Reservation. Interviewed by phone 26 August 1986.

O'Meara, J. W. (Pat). President, National Water Resources Association. Interviewed 12 June 1984.

Osann, Edward. Director, Water Resources Program, National Wildlife Federation. Interviewed by phone 21 January 1986.

Perez, Franklin R. Chairman of the Water Policy Committee of the Fort Belknap Tribal Council. Interviewed by phone 26 August 1986.

Salazar, John. Division of Water and Land Technical Services, Engineering and Research Center, Bureau of Reclamation, Department of Interior. Interviewed by phone 5 March 1986 and 15 March 1986.

Skirbunt, Thomas. Staff, Senate Committee on Environment and Public Works, Subcommittee on Water Resources. Interviewed by phone 21 January 1986.

Stiffarm, Dr. Lenore. Technical Advisor, Fort Belknap Indian Reservation. Interviewed by phone 26 August 1986.

Index

Abourezk, James, 138
Act of February 8, 1887, 50
Administrative agencies, 9; autonomy of, 10, 24; conflicts between, 110–111; credibility of, 10, 211; funding of, 209; image of, 10, 150; in iron triangles, 5, 9–10, 147, 148; stability of, 10. *See also* Army Corps of Engineers, U.S.; Bureau of Indian Affairs; Bureau of Reclamation
Agencies. *See* Administrative agencies
Agrarian populism, 33–34
Ahtanum Irrigation District v. U.S. (1956), 117, 169
Ak-Chin Reservation, 231, 241, 242; bill, 231, 233
Akin Case. See *Colorado River Water Conservation District v. U.S.*
Alaska, 80
American Federation of Labor, 26
American Indian Affairs, Association of, 142
American Indian Defense Association, 150, 158
American Indian Lawyer Training Program, 237–238
American Indian Policy Review Commission (1977), 138, 147
American Indians: assimilation of, 142–143; attitudes toward, 157–158; civil rights movement and, 130; Corps of Engineers programs and,

178–180; current federal water policy iron triangle and, 194; funding problems, 246; government policy toward, 156; immunity to state law, 186–187; impact of expanded activities on, 225; increased political power of, 171, 176, 225, 226; interest groups, 142–144, 146, 243; justice to, 254–255; Reagan endorsed by, 233; relocation of, 175; reluctance to negotiate, 238; self-determination policy and, 227; water as symbol to, 254. *See also* Indian *headings*
American Public Power Association, 84
American Society of Civil Engineers, 81–82
American Society of Engineers, *Proceedings*, 27
Anderson, Mose. See *U.S. v. Mose Anderson*
Andrus, Cecil, 229
Anglos. *See* Non-Indians
Appropriations. *See* Budget, federal; Funding
Arizona, 58–59, 73, 231, 234–236. *See also* Central Arizona Project; Navajo *headings*; Papago Reservation
Arizona Academy, 3
Arizona et al. v. San Carlos Apache Tribe, 240
Arizona v. California (1963), 117, 118,

Designer: U.C. Press Staff
Compositor: Prestige Typography
Text: 10/12 Palatino
Display: Palatino
Printer: McNaughton & Gunn, Inc.
Binder: John H. Dekker & Sons